Delius and Norway

Delius and Norway

ANDREW J. BOYLE

THE BOYDELL PRESS

First published 2017
The Boydell Press, Woodbridge

ISBN 978 1 78327 199 3

The Boydell Press is an imprint of Boydell & Brewer Ltd
PO Box 9, Woodbridge, Suffolk IP12 3DF, UK
and of Boydell & Brewer Inc.
668 Mt Hope Avenue, Rochester, NY 14620–2731, USA
website: www.boydellandbrewer.com

A catalogue record for this book is available
from the British Library

The publisher has no responsibility for the continued existence or
accuracy of URLs for external or third-party internet websites referred
to in this book, and does not guarantee that any content on such
websites is, or will remain, accurate or appropriate

This publication is printed on acid-free paper

I should never think of settling […] too far from my beloved Norway & the light summer nights & all the poetry & melancholy of the Northern summer & the high mountain plateaus where humans are rare & more individual than in any other country in the world; & where they also have deeper & more silent feelings than any other people.

Frederick Delius, 1918

Contents

List of illustrations and tables

Illustrations

Tables

Preface

Frederick Delius travelled to Norway on twenty occasions during his adult life, visiting the south-eastern coast and the central mountains for periods of one to three months. Although he was initially attracted to the country for the same reasons as many other Britons fleeing their industrialised landscape, his Norwegian journeys assumed ever greater significance in his career. He came to regard them as crucial to the health and survival of his artistic process. If prevented from visiting Norway for more than two summers he would become restless, sensing that his creative direction was becoming more difficult to determine. One such break in the chain of visits was caused by the First World War, when submarines and mines made sea crossings too hazardous; in a letter to her husband, Jelka Delius bemoaned the turn of events: 'It is dreadful that we are cut off from Norway, I never felt so strongly that it is really a necessity to you.' On another occasion she described Norway as 'the land of Fred's constant longing'.

Delius identified subtropical Florida as the place where he, as a young man, had determined on a life as a composer. On returning from America he studied at Leipzig and then moved to Paris, where he enjoyed the Bohemian pleasures sought by many artists there in the 1890s. For the last thirty-five years of his life his home was in a French village. Places rich in colour, or exotic nature, or urban energy – such sensual locations always beckoned to Delius. Nevertheless, at regular intervals he needed to flee northwards in order to get his 'old self back again', as he put it. His physical energy was restored by weeks of bathing by the Kristiania Fjord; to reinvigorate his self-belief and to re-envisage his artistic direction he travelled on to the great Norwegian mountains. Again and again.

Norway became an essential active ingredient in his creative processes, easily recognisable in his output. Some thirty-three compositions, large and small, were inspired by his Norwegian experiences or were settings of texts by Norwegian poets. There would be music depicting a Norwegian sleigh ride and Norwegian folk tales; there would be music full of longing for the

Norwegian summer and the call of the cuckoo deep in the birch woods; there would be incidental music for Norwegian theatre bands; and above all else there would be a series of tone poems for orchestra, or orchestra and choir, powered by emotions he associated with journeys in the Norwegian mountains, the greatest of these being *The Song of the High Hills*. A further eighteen compositions using texts by Danish authors can also be said to have directly resulted from Delius's attachments to Norway. My principal ambition for this study has, therefore, been to bring into focus and give perspective to this Norwegian imperative in Delius's art.

A secondary goal has been to determine the composer's place in the history of Norwegian culture. So varied is the chemistry of his creative alchemy that no single country can lay claim to Frederick Delius. The music historians of several countries have, however, celebrated the fact that their culture has formed part of one of the most extraordinary musical personalities of the twentieth century. In England, a cottage industry of Delius research is thriving; in recent years biographical works have appeared in America and significant studies of his music in France and Germany. In Norway, however, his name and his music are practically unknown. An untidy cluster of partial explanations can be offered, including these: Delius lacked a Norwegian champion of his music; his mature chromatic language can appear challenging to audiences; and the inflated instrumentation of his principal works chimes discordantly with the modest budgets of Norwegian orchestras. Most significant, however, was the damage inflicted on Delius's reputation by the events of October 1897 surrounding the production of *Folkeraadet* at the Christiania Theater. After that scandal the composer was *persona non grata* in Norwegian musical circles for the rest of his life.

When Delius sought creative stimulus from culture, rather than nature, he most often turned to Scandinavian artists. His intimate friendship with Edvard Grieg has been well documented. In Paris, Delius was a familiar figure in the artist colonies that gathered in impecunious camaraderie in Montmartre and Montrouge, and also here it was mainly Norwegian artists who attracted the company of the English musician. His close friendship with Edvard Munch started in Paris and blossomed during Delius's visits to Munch on the coast of the Kristiania Fjord. Grieg and Munch were only two of the many artists he knew. In 1899, Norway got its National Theatre, and in a cartoon made of the gala opening night the country's leading cultural celebrities are arrayed in the best seats. One registers with astonishment that almost every one of them was a friend or acquaintance of Frederick Delius: Johan Halvorsen, Bjørnstjerne Bjørnson, Bjørn Bjørnson, Gunnar Heiberg, Tulla Larsen, Ola Thommessen, Christian Krohg, Oda Krohg, Hjalmar Christensen, Vilhelm Krag, Sigurd Bødtker, Hans Aanrud and others.

These two themes form the foundation of this study: Norway in Delius's creative process, and Delius's role in Norwegian culture. It has, however, also been my wish to trace Delius's travels in Norway in as much detail as the often meagre sources allow; his preferences tell us much about his relationship to the country. The extensive periods he spent by the Kristiania Fjord are fully explored here for the first time. For others who also might like to follow in his footsteps, the descriptions of his journeys will be useful. This part of my research brought me to many beautiful parts of the country, and also into contact with a large number of Norwegians who generously aided me in my quest. This is especially true in and around Lesjaskog, where the myths surrounding the composer's final extraordinary ascent of Liahovdane are well known.

I have lived in Norway since 1980 and have been able to make full use of source material in national archives such as the National Library, the Grieg Archives of the Bergen Public Library, the National Archives of Norway and the Munch Museum. Significant new material about Delius's relationships with Norwegians and Norway can be presented in this study.

Norwegian orthography poses challenges for anyone writing about the past history of the country, and for the present volume the most pressing problem was the various spellings of place names that were in active use. It is not uncommon for three different spellings of one place name to have been officially supported in the last hundred and fifty years. (For example, in 1889 Delius stayed at a mountain lodge he referred to as Nystuen. Locals would never have taken this Dano-Norwegian version of the name into their mouths, instead referring to the lodge as Nystova or Nystøgo – versions recognised in standardised rural Norwegian and regional dialect. All three versions occur on maps of the area.) In 1991, the Department of Culture introduced a process, reinforced by a Place Name Law, that would establish one official spelling of each place name. Kartverket (the Norwegian Mapping Authority) administers a *Sentralt stadsnamnregister* (central register of place names), and it is the spelling prescribed here that I use for place names. If, however, an earlier spelling is also in general use, this is acknowledged in a footnote. Where outdated place names occur in letters and diaries, the modern equivalent is given in brackets. In instances where place names have been completely changed – Kristiania to Oslo, Fredriksværn to Stavern, etc. – I have elected to use the name with which Delius was familiar. (The form Kristiania was adopted in 1877, replacing the Danish version Christiania, and the ancient name Oslo was reinstated in 1925. All of Delius's twenty visits fall, therefore, within the period when the city was called Kristiania.)

A further level of orthographical confusion can be caused by the fact that the written language used by most educated Norwegians in Delius's day – including Edvard Grieg and Henrik Ibsen – was to all intents and purposes not Norwegian at all, but Danish. The reasons for this and its implications are explored in some detail at the end of Chapter One.

All translations from Scandinavian languages, including those of poetical texts, are mine where not otherwise stated. Where original correspondence in Norwegian and German has been available, I have made new translations.

Although often originally published with German titles, Delius's works are today mostly performed under and known by their English titles. I have therefore elected to use the familiar English titles throughout the text, as published in the Collected Edition; exceptions are made for works with non-English titles that have become widely accepted, such as *Paa Vidderne*, *Folkeraadet*, *Idylle de Printemps* and *Mitternachtslied Zarathustras*. Original non-English titles are cross-referenced in the index.

It is seldom today that anyone embarks on a project like the present volume, involving extensive research in several countries, without the backing of a university or other research institution. The fact that this book has finally reached publication without these safety nets is partly due to the fact that the officers of the Delius Trust were quick to see the value of the project, and the encouragement they have given the author has been an essential factor in lifting the writing process onwards. Special mention must be made of Dr Lionel Carley, archivist to the Delius Trust, who has been unstintingly generous with his time and advice. At the same time, my indebtedness to his trailblazing research into the subject of Delius in Norway, presented in his two volumes of Delius letters and the single-volume Delius–Grieg correspondence, is gladly stated here.

My thanks are also extended to the staff of various archival institutions, including, in alphabetical order, the Arne Bjørndal Collection in Bergen (Sigbjørn Apeland), the Bergen Public Library (Siren Steen, Leader of Music Department), the British Library (Dr Sandra Tuppen, Curator of Music Manuscripts), the Grainger Museum in Melbourne (Astrid Krautschneider, Curator, and Monica Syrette, Assistant Curator), Gudbrandsdalsmusea (Tor Stallvik, Archivist), Hochschule für Musik und Theater 'Felix Mendelssohn Bartholdy' Leipzig (Anke Hofmann, Head Librarian), Jacksonville Public Library, Florida Collection (Raymond W. Neal, Senior Librarian), Jacksonville University Library, Florida, Kvinnemuseet/The Norwegian Women's Museum in Kongsvinger (Kari Sommerseth Jacobsen, Director), the Munch Museum in Oslo (Lasse Jacobsen, Research Librarian), and Riksarkivet/The National Archives of Norway.

I have benefited from sharing with Roger Buckley our fascination with Delius in Norway, and he has generously shared with me many insights into the Norway diaries written by the composer. Research into Norwegian friends of Delius was also aided by people who have previously delved into these lives, including Dr John Bergsagel (Halfdan Jebe), Øyvin Dybsand (Johan Halvorsen), Merethe Ramm (Camilla Jacobsen) and Mona Lie Thommessen (Mons Lie). Special thanks must be reserved for Professor Asbjørn Ø. Eriksen, who unstintingly shared with me his boundless knowledge both of Edvard Grieg and of Norwegian culture in general.

I would also like to express my gratitude to the many Norwegians around the country who have pointed me in the right direction or helped solve puzzles regarding Delius's journeys by the fjords and on the mountains, including: Trond Braaten, Arild Haglund, Anne Karine Haugsrud and Gunn Erna Løde-mel (Bagn and Valdres); Trygve K. Norman (Finse); Lorenz Hjelle, Emma Hjelle and Anne Mari Aamelfot Hjelle (Hjelle and Sunndal); Anne Wangen (Juvvasshytta); Erik Collett (Leirungshytta); Hans Enstad, Gudrun Haraldsen Faukstad, Jon Faukstad, Sonja Mathisen, Ole Erik Mølmen, Mette Øverli and Per Øven Øverli (Lesjaskog); Sverre Folkestad and Ola Nyhagen (Sandene); Solveig Lund (Skirstad and Nesodden); Astrid Hermansen (Sæli Gård); and Harald Sve Bjørndal (Vågå). In addition, I would like to express my gratitude to Lesja Municipality for financial assistance that made possible the inclusion of several illustrations.

I was fortunate in having the advocacy of Bruce Phillips when this volume was put forward for publication. It was taken under the wing of Boydell & Brewer, and I warmly express my gratitude to editor Michael Middeke, assistant editor Megan Milan and their appointed readers for their many suggestions as to how embarrassing faults might be avoided.

This book is dedicated to my partner Sonja Nyegaard, with whom I travel *paa vidderne*.

Andrew J. Boyle
Gressvik, Norway
Summer, 2016

Abbreviations

BB	Bartók Archive, Budapest
BL	The British Library, London
BOB	Bergen offentlige bibliotek/Bergen Public Library
CB	Collection of Christopher Brunel
DT	The Delius Trust, London
EG1	Finn Benestad, *Edvard Grieg: brev i utvalg 1862–1907, I: Til norske mottagere* (*Selected Letters 1862–1907, I: To Norwegian recipients*) (Oslo: Aschehoug, 1998)
EG2	Finn Benestad, *Edvard Grieg: brev i utvalg 1862–1907, II: Til utenlandske mottagere* (*Selected Letters 1862–1907, II: To foreign recipients*) (Oslo: Aschehoug, 1998)
GD	Lionel Carley, *Grieg and Delius. A Chronicle of their Friendship in Letters* (London: Marion Boyars, 1993)
GM	The Grainger Museum collection, University of Melbourne
JR	Finn Benestad and Hanna de Vries Stavland: *Edvard Grieg und Julius Röntgen, Briefwechsel 1883–1907* (Utrecht: Koninklijke Vereniging voor Nederlandse Muziekgeschiedenis, 1997)
JUL	Jacksonville University Library, Florida
KB	Det Kongelige Bibliotek/Royal Library, Copenhagen
LC1	Lionel Carley, *Delius: A life in letters, I: 1862–1908* (London: Scolar Press, 1983)
LC2	Lionel Carley, *Delius: A life in letters, II: 1909–1934* (London: Scolar Press, 1988)
MM	Munchmuseet/Munch Museum, Oslo
NB	Nasjonalbiblioteket/The National Library, Oslo
PG	Grainger Estate, White Plains, New York
RA	Riksarkivet/The National Archives of Norway
RM	Rodin Museum, Paris
UE	Universal Edition Archives
ØV	Collection of Mette Øverli

Selected glossary of landscape terms used in place names

The following words appear as suffixes in Norwegian place names, for instance Stav*anger*, Vørings*fossen*, Lesja*skog*:

anger	fjord	**angen**	the fjord
berg	hill, mountain	**bergen**	the hill, the mountain
bu	small house	**bua/buen**	the small house
bø	farm	**bøen**	the farm
dal	valley	**dalen**	the valley
fjell/fjeld	mountain	**fjellet/fjeldet**	the mountain
foss	waterfall	**fossen**	the waterfall
gard/gård	farm	**garden/gården**	the farm
haug	hill	**haugen**	the hill
havn	harbour	**havnen**	the harbour
hytte	cabin, lodge	**hytta/hytten**	the cabin, the lodge
li	slope	**lia/lien**	the slope
nes	promontory	**neset**	the promontory
odde	tongue of land	**odden**	the tongue of land
pigg	peak	**piggen**	the peak
seter	mountain farm	**setra/seteren**	the mountain farm
skog	wood, forest	**skogen**	the wood, the forest
stad	place, town	**staden**	the place, the town
støl	mountain farm	**stølen**	the mountain farm
sund	sound	**sundet**	the sound
vang	meadow lawn	**vangen**	the meadow lawn
vann/vatn	lake	**vannet/vatnet**	the lake
vidde	mountain plateau	**vidda/vidden**	the mountain plateau
vik	cove, bay	**vika/viken**	the cove, the bay
øy	island	**øya**	the island
ås	hill	**åsen**	the hill

1

Norway's awakening

'He's either completely lost his mind, or he's English'
Norwegian saying, mid-nineteenth century

In the early afternoon of 28 July 1889, three tired hikers arrived at the mountain cabin at Eidsbugarden. They had been travelling inland from the west coast for several days, but it was here at the portal to the Jotunheim mountains they felt that their summer tour would really begin. The eldest of the three was Edvard Grieg (forty-six), the youngest was Fritz Delius (twenty-seven), and for both this journey was the fulfilment of a long-held desire. Since getting to know Delius two years earlier, Grieg had been seeking an opportunity to introduce him to Jotunheimen. Delius had been under the influence of Grieg's music since his boyhood, and now the Norwegian was to be his personal guide to Norway's most magnificent nature. The third member of the trio was Christian Sinding (thirty-three). Emerging from an obsessive and secret love affair, he was looking forward to this journey as a key to regaining his equanimity.

Around the dinner table that evening a dozen travellers gathered. Among them was a Norwegian with a huge beard, a historian who, in the coming battle for Norwegian independence and national realisation, would have an even greater role to play than Grieg. For three hundred years the country had been governed from Denmark. In the aftermath of the Napoleonic Wars, Norway entered into a union with Sweden in which there was virtual political equality. As the tide of Romantic nationalism swept Europe in the nineteenth century, Norwegian nationalists demanded full sovereignty for their nation. Once independence was achieved in 1905, Norwegian commentators would regard Professor Ernst Sars as the spiritual father of the victory.[1]

Grieg and Sars. At this first, impromptu meeting between two giants of Norwegian cultural life, Delius was a witness. It was a remarkable moment and can serve as a fitting point of departure for this chapter about the Norway

---

[1] Jacob S. Worm-Müller, *Ideer og mennesker* (*Ideas and People*) (Oslo: Aschehoug, 1954), 52.

that Delius would have experienced at the close of the nineteenth century. For here, seated at the table at Eidsbugarden, were representatives of the dualism that came to typify Norway's political and cultural awakening. Everyone in the cabin, Sars and Grieg included, would have been attracted there by Old Norway: the Norway of the free-minded peasant, the mountain shepherd, the summer farm hanging from a seemingly inaccessible hillside. Sars and Grieg were, however, also trailblazers for a New Norway that was politically independent of its neighbours. Aware that the success of their modern project depended on imbuing it with a sense of cultural continuity, they travelled to the mountains to refresh their energies.

Both aspects of this dualism were present in the attraction Delius felt to the country, and seemingly in equal measure. He cultivated Norway's modern men, such as Edvard Munch and Gunnar Heiberg, and modern women, such as Randi Blehr and Ragnhild Juel. At the same time, he experienced the pull of Norway for much the same reason as all other British tourists during the industrial era. Old Norway was the perfect refuge from Britain's crowded cities and polluting industry.

Frederick Delius visited Norway twenty times, ten of the visits were before the turn of the century, ten after.

The English invasion:
'they know they are at the centre of everything'

The surface area of the British mainland is roughly two-thirds that of Norway. In 1900, some 2.2 million people lived in Norway. In England, Scotland and Wales there were seventeen times as many, some 37 million people, a figure that represented a quadrupling of the population in a hundred years.

The British aristocracy had discovered Norway's angling rivers and hunting grounds in the first half of the nineteenth century and had them more or less to themselves. After 1850, the growing British middle class joined in the fun. Many of the *nouveaux riches* would travel south to Greece and Italy on a modernised version of the Grand Tour, often adhering to packaged itineraries along new railway routes. The Romantic desire to glory in mountain nature could also be indulged in the Alps. Many travellers chose, however, to journey north to the wild landscapes of Norway, finding cool, clean air and majestic natural experiences, and without being herded with other tourists on packaged trips. For British people fleeing their industrialised hometowns there was the added draw of experiencing at first hand a pre-industrial rural society. Britons created the Norwegian tourism industry and came to dominate it. One visitor to Bergen in 1888 counted the nationalities of tourists in his hotel register the previous summer: 559 guests came from Britain, 9 from Germany, 7 from Australia, 4 from Denmark, 3 from Holland, 2 from Russia and 2 from Cuba. There were also 119 Norwegians, most of whom would have been in Bergen for commercial reasons.[2] From the middle of the century comes the anecdote of a farmer who, on seeing yet another rambler descending from a mountain edge, exclaimed: 'He's either completely lost his mind, or he's English.'[3]

Walking for sport was itself a recent phenomenon, an expression of the modern spirit. In *The Northern Utopia* (2003), a study of travel books written by British tourists in Norway during this period, Peter Fjågesund and Ruth A. Symes write: 'Whereas in the eighteenth century walking had been regarded as socially degrading, primarily because associated with poverty and vagrancy, the nineteenth century – inspired by Romantic philosophy – had a keen sense of the quality of man's direct contact with the elements.'[4] To these attractions for Englishmen can also be added the romance of Norway as the cradle of Viking culture. Early Nordic settlements in Britain had been the focus of archaeological exploration in the late nineteenth century; the upper classes, engaged in nation and empire building, looked to mythical Nordic forebears as evidence of their own racial superiority.[5]

That Norway functioned as a pressure valve for Britons growing up in an increasingly industrialised society, is a modern reading of the phenomenon. At the time, the perception of the well-educated and well-heeled Englishman – kingpin of the Empire – was, in part, that he was drawn to Norway to enjoy his cultural superiority. One such traveller was Joseph Phythian, who, in his *Scenes of Travel in Norway* (1877), ruminated on having

> felt it an honour to belong to England, for the name, 'Englishman', is rather grander than that of 'Roman'. We scarcely realise this at home, but in a distant land, looking, some way, more broadly upon the world, the fact has more significance. The feeling is not that I, as an individual, am above these other people, but that my country, of which I am part, is above theirs.[6]

The peasants of Norway were considered worthy of much the same degree of wonderment as the benighted tribes of Africa, and for the same reasons. The popular travel writer Frederick Metcalfe, an Anglican vicar, summarised his experiences from a journey to Telemark in 1856: '[The] avidity with which books of travel in primitive countries – whether in the tropics or under the pole – are now read, shows that the more refined a community is, the greater interest it will take in the occupation, the sentiments, the manners of people still in a primitive state of existence.'[7]

---

[2] Quoted by Peter Fjågesund and Ruth A. Symes, *The Northern Utopia: British perceptions of Norway in the nineteenth century* (Amsterdam & New York: Rodopi, 2003), 70.

[3] The origin of the anecdote now seems lost. It is quoted in material published by Den Norske Turistforening (Norwegian Trekking Association).

[4] Fjågesund and Symes, *The Northern Utopia*, 83.

[5] See *ibid.*, 121.

[6] J. C. Phythian, *Scenes of Travel in Norway* (London: Cassell, Petter & Gilpin, 1877), 122.

[7] Frederick Metcalfe, *The Oxonian in Thelemarken; or Notes of Excursions in that Country*, second edition, revised (London: Hurst and Blackett, 1858. First edition, 1856), viii.

Books about Norway were read avidly. There was a market of middle-class consumers enthralled by the prospect of exploring wild and primitive Norway, and a stream of guidebooks and personal travel accounts were penned to inspire and accompany travellers. According to Fjågesund and Symes, from the last decades of the eighteenth century to the end of the nineteenth, British travellers to Norway published around two hundred travelogues, more than half of them between 1870 and 1890. Before the First World War, titles such as *Norway: The Road and the Fell*, *The Adventures of Five Spinsters in Norway*, *The Land of the Long Night* and, most famously, *Three in Norway (by two of them)* adorned the shelves of every metropolitan bookshop in Britain. Among the more significant names was William Mattieu Williams, who, with his two guides – *Through Norway with a Knapsack* (1859) and *Through Norway with Ladies* (1877) – made the country and its culture seem both accessible and exotic. What Williams did for the hiker, Yorkshireman William Cecil Slingsby did for the mountaineer with his *Norway: The Northern Playground* (1904). It is a title forged with the same sense of cultural superiority that Joseph Phythian invoked when he wrote: 'Surely Norway has been made as a playground for the people of other countries, but especially for Englishmen.'[8]

Most accommodation on offer to the tourist was at farmhouses that doubled as post houses, bringing the traveller into close contact with the rural peasantry – and clashes of culture abound in the travelogues. In many, the author expresses his astonishment that the farmer was not in the service of an aristocratic landowner, but was his own lord and master. Insecure in Norway's flattened class structure, travellers of the British middle and upper classes struggled to find a suitable tone when addressing peasants who regarded themselves as their social equals. The travellers were in the habit of addressing the farmer as if he were a servant and were dismayed when they were sharply corrected or simply ignored. One author offered this advice:

> It is advisable to treat every Norwegian, however low in the social scale, with the utmost courtesy, as they are very independent, and do not relish being ordered about. As for the station-keepers and their families, the best plan is to treat them not as hotel-keepers, but as your host, and to ask everything as a favour, and demand nothing as a right.[9]

The absence of a feudal past in Norway, in combination with the ancient udal or odal law governing property rights, had made for an independent and proud class of farm owners for which the only parallels in the British Isles were to be found in the predominantly Nordic cultures of Orkney, Shetland and the Isle of Man. The person first in line to take over the farm was the oldest son,

---

[8] Phythian, *Scenes of Travel in Norway*, 113–14.
[9] Sydney Peel, *Our Trip in Norway* (London: Roworth, 1881), 74.

who was given the right of priority to do so with the farm undivided. Recent commentators have summarised the law in this way:

> He had to buy the farm, and the take-over was termed a sale. The income from the sale was distributed between him and his siblings, according to the portion each was to inherit. If possible, younger siblings were given landed properties or values. This was not always possible, and then the siblings would be allotted an ideal part of the family farm, and the oldest brother would have to pay them yearly rent. There were legal regulations against the splitting of farms, in order to keep the farm viable as an economic unit.[10]

The differences in social conditions attributable to udal property rights gave critically minded travellers of the nineteenth century much to think about. One of these was Samuel Laing, who lived in Norway for several years in the 1830s and noted that, while one in five Norwegians held property, only around one in twenty-two of the rural peasantry of Ireland owned any land. He was well aware that the conclusion he drew, in his *Journal of a Residence in Norway* (1837), would be regarded as 'extravagant or visionary', but stated it all the same; namely, that 'the diffusion of property through society is the only radical cure for that king's-evil of all feudally constructed societies, – pauperism and over-multiplication'.[11]

Travel on Norway's roads was strictly regulated by the Highways Law. This stipulated the number of post houses that were to be found along the main arteries and what the traveller would be charged for use of their horses, carriages, accommodation and food. Tourists expecting the post house to be a well-equipped inn or lodge were frequently surprised by the Norwegian system: 'There appear to be no establishments in Norway corresponding to our publichouse, the French auberge, the German gasthaus, or the Italian osteria: everybody appears to live at home. These posting stations are farmhouses.'[12]

The food on offer usually consisted of bread, milk, cheese and fish, but from the 1850s meat dishes also became more frequent. Apart from potatoes, vegetables were scarce. Travellers often commented on the admirable cleanliness of the post houses, but this was of course on a sliding scale; the further one strayed from the main highways, the less one could expect. Edvard Grieg, on returning from a mountain tour in 1893 with an irritating skin rash, thundered

---

[10] Hans Henrik Bull and Sølvi Sogner, 'Families and Land Ownership in Norwegian Mountain Societies' (abstract), paper delivered at XIV International Economic History Congress, 2006, accessed 1 April 2016 at www.helsinki.fi/iehc2006/papers1/Bull26.

[11] Samuel Laing, *Journal of a Residence in Norway* (London: Longman, Orme, Brown, Green and Longmans, 1837), 480–1.

[12] William Mattieu Williams, *Through Norway With a Knapsack*, new edition (London: Edward Stanford, 1876), 35.

in a letter: 'Oh yes, Jotunheimen is beautiful, but it is also a pigsty! [...] My affliction was caused by *Jotun beds!*'[13]

In the diary he kept of his summer tour in 1887, Delius describes lodging at the Hjerkinn post house as one of the highlights of his holiday, with folk dances demonstrated for the guests by the herd girls (see p. 26). Other travellers had written of the culinary pleasures to be had there:

> The kitchen at Jerkin is justly famous. It is a large wooden hall, a log saloon, whose rich brown smoke-tinted timbers and blazing fire, where something is always frying, form a most enjoyable contrast with the bleak waste outside. Every tourist of sound taste prefers to do all his feeding in this kitchen, and leaves the fine room over the way to the inexperienced visitors.[14]

To cope with the invasion from Britain, the tourism infrastructure was substantially upgraded during the second half of the nineteenth century. In 1856, Williams wrote of his hiking adventures in the country, having travelled *Through Norway with a Knapsack*. Eighteen years later, wishing to update his popular account, he retraced his routes. The changes that had occurred startled him:

> the good hostess of Dombaas had become more like an hotel keeper, the entertainment of guests being now obviously a matter of business routine and no longer an excitement. [...] The domestic welcome of the peasant farmer has departed, the participation in the family meal with the farmer, his wife and farmhands, is no more.[15]

The kitchen and private chambers were now hidden from tourists. Instead, they were more likely shown into 'a special apartment, which in many cases is furnished with downright mahogany and Tottenham-Court-Road upholstery'. Williams added the assurance, however, that the traveller willing to abandon the main arteries for mountain trails would quickly rediscover Norway at its most exotic, more or less unsullied by tourism.

Entrepreneurs exploited the tidal wave of visitors. The old post houses were eclipsed by a type of accommodation never before seen in the villages: splendid wooden hotels of three and four storeys that towered over the boat houses in fjord harbours and over the general store in fertile valleys. At principal junctions these magnificently appointed tourist hotels sprang up to cater to the tastes and demands of the foreign visitor. One such was the imposing Hotel Hardanger in Odda, financed by English entrepreneurs. Delius spent a night there in 1887 (see p. 25), at just the same time as the Norwegian writer Johan Bøgh, who has left us his impressions:

---

[13] Letter from Edvard Grieg to Julius Röntgen, 17 August 1893 (JR).
[14] Williams, *Through Norway with a Knapsack* (1876), 57.
[15] *Ibid.*, 64.

One could immediately see that this was a building created for a specific purpose, it did not give the haphazard impression that typifies many of the afterthought extensions to country hotels, in response to the growth in tourism, which never seem to be either comfortable or solidly constructed. [...] Here there was a buzz and a fuss in all the corridors and on the long verandas a prattle in English, German and French, boys running with suitcases, electric bells ringing and the serving girls in local Hardanger costumes moving through this hubbub as quickly and quietly as would professional hotel staff.

[...]

Dinner is served, as is the English custom, at 7 o'clock, followed by a cup of tea, after which the guests take their strolls in the mild, twilight August evening on the road between the houses. It is as lively as along any large promenade.

[...]

The Englishmen appear to be in their own element, in their own Odde [Odda], where they know they are at the centre of everything.[16]

Norwegians were clearly in a minority in these hotels, but as the century wore on they too began to discover the pleasures of rural and mountain holidays. In 1868, Den Norske Turistforening (the Norwegian Trekking Association) was formed with the aim of acquiring the means 'to ease and develop outdoor life in this country'. In the course of a few years the first mountain lodges had been established, their price tariff and amenities regulated by the association.

If the larger hotels were 'home from home' for the Englishman, he also travelled with enough equipment to feel ready for any eventuality. Johan Bøgh again: 'Sticking boldly out of the countless pockets which they had managed to attach to the most astonishing parts of their costume were travel guides, maps, tobacco, fire steel and God alone knows what else.'[17] The Irish-American author J. Ross Browne was amused to see how much luggage typical English tourists were recommended to bring with them to Norway: 'two suits of clothes, a Mackintosh, a portable desk, an India-rubber pillow, a few blankets, an opera-glass, a musquito-net, a thermometer, some dried beef, and a dozen boxes of sardines, besides a stock of white bread, and two bottles of English pickles'.[18]

From post house to post house the traveller hired a carriole, a light open carriage for one person, often described in that period as 'Norway's national vehicle'. Indeed, Fjågesund and Symes – noting the attention British travel writers paid to the modest vehicle – conclude that the carriole was 'the perfect conveyance in which the romantic and solitary traveller, exposed to wind and weather but still protected by the narrow, coffin-like box, can commune with

---

[16] Johan Bøgh, *Fra Bergenskanten* (*From Bergen and its Surrounds*) (Bergen: Ed. B. Giertsens forl., 1888), 97–100.

[17] *Ibid.*, 106.

[18] J. Ross Browne, *The Land of Thor* (New York: Harper & Brothers, 1867), 317.

1. A carriole-boy waits for a tourist outside Stalheim Hotel. The view is east down
Nærøydalen towards Gudvangen.

the natural surroundings'.[19] How long you might reasonably have to wait at the
post house before a horse and carriole was put at your disposal was regulated
by the price tariff and by the standard of station. At an express station transport
was guaranteed within a quarter of an hour. In remote areas the wait could
stretch up to three hours while a horse was fetched from a neighbouring farm.
The carriole-boys and carriole-girls were an exotic feature of many a traveller's
account. They would sit on a board at the back of the carriage, enduring the
dust storm, in order to drive the carriage back to its home station. Towards the
end of the century, the carriole was superseded by the chaise and roads were
being constantly upgraded. 'The main roads of Norway are admirably made
and kept', noted one visitor. 'They are, in fact, fine specimens of engineering,
which are increased every year, under the wise liberality of the government'.[20]

Up the deep valleys and across the wide fjords of Norway the British tourists travelled, guidebook in hand, map in pocket. But did they look beneath
the surface at larger social trends in Norway, not least in the peasant class with
whom they had daily intercourse? In 1845 only 15 per cent of Norwegians lived
in towns and cities; by 1900 some 36 per cent inhabited urban centres – 'a fact
which suggests that there was considerable pressure on resources', as Fjågesund

[19] Fjågesund and Symes, *The Northern Utopia*, 90.
[20] Edward Spender, *Fjord, Isle, and Tor* (London: Charlton Tucker, 1870), 11.

and Symes aptly reflect.[21] This pressure would, of course, have been considerably worse if not offset by mass emigration. Over 800,000 Norwegians crossed the Atlantic in the period 1825 to 1939; at its peak in the early 1880s, the flight of the Norwegian peasantry amounted to fifteen people per thousand of the population.[22]

For his *Turist i Gudbrandsdalen på 1800-tallet*, Arne Flatmoen made a study of British travelogues and concluded: 'The crisis years, especially those of the 1860s during which the burgeoning class of rural tenants lived in poverty and need, elicited no response from the writers.'[23]

Frederick Delius was also born into the moneyed middle class of British society, the echelon that 'discovered' rural Norway in the nineteenth century. With those among this group who brought to Norway an ingrained cultural arrogance he was, however, to make a decisive break early in his adult life. It was, indeed, the composer's appreciation, not deprecation, of peculiarly Norwegian values and qualities that was to endear him to Edvard Grieg.

A national reawakening

Norway's Constitution was established in 1814. Considerable growing pains – political, economic and cultural – mark the country's rapid advance from that point towards full independence in 1905. Many of these far-reaching and dynamic changes would directly impact on the life of Frederick Delius.

Under the provisions of the Treaty of Kiel of 1814 Denmark ceded Norway, not to Sweden, but to the Swedish crown. This opened the way for a union with Sweden, with Norway as an equal partner – a nation state ruled by its parliament, the Storting, and with its own liberal constitution. After several hundred years of government from Copenhagen, Norway was to all intents and purposes independent. Jan Eivind Myhre writes:

> The most important elements [of the Constitution] were that the country should have its own seat of government at which the people were represented, that there should be equality under the law, and that certain civil rights should be protected, including freedom of expression and the right to pursue trade. The Constitution also enshrined several important social advances. The aristocracy was to be removed after a few years. Furthermore, even though the Constitution, at least indirectly, upheld the power of the civil servants, it also extended the suffrage to landowners, businessmen and other propertied citizens, thereby giving them political influence. In the course of a couple of generations after

---

[21] Fjågesund and Symes, *The Northern Utopia*, 228–9.
[22] *Utvandringsstatistikk: Utgitt av Departementet for Sosiale Saker* (*Emigration Statistics: Published by the Department of Social Affairs*) (Kristiania: H. Aschehoug & Co., 1921), 7.
[23] Arne Flatmoen, *Turist i Gudbrandsdalen på 1800-tallet* (*Tourism in the Gudbrandsdal in the Nineteenth Century*) (Oslo: Cappelen Damm, 2007), 91.

1814, therefore, much of the social and political power in the country passed
from the civil servants to town-dwellers with large commercial interests.[24]

These liberal provisions seem visionary, considering how little the ground for
them had been prepared by preceding generations. A further expansion of
the principles of the Constitution was introduced in 1837 with the Local Government Acts. These enshrined in Norwegian law a far more decentralised
model of governance than in neighbouring countries. To this model can also
be attributed the fact that the effects of the February Revolution that shook
the rest of Europe in 1848 were little felt in Norway. These were developments
in the direction of increased democratisation, and inevitably one result was
that the old model of a civil servant state seemed increasingly out of step with
the spectrum of opinion in the country. Gradually the fronts were mobilised.
On one side stood the church, the government, the civil servants and wealthy
businessmen; on the other, landowners, radical youth movements, artists and
the proponents of an indigenous Norwegian language. 'For the conservatives
this was a battle for morality', writes Karsten Alnæs. 'Christianity, marriage and
the political hierarchy – against forces of chaos, ungodliness and moral dissolution. For many of the radicals it was a fight for truth, justice, transparency,
democracy and national independence.'[25] Oppositional voices clamoured for
the formation of a left-wing party. Finally, in 1884, the government and Swedish monarch were out-manoeuvred and, to avoid a constitutional crisis, the
opposition was asked to form a cabinet. Two distinctive political wings of left
and right (*Venstre* and *Høyre*) had now emerged and a parliamentary system
became the political reality in Norway.

   In the middle of the nineteenth century, modern Norway began to take
shape, both politically and socially. Danish-controlled Norway had suffered
greatly during the depression of the Napoleonic Wars. In their aftermath, the
three generations between 1814 and 1905 experienced a remarkable increase in
population, industrialisation and urbanisation. Jan Eivind Myhre again: 'From
being a country dependent on its export of commodities such as fish, timber,
iron, silver and copper, Norway made huge strides towards becoming an
economy excelling in the production of goods and services, and was in large
part industrialised. Only Great Britain (in particular) and Belgium embraced
the industrialisation of production at an earlier stage.'[26] Better lines of communication were a priority. In 1854, the country's first railway was opened,
and around the same time a new road through the Gudbrandsdal – part of the
principal artery from Kristiania running north to Trondheim. The repeal of

---

[24] Jan Eivind Myhre, *Norsk historie 1814–1905: Å byggje ein stat og skape ein nasjon* (*History of
Norway 1814–1905: To build a state and create a nation*) (Oslo: Det Norske Samlaget, 2012), 12.

[25] Karsten Alnæs, *Historien om Norge, III: Mot moderne tider* (*History of Norway, III: Towards
modern times*) (Oslo: Gyldendal, 1998), 497.

[26] Myhre, *Norsk historie*, 15.

the English Navigation Acts in 1849 ignited an explosive growth in seaborne trade; in thirty years the Norwegian merchant fleet expanded from 290,000 tons to 1,500,000 tons.

It was precisely the importance of the merchant navy to the country's economy that ignited the political conflict that came to dominate all political life in Norway in the last twenty years of the nineteenth century. The conflict set in motion a process that escalated into a fight for full sovereignty and the final dissolution of the union with Sweden. In 1885, the union government decreed that foreign affairs would be fronted by a committee consisting of three Swedes and one Norwegian. The anger this created among Norwegian radicals was enormous, not least because consulates in harbours all over the world were under the jurisdiction of this committee. The consulate issue would bring down a string of governments in Norway in the years that followed. So rebellious was the Norwegian left wing that in 1895 Sweden threatened its 'little brother' Norway with war if it did not fall into line.

It was in this climate that the materials for forging a new Norwegian identity were assembled. The nation had indeed begun to assert itself in many arenas. From 1888 to 1889, Fridtjof Nansen made a crossing of Greenland by ski, an achievement of endurance that put his name on lips all across the world. In 1893, Nansen set sail for the Arctic Ocean with plans to reach the North Pole. His mission failed, but in 1896 he reached the mainland again, reappearing just one year after the humiliation Norway suffered in the consulate issue. Nansen returned south in a blaze of glory, received in every Norwegian harbour as a hero of his people and times. On other fronts, the radical activists of the language movement campaigned to make Norwegians aware of how much their culture had been infected by Danish customs. Gro Hagemann has pointed out that, for the leaders of the movement, 'the language issue was part and parcel of a wider national struggle through which Norwegian culture would be restored after centuries of foreign subjugation.'[27]

With his monumental *Udsigt over den norske historie* (*Overview of Norwegian History*), published in four volumes from 1873 to 1891, Ernst Sars – whom Grieg and Delius encountered at Eidsbugarden – gave his countrymen an image of themselves as proud inheritors of thousand-year-old values. Writing of how liberal the ordinances of the Constitution seemed to Norwegians, Sars pointed out that many 'have been willing to regard them as almost miraculous.'[28] He proposed another explanation that would have far-reaching consequences in the forging of a new Norwegian identity: namely, that the liberality of the Constitution reflected the continuity of the farming class during

---

[27] Gro Hagemann, *Aschehougs norgeshistorie, IX: Det moderne gjennombrudd 1870–1905* (*History of Norway, IX: The modern breakthrough 1870–1905*) (Oslo: Aschehoug, 1997), 166.

[28] J. E. Sars, *Udsigt over den norske historie, I* (*Overview of Norwegian History, I*) (Christiania: Cammermeyer, 1873), 3.

centuries of distant rule from Copenhagen. According to Sars, the greatness represented by the regional kings of the Viking Age had been kept alive and vigorous through the dark centuries of Danish rule. An inexplicable miracle that the 1814 Constitution should be forged in a blaze of liberal values? Not according to Sars, who 'showed us the continuity in our history, the indissoluble continuity that had never been broken, because the people had always been themselves. [...] It is this interpretation of a continuous history that laid the foundations for a broad national consensus.'[29] These are sentiments that, to modern ears, suggest a form of isolationism; but to the British nation-builders of the Victorian age it was exactly the sort of cultural pride with which they wished to identify themselves.

At its most heated the fight for independence was a boiling cauldron of feelings, and it was into this soup that Delius would fall in 1897 – a victim of fervent nationalistic sentiment – with his music to *Folkeraadet*. Norway's leading dramatist at the time, Gunnar Heiberg, had written the play as a satire on the Norwegian parliament's perceived lack of direction. Delius, commissioned to write the incidental music, misjudged how incendiary the political temperature was at the time and wrote humorous variations on the national anthem. As we shall see, the scandal would play its part in uniting Norwegian society and would also have lasting consequences for the composer's career.

In 1905, under the leadership of Christian Michelsen, the Norwegian government resolved to force the consulate issue by passing a unilateral law establishing its own corps of consuls. By good fortune or good planning the timing was excellent; the major European powers had little to gain from a Scandinavian conflict at that moment. A referendum in August revealed that almost all eligible Norwegian voters supported dissolution of the union. At the subsequent negotiations in Karlstad a peaceful agreement was reached and a second referendum showed overwhelming support for monarchy. Prince Carl of Denmark was offered the Norwegian crown and on 25 November 1905 he arrived as King Haakon VII in his capital, Kristiania.[30]

Post-union Norwegian and Danish

Delius wrote eighteen works using texts by Danish authors, including sixteen songs and the opera *Fennimore and Gerda*. In a study of the importance of Norwegian nature and culture to the composer, it might be surmised that such works belong, at best, on the periphery. This would, however, be to attribute to the cultures and languages of Norway and Denmark a far more distinct

---

[29] Worm-Müller, *Ideer og mennesker*, 52.

[30] The ancient town of Oslo had since 1624 been called Christiania, and then, after a spelling reform in 1877, Kristiania. The original name, Oslo, was only restored in 1925. During all of Delius's visits it officially bore the name Kristiania.

segregation than Delius and his contemporaries would have been familiar with. In fact, his attraction to the literature of Danish authors and dramatists grew inevitably from his knowledge of Norwegian culture.

In 1814, when Norway broke free from its union with Denmark, the country's *written* language was not Norwegian – as spoken by the people of Norway – but Danish. To all intents and purposes the written forms of Danish and Norwegian up to c.1900 were almost identical. In fact, written Norwegian *was* Danish. In 1889, Delius wrote to Grieg to tell him: 'I am reading Peer Gynt for the 5th time, only this time in Norwegian with the aid of a dictionary & am coming along quite well.'[31] Despite his assertion, Delius was not reading *Peer Gynt* in Norwegian – but in Danish. Henrik Ibsen had written his epic dramatic poem in Danish, and when it was published in 1867 it was in Danish. The composer was not confused: his mistake was merely a symptom of the fact that, on the page, Norwegian and Danish were almost indistinguishable. Another example might be the famous folk tales collected by Asbjørnsen and Moe and published from the mid-century onwards. Delius was one of the countless admirers of the tales, which were steeped in the peasant culture of the country's forests and countryside; his wife Jelka has related that they spent many winter nights reading the stories 'in Norwegian'. If their version was indeed Norwegian, it was a modernisation of the text, bordering on translation, for Asbjørnsen and Moe had published their collections in Danish, while incorporating peasant words and certain grammatical nuances typical of the countryside dialects of Norway. During the second half of the nineteenth century, Norwegian nationalists and linguists fought to restore the validity of rural dialects as the basis of a modern Norwegian language. Before the turn of the century, however, their efforts had made little impact on the Dano-Norwegian written by the middle classes of the urban centres.

A common language cannot, of course, be equated with a common culture. Nevertheless, in the wake of a three-hundred-year union, the spheres of historical and cultural discourse in the urban middle classes of both Denmark and Norway were so thoroughly and inextricably mingled that authors of both countries nourished Delius's fascination with the aesthetics of the northern world, and in much the same ways. This was a fascination sustained by and always associated with his love of Norway. With this in mind: to exclude *Fennimore and Gerda, An Arabesque* and other of the composer's significant Danish works from consideration in this study for reasons of language or literary culture, would be to exercise an artificial distinction. This said, it must be emphasised that – his efforts to read Ibsen with a dictionary notwithstanding – Delius's familiarity with works by Scandinavian authors came mostly from German translations, not from Danish or Dano-Norwegian texts; likewise, his settings were often of German translations.

---

[31] Letter from Delius to Grieg, undated, early June 1889 (BOB).

*

Delius became fascinated by Norway at the most dynamic period of the country's modern history. It was a time of creative energy, heroic deeds, political bravery and vision – all components in the new Norwegian identity. It was an inspiring and inspired time; from a tiny population of two million came such names as Edvard Grieg, Henrik Ibsen, Amalie Skram, Fridtjof Nansen, Edvard Munch, Harriet Backer, Roald Amundsen and Knut Hamsun.

In such a small society, however, there also existed excellent conditions for the conservative, closed or petty mind to hold sway and thrive. Just before Christian Sinding packed his rucksack to join Grieg and Delius on their trek into the Jotunheim mountains in 1889, he wrote to Grieg to complain about how unbearably provincial he found people's attitudes in Kristiania: 'Everything I come across here strikes me as so petty and narrow-minded that I fall into a black mood every time I have to travel into the city.'[32] Henrik Ibsen lived abroad for twenty-seven years on account of the same bourgeois attitudes in the capital. Had more generously spirited attitudes been typical of Norwegian cultural life around the turn of the century, perhaps Delius would have been forgiven the *faux pas* of *Folkeraadet* and his music welcomed into the Norwegian orchestral canon, where it rightly belonged.

This chapter closes where it began, at the Eidsbugarden table one evening in July 1889. Three remarkable champions of Norway's cultural identity are seated there in lively debate. No one knows better than Edvard Grieg the significance that Ernst Sars's interpretation of Norwegian history will have in moulding a new self-image. No one knows better than Sars how important a pioneer Grieg will be in loosening the paralysis caused by his people's cultural inferiority complex, the result of hundreds of years of subjugation. But they are assembled just here, at Eidsbugarden, to reconnect with nature – with the landscapes that over thousands of years formed the Norwegian character. It is the young and as yet unknown Englishman at the table who will capture in music what Norway's mountain wilderness can release in the human spirit.

[32] Letter from Sinding to Grieg, 3 June 1889 (BOB).

2

1862–1888
Bradford, Florida and Leipzig

'This English-American, musically deep, marvellous Hardangervidda Man'
Letter from Edvard Grieg to Frants Beyer, 20 February 1888

Frederick Delius was born in Bradford in 1862.

Around 1800, Bradford was a rural market town deep in the rolling moorland landscape of western Yorkshire, and with a population of six thousand. Just a half century later, the industrial revolution had transformed the town beyond recognition. Industrialists wishing to invest in wool found there the conditions they sought: sandstone, an excellent building material; large deposits of iron ore and coal; and the soft water that was a prerequisite for scouring wool. By the middle of the century, Bradford was responsible for some two-thirds of Great Britain's wool production and was at the centre of much of the world's wool trade. A large part of the export trade was with Germany and inevitably many of the investors attracted by the town's industrial muscle were German – including Julius Delius. He moved from the textile centre of Bielefeld to Bradford c.1850, when he was twenty-eight years old. At that time the town's eighty textile factories gave work to a population that had risen to 180,000. Julius quickly expanded his export company, Delius & Co., Wool & Noil Merchants, and by 1871 could build new, modern warehouses and offices. He married Elise, also from Bielefeld, and together they had fourteen children. Child number four, the next eldest boy, was christened Fritz. (Only from 1902 would he adopt an English variant of the name, Frederick.)[1]

The head of the family demanded an almost military discipline from his offspring. From an early age the sons were left in no doubt by Julius that they were expected to follow him into the family business. From the culture of his homeland, however, Julius also brought a deep love of music, and Delius recalled that his father 'was a great concert-goer and he often had chamber

---

[1] Much biographical information about the young Delius, his family and his upbringing is to be found in Clare Delius, *Frederick Delius: Memories of my brother* (London: Ivor Nicholson & Watson, 1935).

music in the house'. The children were encouraged to play music: 'I cannot remember the first time when I began to play the piano: it must have been very early in my life. [...] When I was six or seven, I began taking violin lessons from Mr Bauerkeller of the Hallé Orchestra, who came over from Manchester especially to teach me'.[2]

Raised on a diet of masterworks by Haydn, Mozart and Beethoven, Delius could still recall late in life the thrill of discovery when exposed to the new, exotic impulses of Romantic nationalism: 'When I first heard Chopin as a little boy of 6 or 7, I thought heaven had been opened to me – When also as a little boy I first heard the Humoresken of Grieg – a new world was opened to me again'.[3] On another occasion he recalled that when he first encountered the music of Grieg 'it was as if a breath of fresh mountain air had come to me'.[4] The special place Grieg had in the affections of the young Delius is again evident when, seventeen years old, he took part in a family concert during a holiday in Filey on the Yorkshire coast. The programme has been preserved and reveals that, into a watery stew of salon pieces by Flotow, Hummel and Sullivan, Fritz threw a handful of fragrant herbs and spices: a violin sonata by Grieg, probably his first in F major, in which national folk music traits had been lightly used.

On turning eighteen Delius dutifully entered the family firm and bowed his neck to the yoke of the wool trade. He had developed an outgoing and charming personality, personal qualities on which Delius & Co. tried to capitalise in the next three years, despatching him to textile centres. From 1880 to 1883 he found himself in Stroud in the south of England, Chemnitz in Saxony, Norrköping in Sweden and Saint-Étienne in France. On each assignment the young man set out to represent the company, but would become distracted by the rich opportunities to hear music. Wool and commerce were pushed to the back of his mind.

From the music of Edvard Grieg, perhaps also from travel books, Delius had formed at an early age an image of Norwegian culture. In this period as a young commercial representative he got to experience the country with his own eyes. On two occasions he was despatched to Scandinavian textile centres. In 1881, he visited Swedish companies in Gothenburg, Stockholm and Norrköping before travelling into Norway and returning from Bergen. A similar trip was undertaken in 1882, and on both occasions he found it too exciting to be on the latitudes that created Grieg not to explore the culture and nature

---

[2] In Philip Heseltine (pseudonym: Peter Warlock), *Frederick Delius* (London: John Lane, The Bodley Head, 1923; reprinted with additions, annotations and comments by Hubert Foss, London: The Bodley Head, 1952), 30–2.

[3] Letter from Delius to Philip Heseltine, 24 September 1912 (BL). Grieg's *Humoresques*, op. 6, were written and published in 1865.

[4] Undated recollections, probably between 1924 and 1934 (GM). Published as 'Delius: Recollections of Grieg' in LC1, 394.

outside his hotel window. Weeks and months passed with no word from him reaching Delius & Co., and when he was ordered to take the first North Sea ferry home from Bergen he had few new orders with which he might placate his father. Very few details are known of these first northern tours.[5] As was the case during his assignments in France and Germany, the need to satisfy his thirst for music probably became the primary distraction.

Fritz was repeatedly brought to heel by Julius, and the souring of their relationship had the making of a serious conflict. The young man was ever more sure that his future lay in music, his father equally adamant that music was practised as a profession by men who could expect neither the income nor the respect he wanted for his sons. 'I was demoralised', Delius later recalled, 'you can have no idea of the state of my mind in those days'.[6] When an escape route finally opened up, it would not only liberate him from industrial commerce with wool and noil, but transport him away from the factory chimneys and teeming streets of the industrial landscape. In the early 1880s, British investors had purchased large swathes of territory in Florida and advertised widely in the British media the opportunities for advancement that the cultivation of citrus fruit might bring with it. Initially, Julius Delius threw the notion out in anger, but eventually had to acknowledge that textiles were clearly never going to be his son's future. He purchased an option on an orange plantation in Florida, called Solana Grove. In March 1884, Fritz sailed from Liverpool for the New World.

A vocation revealed – and a Norwegian muse

The climate and the flowers are extraordinary and the situation of my grove is lovely and right on the beautiful St. Johns River. [...] The sunsets here are something remarkable and always varying between the most delicate colours on some nights to the most lurid and ferocious hues on others. [...] There is a nice little house on the place with a broad veranda facing the St. Johns River and standing in the middle of the orange trees.[7]

Here, at Solana Grove,[8] Delius lived in relative isolation for a year and a half. It was a period of continual sensual stimulation that was to have a liberating effect on his personality and self-image. If he had ever considered working

---

[5] Most of the few details we have of these first Scandinavian trips are to be found in Philip Heseltine, *Frederick Delius*, 34–5.

[6] In Eric Fenby, *Delius as I Knew Him* (London: G. Bell & Sons, 1936), 164.

[7] Letter from Delius to Jelka Rosen, handwritten transcript dated by the copyist April 1897 (GM).

[8] Due to misunderstandings, the composer's early biographers called the property Solano Grove. In all original documents available to Lionel Carley, archivist of the Delius Trust, the name was given as Solana: see 'Old Grove or New Grove?' in *Journal of the Delius Society* No. 101 (Summer, 1989), 19–20.

the plantation for profit, it was a notion that was quickly modified once he had unpacked his trunk; the running of Solana Grove was left in the hands of a young, black caretaker. For Delius only one thing mattered now: exploring what he might have within him of musical talent. The nearest town, Jacksonville, was fifty-six kilometres to the north, where the St Johns flows into the sea, and, on an excursion there, Delius became acquainted with a capable music teacher. Thomas Ward was ten years older than Delius and had recently come to Jacksonville to take up the post of organist at the Catholic church. There was an immediate rapport between the two men and Ward spent much of the ensuing months out at the grove disclosing to his young protégé principles of counterpoint and composition.[9]

To the alligator-hunting Delius on his citrus grove, would Norway now have seemed impossibly remote? Whatever exotic tones Delius had heard in Grieg's music, would they not have paled when remembered from the veranda of Solana Grove? Apparently not. The romance of the serene, cold north lived in him, stimulated and sustained not least by the young woman who was his neighbour. Here, in the subtropical wilds of Florida, his destiny had ordained that a charming, talented Norwegian singer had taken over the adjoining plantation.

Jutta Bell, née Mordt, was born in Kristiania in December 1860. In 1883, she had married a fourteen years older lieutenant in the Royal Navy, Charles Bell, and the pair had come to Florida to try and make a go of plantation life. Jutta and Charles had little in common and Delius would later recall Bell as a man 'unartistic in feeling' and with tastes 'diametrically opposed' to hers.[10] With the tall, cultivated musician from England, however, Jutta could share passions both for the arts and for Norway's cultural heritage.[11] She would not only become a friend to Delius; surviving letters suggest that Jutta was also an inspiration, a muse. Due to the response his music won from her and the confidence she had in his artistic dreams, Delius's life took a decisive turn. He had fled to Florida in a state of personal crisis; when he left Solana Grove a year and a half later he intended to carve out for himself a career as a composer. Thomas Beecham, in his biography of the composer, was the first to mention the debt Delius owed the young Kristiania woman: 'Mrs Bell became one of the three main influences at this time in aiding the restoration of his self-confidence and a belief in his mission. For years after his return to Europe he maintained a regular correspondence with her in which he more than once admits his

[9] Delius's relationship with and indebtedness to Ward are explored by Don C. Gillespie in his *The Search for Thomas F. Ward, Teacher of Frederick Delius* (Gainesville: University Press of Florida, 1996).
[10] Letter from Delius to Jutta Bell, undated, probably late December 1896 (DT).
[11] In recollections of Jutta Bell written by family members after her death it was suggested that she was a distant relation of Grieg. No evidence has been found to support the claim. She did, however, know well the songs of Grieg when she came to Florida.

obligation to her sympathy and percipience.'[12] It would hardly be surprising – given his state of mind, the wild nature around him and the grove's isolation – if Delius became romantically attracted to Jutta. Late in life, Delius offered advice on love to a young admirer, the composer Philip Heseltine, and wrote: 'I have been in love twice myself – the 2nd time by far intenser than the first – in fact it gave the direction to my life.'[13] In all probability, it is Jutta he had in mind. This seems to be supported by a further letter to Heseltine (who had fallen in love with an older woman who spurned his wish for a sexual relationship):

> I was madly, passionately in love when I was 21,[14] & with evidently a very similar sort of woman – She was, however, not ten years older than me – but just my own age [...] I had just as bad a time of it as you & almost identical. She would not give herself. [...] 7 or 8 years after she came to me of her own accord – but I was no more in love with her & then she became madly in love with me – but all in vain.[15]

Again, there is strong circumstantial evidence that it was to Jutta he was referring. She was born a year before Delius.[16] When they met in Florida, she had newly become a mother; it would be surprising if she had welcomed his advances. Jutta resurfaced in Paris in 1894 after a break-up of her marriage – not '7 or 8 years' later, but eight or nine – and sought out Delius. In letters he wrote to her at that time, he seems to have implored her to put their relationship on a platonic level, expressing gratitude when she had 'put all feelings of the ordinary woman aside'.[17] If Delius suffered from unrequited love in Florida, and she in Paris, their friendship survived the storm: in Paris she would become his trusted adviser on libretto matters (see p. 108).

It was in Florida that the metamorphosis in Delius's life occurred. He was now open to new knowledge and new horizons and, immersed in sensual nature and with a disciplinarian father out of sight and out of mind, Delius turned to composition. Among his earliest efforts – perhaps the first after his new-found goal was established – is a Norwegian song, 'Over the Mountains High' (1885), an English setting of a Bjørnson poem from the stage play *Arne*. Beneath a light melody there are flowing piano arpeggios and a few traces of

---

[12] Thomas Beecham, *Frederick Delius* (London: Hutchinson, 1959), 27.

[13] Letter from Delius to Philip Heseltine, 21 December 1915 (BL).

[14] Delius thought he was twenty-one when he arrived in Florida, but was in fact twenty-two. Until the mistake was discovered late in his life, he believed his year of birth to be 1863, not 1862.

[15] Letter from Delius to Philip Heseltine, 2 January 1914 (BL).

[16] In the official register of her birth the date is given as 10 December 1860. Commentators have previously believed she was considerably older than Delius, and therefore not linked her with his memories of an early lover.

[17] Letter from Delius to Jutta Bell, 11 July 1894 (DT).

Grieg, not least an imitation of a mountain horn call. This is one of only a few small works that exist from his period in America.

Beecham mentions 'three main influences' on Delius; Thomas Ward and Jutta Bell are two of them. The third would leave the most powerful impression on his music. Fortuitously, he was at precisely the right place and at precisely the right moment to experience a style of singing of uncanny beauty – a musical expression that was soon to disappear:

> I would sit out on my veranda in the darkness of evening, and would hear from afar the singing of the Negroes [...] a whole new world now opened up to me. I felt this Negro music to be something utterly new. It was natural and at the same time deeply felt. [...] Their music emerged as unaffected and instinctive, the expression of the soul of a people that had undergone much suffering.[18]

The process by which two incompatible song styles would intermingle had been going on since the first slave ships docked in America two hundred years earlier. On one side was the plantation owner who forced his black workers to learn Christian psalm melodies; on the other was the African-American with inherited indigenous styles of singing. Typical of these was the chanting of melodic lines in parallel, with harmonies arising more as a side-effect. These two styles of melody, initially in conflict, were bonded over time into a unique hybrid – the last phase of which Delius experienced in 1884. Many nineteenth-century musicians attempted to notate the music of the slaves, only to discover that European notation was too limited for the task: 'Their harmony was not that of the hymn-book', wrote Philip Heseltine in his Delius biography, 'but something far more rich and strange which aroused the enthusiasm of Delius and baffled Tom Ward's attempts to analyse it by any methods known to the theorists'.[19] This music, offspring of tribal African music and European psalmody, existed for a short period of maybe eighty to a hundred years. By the close of the nineteenth century it had been watered down, 'corrected' to accommodate white music styles; only some colourful traces of it were still to be heard in early jazz and blues. Today it has completely vanished.[20] For the young and searching Delius the discovery of this music was overwhelming

---

[18] Frederick Delius, foreword to James Weldon Johnson, *Der Weisse Neger. Ein Leben zwischen den Rassen (The White Negro. A Life Between the Races)* (Frankfurt: Frankfurter Societäts-Druckerei, 1928). Translation by Lionel Carley and Evelin Gerhardi published in Jeff Driggers, 'Zu Johnsons Buch: A Forgotten Literary Piece by Frederick Delius' in *Journal of the Delius Society* No. 126 (Autumn 1999), 25.

[19] Heseltine, *Frederick Delius*, 20–1.

[20] Later in life, Delius could become angry if he heard the jazz of the 1920s described as the music of the African-Americans: 'I felt that here was a people who really felt the emotion of music, as I feel now that this mad jazz has nothing to do with the negro. Jazz is an invention of so-called Americans who have taken rag-time and pretended that it is negro music.' *The Daily Telegraph*, 5 October 1929.

and for the rest of his career he would try to recreate the sense of wonder it had given him.

Solana Grove had opened up the vein of creativity in him, and by late summer 1885 the time was right for him to move on. It seems that both musical and personal interests combined to prompt his departure. The awkward situation with Jutta Bell may have been a contributing factor, as may yet another love affair. After Delius's death, the composer's close friend Percy Grainger disclosed that he had told him of a black mistress whom he had got pregnant. Allied to what may have been emotional turmoil was the need to get into musical society. Thomas Ward had taught his student what he could and recommended that he sought a place at the prestigious Leipzig Conservatory. The sudden appearance of Fritz's elder brother at the grove one day, looking for adventure, was a fortuitous turn of events. The plantation was put under his supervision and by the autumn of 1885 Delius had removed to Danville, Virginia, where he performed the duties of a music and language teacher to the young ladies of the town.

Back home in Bradford, his family had heard nothing from him for months and Julius, seriously worried for his son's welfare, hired American detectives: 'If he were found', his sister later recalled, 'he was to be told that his father, while still clinging to his views that music as a career was an absurdity, would permit him to study at Leipzig, if only he would make contact with the family again.'[21] The argument that prevailed was that, with this esteemed qualification under his belt, Fritz would return to America and be in a position to build a profitable career on the strength of his talents as a music teacher.

On 17 June 1886, a cargo ship steamed into New York Harbour carrying the monumental parts of the Statue of Liberty. Once assembled she would forever gaze east towards Europe. Five days earlier, Fritz Delius had gazed longingly in the same direction from the deck of a Cunard liner. He had won the liberty to study music and his eyes were now fixed on Germany.

Leipzig Conservatory

Königliches Konservatorium der Musik zu Leipzig, established by Felix Mendelssohn in 1843, acted like a magnet on young musicians from across the globe. For students from small nations without an institution for higher musical education the Leipzig Conservatory had become the favoured choice. Over 120 Norwegians had studied there before the mid-1880s, one of the largest contingents of foreign students.[22] Edvard Grieg studied there from 1858 to

---

[21] Clare Delius, *Frederick Delius*, 91.
[22] According to information supplied to the author by the archivist of the Conservatory, a surprising number – at least two-thirds – were young women seeking advanced piano instruction. Further information about Delius's time there is to be found in Philip Jones, 'Delius's Leipzig Connections' in *Journal of the Delius Society* No. 102 (Autumn, 1989), 3–14.

1862, Johan Svendsen in the mid-1860s, and in the 1870s Johan Selmer and Christian Sinding had two periods of study at the Conservatory. By the late 1880s, however, the Conservatory was resting on its laurels and Delius would always look back with disdain on his time spent with the Leipzig professors. The musical life of the city, on the other hand, offered students as rich a diet as many a European capital. They had free admission to the famous orchestral concerts at the Gewandhaus and, according to one source,[23] Delius heard Brahms and Tchaikovsky conduct their works there; there were chamber concerts every Saturday; the church choirs were renowned for the quality of their performances; and in the Neues Stadttheater the great music dramas of the age were in the hands of conductors Gustav Mahler and Arthur Nikisch. It is highly probable that Delius would have been in the theatre, for instance, in January 1887 for the production of *Der Ring des Nibelungen* under Mahler's musical direction. And the visits of Nikisch, especially to conduct *Tristan und Isolde*, 'were genuinely red-letter days'.[24]

The Norwegian contingent – ten women, seven men – quickly attracted Delius into its orbit. Among its members were many of the names that would pilot the development of music in Norway for the coming generation. In Delius's year were violinists Johan Halvorsen and Arve Arvesen and pianists Borghild Holmsen and Olaf Paulus Olsen. Composer Hjalmar Borgstrøm and violinist Halfdan Jebe enrolled the following academic year. Sinding, six years older than Delius, had received a state bursary and had come back to the music metropole to work on compositions. Composer and conductor Iver Holter had likewise completed his studies, but returned regularly to the city for inspiration. All of them would strike up friendships with Delius. One other Norwegian student, in Leipzig to study piano, not only gained his friendship, but probably also captured his heart.

Camilla Jacobsen was born in Kristiania in February 1870. Her father, Jacob Jacobsen, had been Norway's first specialist producer of paints. Her cultural bent was also shared by a younger brother, Hans Werner Jacobsen, who became a proficient artist. She was only in Leipzig this one academic year, moving on to Berlin to study with Oskar Raif at the Königlichen Hochschule. No correspondence has survived between Jacobsen and Delius. It is only by reading between the lines of other sources that it seems likely there was an emotional bond between them. In the spring of 1887, as the first academic year was drawing to a close, Delius planned an extended tour of Norway in the summer holiday, a crucial element in his itinerary being a lengthy stay with Camilla. When he left for Norway on 15 July by steamer from Hamburg, he may still not have received confirmation that he was welcome at the Jacobsen summer residence outside Kristiania. Camilla was still in Leipzig, and would matriculate

[23] Heseltine, *Frederick Delius*, 46.
[24] Beecham, *Frederick Delius*, 35.

2. The 25-year-old Delius stayed with Camilla Jacobsen and her family by the Kristiania Fjord for two weeks in the summer of 1887.

on 16 July. Three weeks into his Norway trip, having reached Molde, he got the positive answer he was hoping for, *poste restante.*

Summer 1887: Norway by foot and ferry

In 1887, 1889 and 1891 Delius kept diaries of his Norway travels, but was progressively less conscientious. The third diary consists of little more than dates, names and place names. The first of the three, however – an outpouring of enthusiasm for the landscapes and cultural novelties that filled his days – is a significant document, throwing light on Delius's attraction to the country.[25] Shortly after the holiday he would return to Leipzig, meet for the first time Edvard Grieg and strike up with him a close friendship, not least on the strength of the tales he could relate from this summer tour. His Norway adventure began in Stavanger on 17 July and finished six weeks later when he walked arm in arm with Camilla Jacobsen round the island of Malmøya beneath the glowing night sky of the northern summer.

In 1887, the Stavanger Tourist Association began to promote a tour with the less than catchy title 'The new inland route from Stavanger to Odde in Hardanger through the Ryfylkefiords, Sand, Suldal, Bratlandsdal and Røldal'. Up to the First World War this remained the most popular portal to the western fjords when arriving from the Continent. Delius, too, was travelling from Stavanger to Odda, but had selected his own route through the fjords somewhat further north, from Sandeid to Skånevik and Fjæra, rather than Suldal. His choice was perhaps influenced by recommendations from fellow Leipzig student and composer Georg Washington Magnus, whose family had deep roots in this district. Magnus had been born here in 1863, at Hogganvik, but had grown up in Copenhagen. Delius had noted in advance the address of his family near Vikadal, but did not visit. Instead, his holiday started with a flourish – a traditional Norwegian wedding:

> *Monday 18th July.* [...] Sandeid lies at the top of the Fjord, also beautifully situated. Here I disembarked. A Norwegian school master, who spoke a little German & who was evidently very intelligent had in the meantime invited me to his wedding on the morrow at Ølen.[26] His bride met him at Sandeid so we all 3 got in a skyds [open carriage with one broad seat] & drove on towards his parents' Hof [large farmhouse] near Ølen. His bride sitting on his knee. Now 11.30 pm & raining a little. Scenery very rocky & mountainous.[...] The Hof is very clean & everybody very friendly. I am the first Englishman his parents have

---

[25] Delius's 1887 diary (GM) has been published as 'Appendix III' in LC1, 383–93. If not otherwise stated, the quotations on the next pages from Delius's diaries are from this source (Lionel Carley's transcription), and follow Carley's practice in tidying up the punctuation and orthography, in order to make the diary more easily readable.

[26] The school teacher is Olaf Heggebø (1862–1928). His bride is Britha Eivindsdatter Lien (1860–1931).

yet seen, so cause much interest. His parents are intelligent & kind people, & it really does one's heart good to meet such honest unaffected & unspoiled people. I slept in the large room with the son.

[…]

Today *July 19th* the wedding comes off. On the Hof they have 1 horse, 6 cows & 40 sheep, besides much good land. […] Wedding guests began to arrive at 11 a.m. & at once set to, to eat cake & coffee, piles of cakes all over the long tables in the big room. Honest, straightforward folk these Norwegian peasants. They come in, shake hands & ask all sorts of questions. A batch of 6 or 7 come at a time & after shaking hands all round they sit down at a table & look very solemn, no one speaks a word, it might just as well be a funeral. Then coffee & cake is brought & they set to, after they have finished they shake hands again & say Tak Tak [many thanks]. […] Then Best man reads out the couples who go together to church, 1st a young man, then a young woman. […] The bride in a golden crown goes first then we all follow.

The following day, Delius continued his journey, crossing the mountain ridge of Stølehetta between the villages of Etne and Skånevik:

Excessively steep, & after the last gaard [farm] is passed, scenery becomes more weird & rough. The view down towards Etne is magnificent. The sun for a moment flashes a few rays over the long valley, I from amongst the clouds look now on almost a fairy like scene. The light & shade effects I never saw before, but only for a few minutes, & then all is again bleak & misty […]

By 24 July, Delius had made stops at the Hotel Hardanger in Odda ('of course crammed with English people'), taken the ferry up the Sørfjord and arrived at the Måbø valley. Here he hired a guide and they made their way first to Vøringsfossen (the waterfall described by Delius as a 'magnificent sight'), then got into their rhythm for a challenging trek up to the plateau of the Hardangervidda.[27] Here, on the wide mountain wilderness, their goal was Krossdalen *seter*:[28]

After trudging knee deep thro' swamps & bogs, climbing over rocks & hills, we reached the Sæter after 3 ½ hrs tramp. I was very tired & could not have gone very much further. I walked 36 Kils that day. The Sæter was a hut built of stone, 2 Sæter Jenter [milkmaids] lived there & minded 60 cows. […] We had a rough & tumble time of it. I was wet to the skin, water oozing out of my boots.

---

[27] A *vidde* is an expanse of mountain plateau. Deriving from the word *vid* (broad, wide), it denotes wide open landscape, not the sharp inclines of mountainsides. The *vidde* form of the word means simply plateau, *vidda* means *the* plateau. The plural in the Dano-Norwegian of the time was *vidderne* (the plateaus), in modern Norwegian *viddene*.

[28] A *seter* is mountain pasture for summer grazing with rudimentary buildings to house herd girls and milkmaids (*seterjenter*) and their dairy activities. In Scotland the word shieling has a similar meaning.

Delius had planned a visit to his fellow student from Leipzig, Olaf Paulus Olsen,[29] in Sunnfjord. But first he had to cross the Sognefjord: 'Gudvangen lies hemmed in by enormous rocks 4–5000 ft high, going perpendicularly out of the Sognefjord & Nærøydal. The Nærøydal is the finest I have seen yet, it goes from Stalheim to Gudvangen, the road winding at the bottom of the valley – numerous waterfalls falling from the highest rocks into the valley […]' Olsen's home town was Kristiania, but he was spending the summer near his fiancée Dagny Nitter in the village of Dale. She was a music teacher at the nationally renowned Pigeinstitutt (Girls College), run by the visionary pedagogue Nikka Vonen from a Dale farm.[30] On 3 August, Paulsen Olsen took his English guest on a visit to the college before Delius steamed west down the Dalsfjord towards Florø and the sea: 'Night glorious. Full moon[.] To the left the glowing of the already set sun, to the right the black rocks of the Fjord casting immense shadows. The whole scene never to be forgotten. I never remember a scene so beautiful in light & shade. This is what I came to see in Norway.'

In Florø the next day, Delius went into ecstasies over the panoramic view of coastal islands from the top of Storåsen, only to travel up the coast the following day to Ålesund, take the trip up the Aksla hill, and have to polish his superlatives even brighter:

> The view we got from the top I never shall forget. Certainly the most magnificent I ever saw, or ever shall see – similar to Florø, but grander. We saw over the Romsdalsfjord, & several other fjords, also miles out to sea. The whole forming a magnificent panorama.

In Molde on 6 August, Delius received the letter he had been waiting for from Camilla Jacobsen. From this point his journey moved inland and began to tip southwards again. On 8 August, he was at the post houses Ormem and Stuguflåten in the Romsdal mountains, and the following day passed the Mølme post house at Lesjaskog (where thirty-five years later he would build a summer house), *en route* to Dombås and then the Hjerkinn mountain lodge. At Hjerkinn, entertainment was laid on for the guests: 'We then watched them dance the national dances, such as spring dance & Halling. The only music we had was the singing of the girls. It was very picturesque & the great fire covered everything with a strange glow.'

On 13 August, he arrived in Kristiania and put up at Anne Kure's Privathotel in the centre of town. His thoughts were no doubt focused on being reunited

---

[29] Olaf Paulus (he eventually dropped the Olsen surname) would go on to have a career as a church musician, and was organist in Stavanger Cathedral from 1890.

[30] Nicoline Marie ('Nikka') Vonen ran her school from 1871 until her health failed in 1906. Bjørnson called her 'our soulmate' and sent a daughter and several grandchildren to the school.

with Camilla, and the next day he travelled to the fjord island of Malmøya.[31] Here, the Jacobsens had built a large summer house and for fourteen days the young Fritz Delius enjoyed the good life by the fjord as guest of the family. They took him into town to dine at the Gravesens restaurant, then sightseeing to the Gokstad Viking Ship, temporarily sheltered in a wooden outhouse behind the university. During the summer, the Jacobsens were first and foremost a sailing family and several days of Delius's visit were spent out on the fjord. As his holiday neared its close, Delius was their guest at the regatta, the high point of the summer: 'Very good racing. Then dinner, [and] in the afternoon we all rowed across to the boat house at Ormsund & saw an amateur performance. Then had fine walk round Malmøya, & tea at 8, then we rowed across for the dancing at night. Cam & I took a walk round Ormsund & returned to Malmøya at 11.30.'

On the night of 30 August, Delius boarded the overnight steamer to Kristiansand, where he would change ships for the crossing to Hamburg. Camilla's father, brother and brother-in-law came to the docks to see him off. Her studies in Leipzig were now over, so their friendship would be more difficult to maintain. As the ship steamed down the fjord past Malmøya, Delius may have sorted through many impressions from two summer weeks in her company, and hoped for a lasting relationship. We can only surmise, for all correspondence between him and Camilla Jacobsen has been lost.[32]

Almost the first letter we have in his hand was written in Leipzig the following year: 'For you it will be of little significance if I tell you how much I love & esteem you, but it is true & comes from my heart.'[33] Not to Camilla, nor any other lady friend. These words were directed to the person who had entered Delius's life and given it a new direction. Edvard Grieg.

Edvard Grieg in Leipzig

One day late in 1887, probably in early December, Sinding and Delius were taking their regular walk to Leipzig's Panorama Restaurant to eat lunch. Suddenly the Norwegian said 'There's Mr and Mrs Grieg'.[34] Delius was quickly introduced and the four of them continued on to the Panorama. Many years later, Delius would look back on this happy conjunction: 'Grieg, learning how

---

[31] The islands of Malmøya and Ormøya are on the east coast of the inner Oslo Fjord. They are separated by a narrow strait, the Ormsund.

[32] There is some evidence of Delius being in sporadic contact with her in the succeeding years, but this comes to an end in 1889. Jacobsen returned to Kristiania and took piano pupils, then in 1901 married a doctor, Ernst Ramm. In 1910, they moved to the coastal village of Åsgårdstrand.

[33] Letter from Delius to Grieg, undated, but 18 February 1888 (BOB).

[34] 'Delius: Recollections of Grieg' (GM) published in LC1, 394. The two following quotations are from the same source.

well I knew Norway and hearing that I had just returned from a mountain
tour, naturally took great interest in me and we soon found ourselves comparing notes of mountain trips in Jotunheimen and the Hardangervidda.' In such
a simple fashion it began, the most important friendship of Delius's career.
Edvard Grieg was then forty-four and at the height of his powers.

> [Every] day for months we dined together, played a rubber of whist and then
> took a walk round the Promenade. [...] He had then just finished his C Minor
> Violin Sonata, which had its first performance during the winter season at the
> Gewandhaus chamber concerts, Adolf Brodsky playing the violin and Grieg the
> piano. It was a beautiful performance and I was very enthusiastic, and after the
> concert I wrote Grieg an enthusiastic letter with my impressions, enclosing in
> the letter a sprig of heather which I had gathered on Hardangervidda. Next day
> I was very much moved to see what a deep impression this had made upon him.

Was this gift so precious to Grieg that he even took care to preserve it? The
small account books in which he registered his daily expenditure are today in
the Grieg Archives of Bergen Public Library. Tucked into a pocket at the front
of the book for 1888 is a small sprig of *Calluna vulgaris*, common heather.[35]

Delius, Sinding and Grieg regularly attended operas and concerts together,
and after each performance Grieg would wine and dine the young musicians.
The exclusive group was often expanded to include Norwegian violinist Johan
Halvorsen. A few short weeks after their first meeting, Edvard and Nina Grieg
invited Delius, along with Sinding and Halvorsen, to celebrate Christmas Eve
with them. The following day, Grieg wrote a lively account of the evening to
Frants Beyer, his neighbour outside Bergen and closest friend, assuring him
that he had not been forgotten:

> As the cork popped from the champagne we thought of you, dear friend, and
> many words were spoken that wouldn't be good for you to hear. Only this much,
> that in summer you risk having to open your home to the whole crowd. Delius is
> 'Norway-crazy' and has been to Norway 4 times, camps out on Hardangervidda
> for fourteen days, and that sort of thing.[36]

As a Christmas present, Grieg's publisher had sent him a hamper of choice
wines and foodstuffs and in later years all three composers would recall this

---

[35] According to Bjørn Moe at the Arboretum of Bergen University, the sprig has uncommon
characteristics: 'The plant has had a compact growth with very tight foliage', something Moe
thinks might be accounted for by the harsh climate on Hardangervidda – if the sprig indeed
comes from there.

[36] Letter from Grieg to Frants Beyer, 25 December 1887 (RA). It is possible that Grieg, delighted
with his new friend's enthusiasm for Norway, was gilding the lily. We know of only three visits
Delius had made to Norway at this point, and one visit to Hardangervidda – for one freez-
ing night during the 1887 trip. This might suggest that he had absconded to Hardangervidda
during commercial trips for the family company to Scandinavia in 1881 and 1882. It seems
unlikely, however, that he would have been so familiar with the area and not revealed it in his
tour diaries or any other source.

3. After the first performance of Grieg's Violin Sonata No. 3 in December 1887, Delius sent him a sprig of heather he had plucked on Hardangervidda. It is almost certainly this sprig that Grieg kept safe in the pocket of his account book. (The book measures 8 × 15 cm.)

evening as one of cheerful inebriation. The Griegs had positioned a Christmas tree on the grand piano and the merriment was briefly interrupted when the candles set light to the tree and Sinding, clambering on to the piano to save the day, upset the whole decoration. Each of the party played and sang. Delius presented and performed a piano piece, probably written for the occasion, with the title *Norwegische Schlittenfahrt*.

The original manuscript of this musical sleigh ride has been lost. Some years later, however, Delius would arrange the piece for orchestra, now with the title *Winter Night (Sleigh Ride)*. While allowing for the possibility that he may have revised it, we can with some confidence regard *Winter Night* as essentially the work with which he entertained his friends that unforgettable Christmas. Grieg's English guest revealed himself to be both playful and respectful of the master. He had written a lively trotting march with themes reminiscent of Grieg, and to just the right degree to be taken as humorous tribute rather than parody. The perky main theme is closely related to that of Grieg's 'Bridal

Procession' (op. 19, no. 2) and of no. 3 and no. 4 from *Humoresques* (op. 6) – the Grieg work that first opened Delius's ears to the Norwegian's music:

Allegretto con moto

Example 2.1 *Winter Night (Sleigh Ride), 4–8*

As Grieg does in many of his *Lyric Pieces* for piano, Delius introduces a lyrical middle section with idiomatic folk music traits, including a pedal bass. Then, in a short coda, he borrows a device straight from the Grieg toolbox: chromatically falling lines. We can easily imagine Grieg standing by the punch bowl that Christmas Eve acknowledging with a wry smile the elegant and humorous gift of the Hardangervidda Man.

Yes, the Hardangervidda Man. Grieg had coined a nickname for Delius that evening and used it with affection every time he mentioned his new, young friend in a letter. The Griegs were together with Delius, Sinding and Halvorsen most days and, thanks to his allowance from home, Delius was also able to entertain his friends. Halvorsen recalled later in life that 'Delius had many fine attributes. One of them was that he often invited us […] to his apartment and treated us to the most delicious things. In addition he was so kind as to lend us money. We were constantly in need of money and often had to forgo dinner. Nevertheless, it was a wonderful time.'[37] On 18 January, the friends visited the theatre to see a troupe from Munich present Bavarian folk plays: '[We] enjoyed each others' company so much that we stayed up until 2 o'clock with oysters and wine,'[38] Grieg informed Beyer. A similarly lively evening, fuelled by champagne, occurred a couple of months later when Johan Halvorsen – shortly before his departure from Leipzig to fill the post of concertmaster for an orchestra in Aberdeen – suddenly had a craving for Norwegian *rekling* (strips of dried halibut). The quartet dashed to the telegraph office and shot off an order to Beyer: 'Dear friend, send us some, but quickly, quickly, before Halvorsen has to leave. Our apologies, but we're in high spirits, and expect that to be respected.' Each of them signed the exuberant telegram, including

---

[37] From Halvorsen's unpublished memoir *Hvad jeg husker fra mit liv* (*What I Remember from My Life*), quoted in Øyvin Dybsand, 'Johan Halvorsen (1864–1935). En undersøkelse av hans kunstneriske virke og en stilistisk gjennomgang av hans komposisjoner' ('A Study of his Artistic Activity and an Examination of the Style of his Compositions') (Ph.D. thesis, University of Oslo, 2016), 152.

[38] Letter from Grieg to Frants Beyer, 19 January 1888 (RA).

4. Before they went their different ways in the spring of 1888, the five friends went into a photographer's studio in Leipzig. Left to right: Nina and Edvard Grieg, Johan Halvorsen, Fritz Delius and Christian Sinding.

'Fritz Delius (Hardanger Vidda man)'.[39] The 'clique' (Grieg's name for the five friends) also gathered to give Halvorsen a hearty send-off, with oysters and Rhenish wine in abundance. On one of the spring days before the break-up of the group they went into a photographer's studio to create a memento of their time together (see Illustration 4).

A few weeks later, Grieg would sum up this period in Leipzig: '[When I] consider how fortunate I've been with the company I've kept this winter, and I'm thinking of Sinding, Brodsky and the *admirable Hardangervidda Man*, I can honestly say that the trip was worthwhile, and that's saying something.'[40]

---

[39] Telegram from Grieg to Frants Beyer, 9 March 1888 (NB). Due to bad weather, it would take several weeks for the delicacy to reach the high-spirited group. 'Sinding and the Hardangervidda Man accompanied me to the customs house to collect it [...] and I would struggle to describe the look on their faces when they got wind of the package. The customs officers didn't even bother to weigh it, but just shoved it in my direction with disgust in every crease of their faces.' Grieg in a letter to Beyer, 12 April 1888 (RA).

[40] Letter from Grieg to Frants Beyer, 24 March 1888 (RA).

Grieg and Norwegian dualism

In the four years up to 1892 – the period during which they had closest contact with each other – Grieg would play key roles in the advancement of Delius's career and development of his character. He was a critical and constructive mentor in all aspects of composition; he pushed to get Delius's music published and performed; he opened important doors for Delius in the musical life of Leipzig and Kristiania; and he was a trusted confidant in personal matters – a benevolent father figure. The Norwegian's generous personality would have a liberating effect on the young man. In one letter, written eight months into their acquaintance, Delius broke with the business-like tone that typified his correspondence in order to express to Grieg all the gratitude he felt. Among the hundreds of Delius letters that have survived, this is a unique document; in no other does he express a similar warmth and humility:

> My friendship and sympathetic feelings you captured long ago, and I freely admit that I have never in all my life encountered someone with a personality such as yours. In my life I have been so much left to my own devices that, without being aware of it, I have become egotistic & never been concerned about anyone but myself & worked for my own goals. You are the only man who has changed that & attracted my complete attention to yourself & stimulated the feelings that I now have for you.[41]

While Grieg was in Leipzig, Frants Beyer had inflamed his homesickness by sending him a postcard from Skogadalsbøen, a mountain farm in Jotunheimen, and Grieg had shown the view to Delius. 'This English-American, musically deep, marvellous Hardangervidda Man', Grieg wrote to Beyer, 'he understood the pleasure it gave me. You've got to get to know him. We've got nothing in common except our feeling! But in the end, of course, that's everything!'[42] Grieg's attraction to the young Englishman was of a circular or self-reflexive nature. Grieg was enthused by Delius's love of Norway; but it was, of course, Delius's appreciation of Grieg's music that was partly responsible for igniting those very feelings for Norway. Grieg had, indeed, a compulsive need for recognition by other artists, something that should be seen in the light of the fact that he had defined for himself a project that was unprecedented in Norwegian culture.

There was, of course, a series of Norwegian pioneers who prepared the ground for Grieg's project. One of the first works with stylistic traits similar to those of Norwegian folk music came in 1825, a *syngespill* (or *Singspiel*) by Waldemar Thrane: *Fjeldeventyret* (*The Mountain Tale*). Ole Bull, whose inspiration Grieg readily acknowledged, had brought folk music onto national and international stages in the 1840s, in particular the tunes of Torgeir Augundsson

---

[41] Letter from Delius to Grieg, undated, but mid-August 1888 (BOB).
[42] Letter from Grieg to Frants Beyer, 20 February 1888 (RA).

(nicknamed Myllarguten, the Miller Boy), master of the Hardanger fiddle.[43] Lindeman's volumes of *Ældre og nyere norske Fjeldmelodier* (*Old and Recent Norwegian Mountain Tunes*) were published between 1853 and 1867 and were to be found in all Norwegian homes where music was played. Grieg credited his friend Rikard Nordraak with having defined for young Norwegian musicians what their primary goal should be: 'It was our hope that we both would devote ourselves to the promotion of our national art; although it was not to be, I have stood steadfastly by the promise I gave him, that his mission would be my mission, his goal would be my goal.'[44] Nordraak died in 1866, only twenty-three years old, placing on Grieg's shoulders a responsibility he would regard as formidable, but sacred. He was twenty-two.

Even when these prophets and others are taken into consideration it is evident that little had occurred in Norwegian music that forewarned of the quantum leap in quality of Grieg's finest compositions, their successful alloy of Austro-German method and what his contemporaries experienced as exotic Norwegian colour. Already in his early works, Grieg was taking steps that carried him far beyond these predecessors and into uncharted territory. Precisely because his project was so bold and innovative, he had to reconcile himself at all times to a high degree of artistic insecurity, a state of affairs that could often lead him seriously to doubt his abilities and significance. At his darkest moments he felt his existence had been marked by a never-ending personal struggle and that his life's work was almost without value: '[I] am every other day resolved never to write another note, because I satisfy my own demands less and less.'[45] When he embraced the young Delius it was, therefore, not primarily on account of the Englishman's compositions, but rather his feelings for Norway. It was here that Grieg constantly needed external confirmation: that the culture and character of the Norwegian people had valuable qualities and, by extension, a life devoted to distilling and promoting them would have high meaning. When the cosmopolitan Delius reported that he too had seen and appreciated these essential qualities, it immediately placed him close to the Norwegian's heart.[46]

---

[43] The Hardanger fiddle is a folk instrument characterised by its four or five understrings, which vibrate in sympathy with the upper strings.

[44] Letter from Grieg to Nordraak's father, Georg M. Nordraach, 7 May 1866 (NB).

[45] Letter from Grieg to Gottfred Matthison-Hansen, 20 December 1882. Trans. by Finn Benestad (EG2).

[46] At the close of his life, Grieg would draw sustenance in much the same way from another foreign friend. Broken down by illness and doubt, he was convinced that his music would have nothing to say to coming generations. At this moment, the young Australian pianist Percy Grainger entered his life and lifted up into the light that late composition of Grieg most strongly anchored in folk music, the *Slåtter* (*Norwegian Peasant Dances*), op. 72. Three weeks before he died, Grieg wrote: 'And when [Grainger] played my works to me, the old Adam woke and asked in astonishment: But is it really so beautiful, then, the work you have done?' Letter from Grieg to Alexander Siloti, 16 August 1907 (EG2).

So far removed are we from a time when the exoticism of national folk music was fresh and innovative that we find it difficult to grasp the significance of Grieg's art for his time. For us, it has to be done intellectually: we read up on historical references, study his place in music's development. We comprehend that Grieg took a universally used set of Austro-German composition tools and applied to it melodic and rhythmic styles that his audience would interpret as being similar to traits in Norwegian folk music. In the end, however, we are still left with little sense of the emotional shock that Delius and so many contemporaries felt on encountering the synthesis created by Grieg. What constituted this powerful force was the realisation that there were valid musical expressions beyond the confines of Austro-German models.[47] In recent decades, musicologists – not least when applying aspects of reception theory to music – have pointed out that many traits of traditional music that Norwegians see as defining their folk music are shared with the traditional music of other European regions. This had, however, little or no bearing on the reception of Grieg's music in his lifetime by both Norwegians and the wider world. In fact, as Asbjørn Eriksen has pointed out, Grieg's personal musical style even come to stand as proxy for the true character of Norway's national expression:

> [The] conception of there being Norwegian stylistic expressions had grown out of a historical process. In 1860 there were very few people who would have any notion of how a paradigmatic composition with uniquely Norwegian expression should actually sound, while fifty years later there were many who did – thanks to Edvard Grieg. The weight of Grieg's fame led to his music rapidly being accepted as typically Norwegian both in Norway and further afield, including elements of his personal musical style that had little connection with Norwegian folk music.[48]

Writing about Grieg's place in his national historical context, Daniel Grimley has identified that the drive among Norwegians to promote their culture could even be seen to have a heroic character: 'This tendency towards social improvement and renewal in Norway was simultaneously a form of resistance to Danish (and later Swedish) political and cultural domination, in which music played a significant part.'[49] In the centralised power structures

---

[47] The Hungarian composer Béla Bartók was keenly aware of the contribution Grieg had made in opening up art music to national colour. Once asked by the conductor Antal Doráti why he was studying the score of Grieg's Piano Concerto, Bartók replied: 'Don't you know that he was one of the first of us who threw away the German yoke and turned to the music of his own people?' See Antal Doráti, 'Bartókiana' in *Tempo*, New Series, No. 136 (March 1981), 13.

[48] Asbjørn Øfsthus Eriksen, 'Halfdan Kjerulf (1815–1868), den mangfoldige liedkomponist. Et jubileumsessay' ('Halfdan Kjerulf, the Versatile Song Composer. An Anniversary Essay') in *Studia Musicologica Norvegica* No. 41 (2015), 16.

[49] Daniel M. Grimley, *Grieg: Music, landscape and Norwegian identity* (Woodbridge: Boydell Press, 2006), 53.

of Europe, particularly in France and Germany, the attraction the cultural elite felt towards folk music and other folkloristic expressions was regarded as neo-traditional and driven by bourgeois considerations. Grimley underlines that Norway's fraught relationships with its much more powerful neighbours opened up a more nuanced approach to the adoption of folk culture, a dualism: 'the elevation of a folk culture which was both progressive and retrospective in outlook'.[50] In other words, by taking a stand against city culture, Norwegians not only distanced themselves from industrialisation and the modern, but also from the damage foreign masters had wreaked on indigenous culture.

There was no scarcity of Englishmen with an affection for Norway; as we have seen, the country was swarming with them every summer. It seems, however, that Grieg was instinctively aware that the love Delius had for Norwegian landscape and culture was of a different calibre to that of the typical English mountain tourist drawn by the magnetic pull of the 'Northern Playground', as Slingsby had dubbed it. We shall see in the next chapter that what Delius sought in Norway was essentially different from the inspiration Grieg looked for. His experiences of Norwegian nature and culture were, however, as vital to his art as Grieg's were to his. It was an attraction that would last to the end of his life.

Not only was Delius an untypical Englishman in Norway, it is also likely that he deliberately played down his English origin throughout this period, placing more emphasis on his recent American background. Several Norwegians who met him were under the impression that he was American. And as his time at the Leipzig Conservatory drew to a close, a return to New York or Florida was a realistic alternative.

Two American works: 'scheusslich interessant'

In the year and a half stretching from the day he met Grieg in December 1887 until their Jotunheim tour in 1889, Delius's creative life was intensified with a Norwegian fever. His Romantic concept of the North, present in him from an early age, became now the component of his artistic make-up that he cultivated above all else. With Grieg's friendship now so important to him, his creative compass was attracted towards Norwegian poets, Norwegian painters, Norwegian nature. His first meeting with Grieg had come, however, late in his second year in Leipzig. Before that moment, the compass needle had pointed in an entirely different direction.

Prior to meeting Grieg, Delius drew inspiration from his life-changing experiences in America, in particular the year and a half on Solana Grove by the wide St Johns. The first major work was *Florida*, an extraordinary

---

[50] *Ibid.*, 25.

orchestral suite in four movements (or 'tropical scenes', as he called them). Extraordinary, for several reasons. Firstly, because there was no suggestion in his previous music that this was coming. Delius announced himself as a composer with a work displaying advanced stylistic sense for the orchestra as instrument and palette. There is an almost extravagant melodic richness to the four movements, helping to mask the fact that the composer at that time had a poorly developed capacity for building expansive structures from his melodic ideas. *Florida* is also extraordinary because, as part of the third movement, Delius wrote a dance unlike any that had been written before in European music, giving it the subtitle 'Bei der Plantage' ('On the Plantation'). He employs a folk-like tune that may owe something to songs he heard sung by black workers at Solana Grove or in Virginia. It has a sliding third (from minor to major), with an effect we have become accustomed to associate with blues, and is supported with guitar or banjo plucking, imitated in string pizzicato – as playfully executed as it is strikingly original. While his professors had been striving to push into his head Austro-German counterpoint and harmony, Delius had been composing a work with traits of African-American folk song performed to the rhythm of the dancing feet of plantation workers.

For his next orchestral composition, begun shortly after *Florida*, Delius thought he would expand on his theme. The symphonic poem *Hiawatha* is seemingly as American as the earlier suite, only this time with Native Americans as the source of ethnic colour. On account of his close emotional ties to the black workers and their music, he succeeded in making the music of *Florida* sound fresh and genuine. The exotic rhythms and melodies of the new work sound more like echoes of music he had heard at a Wild West show. Inspired by Longfellow's poem *The Song of Hiawatha* rather than intimacy with Native American culture, *Hiawatha* reflects also the poet's Romantic sentimentality and theatricality. Most artificially ethnic to modern ears is perhaps the dance at its core, gradually whirled up into an energetic and muscular war dance. There are, however, sequences that rival *Florida* in orchestral colour, not least the shimmering conclusion depicting a sunset. Most interesting, as we approach the first compositions Delius wrote that were inspired by his experiences in Norwegian mountain nature, are the pentatonic horn calls that roll and repeat as the music fades into the distance. In his earliest scores for orchestra, he was already experimenting with illusions of spatial distance.

In the spring of 1888, shortly before departing from Leipzig, Delius had the pleasure of hearing his 'tropical scenes', a large military orchestra of sixty players agreeing to play through *Florida* – as long as the beer kept flowing. Delius, Grieg, Nina Grieg and Sinding comprised the audience and after the performance Grieg turned to the composer with an approving '*scheusslich interessant*'.[51]

---

[51] 'Delius: Recollections of Grieg' (GM), published in LC1, 395.

The dilemma facing Delius as he approached the end of his second and final year at the Leipzig Conservatory was what his next move should be. Julius Delius would still expect his son, now with a respected diploma, to return to America and revive his career as a music teacher in a society where qualified pedagogues were in great demand. There is indeed some evidence that Fritz toyed with the notion of crossing the Atlantic again, but now at the head of a small musical troupe. Early in 1888, the Norwegian pianist Martin Knutzen wrote to a friend about an offer relayed to him by Johan Halvorsen: 'He, Sinding, and an American want me to go along with them this autumn on a tour of the American south, giving concerts of chamber music, and this American will guarantee each of us an income of 100 dollars a week.'[52] In all likelihood it was Grieg himself who convinced Delius that only in Europe would his creative ambitions amount to anything. To bring Julius round to this idea, the young composer employed the considerable persuasive talents of the renowned Norwegian. From February of 1888 we have a letter from Grieg to Delius which, considering the intimacy in other letters between them at this time, is markedly formal:

> Dear Sir,
> I was pleasantly surprised by your manuscripts, yes, quite thrilled, and I see in them an outstanding compositional talent in the grand style, a talent that aspires to the highest goal. Your ability to reach this goal is wholly dependent on the manner in which your affairs come to be ordered. If you would permit me – in the interests of your future – to offer you some advice (a privilege I can perhaps be allowed as an older artist), then it would be this, that while you are still young, rather than entering into some external profession, you fully dedicate yourself to the study of your art and pursue your own true nature and inner conviction in your idealistic endeavour.[53]

Delius had rolled out the heaviest ordnance in his arsenal. The formal style suggests that this declaration had been formulated as a reference, perhaps specifically for digestion by Delius senior. While there is no reason to doubt any of the sentiments expressed in the letter, it may well have been knocked up by both men together one convivial evening over a bottle of champagne and a platter of oysters.

With the end of the academic year this chapter of Delius's life, perhaps the happiest, also came to a close. From England he wrote to Grieg: 'I already miss you all very much.'[54] The sentiment was mutual, as we can ascertain from a letter Grieg sent to Beyer: 'Ah yes, the Hardangervidda Man! Him we also

---

[52] Letter from Martin Knutzen to Erica Stang, 22 February 1888. Published in 'Brever fra Martin Knutzen' ('Letters from Martin Knutzen') in *Norsk Musikkgranskning: Årbok 1939* (*Norwegian Music Research: Yearbook 1939*) (Oslo: Tanum), 16.
[53] Letter from Grieg to Delius, 28 February 1888 (DT).
[54] Letter from Delius to Grieg, 12 April 1888 (BOB).

accompanied to the station a few days ago. Now he is in England and our little colony is dispersed. Today we ate dinner all alone and instead of our usual rubber of coffee-whist played a hand of – 101!'[55] On arriving home in Bradford, Delius was pleased to receive from his father the score of Wagner's *Tristan und Isolde*, presented in recognition of the fact that he had stayed the course. Perhaps Julius's resistance was wavering under the influence of Grieg's belief in his son and, early in May, Delius seized the moment to put his father's resolve to the test. Many years later he would relate how he managed to place Grieg, in London on a concert tour, at the same table as his parents: '[We] all had dinner together at the Hotel Metropole and Grieg persuaded my father to let me continue my musical studies.'[56] Grieg's visit to London would have other notable consequences. Edvard and Nina Grieg stayed at the home of his London publisher George Augener, and it is highly likely Grieg introduced him to Delius. In 1890, Augener would be the first to publish the budding composer's music.

On his way to London to spend a few enjoyable days with Grieg, Delius stopped off in Reading to renew his close friendship with his Florida neighbour, Jutta Bell. Shortly after his departure from Solana Grove, Jutta and Charles Bell had also returned to England. That the chemistry between the Kristiania-born woman and the 'Norway-crazy' Delius was still active is supported by the fact that early in the 1890s – her relationship with Bell at an end – Jutta travelled to Paris and sought out Delius, seemingly with a hope of lifting their friendship to another level (see p. 108).

It had been Grieg's fervent desire to take Delius on a mountain tour in Norway in the summer of 1888. From May to the end of the year, however, the Hardangervidda Man was rooted in France. He stayed with his Uncle Theodor in Paris, apart from an extended summer visit to Brittany, and then in November, longing for an environment more conducive to work, rented a house in the village of Ville d'Avray on the outskirts of Paris. Finally free to devote himself to composition, Delius experienced a flood of inspiration, at times working on several large and small scores at the same time. Music poured from him – and most of it was to texts by Norwegian poets.

---

[55] Letter from Grieg to Frants Beyer, 12 April 1888 (RA). For the card game '101' only two players are needed.

[56] 'Delius: Recollections of Grieg' (GM) published in LC1, 395.

3

1888–1889
With Grieg on the heights

'For months our meeting in Wonderful Norway has filled my entire horizon'
Letter from Delius to Grieg, undated, but early June 1889

By the summer of 1888, Delius was established in Paris, but his fascination with Scandinavia was directing his creative impulses. From then until his mountain tour with Grieg a year later there would come Norwegian composition after Norwegian composition:

- thirteen songs to texts by Norwegian poets
- *Paa Vidderne*, melodrama for orchestra and reciter
- *Idylle de Printemps*, symphonic poem originally with a Norwegian title[1] and strongly influenced by Grieg
- sketches for incidental music to Ibsen's *Keiser og Galileer* (*Emperor and Galilean*)

Twelve of the thirteen Norwegian songs written in 1888 and 1889 were quickly published, first in a group of five in 1890, then a further group of seven in 1892 (see Table 1 on p. 40). All were settings of German translations.[2] They were the first Delius compositions to be published and Grieg's influence with the Augener publishing house no doubt played its part. We can see from Table 1 that eight of the twelve texts chosen by Delius had already been set to music by Grieg. From our distance this might seem tactless, but it no doubt attests to Delius's almost blind admiration for his mentor. It should come as no surprise, then, that a handful of musical elements regarded as typifying Grieg's style have also found their way into Delius's songs. Among these can be mentioned sequences of seventh chords, the bass line falling by step, and key modulation

---

[1] The Norwegian title – written in pencil, erased and inked over with the French title – is now illegible. See Robert Threlfall, *Frederick Delius: A supplementary catalogue* (London: Delius Trust, 1986), 136.

[2] Delius was, however, teaching himself Norwegian in this period. Percy Grainger, who got to know Delius some twenty years later, described his Norwegian then as 'moth-eaten'. On the other hand, Eric Fenby, who knew the composer in the last six years of his life, believed that he was more fluent in Norwegian than German, despite his upbringing.

Table 1 Twelve Norwegian songs

Fünf Lieder aus dem Norwegischen (Five Songs from the Norwegian)
Published 1890 with German and English texts.
Most are from 1888, but it is uncertain which, apart from 'Sehnsucht'.

Published title	Author	Poem title and first line	Grieg version
'Der Schlaf' ('Slumber Song')	Bj. Bjørnson	'Søvnens engler' Da barnet sov in	
'Sing, Sing' ('The Nightingale')	Th. Kjerulf	'Syng, syng, nattergal du' Syng, syng, nattergal du	
'Am schönsten Sommerabend war's' ('Summer Eve')	J. Paulsen	'Jeg reiste en deilig sommerkveld' Jeg reiste en deilig sommerkveld	op. 26, no. 2 (1876)
'Sehnsucht' ('Longing')	Th. Kjerulf	'Længsel' Vildeste fugl i flukt endnu	
'Beim Sonnenuntergang' ('Sunset')	A. Munch	'Solnedgang' Nu daler solen sakte ned	op. 9, no. 3 (1865)

Sieben Lieder aus dem Norwegischen (Seven Songs from the Norwegian)
Published 1892 with German and English texts.
Most are from 1888, but it is uncertain which, apart from 'Wiegenlied'.

Published title	Author	Poem title and first line	Grieg version
'Wiegenlied' ('Cradle Song')	H. Ibsen	'Vuggevise' Nu løftes laft og lofte	op. 15, no. 1 (1868)
'Auf der Reise zur Heimat'* ('The Homeward Way')	Aa. O. Vinje	'Ved Rundarne' No seer eg atter slike Fjøll og Dalar	op. 33, no. 9 (1880)
'Abendstimmung' ('Evening Voices'**)	Bj. Bjørnson	'Prinsessen' Prinsessen sad høyt i sit jomfrubur	Work without opus, no. 126 (1871)
'Klein Venevil' ('Young Venevil')	Bj. Bjørnson	'Venevil' Hun Venevil hopped på lette fod	
'Spielleute'*** ('The Minstrel')	H. Ibsen	'Spillemænd' Til hende stod mine tanker	op. 25, no. 1 (1876)
'Verborg'ne Liebe' ('Hidden Love)	Bj. Bjørnson	'Dulgt kærlighed' Han tvær over bænkene hang	op. 39, no. 2 (1873)
'Eine Vogelweise' ('The Birds' Story')	H. Ibsen	'En fuglevise' Vi gik en dejlig vårdag	op. 25, no. 6 (1876)

* later 'Heimkehr'   ** later 'Twilight Fancies'   *** later 'Spielmann'

and harmonic progressions directly from the tonic to the mediant. In a letter written to Delius after receiving some of the songs, Grieg stated that he found 'so many beautiful and deeply felt things in them', but continued: 'And then again there are other things which are difficult to accept [...] in the form and in the treatment of the voice. A Norwegian melody and a Wagnerian treatment of the voice are dangerous things indeed to try to reconcile.'[3]

A comparison of the composers' interpretations offers us some interesting insights, although in two instances, 'Cradle Song' and 'The Homeward Way', Delius's early efforts are being compared to songs that are among the most successful in Grieg's output. Both the Delius versions smile with disarming charm underpinned by unexpected harmonic twists, and in particular the open, lyrical melody of 'The Homeward Way' attaches itself to the memory. Compared to Grieg's versions, however – in which the emotional intensity present in the texts is kept sharply in focus – the creative conviction present at the start of Delius's songs seems to slip away through his fingers. Nevertheless, with these small works Delius often tapped into the same creative originality and imagination of the American scores he had penned in Leipzig. Indeed, when one compares them with many of the works that would follow in the early 1890s, we see him here much bolder, more demonstratively confident of his powers. They also improve on repeated hearings – something Grieg was magnanimous enough to admit in a letter late in 1888: '[On] closer acquaintance I see your songs in a different way. The less flattering this is for *me*, the more flattering it is for *you* and *your songs*. They are filled with such beautiful feeling, and there will never come a time when I am too stupid to see that this is the most important thing.'[4]

Three of the songs deserve special mention. The playful, naïve pleasure of 'Young Venevil' is perfectly captured by Delius's smiling melody. A similarly carefree levity lifts 'The Birds' Story' towards a brilliant close, the piano accompaniment pulsating with the flutter of bird wings. The real pearl of these two collections, however, is 'Twilight Fancies', Delius's setting of Bjørnson's poem 'Prinsessen' ('The Princess'). At an early stage in the composing process he pencilled a note: 'The idea is a Princess sitting *alone* at eventide *not* surrounded by her train. The strains of the Schalmei awaken feelings of love & loneliness. Is it not possible to begin in this wise?'[5] Indeed, the composer begins in exactly 'this wise'. The *schalmei* (or shawm) – the poem's 'horn of a herd boy' – has metamorphosed into a distant, two-voiced call, sounded as if from a forest or hill beyond the castle walls:

---

[3] Letter from Grieg to Delius, 23 September 1888 (DT).
[4] Letter from Grieg to Delius, 6 November 1888 (DT).
[5] See Threlfall, *Frederick Delius: A supplementary catalogue*, 162.

Example 3.1 'Twilight Fancies', 1–6

Throughout the song these remote signals expand the sense of space – near and far, internal and external. On comparing it to Grieg's setting of the text (work without opus number, no. 126) we see that Delius has distilled from the words a psychological depth and emotional pain, while Grieg opts for virginal innocence clothed in a melody similar to a folk song. Delius's harmonies (in particular the half-diminished sevenths) are heavy with unresolved longing. Even the tonality is ambiguous, alternating between B minor (piano) and G minor (voice), and closing in a tantalising blend of B minor (piano) and F sharp minor (voice).

Paa Vidderne and 'Mountain Music'

Delius wrote to Grieg at the end of June 1888: 'I have been working all the time & have got a lot done – further songs, and Ibsen's *Paa Vidderne*, for tenor voice, as well as an orchestral work.'[6] (*Paa Vidderne* means *On the Mountain Plateaus*; for more about the meaning of *vidde/vidda/vidderne*, see p. 25 n. 27). 'One part of me is very curious to see the work', replied Grieg,

---

[6] Letter from Delius to Grieg, 20 June 1888 (BOB).

and yet another part would prefer never to see it, since I've been planning for ages to set that poem. However – my curiosity is too great and I give you my solemn oath that I will not steal from you!! That is to say, no *notes*, as I hope I have stolen your friendship once and for all, and you are never going to get it back.[7]

Later that autumn, Delius hit on the idea that the composition would work better if Ibsen's epic poem was declaimed above the orchestra rather than sung: a melodrama, as the format was known. He reworked the score and early in November sent it to Troldhaugen.

Playwright and poet Henrik Ibsen has to a certain extent been defined by the striking photographs that were taken of him after he had achieved international celebrity: heavy whiskers framing a stern mouth, knitted brow above rimless spectacles and an upward exclamation of hair from the top of his head. It is the earnest artist we associate with searing exposure of Scandinavian social morals, so familiar with bourgeois hypocrisy he could make it the butt of his talent. A man whom we imagine to be in his element behind the closed doors of theatres, libraries and the living rooms of the middle classes. If the image has validity for his later years, it is wide of the mark for Ibsen as a young man, particularly in the happy period during the 1850s when he was attached to Ole Bull's newly established theatre in Bergen. Einar Østvedt has pointed out that Ibsen was a passionate walker: 'In the years prior to 1864 – when, at the age of thirty-six he went into voluntary exile in Italy – he had hiked all over Telemark, made the long mountain crossing from Kristiania to Bergen by way of Valdres and the Filefjell plateau, and been on several hiking tours of the Hardanger fjords and fells.'[8] In 1857, Ibsen moved back to Kristiania to get married, but became overwhelmed by financial and artistic difficulties. It was then, in 1859, that he composed *Paa Vidderne*. 'This strange poem', Østvedt remarks, 'written at a time when Ibsen found himself in the blackest depression of his life, reveals just how much he wanted to get away from it all, how dearly he longed to be back enjoying carefree days among the mountains that had stolen his heart.'[9]

Every word of Ibsen's lengthy poem has been used by Delius, the nine movements following the poet's nine sections. We follow a young hunter who leaves his betrothed and the comfort of his mother's home to go hunting among the peaks. He is also searching for his own peace of mind – 'Mountain air for my thoughts'. Once he is high above the valley, above the claims society has on him, his thoughts are exalted and he gradually becomes more confident about what he wants from life:

---

[7] Letter from Grieg to Delius, 9 August 1888 (DT).
[8] Einar Østvedt, *Henrik Ibsen: Miljø og mennesker* (*Henrik Ibsen: Environment and people*) (Oslo: Gyldendal, 1968), 133.
[9] *Ibid.*, 137.

The demon lust, the passion wild
have fled before the rod;
I stand so blithe and reconciled
to self and to my God!
The fjord, the pineclad ridge, the moors
lie open to my sight,
And then the hills and reindeer-spoors –
my mother, wife – God's peace be yours!
And now, up to the height![10]

Ibsen is exploring paths that he would later map out in dramas such as *Kjær-lighedens komedie* (*Love's Comedy*) and *Peer Gynt*, particularly the conflict between society and personal freedom. His hunter can also be read as a proto-Zarathustra, some twenty-five years before *Also sprach Zarathustra*: a strong man who raises himself above society, cultivating his personal philosophy in exalted isolation. Unsurprisingly, Delius would later develop into a passionate admirer of Nietzsche's thought, as expressed through the prophet.

On reading the score of *Paa Vidderne*, Grieg was left in no doubt that the voice of the reciter, declaiming the poem, would be overwhelmed by the orchestra: '[You] have composed with an unbelievable lack of consideration for the reciter [...] you ought perhaps to have taken a *singing* voice. Am I wrong?'[11] This was no doubt a difficult letter to write and one hears in Grieg's words that he perhaps felt let down by the Englishman. He began the letter assuring Delius that he would not let his mid-winter depression cloud his words, but concluded: 'The pessimism that was to have been avoided has perhaps crept into my discussion of the melodrama!' Having studied and admired the originality of *Florida*, Grieg may have questioned his own powers of judgement when Delius followed up with quasi-Griegian songs and an ambitious melodrama in which the text would disappear behind layers of orchestral colour applied with a heavy brush. For Delius it was also no doubt an unsettling letter to receive, but he tackled it in the best possible fashion, thanking his mentor for honest criticism: 'It has perhaps pleased me more than you would think, and confirms for me that you are the person I have always taken you for.'[12] The score was returned to Delius, who shelved it for good.[13]

Paa Vidderne is the first of several major works Delius composed with experiences of Norwegian mountain nature as his inspiration. We will be looking

---

[10] Henrik Ibsen (trans. John Northam), *Ibsen's Poems* (Oslo: Norwegian University Press, 1986), 82.

[11] Letter from Grieg to Delius, 9 December 1888 (DT).

[12] Letter from Delius to Grieg, undated, December 1888 (DT).

[13] *Paa Vidderne* was first heard in January 1981, edited and prepared by the present author, in a televised performance by the Oslo Philharmonic, commissioned by Norwegian Broadcasting (NRK).

at each of them in due course. It is already appropriate, however, to point out that there is a suite of stylistic elements that is common to all of these mountain works – from *Paa Vidderne* through to the great cairn that is *The Song of the High Hills* (1911–12). These stylistic elements were evidently developed in response to emotions he associated with mountain landscapes or, to be more precise, with the metaphoric content of a mountain journey. The elements are found again and again in Delius's mountain works, and would also later be transferred to other works. Reading from their contexts, we can roughly sort these stylistic elements into two distinct categories: 'Peak'-music and 'Plateau'-music. The first is typified by music that is energetic and striving, the second by music that is reflective and quiet. Together these musical responses constitute what we may term the composer's 'Mountain Music'.

Table 2 'Mountain Music'

Category 1: 'Peak'	
Musical characteristic	**Signifies**
A. Springing, dotted rhythms	Physical energy, endeavour
B. Bold melody with upward thrusting triplets	Strength, conviction
C. Majestic pentatonic horn fanfares	Challenge overcome, goal achieved
Category 2: 'Plateau'	
Musical characteristic	**Signifies**
A. Quiet or diminishing horn calls	Distance, height and expanse
B. Rolling horn call on first three notes of scale, often minor	Reflection; the naked spirit
C. Simple modal melody; often aeolian	Loneliness, timelessness

Category 1, 'Peak'-music, has three distinct music types. 'Peak A' and 'Peak B' are both associated with the physical energy needed to ascend the mountain – by extension the conviction needed to overcome personal challenges. (Wagner's striding heroic themes are a vital influence, particularly on 'Peak B'.) 'Peak C' consists of strident horn calls or horn fanfares and might be presumed to convey songs of exaltation on accomplishing the challenge. The herding call, sounding in the mountains, is also always a spatial signifier; it adds the sense of achieving freedom from constraint and obstacles.

Category 2, 'Plateau'-music, also has three distinct music types. Stylistically quiet and/or reflective, these elements convey a different phase in the metaphorical mountain journey. Again, reading from Delius's mountain scores, they seem to represent the wanderer, now reflecting on panoramas with huge distances, coming to terms with his/her solitude in these vistas – one human in a forbidding universe. 'Plateau A' may employ similar horn calls to 'Peak C', but they are either quiet and distanced, or diminishing. They lift the gaze from the wanderer's person and out towards the distant horizon; the metaphor is not one of height, first and foremost, but of distance. 'Plateau B' is a small, contained horn call, a repeated pattern of a few notes that might roll through the orchestra, metaphorically similar to wind across a plateau or lines of mountain ridges repeating into the horizon – what Norwegians call 'the seven blues'. Alternatively – type 'Plateau C' – the composer might suggest the same mood with short melodies in a minor or, more often, aeolian modality, and with the simplicity of a folk song. Typically these are orchestrated with a transparent texture.

Astonishingly, the composer had already with his first mountain composition, *Paa Vidderne*, defined for himself in some degree this suite of stylistic elements – responses to the mountain metaphor he would go on to develop in all his later mountain works. Here are examples of each of these idiomatic elements in the melodrama:

'Peak A':

Example 3.2 *Paa Vidderne*, Part I, opening

'Peak B':

Example 3.3 *Paa Vidderne*, Part I, 37–40

'Peak C':

Example 3.4 *Paa Vidderne*, Part IX, 747–50

'Plateau A':

Example 3.5 *Paa Vidderne*, Part IV, 335–40

'Plateau B':

Example 3.6 *Paa Vidderne*, Part VI, 422–9

'Plateau C':

Example 3.7 *Paa Vidderne*, Part VIII, 486–90

At least three of the six types were based on the spatial effect of horn calls or herding calls.

The sound of distant horns or vocal herding calls was a widely used metaphor among Romantics – both in music and literature. What a reading or listening audience might derive from the trope would evolve during the nineteenth century; indeed, it has continued relevance into our own time in the guise of the train whistle, ship horn and foghorn. Commentators on the Romantic era,

and in particular researchers into the music of the period, have in recent decades identified the preoccupation among Romantic artists with distance as an
essential trope. Indeed, the loading of distance with Romantic significance was
perhaps the single most distinctive trait of the aesthetic of the era. In his book
Programming the Absolute (2002) – a study which has Robert Schumann as its
focal point – Berthold Hoeckner itemises the fascination Romantics had with
distance in three main categories: spatial distance (as evoked by horn calls),
distance from past events (bringing memory and dreams into new promi-
nence) and the sense of being distant from one's beloved. Summing up these
various strands, Hoeckner writes: 'That music reigned supreme in Romanti-
cism hardly needs new confirmation, but it seems worthwhile to pursue how
the new prestige of music grew, in part, out of the aesthetics of sound dying
away in the distance'.[14] Horn calls are also attributed great significance by
Charles Rosen in his seminal study, *The Romantic Generation* (1995), where
he calls them 'symbols of memory – or, more exactly, of distance, absence and
regret'.[15]

The Romantic aesthetic was, however, flourishing alongside and in the wake
of the Industrial Revolution, and by the middle of the century the essential,
binding characteristic had become a sense of distance from a lost culture. That
is to say, a sense that urban culture had displaced humans – not from a state of
rural harmony, which had always been recognised as mythical, but from the
innocence of spirit which made the myth sustainable. The classical ideal of the
rural idyll, still a trope toyed with by the cultured mind in Beethoven's day,
became for Romantics marked by the sorrow of this cultural distance.

Romantic poets and philosophers strove to create a worthy image of man in
a world where the old hierarchies, both on earth and in heaven, were under re-
evaluation or considered outdated. In 1808, Beethoven depicted the gratitude
of shepherds for the passing of the storm with a melody similar to a folk song
and introduced by a horn call; it is a musical tableau of a classical pastoral
scene. A little over twenty years later, Berlioz wrote his *Symfonie fantastique*
and with the 'Scène aux champs' introduced melancholy into Arcadia. Paradise is lost for ever when, at the end of the 1850s, Wagner preluded the third act
of *Tristan und Isolde* with a shepherd's herding song coupled with a longing for
the unattainable.

In the well-ordered hierarchical society of classical myth, mountains were
a symbol of chaos and disorder. When the Romantic individualist sought the
freedom of the heights, he was no longer the conqueror or capstone of nature,
nor a hunter who considered nature primarily a source of food and sport.

---

[14] Berthold Hoeckner, *Programming the Absolute: Nineteenth-century German music and the
hermeneutics of the moment* (Princeton: Princeton University Press, 2002), 51.
[15] Charles Rosen, *The Romantic Generation* (Cambridge, Mass.: Harvard University Press,
1995), 117.

In the mountains, he found the wildness and grandeur that resonated with the existential dilemmas of his Romantic soul. The herding call, metaphor of the classical idyll, gained revised poetic power. Echoing between the peaks, it served to emphasise the solitude and deep longings inherent in the modern human condition. For Bjørnson in 1868, even the emotional chaos of the first tryst could imply a surrendering of the ego to something greater, a fusion comparable to the oneness with nature of the mountain wanderer listening to distant herding calls:

Det første mødes sødme	(The first tryst's sweetness
det er som sang i skogen	is like a song among the trees,
det er som sang på vågen	is like a song across the fjord
i solens siste rødme, –	at twilight's dying glow, –
det er som horn i uren –	like horns between the mountains
de tonende sekunder,	these sweet resounding moments
forenes i et under.[16]	united in a miracle.)

Delius was no doubt familiar with the ways the horn call, with its implications of spatial distance, had been applied in the works of Beethoven, Schubert, Schumann and Berlioz. None of these, however, would have affected him as did the extraordinary passages for distant horns that open the second act of Wagner's *Tristan und Isolde* (1857–59).[17] Time and again during his formative years Delius returned to the opera house to hear the work, and the impact that Wagner's play with spatial distance had on him can be heard in many of his earliest works, including 'Twilight Fancies' (see Example 3.1) and his first opera *Irmelin*. Wagner's interpretation of the Romantic ethos led him to correlate the trope of distance with the unattainability, not only of classical innocence or perfection, but also of happiness, unless it be attained by erotic conjunction, sublimation and death. It was a paradoxical and crucially egoistic aesthetic to which Delius – while adapting it for his operas *The Magic Fountain*, *Koanga* and *A Village Romeo and Juliet* – never fully subscribed. Essentially, Delius's attraction to the distant horn call was what it intimated of a spiritual sublimation into a higher natural greatness. Not a sharpening of the erotic ego, but a dissolving.

In the same year that *Tristan und Isolde* was completed, Darwin's *On the Origin of Species* was published. In the first edition of his treatise Darwin made it clear that a grasp of geological time was a prerequisite for following his argument, and that any reader who 'does not admit how incomprehensibly vast have been the past periods of time, may at once close this volume'.[18] Geological

---

[16] Bjørnstjerne Bjørnson, *Fiskerjenten* (*The Fisher Girl*) (Copenhagen: 1868), 55.

[17] Isolde and Brangäne stand at night by a brazier, listening to the fading sounds of horns sounded by King Marke's hunting party; only when they are distant enough can Isolde extinguish the brazier – the pre-arranged sign for Tristan to come to her.

[18] Charles Darwin, *On the Origin of Species*, first edition (London: Murray, 1859), 282.

theories were exploding the age of the earth from thousands to millions of years; evolution theory was in the process of dethroning man from what had been regarded as his divinely appointed status. Science was providing ever-expanding perspectives on notions of distance: the creation of Man, the edge of the universe, and the grace of God all now seemed inexplicably distant. If Beethoven and Schubert indulged themselves with spatial signifiers such as the shepherd's horn and the post-horn – playing on the interconnectedness of landscape, memory and absence – it was still against a philosophical backdrop of God in his heaven and Man in his image. By the time Delius came to write *Paa Vidderne*, Man had not so much been deposed, as revealed to have been sitting all along on a throne of his own imaginative projection and, confronted by geological time and an expanding universe, looked quite suddenly small and lost. It was a revolution of existential perspective.

How to compose music that was of this extraordinary time? Much of the force behind Delius's mountain scores was his drive to capture in music the wonderment and loneliness of his times. In the wanderer's meeting with the endless vistas of the Norwegian mountain plateaus he found his metaphor. By the time he wrote *The Song of the High Hills* (1911–12) the man on the mountain plateau had come to represent something larger: disenfranchised Man facing the endless wilderness of the cosmos. With that work, Delius reached the goal of his mountain project, but his early workings are everywhere in *Paa Vidderne*.

Delius's project was distinct from the nationalist project of his Norwegian contemporaries. When looking for a language he associated with his experiences in Norwegian nature, he seldom turned to the stylistic traits used by Kjerulf, Grieg and other Norwegians to imply national exoticism: folk music elements such as rhythms of the *halling* and *springar* dances, bass bourdons in open fifths, etc. In the mountain scores of Delius and Grieg, too, there are few common elements. In Grieg's mountain music the herding call is always *played* by someone, usually a shepherd boy or herd girl. In Delius's music it is lifted away from their hands and mouths, sublimated to a metaphor for solitude, or for oneness with great nature, or for the exalted, uplifted spirit – a symbol of transcendence. An example of the two composers' attitudes is the penultimate motif above (Example 3.6) from *Paa Vidderne*. The motif is strikingly similar to a call that Grieg had noted during a trip to the Jotunheim mountains in 1887. Together with Frants Beyer he had traversed some of the lower Skagastøl peaks and one experience affected him so deeply that he was still writing to friends about it in October. The two men had to find a way over the summit of the Friken mountain and hired the services of two herd girls, one of them a beautiful, young woman called Susanne. Once at the summit the men shared their lunch with their guides, including brandy that they mixed with melt water from a glacier:

But the most wonderful part was still to come. Susanne had a little folk instrument with her, a ram's horn on which you can play just *three* notes, and when the girls had said goodbye to us up there on the summit, because they had to get back down to their milking duties, and Frants and I stood entranced by the beautiful sight of them walking along the ridge, blonde, agile, and upright, with the blue horizon as a backdrop, then suddenly – the girls stood still – Susanne put the horn to her lips – I'll never forget her stance, her body silhouetted against the sky: then it sounded, mildly melancholic as if the mountain nature around us were singing:

When the last, long note had died away we turned to each other – and both stood in tears![19]

Grieg wrote this account just a few weeks before being introduced to Delius and their bonding through a shared love of Norwegian mountain nature. It seems improbable that he would not also have shared with him the tale of Susanne and the horn call, with its overt expression of Romantic nationalism. It is, of course, likely that Delius had heard similar calls on his travels. Either way, Grieg could hardly have read the *Paa Vidderne* score and not reacted to the emotional climax of the work in Part VI where a call very like Susanne's rolls through the orchestra again and again. Before Delius's score had arrived at Troldhaugen, Grieg had vowed not to steal any of its notes; he would then have opened it to discover with astonishment that Delius had perhaps, if not stolen from him, at least been inspired by the Susanne tale.[20]

Later in the same Susanne-letter to Niels Ravnkilde, Grieg ruminated on the powerful reaction her horn call had sparked in him:

There you see, that's how things turn out when a Norwegian musician is lured into the mountains. It's delightful – but whether or not it is something to be desired is another matter. For it seems to me that being overwhelmed to the point of obliteration by the greatness of nature is a risky business, and I know that there is something in my soul that is damaged by it, but I suppose there's no way round it.

Delius and Grieg seemed to have a fairly similar attitude to the Norwegian mountains: they both loved being surrounded by upland landscapes, could not imagine living without their visits there – 'I suppose there's no way round it', as Grieg put it. However, in the significance they attributed as artists to these

[19] Letter from Grieg to Niels Ravnkilde, 17 October 1887, trans. Finn Benestad (EG2).
[20] A similar rolling horn call occurs also in a Delius song contemporary with *Paa Vidderne* – his setting of Ibsen's poem 'Høifjeldsliv' in a German translation, 'Hochgebirgsleben'.

experiences, the two men went their own ways. Grieg was not concerned with trying to capture the emotions he associated with mountain experiences and wrote no programmatic works about mountain nature. His focus was on the people whose lives had been formed by mountain nature: herd girls such as Gjendine (op. 66), Solveig (op. 23), and Veslemøy (op. 67),[21] herd boys (op. 54), and the narrator who in *Den Bergtekne* (*The Mountain Thrall*, op. 32) is lured by the daughters of the mountain troll. Grieg let the people of the uplands be his surrogates, their songs were his – as embodiments of the Norwegian character. At its core, his project was humanistic; he was unsure what advantage there might be in pitting the insignificance of the individual human against the greatness of nature, 'to the point of obliteration'. So, he put to one side the herding call he had heard from Susanne's horn. For his part, Delius believed emotions stimulated by mountain experiences could be constructively projected in art. The more confident he became in his creative tools, the harder he strove to capture precisely the spiritual release involved when personal identity is dissolved in a greater force – the same sense of being 'overwhelmed to the point of obliteration by the greatness of nature' that was anathema to Grieg. For Delius, the lonely call of a horn heard echoing around the mountains was the ideal expression of the human spirit at one with great nature. These differing approaches go a long way to explaining why Delius could readily borrow from Grieg harmonic and melodic traits, but rarely the folk music elements of the older man's work.

Grieg would in fact return to Susanne's horn call in 1895 when he fell under the spell of Arne Garborg's cycle of poems, *Haugtussa* (*The Mountain Maid*). At the close of his melancholic, naked setting of 'Kulokk' ('Cattle Call') he introduced the rolling ram's horn call he had first heard high among the Skagastøl peaks. Perhaps again feeling that alienating sense of personal insignificance, he put the song away and let it gather dust; 'Kulokk' is one of a handful of songs that Grieg wrote for *Haugtussa*, but finally left out.[22]

1888: Longing for Norway

In the late summer of 1888, Delius had to deliver Grieg the disappointing news that he could not afford to visit Norway that year, but would husband his

---

[21] For 'Gjendine's Lullaby' (op. 66, no. 19) Grieg arranged a folk tune sung by the *seterjente* (milkmaid) Gjendine Slaalien (see p. 61). In Ibsen's *Peer Gynt*, to which Grieg wrote incidental music, Peer promises his heart to the *seterjente* Solveig. Veslemøy is the farm girl with mystic powers in the cycle of poems, *Haugtussa* (*The Mountain Maid*), by Arne Garborg, from which Grieg selected poems for his song cycle of the same name.

[22] Daniel Grimley points out that Grieg's use of the melody may be connected with his low spirits in this period: 'The song could concern not just Veslemøy's sense of isolation [...] but Grieg's own sense of creative loneliness and the perceived peripheralisation that recurs in much of his own correspondence around this time.' *Grieg: Music, landscape and Norwegian identity*, 132.

resources towards a trip the following summer: 'How I look forward to walking again on Norwegian moorland and looking out over the great distances.'[23] Grieg replied: 'Alright: next year! Yes! I will do everything in my power to have the pleasure of receiving you here then. No music festivals next summer!'[24] The tone was set for a year's correspondence in which their anticipation of a Jotunheim tour was constantly bubbling to the surface. If Grieg had ever doubted Delius's commitment to the project, he would have been reassured by a letter he received from him in October:

> Do you know what I've been thinking, 'now, please don't faint', to live in Norway. That is, 8 months of the year & 4 months in Leipzig or Paris. [...] Streets and smoke distort our ideas. One has to breathe pure air before one can think purely. I feel so well in mind & body when nature is beautiful.[25]

Grieg, ever the pragmatist, reminded him how brief a Norwegian summer could be: 'Your suggestion flatters both my national feelings and my feelings as your friend, but all the same let's turn it on its head: 4 months in Norway (in the summer) and 8 in Germany and France.'[26] The notion of using Norway only as a summer base was advice Delius followed. On average every other year he would be in Norway for periods ranging from one to three months.

The bonds of friendship were strong in this period. When Grieg assured Delius that, even at their first meeting, his instinct had told him 'our sympathies were mutual',[27] the Englishman replied in kind:

> My instinct has seldom led me astray, my reason often. When I first got to know you, it wasn't instinct any more, for I had already known you for a long time through your music. Nothing reveals the true human more than music. An author can bluff his way through (in my opinion) but a musician has to show his true self or nothing at all.[28]

Around Christmas and New Year both men dwelt on memories of the splendid celebration of the year before, and Grieg wrote to Johan Halvorsen:

> I too recall the previous, wonderful Christmas we spent in Leipzig. No doubt a one-off, never to be repeated. But – never mind! Let's get together one summer evening at Troldhaugen instead. Delius is coming. Sinding doesn't know how the devil he'll manage it, but if the devil can't stump up the resources for such a thing, then it's a poorer devil than I take him for. And Halvorsen is coming! Right, it's a deal?[29]

[23] Letter from Delius to Grieg, undated, mid-August 1888 (BOB).
[24] Letter from Grieg to Delius, 23 September 1888 (DT).
[25] Letter from Delius to Grieg, 19 October 1888 (BOB).
[26] Letter from Grieg to Delius, 6 November 1888 (BOB).
[27] Letter from Grieg to Delius, 23 September 1888 (DT).
[28] Letter from Delius to Grieg, 19 October 1888 (BOB).
[29] Letter from Grieg to Johan Halvorsen, 31 December 1888 (BOB).

Shortly after New Year, Delius was in poor health and had to spend a couple of months with his family in Bradford, keeping warm his longing for Norway by reading Bjørnson and Ibsen. It was probably pneumonia he was struggling with, and Grieg, accustomed to everyone worrying about his frail health, could for once assume the role of concerned party: '*You* must get well! For heaven's sake: Don't do anything stupid! Think of the wonderful summer and our reunion in Norway.'[30] A reunion occurred in fact in February while Delius was still surrounded by the 'streets and smoke' of which he had complained. Grieg was enjoying a triumphal procession of concerts through English cities and when his itinerary brought him to Manchester's Free Trade Hall, Delius was in the audience. In mid-March he was back in France. From then until the summer, the prospects for the mountain tour filled their correspondence. Delius wrote: 'The time is approaching when I can begin the journey I have looked forward to for so long & hopefully the elements will be at their most friendly and send us lovely weather: it will be my first Jotunheimen visit and it gives me so much pleasure that it is you who will be my guide in this magnificent landscape.'[31]

At one point it seemed that a veritable flock of composers would be migrating to the mountains. The participation of Sinding and Halvorsen was taken for granted by Grieg and Delius. For his part, Sinding had mentioned the tour to Johan Svendsen and Ferruccio Busoni and both expressed an interest in packing their knapsacks and following Grieg's trail into the mountain heart of Norway. In the end, they had to decline and Halvorsen was called up for a month of midsummer military service. It was the trio of whist-companions from Leipzig that assembled at Troldhaugen in the middle of July to grease their boots and study timetables and maps: Grieg, Delius – and the man who for several summers provided Delius with an address in Norway.

Christian Sinding

Born in 1856, Sinding was the son of a mining surveyor in the town of Kongsberg, but on the death of his father in 1860 the family moved to Kristiania. He was the youngest of five siblings, three others following an artistic calling: painter and author Otto Sinding, sculptor Stephan Sinding and sculptress Johanna Sinding, who developed mental problems and failed to achieve the renown of her brothers. The fifth sibling was Thora Cathrine, with whom Delius would become acquainted during his Norway holiday in 1889.

Music was the only discipline to interest the young Christian Sinding during his youth, resulting in a first period of study at the Conservatory in Leipzig from 1874 to 1877. Later in life he would disparage the quality of tuition as strongly as did Delius, but it did not prevent him enrolling in 1879 for a further

---

[30] Letter from Grieg to Delius, 4 February 1889 (BOB).
[31] Letter from Delius to Grieg, undated, May 1889 (BOB).

nine months. On his return to Kristiania he devoted himself to chamber music and songs, and with a concert of his works in December 1885 achieved a break-through onto the national stage. The Kristiania critics heaped glowing praises on his music, particularly the Piano Quintet, op. 5. To Grieg, who admired his talent, Sinding wrote: 'I'm beginning to get superstitious. There must be some happy alignment of the stars right now. [...] Here at home I am received with so much goodwill and benevolence that the world no longer seems like a vale of sorrows, quite the opposite.'[32] This favourable conjunction in the heavens had passed the following year. Sinding had lost his mother and the family had more or less broken up. For at least the next decade he had to manage on a tiny income, often only on stipends and bursaries – a period during which the good offices of Edvard Grieg were essential for his advancement. In Sep-tember 1888, Sinding returned to Leipzig on a bursary and soon after would get to know Delius. We have already seen the value Grieg and Delius placed on the time the 'clique' spent together that winter. If anything, Sinding took even more from it. As they each moved on in the spring of 1888, he wrote to Delius – newly arrived back home in Bradford – and laid bare the warmth of his feelings:

> You cannot believe how much I miss you. I have hardly ever before met a person I could trust so completely, and at times an almost sentimental feeling comes over me when I think of you. But I hope you will not laugh too much at me on that account.[33]

Sinding's private life was in turmoil in this period. His pecuniary problems were at crisis point, and he was happy to accept the offer of accommodation from the benevolent professor of violin at the Conservatory, Adolf Brodsky. It was under his roof that Sinding fell in love with Brodsky's sister-in-law. Olga Picard, with her small son, had also sought the protection of Brodsky after her marriage had foundered. Secretly, Sinding and Picard vowed each other undy-ing fidelity. Right up to the Jotunheim tour with Grieg and Delius, a storm was raging in Sinding that threatened to tear him apart. By then, however, Picard had returned home to Odessa and gradually Sinding would reconcile him-self to the fact that his dream would never become a reality. While struggling through this turbulent period, he did in fact enjoy more musical success. Per-haps the most important event of his career was the performance of his Piano Quintet at the Leipzig Gewandhaus in January 1889. The work was hailed as a masterpiece and there quickly followed more commissions than Sinding could accept. Emotionally, artistically and financially his life was in the melting pot

---

[32] Letter from Sinding to Grieg, 18 February 1886 (BOB).
[33] Letter from Sinding to Delius, 19 April 1888 (DT).

around the time of the trio's mountain journey: 'I look forward to this trip as to a turning point in my life. It will be so good to lay aside all cares for a while.'[34]

At the time of writing there are three biographies of Christian Sinding, two in Norwegian by Gunnar Rugstad (1979) and Per Vollestad (2005), and one in Russian by Elena Biterjakova (2007). In Gunnar Rugstad's study the composer is presented as having a difficult and stubborn personality. A more nuanced character emerges from the pages of Per Vollestad's biography from 2005. Here we see that Sinding from an early age learned to take the stones life threw at him with a disarming self-irony and rarely took himself too seriously. He devoted himself totally to his vocation and was zealous in not dissipating his energies unnecessarily. In middle age he married Augusta Gade, who described him as impulsive and warm-hearted, but also absent-minded. Vollestad writes: 'He could easily leave the house with one brown shoe and one black. Once, when he had left the house without [Augusta] checking, he had attended a gala banquet dressed in his old blue work overalls. But had not noticed before coming home.'[35] Even in Vollestad's more sympathetic portrayal we see a personality markedly different to that of Delius. While Sinding on public occasions was content to make his presence felt discreetly in the background, Delius was blessed with both an outgoing manner and the well-bred charm of the English gentleman. How close the two men actually were is difficult to ascertain, since all of Delius's side of the correspondence is lost. Practically everything we know of their friendship comes from surviving letters written by Sinding. That there existed a strong mutual respect and attraction is, however, testified to by the fact that Delius wished to take Sinding with him on two projected tours to America that never materialised. During Delius's three long sojourns in Norway in 1889, 1891 and 1893 much of his time was spent with Sinding, and they also saw a lot of each other in Leipzig and Paris during this period.

Summer 1889: 'Living the wild life' in the mountains

From the first days of their acquaintance, Grieg had longed to show Delius the Jotunheim mountains. In the summer of 1889, that wish was fulfilled, and, thanks to the diary Delius kept of his Norway trip, we can follow his movements in some detail.[36] His ferry arrived in Kristiania at 2.00a.m. on Monday 24 June. Despite the late hour, he was met not only by his Leipzig friend, violinist Arve Arvesen, but also by a cultural celebrity, Arve's father Olaus Arvesen,

---

[34] Letter from Sinding to Grieg, 13 June 1889 (BOB).
[35] Per Vollestad, *Christian Sinding* (Oslo: Solum forlag, 2005), 111.
[36] Delius's 1889 summer diary (GM) has been published as 'Appendix V' in LC1, 397–401. If not otherwise stated, the quotations on the next pages from Delius's diary are from this source (Lionel Carley's transcription), and follow Carley's practice in tidying up the punctuation and orthography, in order to make the diary more easily readable.

one of the foremost radical pedagogues in Norway. The following day, he had a run-through of Grieg's Violin Sonata No. 3 at the offices of music publisher Warmuth, accompanying Arvesen; this was in preparation for a planned concert in Hamar on 7 July, but in the end Arvesen would not be accompanied by Delius (see below). Then on to dinner. At his table at the Gravesens restaurant in Stortingsgate were assembled several bright lights of Norwegian cultural life. In addition to Arvesen were two artist friends with whom Delius had become acquainted in Paris. Sculptor Jo Visdal and painter Eyolf Soot had both been awarded bursaries in 1888 which enabled them to travel to the French capital. Two friends from Leipzig were also in attendance: Iver Holter and Johan Halvorsen, the latter passing through town on his way to a month's military duty.

Delius then travelled by local ferry to the Nesodden peninsula in the inner Kristiania Fjord with lawyer Glør Thorvald Mejdell, who was married to Sinding's sister Thora Cathrine. They had their summer house, Skirstad (today known as Gamle Haslum), at Blylaget and the permanently hard-up Sinding was staying with them for the summer. Mejdell would make a name for himself as a defender of workers' rights. Delius relaxed at this fjord retreat from Monday through to Sunday, bathing, sailing and making excursions, such as this one on Friday 28 June:

> Got up at 6, & walked over to Drøbak with Sinding. Most delightful walk thro pine forest […] arrived at 10 […] at the Gades. Had a bathe, a sail – then dinner, a sleep, another bathe, a walk on the hills above the town, then supper. On my way to the Hotel, got into conversation with a Mr Parr, large in shipping.

Drøbak, on the east coast of the fjord, was a quiet fishing village that filled in the summer months with artists and Kristiania's well-to-do wishing to escape the city. Sinding's friends Augusta and Fredrik Gade were among these and had their summer house at Husvik, a bay to the north of the town. Husvik was also the base for two shipping magnates, brothers Søren Angell Parr and Hans Henry Parr, who had made their fortune carrying ice to England. Delius's conversation with one of the elderly brothers may well have been about their common origins, as the Parr family had emigrated from Yorkshire.

On Sunday 30 June, Delius and Sinding travelled back to Kristiania and continued by train to Hamar, some hundred and thirty kilometres north of the capital, beautifully sited on the shores of Mjøsa lake. Delius and Sinding were to stay with the Arvesens at Sagatun, high above the town. Established in 1864 by education reformers Herman Anker and Olaus Arvesen, Sagatun was the first folk high school in Norway.[37] Arvesen was rector of the school and his residence was on the same site. He had planned to take Delius to visit Bjørnstjerne Bjørnson at the great man's home some eighty kilometres north

---

[37] Anker's daughter Katti was born at Sagatun in 1868. Katti Anker Møller (her married name) would become one of Norway's foremost campaigners for women's rights.

of Hamar. In a recent letter to his daughter Bergliot, Bjørnson had sighed: 'Arvesen has announced that he is bringing an American friend of Arve's, as well as Arve. I can't be bothered with all the fuss. The older I get, the less I like it.'[38] The plan was probably displaced by national events. In these first days of July, the left-wing government of Johan Sverdrup was in crisis, and Bjørnson was quickly and fully caught up in the whirl of political debate and commentary. Instead, Arvesen introduced Delius and Sinding to one of the region's most prominent families at Sæli Gård, 'a magnificent farm, 3 kilometres from Hamar, overlooking the lake Mjøsa', as Delius noted in his diary on Tuesday 2 July. The estate has been in the same family from 1798 to the present, and at the time of Delius's visit was owned by Andreas Sæhlie, previously mayor of the municipality and county representative at parliament.[39] One of his daughters, Ingeborg Sæhlie (twenty-six), was engaged to doctor Vollert Hille, son of Arnoldus Marius Hille, Bishop of Hamar. A talented singer who had received tuition in Paris, she was due to perform Grieg songs at the approaching Arvesen concert and Delius, who was to accompany her, came to Sæli Gård every day this week to rehearse. One of the local newspapers, *Oplandenes avis* (editor: Olaus Arvesen), carried prominent advertisements for the upcoming event.

It is from a rival organ, *Hamar Stiftstidende*, that we learn that things did not go quite to plan. 'Mr Arve Arvesen's concert this evening (Sunday) was remarkably well attended, considering the rain, and the concert arranger was repeatedly called to the stage to receive the applause of the audience.'[40] In Grieg's Violin Sonata No. 3 and Mendelssohn's concerto he was accompanied by a Mr Gasmann. The review continued: 'Unfortunately Miss Sæhlie was at the last moment prevented from attending due to illness in her family. In a commendable act of goodwill, Mrs Geelmuyden stepped in at two hours' notice to perform the vocal part of the programme which she, accompanied by Mr Delius, executed in a beautiful way, and was rewarded with the warm gratitude of the audience.'[41] This was Delius's first public performance in Norway.

On Monday 8 July Delius returned to Kristiania, meeting up again with Sinding who had returned early from Hamar. Then he continued alone by fjord steamer down to Fredriksværn, probably invited by Iver Holter, who spent his summers there fishing and sailing. Since 1886, Holter had been conductor of the capital's principal orchestra, Christiania Musikforening, a position he would hold for twenty-five years. Fredriksværn (today's Stavern) would become a favourite summer resort for Delius in the coming years, an

---

[38] Letter from Bjørnstjerne Bjørnson to Bergliot Bjørnson, June 1889 (NB).
[39] The farm would also play a role in national history fifty years later. As the Germans invaded Norway in April 1940, the royal family and government had to flee Oslo and their first refuge was Sæli Gård.
[40] *Hamar Stiftstidende*, 9 July 1889.
[41] Anne Elisabeth Geelmuyden was the wife of one of the teachers at Sagatun.

ideal haven for bathing and sailing. On the west side of the Kristiania Fjord, so far south that the fjord here opens into the Skagerrak, the village doubled as a fishing community and naval base; from 1814 until 1896 it was the home port of Norway's defence fleet. Delius's letters from the village that summer indicate that he stayed at the renowned Hotel Wassilioff on the seafront. The quality of the hotel, as much as the splendid coastal nature, explains the popularity of Fredriksværn in this period, despite the fact that hotel guests were regularly vetted by the local lord of the manor, Baron Finn Wedel-Jarlsberg.[42]

On Wednesday 10 July Delius was joined in Fredriksværn by Sinding, and then on Saturday the two friends took the coastal steamer west towards Bergen, finally arriving there at midday on Monday – the three composers reunited for the first time since the Leipzig 'clique' was disbanded. Delius writes: 'Met by Grieg on the pier, went at once to Troldhaugen, delightfully situated on a fjord.'[43] Late in life, Delius dictated recollections of his days at Grieg's home, describing 'a very agreeable week fishing and walking, Grieg playing some of his latest compositions to us, and making excursions to Bergen to buy the necessary knapsacks and provisions for our projected walking tour in Jotunheimen'.[44]

On Wednesday 17 July the party travelled into Bergen to procure supplies and, while there, Delius ran into 'a Miss Anna Mohn, who I had met in Eide 2 years before. Very nice.' The following day he noted: 'Went to Mohns to dinner. Went over their stores of stockfish.' On board the ferry from Hamburg to Norway to start his 1887 holiday, Delius had shared a cabin with a member of the Mohn family of Bergen, probably Wilhelm, then seventeen years old. He had joined the Mohns a few days later on the Granvin Fjord at Eide, where the family were gathered for the summer, and enjoyed a day's walking and bathing with them.[45] This new meeting with Wilhelm's sister, Anna Mohn, is presumably a chance encounter, as she was only fifteen. The Mohns were one of the old Hanseatic trading families that had built up Bergen's position as a commercial centre over many centuries, with the famous Bryggen as their trading base. The Mohns conducted their stockfish business from the oldest and most famous of the Bryggen buildings, Enhjørningsgården (The House of the Unicorn), with the figure of a prancing unicorn above the door. The house was owned by a different branch of Anna's extended family; however, since Delius was given a tour of the stockfish stores, it was probably also here

[42] See Vilhelm Krag, *Den gang vi var tyve Aar* (*When We Were Twenty Years Old*) (Oslo: Asche-houg, 1927), 152–6. Born in 1815, the baron was one of the last people who could rightfully bear an aristocratic title; titles were abolished in Norway in 1821.

[43] Edvard and Nina Grieg had built their house in 1885 on a promontory above the waters of Nordåsvatnet, a fjord arm some ten kilometres south of Bergen. They chose the site because they would become neighbours with Grieg's closest friend, Frants Beyer.

[44] 'Delius: Recollections of Grieg' (GM), published in LC1, 396.

[45] Delius's 1887 diary (GM), published as 'Appendix III' in LC1, 386–7.

the dinner was held.[46] In her correspondence with Delius in the following year, Nina Grieg teased him about his holiday flirtations. Not only Anna Mohn, but also a Petra Vogt seems to have fallen under his charms during these days in Bergen. Petra, nineteen years old, was the daughter of Peter Herman Vogt, one of Bergen's foremost medical practitioners, author of the standard Norwegian textbook for aspiring midwives.

A lazy week of bathing and fishing was passed as the guest of Edvard and Nina Grieg, and in his diary Delius noted that they were joined for dinner some evenings by Frants Beyer and his wife Marie, or rowed across to the Beyer house on the next promontory.

In the afternoon of Tuesday 23 July, the three composers left from the Bergen railway station for Voss, 'the train crowded with English'.[47] After Voss, Delius, Grieg and Sinding travelled by steamer on the Sognefjord to Lærdalsøyri and from there climbed eastwards up to Nystuen, a thousand metres above sea level:

> *Wed.* Left at 7 a.m. in carriage for Gudvangen & Laerdalsøyri. Delightful day. Dinner at Gudvangen. Laerdalsøyri at 7.30. Nice hotel. Drank Toddy on the balkony.
> *Thurs.* Left in carriage at 8 a.m. for Nystuen via Maristova [Maristuen]. Delight-ful scenery. Stopped for dinner at *Borgund* (a very interesting church). Arrived at Nystuen at 8 p.m. after a magnificent drive over a Vidde. Slept on the floor in the drawing room.

Borgund stave church is from c.1150–1200, and is regarded as the best pre-served of Norway's medieval stave churches. The *vidde* crossed by the party is Filefjell. The Nystuen lodge looks out on the waters of a small lake, Otrøvatnet, but its backdrop is the almost perpendicular cliff face of the Støgonøse hill. On Friday, the three travellers climbed to the top by a more circuitous route, '& had a great panorama of Jotunheim', Delius noted.[48] In his later recollections he recorded that 'Grieg and Sinding went down the proper way, but I went down a more direct and very much steeper way and almost came to grief. When I arrived at Nystuen they were just on the point of sending after me.'[49]

The trunk road to Bergen was still being constructed in these years, so next day Grieg and friends had to walk or ride the eight kilometres from Nystuen to Tyin lake, spending the night at Framnes, a recent addition to the rapidly expanding catalogue of tourist accommodation in the central Norwegian mountains. The travellers were now in the foothills of Jotunheimen. The next

---

[46] The Mohn house has been faithfully restored and is today, appropriately, a popular restaurant.

[47] This first stage of the huge engineering project to connect Bergen to Kristiania – 107 kilome-tres to Voss – had opened as a narrow gauge line in 1883.

[48] The Romantic wildness of the landscape here is captured in one of the most well-known paintings by J. C. Dahl, *Stugunoset paa Filefjeld* (*Stugunoset on the Filefjell*), from 1851. In his diary, Delius calls the hill Stugunøsi. Today the official name is Støgonøse.

[49] 'Delius: Recollections of Grieg' (GM), published in LC1, 396.

leg of the journey was by rowboat up the lake to the Tvindehaugen lodge, from there up and over the Skjenegge[50] hill – 'Grand view of Bygdin & mountains from the top', noted Delius – and down to the shores of Bygdin mountain lake. At the western end of Bygdin lay Eidsbugarden, the cabin at which the renowned historian Ernst Sars was also staying (see p. 7). He had become friends with a Dutch tourist, Vrouke Titsingh, when she was in Norway in 1887, and had now undertaken to introduce her to Jotunheimen. Although Eidsbugarden had been open to tourists since its construction in 1868, it had been built on a private initiative by four friends, including Ernst Sars and Aasmund Olavsson Vinje, the famous poet, journalist and campaigner for the rural Norwegian dialects. Vinje, who died in 1870, is celebrated today at Eidsbugarden by a monumental sculpted head.

In his diary, Delius has left us a few words to describe his progress to Leirungshytta, the cabin Grieg had hired for their Jotunheim holiday:

> Left at 12 next day, *Mond.*, for Gjende. Grand march on a vidde. Arrived at Gjendebu 6 p.m. Dinner 7.30. Quiet chat with Grieg & Sinding. Slept with Grieg. Bathe in the morning. Met by our guide, Vistikleivin [Vistekleiven], & left in a boat for the hut of Dr Nicolaysen. After delightful row, arrived at 2.30. Dinner I cooked.

Gjendebu, at the western end of the Gjende lake, was a simple *seter* belonging to the Slaalien family from Bøverdal, and from 1871 the Turistforening (Trekking Association) had a lodge here under the family's auspices. Gjendine Slaalien, the one herd girl whose name is known to most Norwegians and to many music lovers outside of Norway, spent many summers here. She was christened in the lake and named after it. Gjendine recalled vividly the summer of 1889 because from the end of May she spent fourteen days here completely alone, apart from her herd.[51] She was eighteen years old. The event that secured Gjendine's fame took place two summers later when she was helping out at another Jotunheim *seter*, Skogadalsbøen, where her sister had just given birth. Edvard Grieg, Frants Beyer and the Dutch composer Julius Röntgen stopped there on their mountain holiday. In the small hours of a light summer night, Gjendine and her two fellow herd girls joined the men in their hut and, enlivened by a tipple the tourists had with them, sang all the old folk songs they knew. Beyer wrote them down and later Grieg would bring 'Gjendine's Lullaby' (op. 66, no. 19) out to the musical world. This extraordinary meeting in 1891 has always been regarded as the first between Edvard Grieg and Gjendine Slaalien, but it is

---

[50] Skjenegge is called Skineggi in Delius's diary, one of several earlier forms that are now no longer in official use.

[51] Arvid Møller, *Gjendine* (Oslo: Cappelen, 1976), 17–18.

highly probable that Grieg, in the company of Delius and Sinding, met her in July 1889.[52]

For the next nine days, the three composers enjoyed the life of hunters in a cabin by the shore of Gjende. The lake stretches eighteen kilometres, roughly east–west, and, on its southern shore some fourteen kilometres east of Gjendebu, the Leirung stream falls from an upper valley into the lake. Here at the foot of the waterfall is the Leirungshytte, a hunting cabin loaned to Grieg by a Kristiania friend, surgeon Julius Nicolaysen. Nicolaysen had also recommended to Grieg as guide and bearer the local hunter he employed when tracking reindeer. Hans Christensen Vistekleiven was from the village of Vågå to the north of Jotunheimen. He married in 1859 and had a large family which he supported through casual farming jobs and his prowess as a tracker and marksman. To most people he was known simply as Hans the Hunter.

Of a multitude of travel accounts written by English authors of their Norwegian holidays, the most famous, dating from 1882, is *Three in Norway (by two of them)*. In this humorous account by J. A. Lees and W. J. Clutterbuck there are interesting parallels to our three composers, not least the fact that an extended stay by the shore of Gjende is the highlight of the trip. Julius Nicolaysen, whom the authors refer to as Professor N., is staying across the lake from the Englishmen at his hunting cabin, which they describe as 'an extremely comfortable and convenient little dwelling, in a most charming situation.'[53]

From Monday 29 July to Thursday 8 August our three pillars of musical society abandoned themselves to 'living the wild life', as Grieg would write in a letter some years later.[54] 'Our principal food was trout from the lake, wonderful trout', recalled Delius. 'We ate flatbrød, the flat Norwegian oatcakes, and every evening we had hot whisky toddy and played cards.'[55] On fine, sunny days they indulged in fishing, hiking and rows across the lake to the Memurubu *seter* and tourist lodge to buy eggs and milk and to the Gjendesheim tourist lodge at the eastern end of the lake to collect letters.

---

[52] There is, in fact, considerable confusion in the sources about Gjendine's first encounters with both Delius and Grieg – confusion to which she herself contributed in the course of a long life (she died in 1972, a hundred years old). Arvid Møller interviewed Gjendine extensively before her death, and it is on the basis of these discussions that he wrote in his book *Memurubu* (Lillehammer: Thorsrud lokalhistorisk forlag, 2010, 44) that the young woman had sung for Delius, Grieg and Sinding in 1889. In a radio interview in 1947 she implied that it was at Gjendebu, not Skogadalsbøen, that she had first met Grieg and that she was at first too shy to sing for him: 'But then he suggested that I stand behind a door, with him on the other side – and that did the trick!' (*Rolf Kirkvaag i samtale med Gjendine på Elveseter*, NRK, 1947. NB). Most commentators, including Grieg's biographers Benestad and Schjelderup-Ebbe (*Edvard Grieg*, 1980), have held to the prevalent narrative of her meeting with Grieg for the first time at Skogadalsbøen in 1891, together with Beyer and Röntgen.

[53] J. A. Lees and W. J. Clutterbuck, *Three in Norway (by two of them)* (London: Longmans, 1882), 194.

[54] Letter from Grieg to Julius Röntgen, 20 June 1900 (JR).

[55] 'Delius: Recollections of Grieg' (GM), published in LC1, 396.

5. The hunting cabin on the south bank of Gjende, where Delius, Grieg and Sinding stayed for nine days in 1889, is almost unchanged.

On rainy days, the composers took manuscript paper from their rucksacks and did a little work. Delius started on a small set of variations, but never completed them. The sketches are marked 'Leirungs Hütte, Jotun heim/Norge/August 1889'. In an inventory made of the manuscripts at Delius's home after his death there was indeed listed a 'Small piece composed in Jotunheim (Norway) jointly by Grieg, Sinding and Delius, MS'. Whether this had any connection with the unfinished variations must remain a mystery, as the whereabouts of this manuscript are now unknown. Although the piece was probably a bagatelle to while away the time, the very idea of these great musical imaginations setting each other composing conundrums is fascinating.

On the evening of Thursday 8 August they were back at Eidsbugarden, and the following evening at Nystuen. Delius wrote: 'Last night with Grieg, he going next day back to Laerdalsøyri. We (S & I) to Valdres. Cards & portwine, for last time.'

On Saturday, he and Sinding travelled down to Fagernes, the only event of note in his diary being their meeting along the way with Queen Sophie of Norway and Sweden. The queen spent many of her summers in the Norwegian countryside, choosing much the same degree of spartan comfort that Delius, Grieg and Sinding had experienced. This summer, she stayed for several months at Gjevle farm, north of Dokka. By way of the Randsfjord lake and the towns of Hønefoss and Sandvika they finally arrived back in Kristiania on the afternoon of Tuesday 13 August, and here Delius and Sinding went their own ways. Delius returned to the coastal delights of Fredriksværn for a week, crewing for Iver Holter on 'two or three dangerous sails'.

On his final day, Thursday 22 August, Delius was back in Kristiania, where he and Sinding indulged themselves at a Turkish baths before Delius boarded his ferry for the journey homewards.

During their weeks together Grieg and Delius had acknowledged the intimacy of their friendship; from their first letters after the tour they replaced the formal address forms *Sie* and *Ihr* with the informal *Du* and *Dein*. Paradoxically, their friendship would never be quite as warm again, their letters never quite so effusive, as in the weeks and months prior to the trip. We will see that, during the 1890s, there was a steadily decreasing level of contact, and it seems that the glow of sympathetic sentiment, previously so candidly expressed, had faded a little during their Jotunheim expedition of 1889. For almost a month they had been together, and nine days were spent in a tiny, isolated and primitive cabin. For two strong personalities there may well have been some rather testing moments.

It is also possible that Delius's attitude to money would become a wedge between them. In Grieg's account book we see that, on Delius's arrival in Bergen, he had to lend him 128 crowns, a sum equivalent at the time to a month's wages for a trained industrial worker.[56] In other words, the Englishman's participation was dependent on Grieg's generosity, a situation that seems to repeat itself in 1891 (see p. 78). Although unstintingly munificent when friends and relations were involved, Grieg was also meticulous, entering into his account book even the tiniest expenditure. It was an attitude to financial matters he shared with his dearest friend throughout his life, Frants Beyer, who, at the peak of his career, was Bergen's tax commissioner. Delius, on the other hand, was far more carefree about money and, though he did not live beyond his means, these were almost exclusively made up of contributions from family and friends. 'We've got nothing in common except our feeling', Grieg had written to Beyer on first getting to know Delius in Leipzig, and the value they placed on thrift and frugality may have partly defined the distance between their characters and Delius's.

Whether or not the prolonged contact Grieg and Delius had with each other in Norway had taken the shine off their mutual attraction, other concerns would soon fill their days and minds. The deteriorating state of Grieg's health made him progressively less gregarious. In contrast, Delius's whole-hearted

---

[56] It may also have been in connection with Delius's financial situation that Grieg had written to Julius Delius in April. The letter no longer exists, but if Delius's lack of resources was threatening to upset their Jotunheim plans, it may have contained a request from Grieg, on Delius's behalf, that Julius proffer some extra support to his son. On returning to Troldhaugen from the mountains, Grieg wrote up his expenses in his account book under the oddly incomplete heading: 'Tour in Jotunheimen with Sinding'.

involvement in the artistic and aristocratic circles of Parisian society would weaken for several years the magnetic pull of the mountains. He would return to Norway in 1891 and 1893, but not to Jotunheimen until 1896.

4

1890–1891
'C'est de la Norderie'

'It seems radiant with glory, that time'
Letter from Nina Grieg to Delius, 22 May 1909

While young Norwegian musicians had sought an education in Leipzig in the first half of the nineteenth century, painters were drawn to the academies in Düsseldorf and, later, Munich. With the emergence in France of the early impressionists and the Barbizon school, however, the European art map was redrawn. In the last two decades of the century, German academies lost much of their attraction for Norwegian art students, who elected rather to submerge themselves in *la vie de bohème*. In 1878, as part of the Exposition Universelle – the World's Fair in Paris – a huge exhibition of art was staged that revealed to Norwegian artists the pre-eminence of contemporary French art. Among the Norwegians who moved to Paris after the exhibition were Christian Krohg, Hans Heyerdahl and Erik Werenskiold. Attracted by liberal Parisian society, many female Norwegian artists – including Kitty Kielland, Harriet Backer and Asta Nørregaard – also fled there from petty bourgeois Kristiania.

Radical Norwegian authors, too, turned their backs on the classical inspiration of Rome in favour of Paris, as Torleiv Kronen has pointed out: 'The new republic rekindled the hope of fulfilling the old promise: freedom, equality and brotherhood. A generation of writers with Flaubert, Zola, Maupassant and the brothers Goncourt at its head augured well for a wholly new way of thinking. The arts, in particular literature, were expected to serve reality. For Norwegian writers, realists as they were, this was irresistible.'[1] Bjørnstjerne Bjørnson lived in Paris for five years (1882–87) and Jonas Lie for twenty-four years (1882–1906); the homes of these literary beacons became rallying points for Norwegian thinkers and artists.

---

[1] Torleiv Kronen, *De store årene: Fransk innflytelse på norsk åndsliv 1880–1900* (*The Great Years: French influence on Norwegian arts and letters 1880–1900*) (Oslo: Dreyer forlag, 1982), 104.

These and other Scandinavian figures prepared the ground for the extraordinary obsession with everything Nordic that swept Paris in the 1890s. It was the second generation of Norwegian painters – those who arrived there around the same time as Delius – that would harvest the fruits; they came to a city whose art lovers could not got enough of chill northern landscapes in either naturalist or later neo-romantic styles. Here is Parisian music critic Adolphe Boschot describing a gallery visit:

> We enjoyed meditating in front of the winter landscapes where snow has a bluish sheen under a pale and yellowish sky; other times, surrounded by mountains, by the shore of a sky-blue lake, there would be a cheerful play of lively colours, vibrant, the reds of painted swings, the purplish heather, the emerald moss that was shooting new growths around the base of the trees.[2]

As an antithesis to the industrialisation of the cities, and as a counterbalance to the prevailing *fin de siècle* fatalism of the political classes, the myth of the exotic and pristine landscapes far out there on Europe's periphery had a powerful influence on Frenchmen. When, in addition, Ibsen conquered the Parisian public in 1890 with a groundbreaking production of *Gengangere* (*Ghosts*), little Norway cemented its new position as a potent symbol of free-thinking and liberal values. Experienced society watchers assumed, however, that it was a fashionable trend like any other, actress Sarah Bernhardt acidly dismissing it: 'C'est de la Norderie'.[3]

Norwegian friends in Paris and St Cloud

Shortly after returning from his Norwegian holiday in the summer of 1889, Delius moved to an apartment in the village of Croissy-sur-Seine on the outskirts of Paris. He worked intensively on new compositions and made forays into the metropolis to cultivate social and cultural interests. Throughout the 1890s he moved in a circle of friends primarily made up of Norwegian painters. We saw that, on his arrival in Kristiania in the summer of 1889, he ate dinner with Norwegian friends – among them two new friends from Paris, Eyolf Soot and Jo Visdal, painter and sculptor respectively. In addition, he knew art students Gudmund Stenersen and Agnes Steineger, as well as her Norwegian teacher from Munich, Marcus Grønvold. It is probable that as early

---

[2] Adolphe Boschot, 'Le Charme de Grieg' in *Carnet d'Art* (Paris, 1911). Quoted by Harald Herresthal and Ladislav Reznicek in *Rhapsodie norvégienne: Norsk musikk i Frankrike på Edvard Griegs tid* (*Rhapsodie norvégienne: Norwegian Music in France in Edvard Grieg's Day*) (Oslo: Norsk musikforlag, 1994), 138. Herresthal and Reznicek's book is a rich source of information about Norwegian music and musicians in Paris in this period.

[3] Quoted by Kela Nyholm in 'Henrik Ibsen og den franske scene' ('Henrik Ibsen and the French Stage'), in *Ibsen Årbok 1957–1959* (*Ibsen Yearbook 1957–1959*) (Skien: Ibsenforbundet, 1959), 49–50.

as his first year in Paris, Delius also became a close friend of the nervous young man who was destined to become Norway's most famous artist.

'I got to know Delius at the end of the eighties', Edvard Munch recalled in a memoir note late in life, adding: 'Delius was a fine person'.[4] Munch arrived in Paris on a study scholarship in October 1889, but it is possible the two had got to know each other during the composer's long stay in Norway that summer – they were both friends with Arve Arvesen, with whom Delius spent several days in Kristiania and Hamar. Munch also knew Eyolf Soot well and any contact with Soot's circle in Paris would quickly have led his and Delius's paths to cross. Munch was carried to France on a wave of personal creative development. Having several times been overlooked by the committee that awarded the annual state bursary, Munch was now considered a worthy recipient on account of an exhibition he had held in Kristiania in April. The modern approach he adopted in several works, not least the symbol-heavy *Vår* (*Spring*), sparked mixed reactions in both public and critics. Not that these were the artist's target groups: 'This fine, effortless, symbolically charged picture', writes Atle Næss in his biography, 'should perhaps be regarded first and foremost as a bursary application'.[5] One of the most influential names in Norwegian cultural life, Christian Krohg, threw his authority behind the 25-year-old painter: 'Munch resembles no one. [...] He paints – that is to say – he *sees* in a different way than other artists do. He only sees the essentials and therefore only paints those.'[6]

Munch's first months in Paris were a hard struggle; he had little to live on, his health was poor, and at the end of November his father died. After this blow, he moved out to St Cloud, leaving – as Delius had done before him – the temptations of Paris for a quiet environment on the city's outskirts more conducive to work. It is one of his sketchbooks from this period that contains the first of several studies he made of Delius in the course of their 45-year, always warm, friendship. The portrait is of the composer's head and shoulders in three-quarter view.[7] For Munch, this was a time of personal and creative upheaval and he met full-on the challenge of trying to establish for himself an artistic credo. It was in fact in this same sketchbook that he noted down a thought that might be regarded as a dictum guiding his production in the coming years: 'Symbolism – nature is shaped by one's state of mind'.

*

---

[4] Note by Munch (MM N 222) (MM).

[5] Atle Næss, *Munch: En biografi* (Oslo: Gyldendal, 2004), 91.

[6] *Ibid.*, 92.

[7] Sketchbook (MM T 127) (MM). A similar sketch of Delius would be used by the Kristiania newspaper *Verdens Gang* in 1891 to illustrate its review of the première of the *Paa Vidderne* symphonic poem (see p. 89). It is possible that the two drawings were made at the same time.

The painters and authors who injected *la Norderie* into French veins have been mentioned. What about music? Young Norwegian composers were in fact a rare commodity in Paris, they still preferred German conservatories, and their absence is of course one of the simpler explanations for Delius's attraction to Norwegian painters. This is not to say that there was any lack of Norwegian *music*. On the contrary, Norwegian music was everywhere, its influence was huge and it contributed as much as did visual arts to the warm reception in the French capital for Nordic culture. The credit for this positive attitude can, however, be ascribed to all intents and purposes to one composer, a man who in fact avoided Paris for as long he could: Edvard Grieg.[8]

While trends in contemporary painting, then as now, were followed by a small cultural elite, Grieg reached, with his many volumes of *Lyric Pieces* for piano, the living rooms of countless middle-class homes. In the course of the 1880s, Grieg's music, with its exotic colours drawn in part from folk music, acted with great power on a wide French public. Here is more from Boschot's visit to an exhibition of Scandinavian art:

> The dreams we spun in front of those paintings were conjured up again through Grieg's music. We envisaged a Scandinavian landscape, almost everything was a product of our imaginations, but even softer and more beautiful in our dreams because it had something of that landscape in it. His *Lyric Pieces*, the andantes of his sonatas, the *Humoresques*, the song of the trembling Solveig [...] We were beguiled by these melodies created by the fjords; they invited us to travel on dream journeys to regions full of mysticism and legends; and in some misty light we found our dream, our own longings.[9]

For French composers, Grieg's unique fusion of Norwegian folk music with conventional Austro-German composition tools was a revelation. A typical figure was Édouard Lalo who, in 1878, composed for violin and orchestra a *Fantaisie Scandinave*. The work was rechristened first as *Fantaisie Norvégienne* and later as *Rhapsodie Norvégienne*, now in a version for orchestra alone. Lalo was convinced he had based his fantasy on genuine Norwegian folk tunes, but Edvard Grieg knew better. In 1899, he wrote in a letter: 'When the late and talented French composer Ed. Lalo in his Norwegian rhapsody borrowed a melody from the first movement of my op. 19, thinking it to be a folk song, I allowed myself the pleasure of regarding it as a compliment rather than as a theft'.[10]

Not all French robberies were accepted by Grieg with the same equanimity. Despite the interest in his music throughout the 1880s and numerous

---

[8] If Grieg was the musical god of *la Norderie*, then Johan Svendsen (b. 1840) was his prophet. At least two of Svendsen's Norwegian rhapsodies for orchestra had their premières in Paris in the late 1870s.

[9] Quoted by Herresthal and Reznicek, *Rhapsodie norvégienne*, 138-9.

[10] Letter from Grieg to Henry Theophilus Finck, 17 July 1899, trans. Finn Benestad (EG2).

invitations from French orchestras and producers to grace their halls, he resisted adding Paris to the route of his concert tours. The reasons were mostly financial; the price of living in the French capital grated with his thrifty nature. In addition, however, he was exasperated by the fact that the success he had achieved was due to illegal publications of his music from which he earned nothing. He was a victim of what we today call copyright piracy.[11] Time and again he was tempted by conductors and impresarios, only to withdraw at a late date, often with his frail health as an excuse. All resistance was, however, finally overcome in December 1889. Edvard and Nina Grieg came to Paris and stayed six weeks, received everywhere as if they were royalty.

Delius wrote several letters to Grieg in the autumn of 1889, but only on his third attempt did he get a reply. Not only was the Norwegian up to his ears in work, he was also depressed about the health of Nina, who, in addition to a lengthy and painful kidney stone complaint, was suffering a throat problem that prevented her singing. If Delius suspected he had been cold-shouldered by Grieg, the feeling would have been reinforced once the Norwegian arrived in Paris. No doubt Delius had looked forward to receiving the Griegs during their first visit; he had even prepared for the event by making an arrangement for orchestra of one of Grieg's most popular pieces, perhaps as a welcome gift or Christmas present: 'Bridal Procession' from *Pictures from Folk Life* (op. 19).[12] They arrived in Paris on 9 December and a few days later Nina felt obliged to send Delius a letter assuring him that they were not ignoring him: 'Grieg asks me to tell you that had he not been ill already on arrival in Paris, he would have written to you at once. The worst seems to be over, but he is still too weak to see anyone. When he is better you will hear from him.'[13] Grieg had recovered sufficiently to take part in his first concert duties on 22 December. He had also received an invitation from Delius once again to spend Christmas Eve together, and sent a perfunctory reply: 'We are invited to Jonas Lie's tomorrow, Christmas Eve. So I am afraid it is not possible. What a pity that you live so far away that everything has to be worked out so far in advance, as I find that very difficult.'[14] For much of Grieg's six weeks in the French capital he was troubled with stomach and nervous problems. While it is likely that he and Delius eventually got together, there is no actual evidence of a meeting.

Delius's friendship with Grieg would undoubtedly have given him a good deal of prestige in the circles in which he moved, circles made up of artists

[11] See Herresthal and Reznicek, *Rhapsodie norvégienne*, 132.

[12] The arrangement exists in a complete version in pencil, dated 2 December, that remained in Delius's possession. It is not known whether he presented a finished copy to Grieg. The arrangement was posthumously published in the *Collected Edition of the Works of Frederick Delius* (London: Boosey & Hawkes, 2009), Supplementary Volume 2.

[13] Letter from Nina Grieg to Delius, undated but mid-December 1889, trans. Lionel Carley (GD).

[14] Letter from Grieg to Delius, 23 December 1889, trans. Lionel Carley (GD).

who regarded Grieg as the flag-bearer for Norwegian influence on European culture.

Edvard and Nina Grieg left Paris for Leipzig and stayed there all spring. Sinding was also on one of his prolonged visits and once more there were pleasant evenings around the whist table, composer Hjalmar Borgstrøm now seated on Delius's chair. An invitation was also extended by Grieg to Delius, for we have his reply: 'As yet I have not got an answer from home, so I won't be able to come.'[15] (If he lived frugally, Delius could get by on the regular allowance he received from his family in England, supplemented by his uncle in Paris. If he wished to go beyond these means, he was obliged to write home and apply for further assistance.) In this same letter, he could also inform Grieg that he was in high spirits, and that long walks around Croissy and the arrival of spring had helped him to crystallize a life philosophy. From now on he would live according to his own nature and be governed by World Joy rather than World Sorrow.

In May 1890, Delius experienced a high point in his early career when the first collection of his Norwegian songs was published by Augener: *Fünf Lieder aus dem Norwegischen* (*Five Songs from the Norwegian*). As we saw (Table 1, p. 40), of the twelve Norwegian poems Delius used in this and its companion album (1892), eight had been previously set by Edvard Grieg. Would it not perhaps also have been regarded as a *faux pas* that Delius dedicated the albums to Grieg's muse, Nina? On sending her the 1890 album, Delius wrote: 'When I first got to know Grieg's music it was not just that it made a deep impression on me, it was as if I heard something new. A curtain was lifted. The same happened when I heard you sing. I had never heard such singing, so it was something new to me.'[16] With her letter of thanks, Nina initiated a correspondence with Delius that from the outset adopted a playful and candid tone, no doubt mirroring the easy familiarity the three friends enjoyed whenever together. Now back in Bergen, she wished Delius a pleasant trip to Leipzig and stimulating days there with Sinding. The financial means had evidently been scraped together after all, and Delius was to spend a month in the musical Mecca. Sinding and Holter looked forward to his arrival, as did a new Norwegian friend from Paris, Johan Selmer, who wrote: 'We are waiting with impatience for your arrival'.[17] Delius's return to Leipzig would, however, ensure that this latter friendship was not prolonged.

[15] Letter from Delius to Grieg, 1 April 1890 (BOB).
[16] Letter from Delius to Nina Grieg, 26 May 1980 (BOB)
[17] Letter from Selmer to Delius, 24 May 1890 (NB).

Delius and Selmer – friends and rivals

In his first Paris years, there were two Norwegian musicians whose friendship Delius cultivated: violinist Arve Arvesen and composer Johan Selmer. After their time together as students in Leipzig, violinist Arve Arvesen left for Paris around the same time as Delius, studying with Martin Pierre Marsick from 1889 to 1892. However, the fallout from a scandal in 1891 cast a shadow over his reputation and perhaps explains why from 1892 he preferred to work first in Brussels, then Helsinki – well away from the colony of prominent Norwegians in Paris. It was a scandal involving the Bjørnsons. As we saw during Delius's summer holiday, the Arvesen family in Hamar had a close relationship with the Bjørnson family. Nevertheless, on meeting the painter Oda Krohg in Paris, Arve Arvesen told the artist that Bjørnson's wife, Karoline, thought her 'to be a cocotte' – a woman of loose morals. An indignant Oda Krohg immediately sent a telegram to Mrs Bjørnson: 'In setting out your opinion of me, you have used words I would neither utter or write to anyone apart from my husband.'[18] Her husband was Christian Krohg, whom she apparently had instructed to instigate libel proceedings. Two months later, Arvesen grasped the nettle: 'Mrs Krohg! The stories that I told you did not in fact come from Mrs Bjørnson but from *me*. It was all fabricated by me.'[19] This was no doubt deeply humiliating for the young violinist; ten years later he renewed his correspondence with Bjørnstjerne Bjørnson, regretting in the strongest terms 'the stupidity of which I was guilty in Paris.'[20]

Arvesen was forced to learn the hard lesson that it was unwise to cross powerful figures in the Norwegian colony. It was a similar moral Delius would eventually draw from trying to establish a friendship with Johan Selmer. Eighteen years older than Delius, and strongly influenced by the orchestral music of Berlioz, Selmer had chosen to study in Paris rather than Germany. During the Paris Commune of 1871 he had allied himself with the revolutionary cause, organising musical events to support *les communards*. One of the works planned for performance was the orchestral *Scène funèbre* (op. 4), a sombre funeral march at the end of which 'La Marseillaise' breaks out in triumph. Before it could be performed, the government forces had rallied and Selmer, with a death warrant hanging over his head, had fled to Norway. In the late 1870s, the French authorities re-evaluated the damage of his actions and allowed him to return. Delius got to know him in the spring of 1890 and expressed in a letter his admiration for Selmer's op. 5, *Nordens Aand* (*The Spirit of the North*) for choir and orchestra: 'I am very taken with the work & it must make a great impression.'[21] The Norwegian was flattered by the interest shown

---

[18] Telegram from Oda Krohg to Karoline Bjørnson, 19 March 1891 (NB).
[19] Letter from Arve Arvesen to Oda Krohg, 20 May 1891 (NB).
[20] Letter from Arve Arvesen to Bjørnstjerne Bjørnson, 1 October 1902 (NB).
[21] Letter from Delius to Selmer, 9 April 1890 (NB).

in him by the younger composer and they spent a good deal of time together
before Selmer left for Leipzig. When Delius followed in May, they attended
together concerts and operas, and both arranged to have a professional orchestra rehearse a selection of their compositions. What then happened left Delius
so incensed that his anger was still evident a couple of months later when he
wrote to Grieg (the letter has been damaged and some words are missing):

> I wanted to have an [orchestral] rehearsal & had to pay 50 marks for it, which
> is a very good idea; you get to rehearse much better. [I] wanted to set it up so
> that I could rehearse for at least 2½ hours, as I had 5 things to rehearse. Selmer
> had already rehearsed 2 or 3 times with […] a Finnish March or something.
> Nevertheless [he visited] me & asked if he could rehearse his march […] he
> wanted to, heaven knows, to make it popular etc! I said I only had enough time
> [to rehearse] my own music. So I went out to Gohlis where [the run-through]
> was to take place. The orchestra was an hour & a half late & just when I had got
> started Selmer [came] & asked me if he could rehearse his […] once. I said, 'You
> know what I said [before]', so he then takes the baton & […] begins to rehearse.
> Not merely a [run-through] but the violins on their own, the violas on their
> own etc. […] 25 minutes of my time that was already [foreshortened]. As he
> walked away, he said to me, 'You know that [everyone] has to know how to help
> themselves'.[22]

It did not help matters that Selmer then penned in English what Delius called
'a crawling letter', apologising for his behaviour: 'Trusting in your friendship
and noble collegiality I dared to do it'.[23] Selmer reappears in Delius's story
during the *Folkeraadet* scandal of 1897, one of few Norwegian musicians who
came out in support of the beleaguered Englishman.

1890: A summer by the coast

No letters from Grieg to Delius exist from the first five months of 1890. The
closer he got to summer, however, the more impatient Grieg became to escape
to the mountains in the company of like-minded friends. The first invitation
to Delius was sent by Nina, who, writing in early June, asked him not to forget
them at Troldhaugen and, spicing up her entreaty, pointed out that 'the rat-
tlesnake' of the previous year would no doubt be visiting again.[24] This was the
now sixteen-year-old Anne Mohn (see p. 59). With her choice of metaphor
here, Nina introduced into their correspondence code words she would subsequently adopt when discussing Delius's amorous life – his 'rattling', as she
termed it. The invitation to spend the summer in Norway was reinforced in
mid-June by Grieg himself, then in July by Delius's Paris friend, the painter

---

[22] Letter from Delius to Grieg, undated, probably July 1890 (BOB).
[23] Letter from Johan Selmer to Delius, 21 June 1890 (DT).
[24] Letter from Nina Grieg to Delius, 6 June 1890 (BOB).

Gudmund Stenersen, who sent him a greeting from Skogadalsbøen: '*Come here and feel the fresh wind from the fons* [glaciers] *and be like me a new man*.'[25] Even this appeal was unable to bring Delius to Norway. He was intent on finding a seaside town where he could combine work and leisure. His first choice was Saint Helier on Jersey, and then he extended the summer into early October with a stay at Saint-Malo on the Brittany coast. Grieg did not try to hide his disappointment: 'How regrettable that you are not coming to Jotunheimen.'[26] He suspected that Cupid's arrows had punctured Delius's serenity, but received this retort: 'You write about my nerves. I can assure you I don't have them any more & have never felt more hale & hearty. The god Cupid has been very quiet, never wholly absent, but more Platonic.'[27] He had by no means banished Norway from his thoughts. This period without a visit to the country had an effect on him that would be repeated throughout his life every time he was prevented from travelling north. He assured Grieg: 'I'm really sorry not to be coming with you! to Jotunheimen the holy of holies & glory of glories [...] I now have a double longing for Norway (as Bjørnson would have put it)[28] & must definitely come next year.'

His high spirits carried over into October when he returned to the Croissy apartment, and throughout the next months he worked assiduously on a series of large scores. The winter of 1890–91 was, however, mercilessly hard in both France and England; an intense freeze set in at the end of November and lasted through January, dragging 'a good many artists along with it into eternity', as Delius wrote to Grieg.[29] In March, he travelled to the family home in Bradford to recuperate. His thoughts were now turning to summer and Norway, but when he wrote to Grieg, he emphasised that he was hoping for a quiet and relaxing stay: 'How I would love to get back to Norway this summer & wander about a little in Jotunheimen. Without all the big storm marches etc. I would be there at the drop of a hat. We must go together, that would be nice!'[30] As we noted earlier, after their joint tour of Jotunheimen in 1889 there seemed to come something of a chill in their friendship. If this was the case, then between the lines here we might read one reason: Delius would have preferred a more easy-going type of holiday than the *Sturmmärsche* up mountains and down valleys favoured by Grieg. (Ironically, when Delius reached the same age as Grieg he too felt driven to take hikes in the mountains that were so lengthy

---

[25] Letter from Gudmund Stenersen to Delius, 12 July 1890 (DT) (emphasis in original).
[26] Letter from Grieg to Delius, 11 August 1890 (BOB).
[27] Letter from Delius to Grieg, 14 September 1890 (BOB).
[28] The reference is to Bjørnson's peasant-tale *Arne*, in which Arne remarks that he has 'a double longing – to find someone worth loving and to become something important'. As we saw (p. 19), Delius had set the text of Arne's song 'Over de høje fjælle' ('Over the Mountains High') in one of his earliest compositions.
[29] Letter from Delius to Grieg, 10 March 1891 (BOB).
[30] *Ibid.*

and challenging he had trouble enticing friends to join him – including the now ailing Grieg!) In his reply, Grieg assured the young man that the summer's sensual and sporting pleasures would not be neglected, that they could look forward to 'a splendid time fishing, bathing and climbing'.[31] Once again, Grieg envisaged a caravan of musician friends making their ascent from Troldhaugen to the inland mountains. Apart from Delius and Sinding, he invited Frants Beyer, composer Ottokar Nováček, publisher Max Abraham, violin professor Adolf Brodsky with wife and sister-in-law (Sinding's old flame, Olga Picard), and conductor Iver Holter.

Holter had promised Delius that he would perform one of his scores with Christiania Musikforening when the new season started in October. So, before leaving Croissy-sur-Seine for Norway, Delius relinquished his apartment, planning to live in Norway from the end of June until the première – over four months, his longest-ever stay in the country. The work that had piqued Holter's interest was a symphonic poem to which Delius had transferred a title he had first used for the spurned melodrama of 1888: *Paa Vidderne*. To distinguish it from the melodrama, it is hereafter referred to by its English title: *On the Mountains*.[32]

Summer 1891: Aulestad and Troldhaugen

Delius sailed from Antwerp and arrived in Kristiania on the evening of 28 June 1891. This much is divulged by his diary notes. Of the next five days, however, there is not the slightest hint. This Norway diary, the third and last that he was to keep, begins in a fragmentary and sporadic fashion, only to grind to a complete stop at the end of August.[33] What occupied Delius during these first days? Perhaps he visited Edvard Munch at the painter's favoured summer haunt, the fjord village of Åsgårdstrand, or Iver Holter further down the coast in Fredriksværn. Perhaps he renewed his close friendship with Camilla Jacobsen and family on Malmøya. He was constantly involved in new romances in this period, and missing links in the chain of correspondence between him and the Griegs suggest that letters containing intimate disclosures were destroyed. It is probable that this diary, seemingly written up at a later date, was also marked by a high degree of self-censorship.

On Friday 3 July, Delius left Kristiania and spent the weekend at Gjøvik on his way to an eight-day stay at Aulestad, Bjørnson's home. Two years earlier,

---

[31] Letter from Grieg to Delius, 1 May 1891, trans. Lionel Carley (GD).

[32] This practise was adopted by the Delius Trust in its publication of the work in the *Collected Edition of the Works of Frederick Delius*.

[33] Delius's 1891 diary (GM) has been published as 'Appendix V' in LC1, 401–2. If not otherwise stated, the quotations on the next pages from Delius's diary are from this source (Lionel Carley's transcription), and follow Carley's practice in tidying up the punctuation and orthography, in order to make the diary more easily readable.

in 1889, Olaus Arvesen's plan to take Delius to Aulestad had been derailed by political events (see p. 58). This time, the invitation was extended to Delius by Bjørnson's 22-year-old daughter Bergliot. Since 1887, she had studied singing with Mathilde Marchesi in Paris, and Delius might have got to know her through Arve Arvesen. There is nothing to suggest a romantic connection between Bergliot and Delius; it was in fact during this summer at her home that Bergliot first met and fell in love with Ibsen's politician son, Sigurd.

The preliminary stop in Gjøvik was occasioned by the National Rifle Championship, an event that carried heightened prestige in this period of strained relations with Sweden. On the evening of 4 July, the soprano Gina Oselio (real name Ingeborg Aas) was to entertain the participants. In November 1890, Bjørnson's eldest son, actor Bjørn Bjørnson, had divorced his wife in order to court Oselio, but his parents – especially Karoline – still had some way to go before they would accept her into the family fold. Arve Arvesen was also booked to play at the same concert; he was *persona non grata* at Aulestad since his indiscretion involving Oda Krohg and Karoline Bjørnson. With this pair of 'toxic' performers on the bill, it was most likely the younger members of the Bjørnson clan who received Delius in Gjøvik: Bjørn and his sisters Dagny and

6. On 8 July 1891, Delius (insert) was photographed in the fields below Bjørnson's farmhouse at Aulestad. He was out walking with (from left to right) Anna Finsen (b. 1864, daughter of the great Danish-Icelandic politician Hilmar Finsen), Dagny Bjørnson (b. 1876), Mia Hedlund (b. 1880, daughter of Swedish newspaper editor and politician Sven Adolf Hedlund) and Nulle Finsen (b. 1869, younger daughter of Hilmar Finsen).

Bergliot. On the day after the concert, the party travelled on to Aulestad farm, though presumably without Arvesen.

From his week as the guest of one of Norway's foremost personalities and political thinkers, Delius has left us only a few scant words in his diary. On one evening when the family were gathered, Bjørnson read aloud his unfinished *Fredsoratorium* (*Peace Oratorio*). On two consecutive days Delius joined Bjørnson in the natural water hole near the house where the author took his daily bath before dinner. One remarkable photograph was taken in the fields below the farmhouse. It captures a spontaneous moment (see Illustration 6), the composer in stylish summer attire together with four women who are plucking wild flowers, the farm buildings of Aulestad in the background. From his diary we know it was taken on 8 July. On 11 July, it was time to travel south again. Taking his farewell, Delius expressed his gratitude with a musical quotation that held special significance for both guest and host, jotted down on a sheet of paper torn from his notebook: the first four bars of his setting of Bjørnson's 'Skogen gir susende langsom besked'. In March 1890, Bergliot in Paris had received a letter from her father containing some old verse lines that had come to light when tidying his papers:

Skogen gir susende langsom besked.	(The wood soughs slowly what it knows.
Alt, hvad den saa i de énsomme tider,	All it saw in those lonely ages,
alt, hvad den led, da den fantes omsider,	all it has suffered since being found,
klager i vinden, som tar det med.	is wailed in the wind and lost.)

'Aren't those lines lovely? Someone should set them to music', Bjørnson had suggested to his daughter.[34] Whether Delius had got them from Bergliot in Paris or from Bjørnson during his stay is unknown, but as a parting gesture it was a happy idea.

Delius broke his journey with a stop in Lillehammer at the head of the Mjøsa lake. The dry inland climate of the region attracted a colony of artists, particularly those suffering from tuberculosis, and their meeting place was a restaurant on the roof of the Hotel Victoria, with a panoramic view of the lake. Here, Delius enjoyed a stimulating evening in the company of Bergliot Bjørnson, Julie Nilsen (a teacher who was a regular summer guest at Aulestad), and painters Halfdan Strøm and Ole Molnes. Both would have known well Delius's Paris friend Eyolf Soot, who also spent summers here.

In Kristiania on 12 and 13 July, Delius devoted himself to a certain 'Miss Bötger of Christiansand'. On the first evening they travelled out to the island

---

[34] Letter from Bjørnstjerne Bjørnson to Bergliot Bjørnson, 30 March 1890. Delius's setting of 'Skogen gir susende langsom besked' was not published until 1981, then as a supplement to the *Collected Edition of the Works of Frederick Delius*. It included an English text by Lionel Carley with the title 'Slowly the Forest'.

of Bygdøy to explore the pleasure gardens at Fredriksborg (described in an 1893 travel guide as 'shabby'). The next evening, they ate dinner at the Grand Hotel. From later correspondence we can deduce that this was pianist Charlotte Bødtker (twenty-three), who, like Delius, had several years in the United States behind her. In 1892, she would marry a Norwegian businessman and cross the Atlantic again, settling first in Ohio, then in Chile.

The next three days were spent with Sinding, who was staying with his friends Augusta and Fredrik Georg Gade at Husvik outside Drøbak, an hour by steamer down the east coast of the Kristiania Fjord. On 15 July, Delius crossed the Kristiania Fjord and continued south down the western coast, returning to Fredriksværn and the fashionable Hotel Wassilioff. The small, sunny fishing village and naval station, with the open Skagerrak just beyond its harbour, would be the composer's base until the end of October. The summer tranquillity here was dramatically broken on his first night when the large bathing house outside the hotel burned down and the whole population dashed to watch or help.

The group of musicians Edvard Grieg had envisaged assembling in Bergen prior to the mountain tour never materialised. One after another they sent their apologies. As late as 3 July, Grieg had written to friends mentioning that Delius would be arriving at Troldhaugen on the fifteenth. But then it was the Englishman's turn to reconsider his options, writing on 16 July to Grieg from Hotel Wassilioff:

> I'm afraid that I don't have enough money to go to Jotunheimen this year. It's quite certain that you will be going? I really don't know what I should do. Could I not perhaps stay with you on your return from Jotunheimen, I could stay here and take it easy until then. […] I would very much like to see you and stay with you for a while.[35]

Grieg replied immediately. Although his letter is no longer extant we can make some assumptions about its content from Delius's movements in the coming weeks. He probably urged Delius to come at once and enjoy some carefree days with him at Troldhaugen; on the way, he could pick up Iver Holter, who was out sailing along the coast of Southern Norway; as for the expenses of a trip to the mountains, perhaps Grieg offered some assistance. So on 19 July, Delius boarded the coastal steamship *Motala* in Fredriksværn, and in Kristiansand Iver Holter came aboard. There were rough seas, so around the perilous cape of Lindesnes the friends elected to travel by train, rejoining the *Motala* at Stavanger.

From Delius's diary we know that Grieg laid on for his guests 'a delightful week sea-bathing, fishing & taking walks'. From Grieg's account book we also know

---

[35] Letter from Delius to Grieg, 16 July 1891 (BOB).

7. Left to right: Bjørnstjerne Bjørnson, Nina Grieg, Karoline Bjørnson and
Edvard Grieg, c.1903.

that there were cultural pleasures. On 27 July, Grieg took Holter and Delius
to the summer exhibition of the Bergen Kunstforening (Art Society), the first
time the society exhibited works of a French painter. On one occasion there
was a trip up from the town centre to the summit of the Fløyen mountain,
probably by carriage; on another they enjoyed a long walk from Troldhaugen
to the nearby Tveterås Wood. Here Delius picked a bouquet of flowers that
Nina Grieg displayed around the mirror in the Troldhaugen dining room.
While in Bergen, Delius bought a British flag and sent it to Aulestad. (It was
Bjørnson's custom to greet the arrival of international guests at his home with
the flag of their country, but in the case of Delius he did not have one.) To
accompany the package Delius wrote the following note: 'The English flag will
very soon arrive at Aulestad; use it with care if you don't want to be up to your
neck in English tourists.'[36]

As late as 23 July, Grieg's plan was to travel to Jotunheimen with Delius.
They never got that far. Instead, all four – Nina and Edvard, Holter and Delius
– left around 29 July for Lofthus on the Sørfjord in Hardanger. Grieg never
needed an excuse to visit Lofthus; during many summers in the 1880s this
fruit cultivation district with stunning views across the fjord to the Folgefonna
glaciers was almost his second home. As an added incentive in 1891, however,
his friend, the Dutch composer Julius Röntgen, was holidaying there with his

[36] Letter from Delius to Bjørnson, 29 July 1891 (NB).

family. It was probably here that the plans were overhauled. Röntgen longed to visit Jotunheimen with Grieg, while Delius and Holter longed to be back under sail on the Kristiania Fjord; so, while in Lofthus, Grieg and Röntgen plotted out an extensive tour of the Sognefjell mountains, with departure a fortnight later. As an alternative trip, the Griegs, Delius and Holter set off on a four-day excursion, starting sometime around 4 August. Their first stop was Odda, then on to Røldal, where they visited the church, and then next day, Delius noted in his diary, 'a heavenly drive in the sunshine to Haukeliseter, where we had a good dinner & a good bottle of Burgundy'. At a thousand metres, the Haukeliseter mountain farm and post house was at the highest point of the main road between East and West Norway.

The day after their arrival at Haukeliseter found Grieg bedridden with his recurring stomach complaint, so Nina and Delius went exploring on the mountain plateau, plucking 'lovely blue & brown gentian flowers'. These hours spent together are indicative of the warm friendship that existed between the two. Today, visitors to Troldhaugen can find a framed photo of Delius on the wall, with a greeting in the composer's hand: 'Minne om en sommermorgen paa Haukelifjeld' ('A reminder of a summer morning on Haukeli Mountain') (see Illustration 22). He sent Nina the portrait in 1909, a couple of years after Grieg's death – and eighteen years after their walk on the plateau. She wrote back:

> You recall that summer morning on Haukeli mountain, so do I! Those gentians, the blue flower, so clearly I see it all. Those were happy days. But on our return journey Edvard fell ill, as so often, and we had to stop in Odda. We were however grateful for 5 bright summer days roaming about. It seems radiant with glory, that time, now vanished![37]

On their third day at Haukeliseter, around 7 August, there was a change in the weather and in pouring rain Delius and Holter, who were headed for East Norway, bade farewell to Nina and Edvard Grieg, who intended to return to Lofthus via Odda. In fact, Grieg's stomach ailment stranded the couple in Odda for four days.

At this point, some forty-one days into a Norway stay of a hundred and thirty days, Delius's 1891 diary stutters to an end. From near the end of his life, however, we have some lines he dictated that fill in a few details of how the summer trip ended: 'From Dalen we went to Skien over inland lakes and by carriole, where we spent the night. Holter left for Xania and I stayed alone to see the Exhibition. Going from there back to Fredriksværn where I stayed till the beginning of November associating a great deal with the painter Hjalmar Johnsen.'[38]

---

[37] Letter from Nina Grieg to Delius, 22 May 1909 (DT).
[38] Dictated note from c.1927, published in Rachel Lowe, *A Descriptive Catalogue with Checklists of the Letters and Related Documents in the Delius Collection of the Grainger Museum* (London: Delius Trust, 1981), 224. The exhibition was *Den almindelige norske Landsudstilling*, a

A threesome by the sea – and plans for an artist colony

Delius did indeed 'associate a great deal' with Hjalmar Johnssen this summer and autumn. They were, however, only two-thirds of a friendly threesome or 'triangle' – Johnssen's word – and the third member was the State Minister's wife, Randi Blehr. Delius's attractive personality had won him a secure position in the heart of Nina Grieg, nineteen years older, the wife of one of Norway's most powerful artists. In Fredriksværn this summer he cultivated a close relationship with the eleven-years-older Randi Blehr, wife to one of Norway's most powerful politicians. It is principally from three letters from Johnssen to Blehr that we gather an impression of the strong bond that, for a few months, connected these three extraordinary people.

Born in Stavanger in 1852 and brought up in Bergen, Johnssen went to sea as a young man and only took up painting seriously in 1875. After marrying, he lived in a variety of coastal towns, including Fredriksværn in 1891–92, and specialised in maritime paintings or scenes from the harbours along Norway's south coast. He was represented at the first Autumn Exhibition in Kristiania in 1882 and the World's Fair in Paris in 1889. In the months during which Delius and Blehr kept him company in Fredriksværn he prepared canvases for that year's Autumn Exhibition, one of which was purchased by Delius.

Randi Blehr hailed from Bergen, and in her youth had taken music lessons from Nina Grieg; at her wedding to Otto Blehr in 1876 it was Edvard Grieg who played the bridal march. Otto Blehr, one of the sharpest minds on the political left wing, had in 1883 been the architect of the judicial challenge to the right of veto held by the Norwegian-Swedish crown. It was a manoeuvre that a year later would usher in the formation of party politics in Norway (see p. 10). Since March 1891, he had filled one of the most important posts in Johannes Steen's first government, that of State Minister in Stockholm.[39] If Otto Blehr was in the vanguard in the fight for Norwegian independence, Randi Blehr was no less a pioneer in an equally important struggle: the fight for social and political rights for women. In 1884, she was one of the founders of Norsk Kvinnesaksforening (Norwegian Association for Women's Rights), which she led for twenty-five years, and in 1889 she established the first school of weaving and tapestry in Norway. Parallel with her own visionary work, she was also frequently called upon to perform in an official capacity as wife of the State Minister. Even on the most formal occasion her wit and charismatic personality was an icebreaker. A typical anecdote relates to a reception Otto Blehr gave

national trade fair. Hjalmar Johnssen's surname is often spelt with one *s*. However, the artist signed his name Johnssen.

[39] The union with Sweden was administered from state buildings in Stockholm. During the final decades of the union, the highest-ranking Norwegian official appointed to oversee Norway's interests was called the *Norsk statsminister i Stockholm* (Norwegian State Minister in Stockholm). His political authority was second only to the Prime Minister (the *Statsminister*) in Kristiania.

8. Female rights activist Randi Blehr in 1899, eight years after Delius
got to know her.

for members of parliament. Randi, circling with the wine tray, stopped in front
of one of the politicians:

> Mrs Blehr: Now, I don't think I can offer you any wine. You're a teetotaller, I
> believe?
>
> Member: No. I'd quite like a glass of wine.
>
> Mrs Blehr: Oh, I was sure that you …
>
> Member: Mrs Blehr has perhaps in mind that I am Chairman of the Associa-
> tion for Decency and Morality.
>
> Mrs Blehr: That's it. I knew there was something I couldn't offer you.[40]

Otto Blehr's third cousin, Cathrine, lived in Fredriksværn with her husband,
shipping broker Nils Backer. It is probable that Randi Blehr stayed with them
in Larvikgate, adjoining the naval station, when she came to Fredriksværn in
August 1891 to take a bathing cure for a persistent health problem.

Throughout August and September 1891 Delius, Randi Blehr and Hjalmar
Johnssen went on excursions to nearby inlets or fished in the fjord, spending

---

[40] Retold in Jon Dørsjø, *Levende anekdoter* (*Lively Anecdotes*) (Oslo: H. Aschehoug & Co., 1959),
25.

their evenings in lively debate about politics and art. At some point, Delius suggested to his friends an extraordinary project: a collaboration of like-minded artists in a colony. Everything we know about this radical idea is to be found in a few sentences in Johnssen's first letter to Blehr after she had returned to Kristiania. Frustrated by the poor treatment of artists by the Norwegian authorities, he concluded:

> No, madam, we will really need to give the colony serious consideration. *I'm in* – from the very start; for during my lonely excursions down here I have been thinking deeper about it and find the idea superb. And not only that, I am in no doubt – that it could be realised. Funnily enough the local sexton Kirkeroed (you met him at my house one evening) quite coincidentally suggested a similar idea, of course conceived in a more popular way than Delius's. This latter's noble and charitable thought processes were not present in the sexton's notion – but the idea was, however, analogous, roughly in the same relationship that butter has to margarine![41]

For artists in the latter half of the nineteenth century, the concept of some form of collective community was one that bubbled to the surface in many places and forms. This was one of the first generations of creative professionals to try and make its living independent of aristocratic patronage, embracing as far as possible the freedom to interpret contemporary society. In her study of artistic communities, Nina Lübbren has calculated that over three thousand artists were members of the eighty most celebrated colonies between 1830 and 1914: 'By the 1880s, settlement in an artists' village, on a temporary or permanent basis, had become a serious career option for artists, and a steady stream of painters migrated from city to country.'[42] Perhaps the most influential of these was the Barbizon school in France, active c.1830 to 1870. In Denmark there were several such colonies, the most renowned being the group of landscape painters centred around Brøndums Hotel in Skagen during the 1880s. The short summer in Norway, allied to the fact that there were relatively few professional artists, goes a long way to explaining why the colony concept was less developed there. However, throughout the summers of the 1880s and 1890s there were clear advantages for artists to group together in the coastal villages and towns of the Kristiania Fjord – including Drøbak, Åsgårdstrand and Fredriksværn – to prepare their entries for the Autumn Exhibition. And on his coastal holidays Delius encountered many of them. The annual exhibition had come into being in 1882, organised by the artists themselves as a riposte to the power of the private galleries. In 1891–92, Hjalmar Johnssen threw himself wholeheartedly into a campaign for a permanent exhibition space for contemporary art, and it was his frustration at meeting

---

[41] Letter from Hjalmar Johnssen to Randi Blehr, 3 October 1891 (RA).
[42] Nina Lübbren, *Rural Artists' Colonies in Europe, 1870–1910* (Manchester: Manchester University Press, 2001), 1.

huge resistance to the notion that boiled over in a letter to Randi Blehr: 'How despicable they seem to me, those Kristiania swells who 'manage' our artistic well-being. […] I have become ever more convinced that Kristiania is a thoroughly despicable city with regard to all things artistic, and does not deserve, God knows, that we do anything for it.'[43] About the Delius colony – apart from it being the brainchild of his 'noble and charitable thought processes' – we know nothing. However, in Johnssen's conviction that 'it could be realised', we might read that it was intended to be more formally organised than a loose summer gathering of painters.

The artists' colony ideal was one that would resurface at a much later date in Delius's life, but is worth mentioning here. In 1915, it was the author D. H. Lawrence who was father to the noble thought, as he explained to a friend: 'I want to gather together about twenty souls and sail away from this world of war and squalor and found a little colony where there shall be no money but a sort of communism as far as necessaries of life go, and some real decency.'[44] On learning that Delius's old orange plantation in Florida had fallen into disuse, he got in touch with the composer through mutual acquaintances. Delius quickly threw sand on the fire: 'My orange grove has been left to itself for 20 years & is no doubt only a wilderness of gigantic weeds & plants. […] I should have loved to be of use to Lawrence whose work I admire – but to let him go to Florida would be sending him to disaster.'[45]

Whatever ailment it was that brought Randi Blehr to Fredriksværn, it was not cured by saltwater treatments, and at the end of September she returned to Kristiania and put herself under medical supervision at a sanatorium. Shortly after, Delius too moved to a temporary address in the capital to oversee the rehearsals by the Christiania Musikforening of *On the Mountains*. Writing to Blehr, Johnssen told how much he missed them: '[You] can hardly know just how lonely it is here after you (and then Delius) left. Can you envisage how I feel down here all alone on these long evenings? With no one to exchange thoughts with, oh! I'm going almost mad with longing to get away.'[46]

On the same day that Johnssen penned this, Blehr had checked in at the Holmenkollen Turisthotell (built 1889, burned down 1895), where many of Kristiania's affluent inhabitants sought convalescence in a beautiful landscape high above the city and the fjord. The correspondence that survives between Delius and Blehr consists of ten letters, and nine of these were written by him. The first, however, is from Blehr – penned on her first evening at the hotel and

[43] Letter from Hjalmar Johnssen to Randi Blehr, 3 October 1891 (RA).
[44] Letter from D. H. Lawrence to William Hopkin, 18 January 1915, published in George J. Zytaruk and James T. Boulton (ed.), *The Letters of D. H. Lawrence, II* (Cambridge: Cambridge University Press, 1981), 259.
[45] Letter from Delius to Philip Heseltine, 24 November 1915 (BL).
[46] Letter from Hjalmar Johnssen to Randi Blehr, 3 October 1891 (RA).

the following morning. The main body of the letter is quoted here for it gives us – in addition to a clear impression of her warm personality – some insights into the way women related to Delius, how their personal lives were touched by his charm.

> Delius!
> On my first evening here I really feel I must send you a greeting. I've already enjoyed some eleven hours here! I can't say: *Alas*, what a day! When I arrived here this glorious morning all *alases* and woes and sorrows started to creep little by little out of my soul. I'm left with feelings of great exaltation over the scenery and self-contentment that I had finally plucked up enough courage to come up here.
>
> The wonderful scenery! – Yes, you'll understand 'what I mean'. I went immediately for a long walk. Sun-drenched air. Golden, glowing, purple trees. And then the quiet, dark, faithful firs. Between their trunks the Kristiania Fjord shone like an open road. And then I saw the city under its smog and smoke, trivial and poor. I stood 'på vidderne' and from there I sent my greetings to you *above* the Xania smog, over to Nordstrand. I was so happy that, on this glorious day, you were not *beneath* it.[47]

From Grieg's account book we know that on 26 October – the last weekend before Delius left Norway – he visited Holmenkollen. He was almost certainly accompanied by Delius on a visit to Blehr.

The special Delius–Blehr–Johnssen relationship this summer would never be rekindled in the same way. In March 1892, Blehr wrote Johnssen a letter thanking him for a painting, to which he replied:

> I am so pleased that my little picture has won your approval and, in all its modesty, will serve to remind you of our time together down there in Fr.værn, from the bottom of my heart I would like our 'triangle' to be reunited there again the coming summer and become established for many years to come.[48]

In the summer of 1892, however, Delius could not afford to come to Norway. Neither did Johnssen have the funds to get him to Paris, as he makes clear in this same letter: 'He implores me to come down to visit him', he sighed to Blehr, 'but what is a poor soul to do who has absolutely none of the wherewithal for the most basic necessities, far less for "the salons of Paris"'. Delius's friendship with Randi Blehr would continue to develop on his two next trips to Norway, in 1893 and 1896.

---

[47] Letter from Randi Blehr to Delius, undated, probably 3 October 1891 (DT).
[48] Letter from Hjalmar Johnssen to Randi Blehr, 14 March 1892 (RA).

Delius's 'summer music' – as much Norwegian as English

In the first years of the 1890s, Delius preferred restorative vacations by the Kristiania Fjord – sunbathing, swimming and sailing – to exhausting day-long marches across mountain plateaus. This is an aspect of his attraction to Norway that has generally been overlooked by his biographers. During his Norway holiday in 1889, Delius was in the mountains for seventeen days, but fished, bathed and sailed by the coast for twenty-six days. Probably only two days of his four months in Norway in 1891 were spent in the mountains; the rest of the time was by the Kristiania Fjord or in the capital. In 1893 he returned to Norway, with coastal villages like Drøbak and Åsgårdstrand as his bases. Time and again, Grieg invited Delius to join him on expeditions to the mountains, but here Delius was to disappoint. Not until 1896, after a serious bout of ill health, did he again make plans for an extended stay in the mountains, and then he would seek in vain the company of Grieg.

A second misconception that prevails about Delius's Norwegian summers is more significant. It is, of course, appropriate that Delius commentators have associated his mountain music exclusively with his love of Norwegian landscapes. He did not travel to the Alpine regions of other countries. Works like *Paa Vidderne, On the Mountains, Over the Hills and Far Away* and *The Song of the High Hills* are self-evidently an artistic exploration of a part of his personality that could be expressed through metaphors of the mountainscape and the mountain journey, such as he knew them from the highlands of Norway. Rather more surprising is the fact that commentators have associated what we might call the composer's 'summer music' with English, or in certain instances French, rural landscapes, but never with the Norwegian coastal region where he chose to spend so many summers. The subjective reception any listener has of music is not the issue here; one individual's reception of a work is as valid a subjective response as any other listener's. However, insofar as a work, at time of composition, is informed by moods and emotions that were experienced in a particular place, the simple facts of where Delius enjoyed his summers ought to have some bearing on how his 'summer works' are described.

The music of his that has come to be associated with the richness of summer is characterised by calmly flowing orchestral textures, a warm instrumental palette, melodic lines decorated with idiomatic imitations of birdsong and the harmonic sensuality of the tonal language he cultivated from the late 1890s. When the myths of Delius and his music were being established by early commentators, it was typical to relate this style of music to an ideal of idyllic pastoral life in the English countryside. Bernard van Dieren, for example – writing in *The Musical Times* in 1934 – maintained that the composer's English admirers 'could hear it in every note. The English lawn and the English ale, the green pleasant land, and the exquisite harmony of rural life reappeared in his music.'[49] Eric Fenby, in his book *Delius as I Knew Him*, quotes composer and critic Cecil Gray:

> '[Nothing] could be more unmistakably English than such things as the Dance Rhapsody No. 1 or *In a Summer Garden*, or the two lovely pieces for small orchestra – in spite of the fact that the first of these two latter [*On Hearing the First Cuckoo in Spring*] happens, quite irrelevantly, to be based on a Norwegian folk song. How magically, too, do the first pages of *Brigg Fair* evoke the atmosphere of an early summer morning in the English country, with its suggestion of a faint mist veiling the horizon, and the fragrant scent of the dawn in the air!'[50]

There is strained logic here. When Delius borrows an English folk song for *Brigg Fair*, it contributes to a musical mood picture of English landscape; when Delius borrows a Norwegian folk song it is irrelevant: the landscape is still idyllic England. Even the most meticulous of Delius researchers, Robert Threlfall, subscribed to this attitude, describing *On Hearing the First Cuckoo in Spring* as 'an English spring-song' and 'usually considered quintessentially English' (this is further discussed on p. 260).[51] This reception of the music tells us something of who is listening to it, but little about how it came to be written.

From the year he enrolled at the Leipzig Conservatory until his death, Delius never chose to spend an entire summer in his homeland. During the war, he was compelled to take up residence there for extended periods, in exile from his French home. As a matter of choice, however, he always preferred to be in Norway in the summer, and if that were not possible, then on the French or Dutch coast; but never in England. If concrete memories and experiences of moods and emotions associated with the life-affirming sensuality of summer have been sublimated in his summer music, then fjord regattas with the Jacobsen family, sailing trips with Iver Holter around Fredriksværn, diving into the sea off Drøbak's sun-warmed rocks and radiantly light summer nights in Munch's garden by the sea at Åsgårdstrand must be at least as significant as some distant dream of an English pastoral utopia.

In discussions of Delius's Norwegian music, the exclusive accentuation of his attraction to the mountains has obstructed a view of the whole picture of what he sought and found in Norway.

On the Mountains in Kristiania

The high-water mark of Delius's long visit to Norway in 1891 was the première on 10 October of the symphonic poem *On the Mountains*. Grieg, who was booked for concerts in Kristiania a little later, was determined to be present.

---

[49] Bernard van Dieren, 'Frederick Delius', *The Musical Times*, Vol. 75, No. 1097 (July 1934), 598.
[50] Fenby, *Delius as I Knew Him*, 208.
[51] See Robert Threlfall, 'Delius: A Fresh Glance at Two Famous Scores' in *The Musical Times*, Vol. 125, No. 1696 (June 1984), 315.

On 5 September, he wrote to Holter, the conductor of Christiania Musikforen-ing: 'Be sure to let me know the date for the 1st concert, so that I can be present if at all possible and hear Delius's thing'[52] – an entreaty that could have been more deferentially worded, considering that a substantial 'thing' composed by Holter was also on the programme. On 23 September, he wrote again from Troldhaugen to Holter: 'Pass on my regards to Delius. I am looking forward to seeing you both and will do everything I can to get there by the 10th.'[53] He kept his word; Nina and Edvard arrived in the capital three days before the concert.

It was also likely that Delius's close friend from Paris, Edvard Munch, was at the event. As we saw in Randi Blehr's Holmenkollen letter, Delius lived in Nordstrand on the outskirts of Kristiania during the concert preparations. Munch's foster aunt lived in a flat in Nordstrand and when the artist was in the Norwegian capital, it was here that he stayed. In 1891, he was at home from the end of May until the Autumn Exhibition in November and indeed painted a number of works with Nordstrand motifs, often with the fjord as a backdrop. It is reasonable to assume not only that Delius stayed with Munch, but that the friends saw a lot of each other during the composer's Norway stay. Munch was also to profit in his own way from the Delius concert.

For the capital city's music lovers there were two obstacles to enjoying the concerts of the Christiania Musikforening. It had a decidedly provincial standard, despite being the capital's foremost orchestra; and it lacked a proper concert hall. Concerts were held in the circus auditorium in Christiania Tivoli, a popular city centre amusement park modelled on Copenhagen's Tivoli. Beneath an impressive dome, the circular arena could house an audience of up to 2,600 visitors. For orchestral concerts, 1,400 tickets were put on sale. The acoustics were atrocious and, even after attempts were made to rectify the worst failings before the 1891 season, were likely to 'cause the orchestral texture to unravel'.[54]

The concert, which was well attended, opened with an orchestral suite by Iver Holter. And although the penultimate work was a song entitled *Jeg vil ud* (*I Have to Get Out*), the Kristiania critics stayed for the finale, *On the Mountains*, described in the programme as a 'Concert overture for large orchestra. (1st performance) Manuscript.' Delius's debut was greeted with a mixed response by the city's newspapers. *Dagbladet* thought the work 'significantly influenced by our own leading composers and here and there peppered with a specifi-cally Norwegian colouring', but conceded that 'there were moments, in fact many, that were strikingly appealing and atmospheric and won its composer the audience's unconditional favour'.[55] *Morgenbladet* felt the work 'should be

[52] Letter from Grieg to Iver Holter, 5 September 1891 (NB).
[53] Letter from Grieg to Iver Holter, 23 September 1891 (NB).
[54] *Morgenbladet*, 11 October 1891.
[55] *Dagbladet*, 12 October 1891.

9. In 1891, the first performance of orchestral music by Delius was given in the domed circus building of Christiania Tivoli.

regarded more as a sequence of mood pictures, with Ibsen's poem as a guide, than as a fully developed orchestral work, and we readily admit that it is not short on winning ideas; but these are not fully formed, as if the composer in too great a degree lacked a plan for the work's structure'.[56] The liberal *Verdens Gang* set itself apart in welcoming the debutant with an overwhelmingly positive review, and the writer had taken the trouble to acquaint himself with Delius's background. It is no doubt relevant that Delius in the course of the summer had become acquainted with the paper's powerful editor, Ola Thommessen – perhaps introduced by radical friends such as Randi Blehr. Was it also Delius who suggested to the editor that his paper should use a drawing by the promising young artist Edvard Munch to embellish the review? *Verdens Gang*'s generous coverage of the Delius debut was indeed accompanied by a portrait of the composer drawn by 'E. M.'.

> The composer [...] is English by birth; but in temperament and after an education gained from long periods in America, France, Germany and Norway he is a cosmopolitan. Through his admiration for our art and landscape he has come to love our country, and few foreigners know it and its people so well. *On the Mountains* [...] is a fine and appealing composition rich in imagination and

---

[56] *Morgenbladet*, 11 October 1891.

colour, which both in its musical content and partially successful structure far
exceeds what one might expect of a novice.[57]

We will soon look closer at this and other compositions from the period.

Autumn storms blew in over Norway, perhaps delaying Delius's departure.
He returned after the excitement of his debut to the tranquillity of Fredriksværn, now deep into low season. Shortly after, from 17 October, Nina and
Edvard Grieg came to visit him for a few days. Both of them had connections
to the coastal town through Aunt Edvardine – sister to Edvard's mother and
Nina's father. As a boy, Edvard had stayed with her in Larvik and made excursions to Fredriksværn; his drawings of the town's fortifications still survive.
Back in Kristiania on 24 October, Nina wrote to Delius, and it is clear that, in
their response to the coastal scenery, they had enjoyed a similar bonding to
that shared by them on the Haukeli hills:

> It was so glorious in Fredriksværn that I am quite unable to forget it. Such scen-
> ery is very much to my taste, how I would love to live there for a while! Such
> contrasts as 'Krabbehullet' in a storm, 'woodbines' smelling so sweetly, moon-
> light through wild, hurrying clouds and sunshine through trees in gold – God,
> isn't it all wonderful! And then to look out far, far into the sea![58]

Shortly after, Delius too returned to Kristiania and bade the Griegs farewell. He then travelled back to Paris, probably staying with his uncle while
he looked for a suitable apartment. In November, he received a further letter
from Nina Grieg, and their shared time by the coast was still very much on
her mind: 'How often I think of our companionship in Fredriksværn, it still
seems like a fairytale to me, a wonderful one.'[59] At the same time, she rebuked
him for not having written since leaving Norway, suspecting female distractions – her code words were again activated: 'I suppose that you have finally
become so absorbed in rattling that you can think about nothing but the
mutual rattle. Well, – if that is the case I suppose I must be patient and wait
until you have calmed down enough to be in a position to spare a few thoughts
for us again.' Grieg had taken a back seat; in the next years it was Nina who
answered Delius's letters, from time to time with a little postscript in Edvard's
hand. She became an intermediary between the two self-absorbed composers.
If the father figure that Delius had found in Leipzig was now too preoccu-
pied with his own interests, his place was to a large degree supplanted by an
equally understanding and humorous mother figure. Nina's correspondence
with Delius was often a strange mixture of charming chatter and an interest
in his love affairs that could border on the intrusive. As 1891 was drawing to a
close, there were further exchanges – a (now-lost) letter from Delius in which

[57] *Verdens Gang*, 12 October 1891.
[58] Letter from Nina Grieg to Delius, 24 October 1891, trans. Lionel Carley (GD).
[59] Letter from Nina Grieg to Delius, 16 November 1891 (BOB).

he mentioned his resolution to break with his 'rattling' habits, and a sceptical response from Nina: 'Would you not rather give up eating and drinking? I don't think you would agree with Heine: without some rattling of teeth there would be no point to life, but – one is only young once.'[60]

Songs of a Nordic summer

There are two large manuscripts bookending the years 1889–91, two works full of emotions Delius associated with experiences in the Norwegian highlands: *On the Mountains* and Violin Sonata in B Major. The first of these was in Iver Holter's hands about a year before he conducted it in October 1891. The other was completed in the autumn of 1892 and as such falls outside the remit of this chapter; musically, however, the sonata is a sister composition to *On the Mountains*, the works so related in temperament and themes that they seem products of a continuous creative process. In the lowlands between these are many smaller compositions, and at least two of them may be motivated by memories of the Norwegian summer, its glowing and sensual evenings. The first is 'Dreamy Nights', to a Holger Drachmann text – and not for the first time Delius would fall for a poem earlier set by Christian Sinding:

Paa Stranden skælver ej det mindste Blad;	(No branch or leaf is trembling on the shore;
Her ruller Søen sølvblank ud sit Bad,	from sea to beach the silver ripples pour,
Og Solnedgangen lejrer sig derover.	Above your head the waves of sunset lie.
[…]	[…]
De lyse Nætter, ak de lyse Nætter!	Those radiant nights, oh those radiant nights!)

With a lulling, barcarolle-like 6/8 pulse, Delius's setting seems to capture the soft ripples in the shallows. Indeed, Drachmann's mood painting of the beach by the fjord stirred something deep in the composer, perhaps touching on his experience of summer nights around Malmøya, Drøbak and Fredriksværn. He would return to the poem several times in the 1890s, first with revisions of the original interpretation, later with a new setting.

---

[60] Letter from Nina Grieg to Delius, 21 December 1891, trans. Lionel Carley (GD). Nina seems to have misinterpreted or faultily recalled Heine's metaphor of a chilled Cupid. The poem in question is 'Kalte Herzen' ('Cold Hearts'):

Und ich darf ein schneeig Kissen	(All I had, a snowy pillow
An das heiße Herz mir drücken.	to my burning heart to hold.
Amor klappern alle Zähne,	Cupid's teeth were set to rattling,
Jessica kehrt mir den Rücken.	Jessica had turned him cold.)

Around the same time as he composed the song, Delius was sketching a short tone poem with the working title 'Summer Night' ('Lyse nætter'), but it was never completed. It reinforces the suspicion, however, that an unrelated mood piece he wrote in 1890 with the title 'Summer Evening' also drew for its emotional source on memories of warm evenings by the Kristiania Fjord. This short piece (seventy-four bars) belongs to Three Small Tone Poems:

1. *Summer Evening*
2. *Winter Night* (*Sleigh Ride*)
3. *Spring Morning*

No. 2 is in all probability an orchestration of the musical sleigh ride Delius had played for Grieg on Christmas Eve 1887, *Norwegische Schlittenfart*. It would be reasonable also to expect a fourth 'season'; Delius's friend Sir Thomas Beecham did at one time have a manuscript in his possession that he referred to as 'Autumn (Tone Poem)', but there is now no trace of this work. With 'Summer Evening', Delius took large strides away from the bold and majestic sweeps of his mountain music in the direction of the warmly chromatic tonal language of his maturity. The plastic pulse of the music with its constant shifts in time signature, the quietly rolling 6/4, the lyrical, almost ecstatic climax, and not least the melodic fragments with pentatonic coloration – these were all portents of idiomatic characteristics of the composer's highly individual style, a language that only fully developed ten years later.

Apart from Drachmann's 'Dreamy Nights' and the Bjørnson verse that became the melancholic 'Skogen gir susende langsom besked', the texts Delius chose for his songs in this period are by non-Scandinavian poets. This may have been a deliberate strategy to position himself beyond the shadow cast by Edvard Grieg. In 1891, he completed an uneven song cycle for tenor and orchestra to poems from Tennyson's *Maud*. Far more solidly cast were his settings of Shelley and Heine (three songs each).

On the Mountains symphonic poem – and a 'mountain sonata'

With his mountain scores Delius strove to convey ideas about the human spirit as something essentially pure, exalted, strong and free. Before he read Nietzsche's philosophical novel *Also sprach Zarathustra*, it seems to have been in Ibsen's epic poem *Paa Vidderne* he found these values best expressed. When, in the summer of 1890, he felt a deep longing for Norway – something that recurred in those years he did not travel to the country – he revisited the emotions kindled in him in 1888 when he had composed the melodrama *Paa Vidderne* to the poem. The result was the symphonic poem *On the Mountains*. (The description 'concert overture' disappeared when Delius later revised the manuscript for an 1894 performance in Monte Carlo.) The new work shared with the melodrama of 1888 almost nothing, apart from the original Norwegian title, *Paa Vidderne*, one motif, and an Ibsen verse on the title page, the final lines of the epic poem (quoted by Delius in German):

> I'm clad now in steel, I follow full-shod
> the high-country summons to wander!
> I've lived out life on the lowland clod;
> up here on the heights there is freedom and God,
> the rest are groping down yonder.[61]

The work is full of the types of Mountain Music we first registered in the melodrama (see Table 2, p. 45) with six idiomatic types in two categories: 'Peak'-music and 'Plateau'-music. However, the composer lets his musical motifs impregnate each other far more than in the early work; from one type of melody another seamlessly arises. In bars 1–4 (Example 4.1) he presents a subdued phrase corresponding to type 'Plateau C' – melancholic and modal. It comprises two cells, marked *x* and *y* – from these threads most of the material is spun. Out of the *x*-cell there immediately (bar 13) grows a motif strengthened by the resolve of type 'Peak B'. The dotted *y*-cell becomes ever more insistent and soon breaks into a muscular motif (fig. A, bar 9) that corresponds to type 'Peak A'.

Example 4.1 *On the Mountains*, 1–4

The work's first bridge section conforms to type 'Plateau C', melancholic and modal:

Example 4.2 *On the Mountains*, fig. B, 5–6

In the central section of his symphonic poem, Delius gives us two driving, majestic themes. First comes type 'Peak B' striving up towards the light:

---

[61] Ibsen (trans. Northam), *Ibsen's Poems*, 90.

Example 4.3 *On the Mountains*, fig. C2, 1–4

From here it is not a huge leap before the horn calls break out, type 'Peak C'. Across the climactic summit of the work, these pentatonic fanfares sound again and again.

For 'Plateau A' – majestic horn calls vanishing into the horizon – we have to wait until the work's final bars. Here, almost as a salute to his younger self and to the melodrama he so optimistically sent to Grieg for appraisal, Delius quotes for the first and last time from the earlier *Paa Vidderne* manuscript (see Example 3.5). Only one significant melody falls outside the Mountain Music types: the work's broadly fashioned secondary theme.

While Delius was now much more competent in evolving material from small melodic cells, it has to be said that, structurally, the symphonic poem is less convincing – as indeed is pointed out by all the Kristiania critics. The composer struggled to sustain the development of his thematic material. The expansive cantabile secondary theme is beautiful, but does not open itself to development; the central climax consists of repetitions of the fanfaric horn call with increasingly heavy layers of brass and percussion, and soon tends towards the bombastic. All the same, with *On the Mountains* we see Delius move on in leaps and bounds in the art of cultivating plastic thematic material – melodic building blocks that allow for motivic development over longer sequences. Here, the real breakthrough came with his Violin Sonata in B Major.

Delius's first violin sonata could justifiably be called his 'mountain sonata'. It was a third substantial opus in four years with most of its melodic material true to the set of stylistic formulas we have identified as his six types of Mountain Music. Once again we meet energetic dotted motifs, pentatonic 'horn call' figures, and majestic climbing themes striving up towards the light. One instance of the latter opens the sonata's finale, and by comparing Example 4.4 with Example 4.1 we quickly discover just how intimately related the sonata is to the symphonic poem:

Example 4.4 Violin Sonata in B Major, 3rd movement, opening

Both in his ingenious structural solutions and in his ability to generate from melodic cells large stretches of music, we see the fruits of an intense period (winter 1891–92) when Delius was seriously at work on the challenges of his craft. In its way equally remarkable – especially when compared to the waves of bombast that flooded the middle section of the Lisztian symphonic poem – is what Delius creates in his second movement from two simple phrases, similar to horn or herding calls: Example 4.5 and Example 4.6. In contrast to the metamorphosis of rhythmic and melodic cells in the outer movements, the music here subsides into tranquillity. In the context of the work seeming to have emerged from emotions and moods Delius expressed with mountain metaphors, we might imagine here that this is the contemplative peace of the mountaineer looking out across the endless plateau and hearing a distant herding call:

Example 4.5 Violin Sonata in B Major, 2nd movement, 54–7

Example 4.6 Violin Sonata in B Major, 2nd movement, 72–3

*

Initially, the sonata was dedicated to the French violinist Charlotte Vormèse. At the Paris conservatory, she was awarded first prize for her playing, and by critics she was awarded adjectives such as 'délicieuse', 'jolie et distinguée' and 'le talent plein de charm'. It is indeed possible that she caught the attention of Delius through both musical and non-musical qualities, but nothing more is known of her place in his life. At some later date, her name was covered over in the manuscript. Perhaps the sonata did not find favour with her – in which case it was an opinion that would come to be shared with Max Abraham of Edition Peters (see p. 102).

Delius had now filled three expansive scores with his Mountain Music: a melodrama (1888), a symphonic poem (1890–91) and a violin sonata (1892). None was published in his lifetime. The idiom had brought him little success but, far from abandoning it, he seems assured in his conviction that the music that expressed this segment of his personality – explored through metaphors of the mountainscape and the mountain journey – was distinctive creative material. He would have sensed that, with every new composition in the sequence, he was refining a personal language with which he could structure and communicate those experiences. On his next 'mountain ascent' he would really achieve success: the overture *Over the Hills and Far Away* (1896–97). Subsequent summits are the mountain intermezzi that bring up the curtain on Scenes III and VI of *A Village Romeo and Juliet* (1900–02) and the opening movements to the two parts of *A Mass of Life* (1904–05). Six years after the *Mass* would follow the work that crowns the composer's endeavours to express himself through mountain metaphors: *The Song of the High Hills*.

If he had made huge advances in composing material with intrinsic motivic development, his music was still mostly bound to rigid phrases. The rhythmic freedom, the rhapsodic flow of ideas and the great lyrical climaxes that typify his mature language were still no more than suggested. These would be prizes of the following years, when Delius recalibrated his talent to meet the challenges of music drama. Life on the mountain plateaus – *paa vidderne* – he was done with for a while. Now his creative dreams were all focused on the opera stage.

5

1892–1895
Norway lost

'For me dramatic art is almost taking the place of religion'
Letter from Delius to Jutta Bell, 29 May 1894

Shortly after returning to Paris from Kristiania and the première of *On the Mountains*, Delius moved to a small apartment in the Petit-Montrouge quarter, bounded by Montrouge to the south and Montparnasse to the north. After a few years in rural surroundings, he was now in a densely populated working-class neighbourhood to which many young artists were moving.

Some notion of Delius's personality and appearance at that time is to be gained through the eyes of those who observed him. Artist Jelka Rosen, his future wife, gives us this portrait:

> an aristocratic looking, rather tall, thin man with curly dark hair with a tinge of auburn and an auburn moustache which he was always twisting upwards. […] An old grey hat, his blue vivacious eyes, pale face and red tie, accentuating the pallor. […] I remember the pang of anxiety his pallor gave me. He worked half the night, smoking and drinking red wine, and then stayed in bed late, but disturbed by all the noises in that populous courtyard.[1]

The English composer Isidore de Lara was also in Paris and found Delius 'ascetic and unworldly', but, on getting better acquainted, concluded: 'I never saw a man with such irresistible will, and as it is directed with intelligence, he is sure to come to the front. […] He seems to have the working capacities of a brewer's horse.'[2] Delius was still living on allowances from his father in Bradford and his uncle in Paris, and could rarely allow himself luxuries. 'His means were very small, and he cooked his own meals', recalled de Lara. 'I have often dined with him in his room on a couple of eggs.'[3] A young English-American

---

[1] From a typescript in the Gerhardi/Steinweg collection, published as 'Jelka Delius: Memories of Frederick Delius' in LC1, 408–10.
[2] Richard Whittington-Egan and Geoffrey Smerdon, *The Quest of the Golden Boy: The life and letters of Richard Le Gallienne* (London: Unicorn Press, 1960), 187–8.
[3] Isidore de Lara, quoted in GD, 147.

pianist, Harold Bauer, lived nearby, and half a century later his encounter with
Delius was still clear in his memory:

> [His] tastes in art were as wide and liberal as could be imagined; but he had the
> strongest feeling that the first duty of any artist was to find ways in which his
> own personality could be expressed, whether or not the process conformed to
> traditional methods. 'An artist', said Delius, 'will finally be judged by that and
> nothing else. He must have' – here he hesitated and finally found the expression
> of his thought in French – 'une note à lui.'[4]

A musical language that was his own. Seen with the perfect vision of hind-
sight, Delius's struggle to refine this language is clearly the defining dynamic
of his life in the years 1892 to 1895. Almost everything he wrote from 1896
onwards would sooner or later find admirers and sponsors, and in the years
up to the First World War his star would rise dramatically in the European
firmament. In 1892 to 1895, however, he devoted himself to two large scores
that would not be performed in his lifetime: the operas *Irmelin* and *The Magic
Fountain*. If his all-encompassing goal was uncompromisingly to cultivate a
creative language through which he might express the qualities he knew he
had within him, then his determination to attain it was exhaustively tested by
years of rejection and a distressing disease.

During this transitory period, he found himself near the inspiring core of
artistic life in Paris, an admired figure in a creative colony that also counted
Paul Gauguin, August Strindberg and Edvard Munch among its members.

Parisian salons

1892 began with Delius conscientiously working on the violin sonata and his
first opera. He wrote regularly to the Griegs, and Nina could relay in a letter to
Iver Holter that the Parisian women were being spared Delius's attentions: 'He
seems to have suspended his "rattling" in the winter months, but I rather sus-
pect that the spring will revitalise it again.'[5] The Griegs had high hopes of seeing
their English friend in Norway in the summer, so Nina was clearly upset when
he made his apologies, citing the expense of the new apartment. Particularly
pained by his brusque manner, she replied: 'Well, well – something stronger
than the mountains! "I'm afraid I can *not* come to Norway this year" was really
to make a long story short.'[6] Perhaps to wound Delius in return, Nina implied
that she interpreted his action as a sign that their friendship was on the ebb:
'Now farewell, dear Delius, perhaps we will run into each other again later in
life; I would not like it to end like this, we have had too much mutual pleasure

---

[4] Harold Bauer, *Harold Bauer: His book* (New York: Norton, 1948), 59–60.
[5] Letter from Nina Grieg to Iver Holter, 3 May 1892 (NB).
[6] Letter from Nina Grieg to Delius, 29 June 1892 (DT). The first sentence was written in French
in the original: 'quelque chose plus fort que les montagnes!'

for that, don't you think?' In a postscript, Grieg too expressed his unhappiness with his friend's decision. Instead of in the Jotunheim mountains, Delius once again spent the summer in French coastal towns.

In June, there was a political crisis in Norway. The left-wing Venstre engaged in what became known as its 'clenched fist politics', unilaterally declaring an end to the shared consular service of the union.[7] This was a dangerous development and in the late summer Nina, realising that Delius was not keeping abreast of the news, teased him: 'I really thought that you had your own source of information.'[8] It was a well-aimed gibe; in August, Delius had indeed asked Randi Blehr, wife of the State Minister, for some insights into the situation:

> I am very interested in Norway – not only in its politics but especially in the development (spiritual) of a country of which I am very fond and where great power in art and science is slumbering. [...] Why not start a revolution straight away and become a republic, wholly independent of Sweden. You must explain some of this to me, as I really don't know what's going on.[9]

In the late autumn, Delius had further dealings with Randi Blehr and family. She was aunt to two radically minded young women, Dagny and Ragnhild Juel, who had left their liberal home in Kongsvinger to study music in the capital, using the home of Otto and Randi as their base. Dagny was then twenty-five and Ragnhild twenty-one. In the summer of 1892 they constituted a dazzling double star at the centre of Edvard Munch's cirle in urban Kristiania and coastal Åsgårdstrand, a new generation of Bohemians that Atle Næss describes as being 'more concerned with music, poetry and symbolism than with absinthe, "free love" and "writing the story of their lives"'.[10] Munch captured the young women in his painting *Musiserende søstre* (*Musical Sisters*), Dagny on the piano stool and Ragnhild enraptured in song. To further her education, Dagny Juel moved on to Berlin and to a new set of Bohemians, her liberated personality seemingly provoking the carnal instincts of every male artist she met; both Strindberg and Munch had affairs with her in Berlin before she finally committed herself to the Polish author Stanislaw Przybyszewski. Ragnhild Juel was instead sent in October 1892 to Paris – with a visiting card for Fritz Delius – and just after Christmas wrote to Aunt Randi:

> I spend a lot of time with Mr Delius, and like him very much. He strikes me as a fine, intelligent man, and also extremely musical. Through him I have been included in a little Wagner society which is terrifically interesting – there are four gentlemen, including Delius, who play Wagner's operas in versions for

---

[7] See Narve Bjørgo, Øystein Rian and Alf Kaartveidt, *Selvstendighet og union: Fra middelalderen til 1905* (*Independence and Union: From the Middle Ages to 1905*) (Oslo: Universitetsforlaget, 1995), 347–50.

[8] Letter from Nina Grieg to Delius, 1 September 1892 (BOB).

[9] Letter from Delius to Randi Blehr, 7 August 1892 (DT).

[10] Næss, *Munch*, 125.

eight hands, while I and an excellent baritone add the vocal parts. It is terrifically interesting and educational for me – all the gentlemen are excellent musicians and a couple of them first rate pianists. – Christmas Eve was spent at the home of Mr Delius's uncle, who also lives down here, and there we had a frightfully good time. In fact, Delius has been a terrific friend to me down here.[11]

It would appear that Randi Blehr had appealed to Delius to facilitate Ragnhild's entry into the musical life of Paris, and from time to time he sent back a report to her. In the new year, the singer became part of the artistic circle orbiting painter Frits Thaulow and Delius saw less of her.

In his monograph *Delius: The Paris years*, Lionel Carley writes: 'Until now he had worked hard and on the whole lived quietly since settling in France. [...] He was to find himself almost suddenly in a circle of superbly creative, extraordinary and sometimes eccentric people, whose art and experience were to enrich his own.'[12] On two planes – among young artists and in high society – Delius now moved in constantly widening circles. As early as 1889 he had got to know in Paris the Swedish sculptress Ida Ericson and her husband William Molard, who composed in his spare time. Molard, born in 1862, had spent the first years of his life in Norway.[13] Ida Ericson, ten years older, was very taken with Delius, describing him as 'one of the most intelligent people' she had ever met,[14] and sculpting a bust of him. In 1889, Ericson and Molard moved to a new home and studio on the Rue Vercingétorix in Montparnasse, a district almost exclusively inhabited by young, penniless artists, and here the hospitable couple kept open house. In his book *Molards salong*, Thomas Millroth has depicted the unique milieu:

> People came and went and soon Thursdays had become the day for meeting people and everyone was welcome. [...] It was not a salon in the usual sense, for here there were no rich patrons, no influential publishers or members of the Académie [...] All in all, the guests at Rue Vercingétorix 6 were without means and more often than not were to remain so. The significance of this group was of a different calibre, difficult to weigh and measure, but the thoughts and ideas that were conceived here would colour the artistic life of Paris.[15]

Delius was a regular member of this loose assembly of painters, poets and musicians – many from Scandinavia – and among these friends was often

---

[11] Letter from Ragnhild Juel to Randi Blehr, 27 December 1892 (RA).
[12] Lionel Carley, *Delius: The Paris years* (London: Triad Press, 1975), 32.
[13] William Molard's mother, Rachel Anette Hamilton, had met his father, the French musician Victor Molard, in Halden in Norway's south-east. From 1868 to 1879 they ran a music shop and hire library in Kristiania.
[14] Quoted by Thomas Millroth in his *Molards salong* (Stockholm: Forum, 1993), 109.
[15] *Ibid.*, 97.

referred to as 'Le grand Anglais' of the Latin Quarter.[16] On Saturdays, music was given priority; when Ragnhild Juel mentioned a 'terrifically interesting' Wagner Society, she was probably referring to a gathering of enthusiasts at Rue Vercingétorix. Millroth writes: 'No doubt every aspect of Wagner was turned inside out when Molard and his composer friends got together on Saturdays – a circle that embraced Maurice Ravel, Léon Moreau, Florent Schmitt, Déodat de Séverac, Fritz Delius and others.'[17]

At the Molard salon there was also fertile soil for radical political thought. In 1892–93, a series of bombs was detonated in Paris by anarchists. Writing in his autobiographical *Inferno*, August Strindberg states that 'the whole circle of anarchistic artists could be met' at the Molards.[18] As we saw in his letter to Randi Blehr above, Delius's political leanings were also to the left and he advocated radical renewal of the social order; his red necktie was thought to have signalled his political sympathies. This notwithstanding, in the winter of 1892–93 Delius was introduced by influential friends into the finest salons in the city.

Anyone familiar with the works of Marcel Proust will feel they have a grasp of the personality types, the values and the power plays that comprised the *modi operandi* of the aristocratic Parisian salon, and also of its isolation from the rest of society. It is not unreasonable to wonder how comfortably the 'red' Delius fitted in here, when he obediently answered the beck and call of one princess or baroness after another. A seemingly discordant clash of values more than likely has its explanation in the fact that a struggling composer was compelled to expand his network to include moneyed and influential members of society; unlike painters, who for a small outlay could exhibit their works, a composer's music would remain unheard without a sizeable investment of money and confidence.

Music was an essential ingredient of the salon, and Delius may have performed on the violin and piano. Of greater fascination for salon guests, however, would have been the astonishing skills he had developed in the course of this winter as an earthbound interpreter of the cosmos: he had learned how to construct horoscopes. The most celebrated opera singer in Paris, Emma Calvé, was just one of the society celebrities waiting their turn to supply him with details of when and where they were born, and then to receive in return divinations regarding how their lives would develop and, even more tantalising, when they would end. In his diary for 1905 the Norwegian author Arne Garborg joked: 'At least I'll be around until 1911, at which point I will be released

---

[16] According to composer Florent Schmitt, quoted by Felix Aprahamian in 'A Promise Fulfilled' in *Journal of The Delius Society*, No. 147 (Spring, 2010), 60.

[17] Millroth, *Molards salong*, 223.

[18] August Strindberg, *Inferno* (1897) from the translation by Jan M. Claussen (Oslo: Bokvennen 2000), 21.

from this world, according to the prediction'.[19] And who had read Garborg his
horoscope? None other than Delius, entertaining guests after a dinner in Paris
in 1896. There is no doubt that he was fascinated with the contemporary occult
craze, but there was also a prankster vein to his sense of humour; he enjoyed
nothing more than thumbing his nose at pomposity. If the socialist part of
Delius had to swallow some pride in entertaining the well-to-do, perhaps
some balance was after all achieved in the practice of his 'clairvoyant' skills.

Summer 1893: Juel, Munch and Rode

In the summer of 1893, Delius returned to his beloved Kristiania Fjord. His
shaky finances did not stretch to a mountain excursion and the fact that he got
as far as Southern Norway at all is probably due to Christian Sinding pulling
strings with the ferry company to get Delius free passage from Antwerp. At the
beginning of July, Delius and Sinding hired a small house in Drøbak on the
east side of the fjord where they could compose between bathing and cycling
trips, and their neighbour Augusta Gade – with whom Sinding enjoyed an
ever more intimate relationship – took care of their meals and other practical
needs. That Randi Blehr visited Delius in the coastal town we know from a
letter sent to her on 8 August by the Drøbak artist Edvard Diriks: 'It has been
lovely weather here recently, so I have been busy at my easel, and therefore have
hardly seen anything of Delius or the Gades since you yourself were here.'[20]

It seems as if the tone between Delius and Sinding was as warm as ever.
However, Sinding, who often seems to have reacted in an over-sensitive way
to perceived slights, had begun to cut many ties of friendship. In the autumn
of 1892, Iver Holter had fallen from grace. During preparations for the première of his first symphony by the Christiania Musikforening, Sinding had
demanded a fee for writing out the orchestral parts, but Holter had refused to
pay. The composer lost his temper, and when the symphony was subsequently
sent to the printers, the dedication to Holter had been removed. 'I certainly
behaved in a despicable way', Sinding later confided to Delius.[21] By the end of
1893, he had also managed to alienate Edvard Grieg. It may be that Sinding felt
he no longer needed the assistance of a 'support team'; he had recently signed a
contract with Max Abraham at Edition Peters that made his future financially
secure.

In February of 1893, Abraham rejected Delius's Violin Sonata in B Major.
In part-explanation of his decision he referred to critical comments about the
manuscript Grieg had offered him. This may well have cooled any enthusiasm
Delius had felt for visiting Western Norway, even if he could have afforded

[19] Arne Garborg, *Dagbok 1905–1923* (*Diary 1905–1923*) (Kristiania: Aschehoug, 1924), 1.
[20] Letter from Edvard Diriks to Randi Blehr, 8 August 1893 (RA).
[21] Letter from Sinding to Delius, 17 December 1892 (DT).

it or if Grieg had been well. In fact, the Norwegian had been ill all spring and spent much of June recuperating at a sanatorium. It is uncertain whether Delius even informed the Griegs that he was in the country.

From Drøbak, he would have been able to keep in touch with friends by making short ferry journeys up to Kristiania – where he visited editor Ola Thommessen and probably Randi Blehr – or across the fjord to Edvard Munch in tiny Åsgårdstrand and Iver Holter in Fredriksværn. In early August, he left for Kongsvinger near the border with Sweden to visit Ragnhild Juel at the family home, Rolighed, perched high above the town.[22] The family was assembled for a summer gathering and, before leaving Drøbak, Delius wrote to Randi Blehr to make sure that she would be present. After his stay at Rolighed, he continued east for a two-week visit to Sweden, his first since his days as a young wool merchant. Little is known of his movements, but one hint comes in a letter of 25 August written by Ragnhild Juel's sister, Astrid, to her Aunt Randi:

> I haven't heard anything from Mr Delius either but we presume that he has seen in the newspapers that Ragnhild is on a concert tour with Mrs Nissen,[23] and that he therefore has travelled straight past without leaving any message. There is no possibility of his coming now anyway, for in Mr Waern's telegram it said that he would be leaving on the 20th. I will write straight away to Ragnhild that she should get in touch with Mr Delius in Drøbak.[24]

To the Molard circle in Paris belonged the Swedish art historian Cecilia Waern, who penned lively accounts of studio visits for both American and Swedish periodicals. It seems likely that Delius paid her a visit at her family home in Sweden.

Here the contribution of the Juel sisters to the Delius story comes to an end. After a hard struggle with herself, Ragnhild decided to withdraw from her musical career in favour of the security of a marriage to a Swedish doctor. She died young of cancer, thirty-eight years old. Dagny pursued a career as an author, only to meet an equally tragic death, murdered by a jealous admirer in 1901.

Back by the Kristiania Fjord, Delius 'swapped sides' and had his mail addressed to Åsgårdstrand on the west bank, where he stayed with Edvard Munch – the first Delius visit of which we know to the fishing village so beloved by the painter, and so crucial to his development. Hans-Martin Frydenberg Flaatten

---

[22] The Juel family home is today the Norwegian Women's Museum.

[23] On 19 August, Ragnhild Juel and pianist Erika Nissen had embarked on an extensive tour of Norway. Bjørnstjerne Bjørnson had recently broken off a lengthy affair with Nissen and would stay in foreign exile for three years to save his marriage.

[24] Letter from Astrid Juell to Randi Blehr, 25 August 1893 (RA). The family surname was spelt variously with both one and two 'l's.

has described the 'fascinating narrative of how this unique artist methodically captured a special stretch of East Norwegian coastal nature and transformed it into his own mystical landscape of the spirit'.[25] He continues: 'In the great depths of the fjord and in the human microcosm of the village Munch finds strong and clear contrasts that he wants to explore'.[26] The painter was in the most fertile period of his career and from these months by the coast in 1893 we have works such as *Soloppgang i Aasgaardstrand* (*Sunrise in Aasgaardstrand*), *Stjernenatt* (*Starry Night*) and *Stemmen* (*The Voice*). His masterpiece, *Skrik* (*The Scream*) – a Kristiania motif – also belongs to this same intense burst of creativity.

In addition to Delius, Munch had also invited to his summer paradise the poet Helge Rode (twenty-two), who the previous year had made a name for himself with his first collection. Many years later, the art historian Jens Thiis would recall this gathering of friends: 'The summer after his *Hvide Blomster* was published, I met Helge again in Åsgårdstrand. It was his friend Edvard Munch who had tempted him there. Munch's German-English composer friend Delius was also there. We enjoyed some beautiful, sun-drenched late summer days'.[27] It was probably Munch who had introduced Rode to Delius on some earlier occasion. As early as 1890, Munch and Rode had belonged to the same band of brothers who drank at the Grand Hotel in Kristiania. Certainly Delius had broken his trip home from Norway in November 1891 to spend an evening in Copenhagen with the 21-year-old Dane. A warm friendship ensued that would last their whole lives.

Helge Rode was born in Denmark and formed in Norway. His mother was Danish; she separated from her husband at a young age and followed her new partner, Norwegian journalist Erik Vullum, north to Kristiania. Helge Rode was then eight. Around the dinner table in the Vullum home he would hear many of Norway's most radical voices in lively debate. Margrethe Vullum would herself become a fearless activist for women's rights and the first woman to gain a permanent position as a journalist for Norway's most radical newspaper, *Dagbladet*. In winter, the family usually left the smog-ridden capital in favour of the beautiful valleys of Valdres. Here, in the snow-covered village of Bagn in May 1891, Rode experienced a form of spiritual awakening that would define his path: 'Something happened to me here. The huge and gleaming white nature, the pure air, the complete silence, the long solitary tours [...]

---

[25] Hans-Martin Frydenberg Flaatten, *Måneskinn i Åsgårdstrand: Edvard Munch. Edvard Munchs sjelelandskap, scener, stemmer og stemninger i en småby ved sjøen* (*Moonlight in Åsgårdstrand: Edvard Munch. Edvard Munch's creative landscape, scenes, voices and moods in a small coastal town*) (Oslo: Sem & Stenersen, 2013), 12.

[26] *Ibid.*, 67.

[27] Jens Thiis, 'Minneord om Helge Rode' (In Memory of Helge Rode) in *Festskrift til Francis Bull på 50-årsdagen* (*Festschrift on the Occasion of Francis Bull's 50th Birthday*) (Oslo: Gyldendal, 1937), 307.

engineered an upheaval in my being [...] A recognition of being in harmony with natural forces that were independent of death.'[28] This was very likely an experience he retold to the gathering of artistic friends in Åsgårdstrand two years later. And, if so, it would be no coincidence that the next time Delius was in Norway, in 1896 – seeking a renewal of his creative powers – he chose Bagn in Valdres.

Great artists at the Molard salon

In his years at Petit-Montrouge, Delius spent much of his leisure time in the company of three of the foremost artistic geniuses of the epoch, fragmented personalities that each embraced as much psychological darkness as intensely burning creative fervour. All three belonged to the Molard circle during their overlapping stays in Paris in this period:

Paul Gauguin	January 1894 – July 1895
August Strindberg	August 1894 – July 1896
Edvard Munch	February 1896 – May 1897

An art connoisseur of a later epoch, Osbert Sitwell, would recall that Delius was 'the one Englishman I have ever met who knew personally the giants of the post-impressionist movement, recognised them for what they were, and was privileged to frequent their studios'.[29] Recently returned from a Pacific island journey, Gauguin established a studio on the first floor of Rue Vercingétorix 6, above Ida Ericson's studio. Delius has left us some lines regarding his daily contact with this circle:

I met Strindberg in Paris in the early nineties at the studio of Ida Ericson, a Swedish sculptress married to William Molard, a French-Norwegian composer. Later on I met him quite frequently at the 'Crémerie' of the Mère Charlotte, Rue de la Grande Chaumière (Montparnasse), where artists received unlimited credit. [...] Among the *habitués* of the Mère Charlotte at that time were Strindberg; a Polish painter named Slewinsky; Mucha, a Czech designer of decorations and *affiches*; Paul Gauguin, the great painter; Leclercq, a poet; the *maître de ballet* of the Folies Bergère, also a Czech; and myself. [...] I occasionally lunched or dined at Madame Charlotte's to meet Gauguin and Strindberg. Or I would sometimes fetch Strindberg for a walk in the afternoon.[30]

Strindberg's mental state was precarious, something that he made no attempt to conceal in his autobiographical novel of that period, *Inferno*. Indeed, Delius

---

[28] Hanne Engberg, *En digters historie: Helge Rode 1870–1937* (*History of a Poet: Helge Rode 1870–1937*) (Copenhagen: Gyldendal, 1996), 54–5.

[29] Osbert Sitwell, *Great Morning* (London: Macmillan, 1948), 252.

[30] Delius's Strindberg memories were first published in *The Sackbut* (December 1920). Republished as 'Delius: Recollections of Strindberg' in LC1, 404.

was at times drawn into the eccentric Swede's experiments with alchemy and flirtations with spiritualism.

Another cultural giant, although diminutive in stature, visited Paris in 1894, and Delius seized the opportunity to present him to his friends at the Molard salon. Edvard Grieg was back in Paris to conduct a concert of his own compositions. It was a signal honour for the artists of Rue Vercingétorix 6 to have this musical luminary among them and William Molard made sure to invite his most valued musician friends, including Maurice Ravel, then nineteen years old. Grieg had for some time been trying to find someone with linguistic talents who might translate his songs into French. During this visit the problem was resolved: Molard and the poet Leclercq undertook the task, with assistance from Delius, devoting to it the summer of 1894.

Many of the Norwegian artists who were in Paris for a shorter or longer stay got to know Delius and the Molards. In April 1893, Sinding wrote to him: 'Vilhelm Krag is leaving for Paris this evening. I have given him your address and promised him that he would find you very pleasant company.'[31] The 22-year-old poet had made his sensational debut on the Norwegian literary scene two years earlier, and his muse had been Ragnhild Juel. Now she was in Paris under Delius's supervision. Krag and Delius hit it off straight away and in 1894 the composer would set to music the poem 'Jeg havde en nyskaaren seljefløjte' ('I once had a newly cut willow pipe') from Krag's fairy tale play *Vester i Blaafjeldet*.

Knut Hamsun also arrived in Paris in April 1893. Thirty-three years old, he had behind him the successes of *Sult* (*Hunger*) and *Mysterier* (*Mysteries*) and in Paris he would make headway on *Pan*. Even though the names of Delius and Hamsun are not directly connected in any surviving correspondence, it is likely that they spent time together, for they shared many friends and acquaintances: Gauguin, Strindberg, the French poet Paul Verlaine, Vilhelm Krag and the Danish author Herman Bang, to mention just a few. Hamsun and Strindberg also had the same habit as Delius and Strindberg – they enjoyed taking long walks around Paris.

Munch, Grieg, Krag, Hamsun, Strindberg, Rode – these and other shining names in the history of modern Scandinavian arts played greater or lesser roles in the story of Frederick Delius. It is not, however, one of these whom he would describe with the following words: 'He is the only one that is worth something and the only man I really love.'[32] Violinist and composer Halfdan Jebe is today forgotten by his native Norway. Indeed, he had too restless a soul to make his mark on Norway during his own lifetime, and experienced the conformity of society there as a straitjacket. For Delius, however, it was

---

[31] Letter from Sinding to Delius, 11 April 1893 (NB).
[32] Letter from Delius to Jelka, 18 December 1898 (GM).

10. 'Jebe is the only man I ever loved in all my life', wrote Delius. In 1902,
Halfdan Jebe entered into a creative partnership with painter and author
Christian Krohg (at piano) and author Peter Egge with the aim of writing an opera.

precisely the constantly smouldering spirit of dissent and iconoclasm in Jebe that made him so valued a friend. He came to personify for Delius his own urges to break with social orthodoxy.

Halfdan Jebe was born in 1868 in Trondheim to a father who was a respected military doctor and a mother who came from a long line of high-standing bureaucrats. Jebe moved as a teenager to Kristiania where he studied music with Iver Holter and Ludvig Mathias Lindeman. He enrolled at the conservatory in Leipzig in the autumn of 1887, Delius's second year there, moving on to further violin studies under Joachim in Berlin and subsequently composition in Paris under Massenet. From 1894 to 1897 he played in the Colonne orchestra, the Paris ensemble most favourable to contemporary music. His younger sister Martha Caroline (known to everyone as Tupsy), a talented painter, was also studying in Paris in this period, and would soon be drawn into Delius's artistic circle. Halfdan Jebe and Delius were often together in these years, the free-living lifestyle of his younger Norwegian friend seeming to confirm or release parts of Delius's personality. There was a good deal of common ground: both were non-eldest sons of wealthy bourgeois parents in provincial cities, both moved on from playing the violin to composing, both would use these talents as a springboard to escape conventional backgrounds. Jebe was, however, of far less resolute stuff and the course of his life, marked by restlessness and neuroses, suggests psychological scars – though what their cause might have been is unknown. Once free of his father, Delius grasped the matter of moulding his artistic career with both hands. Jebe's career would instead develop into an unending sequence of escapes. Comfortable positions in orchestras and colleges were abandoned after two years or less; many years would be spent as an itinerant musician in Europe, Asia and the USA. Always searching for some greater cause worthy of his talent, Halfdan Jebe would finally settle in revolutionary Mexico in 1923, devoting himself to the promotion of human and civil rights for the indigenous population.

In 1894, Jutta Bell reappeared in Delius's life. Jutta had been his Norwegian muse at Solana Grove in Florida. While Jutta did not separate from her husband until 1896, the marriage was already on the rocks when she, with two small children in tow, moved to Paris. She had quickly needed to develop her singing talent into paid employment and had therefore sought vocal tuition in the French capital. It is, however, likely that Delius's presence in Paris was also an influential factor. As we saw in Chapter Two, it was probably about Jutta that he later wrote these words:

> I was madly, passionately in love when I was 21 […] [She was] just my own age […] She would not give herself. […] 7 or 8 years after she came to me of her own accord – but I was no more in love with her & then she became madly in love with me – but all in vain.

If the flame of love for her had died in Delius, he still recognised a person whose resources he might find useful. His artistic passion was now opera and in his constant search for source material for a libretto he turned to Jutta, who knew many of the old Norwegian folk tales:

> Please tell me some more fairy tales. I love them as much as you do, and we might weave some together for our purpose. I should, as I said before, like to give all my works a deeper meaning. I want to say something to the world very serious & music & poetry are my only means. You might really be of great help to me, as I see in you a sister nature to mine.[33]

If he were to collaborate with Jutta on an opera, however, it would have to be purely on his conditions:

> I am really most happy that you now see things in the right way and put all feelings of the ordinary woman aside. I feel also that for the first time a woman understands me thoroughly – Believe me when I tell you that I understand you

---

[33] Letter from Delius to Jutta Bell, 29 May 1894 (JUL).

also and have the greatest admiration for you – Don't search any more for the truth. It will come to you in working for a great cause.[34]

With this, Jutta Bell and Fritz Delius began work on a libretto – capitalising not, in the end, on her knowledge of Norwegian folk tales, but on his of Native Americans. It would become his second opera, *The Magic Fountain*. 'For me dramatic art is almost taking the place of religion', he wrote to Jutta.[35] And in the summer of 1894 he forsook both Norway and the coastline of France to travel to the temple of his religion, Bayreuth. Here, and in the Munich opera houses, he heard *Tannhäuser* once, *Parsifal* twice and *Die Meistersinger*, *Tristan und Isolde* and *Der Ring des Nibelungen* all three times. '[It] will no doubt be of great benefit to me', he wrote to Jutta, who had borrowed his apartment in his absence.[36]

In mid-1895, *The Magic Fountain* was complete, as was Jutta Bell's period of vocal education in Paris. She returned to London and, now independent of her husband, established her own vocal studio. She quickly gained for herself a respected name as a voice trainer and later as an author (see p. 174).

1895: The dark year

The year 1895 is a low point in Delius's life. If there was originally a good deal of correspondence from the period, little of it has come down to us. There seems, therefore, to hang a veil over 1895 that hinders scrutiny of his life events. It is nevertheless evident that serious problems mounted up on three sides, threatening his musical development, his financial situation and his health.

Delius had managed to get songs published in London and Paris, and in February 1894 he had succeeded in getting *On the Mountains* performed for the second time, now at a prestigious concert in Monaco. Subsequently, he had devoted himself to opera and much of his time and resources in 1894 were channelled into stimulating the enthusiasm of operatic conductors and impresarios. While in Munich and Bayreuth, for instance, he had arranged to meet the conductor Hermann Levi and show him *Irmelin*; Levi sent Delius on to Richard Strauss, but nothing came of the campaign. The manuscript of *The Magic Fountain* was considered first in Prague and Weimar, later by publisher and producer Henrik Hennings in Copenhagen, and by conductors Felix Mottl in Karlsruhe and Alfred Hertz in Elberfeld. After initially favourable responses it always ended in the same way, with rejection.

---

[34] Letter from Delius to Jutta Bell, 11 July 1894 (JUL).
[35] Letter from Delius to Jutta Bell, 29 May 1894 (JUL).
[36] Letter from Delius to Jutta Bell, 12 August 1894 (JUL). While in Munich Delius happened to run into Bjørnson with his wife Karoline and daughter Dagny. Bjørnson was living at the time in the Tyrolean town of Schwaz and invited Delius to stay with them for a few days. It is not known whether he accepted the offer.

The chances of putting *The Magic Fountain* on stage were also weakened by financial setbacks. In 1895, Delius's uncle in Paris, generous up to this point, put his foot down when approached about subsidising a production of the opera. The return on his investment of confidence and resources in his nephew had been meagre. In a pincer movement by Delius's father and Uncle Theodor, probably coordinated with the intention of forcing him back to a respectable career as a teacher in America, his allowance from Bradford was also cut back to the bare minimum.

The darkest cloud over his life, however, was the disease with which he was diagnosed in the course of 1895. A syphilis diagnosis would hardly have come as a shock to any of the Bohemians who gathered under the Molard roof. In one of his more hypocritical moments, Strindberg, with Lutheran disdain, criticised the members of the Molard circle for cultivating 'free and easy manners, loose morals, deliberate and fashionable irreligion'.[37] The truth is rather that, for him as for other artists who elected to live *la vie parisienne* in the cafés, salons and studios of Montparnasse and Montrouge, the magnetic attraction of the area had as much to do with the uninhibited lifestyle as with the opportunities for professional development. The available treatments for syphilis, especially those preparations based on mercury, had only a temporary effect and unpleasant side-effects. On the first serious occurrence of the ailment, it would seem that Delius avoided these treatments, placing instead his confidence in recent alternative developments in homeopathic remedies. In 1891, the German homeopath Martin Glünicke had published *Mein Heilsystem oder die Heilung der Krankheiten mittelst giftfreier pflanzlicher Säfte* (*My Therapeutic System. Or: How to Cure Disease with the Aid of Non-Poisonous Plant Extracts*). The fact that Glünicke had made a study of the way Native Americans had utilised plants in their medical remedies possibly carried more weight for Delius than the fact that he was educated as a lawyer rather than as a chemist. 'I really had to laugh at your enthusiasm for Glünicke', was Grieg's mocking response a few months later. 'I am very ready to believe that you feel fit and healthy after his extracts, because you were fit and healthy before too!'[38]

This is the disease that fifteen years later would cause Delius's first physical breakdown, would later render him blind and paralysed, and finally would take his life.

Delius had been in Norway in 1887, 1889, 1891 and 1893. No matter what other things were going on in his life, he returned to Norway and – to use his own words – got his old self back again. Never did he need a Norwegian holiday more than in 1895, but that year the sequence was broken, probably for financial reasons. Towards the end of 1895, his inherently optimistic life force was

---

[37] August Strindberg, *The Inferno*, trans. Claud Field (New York: G. P. Putnam, 1913), 26.
[38] Letter from Grieg to Delius, 12 January 1896 (BOB).

again in evidence. In September, Christian Sinding was in Berlin and persuaded Delius to leave his troubles behind in Paris for a while; their old Leipzig
colleagues, Hjalmar Borgstrøm, Ferruccio Busoni and Ottokar Nováček, were
in the German city for the winter. The invitation may also have coincided happily with a notion Delius had formed for pleading the case for an allowance
with a wealthy aunt who lived in Berlin.

Irmelin and *The Magic Fountain*

An artist must have his own voice, 'une note à lui', thought Delius. He once
stated that: 'If you devote yourself to music, there is only one way to attain to
anything at all, I mean any originality, and that is by working right through
your influences'.[39] Daniel Grimley, in an evaluation of Grieg's influence on the
succeeding generation of composers, has pointed out that artists who are in the
process of working through their influences often experience periods of creative anxiety connected with issues of identity and self-image: 'It is a process
of simultaneous attraction and rejection (or, more properly, suppression).'[40]
Young artists can be debilitated by the sense that their predecessors have said
so much, taken up so much room, that there is no longer enough space for
them to develop an original musical identity or poetic voice. Under Edvard
Grieg's influence, Delius had created the *Paa Vidderne* melodrama and a
couple of handfuls of songs to Norwegian poets. He then toyed with the idea
– perhaps inspired by Grieg's success with *Peer Gynt* – of incidental music to
Ibsen's *Keiser og Galileer* (*Emperor and Galilean*). Eventually, the sketches were
discarded in favour of an opera based on Ibsen's *Gildet paa Solhaug* (*The Feast
at Solhaug*), the German translation of which had appeared in 1888. Delius had
direct contact with Ibsen about the rights, who sent him on to the translator;
the rights had, however, already been assigned to Hugo Wolf, whose *Das Fest
auf Solhaug* appeared in 1890–91.[41] Grieg's influence does indeed seem for a
period to have weakened Delius's individuality. Around 1892, however, significant processes were bubbling through his creative work; he was moving away
from his Scandinavian influences. This point can be identified as a crucial
moment in his career, a watershed in his development. New gods, Wagner in
particular, filled the vacuum and the challenge of assimilating them – forming
them into an element of his own 'note à lui' – comprises much of the story of
his artistic development in the 1890s. 'I want to tread in Wagner's footsteps',

[39] C. W. Orr, 'Frederick Delius: Some Personal Recollections', reprinted in Christopher Redwood (ed.), *A Delius Companion* (London: John Calder, 1976), 58.

[40] Grimley, *Grieg: Music, landscape and Norwegian identity*, 207.

[41] Early in 1892, members of the Molards' circle were invited by Swedish sculptor Christian
Eriksson to a studio-warming party. Delius contributed a lively, but insubstantial, part-song
to a text from *Gildet paa Solhaug*, utilising Ibsen's original Dano-Norwegian: 'Her ute skal
gildet staa' ('Here We Shall Feast').

he had told Jutta Bell in 1894, 'and even give something more in the right direction.'[42]

Once he had abandoned the Ibsen dramas, Delius's search for a theme for an opera took him down several routes, including that of Greek mythology (the story of Endymion), before a poem by Danish author J. P. Jacobsen channelled his thoughts in the direction of folk tales. Most of Jacobsen's poems were published in 1888, three years after his death, and achieved immediate success. *Irmelin Rose*, which quickly became one of the most popular, begins:

Se, der var en Gang en Konge,	(Now, once upon a time there was a king,
Mangen Skat han kaldte sin,	with treasures priceless and rare
Navnet paa den allerbedste	and all knew that the jewel of them all
Vidste hver var Irmelin	was Princess Irmelin the fair)

The narrative Delius fashions from this source and from tropes in Germanic and Nordic folk myths tells of the Princess Irmelin, who scorns her knightly suitors, and Nils, a prince who as a child was kidnapped by bandits and has grown up as their servant. With the aid of a magical stream, Nils finds his way to Irmelin's castle and to her heart. Conductor Thomas Beecham, Delius's champion and close friend, regarded the opera's narrative strands as an expression of the composer's longing to escape the ugliness of modern life: 'Norway and the influence of the Norwegian way of life, simple and unspoilt by over-urbanization, cleansed his mind of the perilous stuff which had for too long been haunting it, and brought it back again into the enchanted world of folklore and fairyland.'[43] As the scaffolding of an opera, the story is not intrinsically any less promising than others of the day based on folklore and Nordic myths. Where *Irmelin* fails is in Delius's treatment of the story – that is to say, in its libretto. He elected to write the text himself, perhaps with Wagner as his model, but more likely because he struggled to find a suitable collaborator. The text offers little in the way of character development or psychological insights into the actions of the protagonists. Apart from the romantic love duet near the end, the story – with its enchanted stream, prince in disguise and uproarious bandits – would have been better suited to an opera for children. At times the literary quality of Delius's libretto also jars:

IRMELIN	Knights for thee but not for me.
MAID	Why not for thee … and why for me?
IRMELIN	Some are young and some are bold,
	Some are rich and some are old,
	But they all leave me cold.

In this period he was, of course, far from alone in wishing to develop a post-Wagnerian operatic universe without its mythological gods and larger-than-life

---

[42] Letter from Delius to Jutta Bell, 29 May 1894 (JUL).
[43] Beecham, *Frederick Delius*, 55.

heroes. At the same time as Delius was writing *Irmelin*, Mascagni in Rome was in the process, with *Cavalleria rusticana*, of presenting one solution: realistic social drama wedded to lyrical music – the style known as *verismo*. Initially attracted to the realism of Ibsen, Delius was now seeking a different solution. The concept of a fairy tale opera was in itself both an imaginative and an audacious experiment. Humperdinck was at that very moment exploring a similar path through the enchanted wood, and had Delius worked to a libretto as accomplished as that provided Humperdinck by his sister, then *Irmelin* might have found a place in the repertoire alongside *Hänsel und Gretel*. All six of his scores for the opera stage, from *Irmelin* (1890–92) to *Fennimore and Gerda* (1908–10), are to a greater or lesser extent handicapped by their libretti, and demand of an audience a willingness to accept that the wonderful nourishment of the music comes with the grit of textual banalities. It is perhaps the principal reason that the composer's often wonderful operatic music is not better known today.

The weakness of *Irmelin*'s text must not, however, impede our view of the fact that with this work Delius took huge strides away from his influences and in a bold direction. Grieg's fingerprints are rarely to be seen in the music, nor has the composer surrendered to using Wagnerian hero melodies of the type that emboldened the heart of *On the Mountains*. The largest advance made with *Irmelin* is in the composer's new-found ability to render his music fluid over extended passages and with great rhythmic flexibility. In earlier works, such as *On the Mountains* and the violin sonata, Delius's melodic phrases were still to a large degree four-square, and rhythmic fluidity was governed by these same rigid parameters. With the concluding love duet between Irmelin and Nils he hurdles a barrier. While illustrating the fluctuating emotions of the characters, he imposes impressive control on a stream of emotional intensity – constantly tensing and relaxing, holding back the flood then slipping it free. He builds up and then rounds off large lyrical climaxes. This emotional tension is so distant from the childish play of the first two acts that it provides the listener with a disorienting experience, as if moving from a fairy story told in black-and-white film to a steamy romance in full Technicolor. With this duet Delius offers us the first signs of the rhapsodic freedom and rhythmic flexibility that would come to typify his finest works.

After his 'Norwegian' fairy tale, Delius chose themes for his next two operas that played on experiences he could draw on from his American years, and which thereby offered him, to a greater degree, colourful opportunities for developing the individuality of his voice. *The Magic Fountain* and *Koanga* are among the furthest points he arrived at in a process partly designed to distance him from Griegian/Norwegian influences, and are therefore peripheral to the theme of this book. Their significance for his development must, however, be mentioned as we come to them. Even before he had got down to work on *The Magic Fountain*, Delius had expanded his vision to a trilogy of music dramas, and at the core of these works would be three ethnic groups that each in their own way challenged the values of Western civilisation: 'I have a vague idea of writing 3 works', he confided in Jutta Bell, 'one on the Indians, one on the Gypsies and one on the Negroes & quadroons'.[44] African slaves on an American plantation form the backbone of *Koanga*. Gypsies, or their equivalent, came to play a vital, if subsidiary, role in *A Village Romeo and Juliet*. For *The Magic Fountain* Delius chose the partly historical account from 1513 of the Spaniard Ponce de León, leader of the first European expedition to Florida, who, according to legend, was searching for a magical water source that could bestow eternal youth on those who drank from it. Delius gave Ponce a different Spanish name, derived from his own orange plantation in Florida: Solana, later changed to Solano. In the opera, Solano, shipwrecked on the Florida coast, is found and nursed back to health by the local Indians. Between the beautiful Indian girl Watawa and the Spaniard there grows a forbidden bond of love.

In several ways, Delius moves his operatic music forward here in comparison with *Irmelin*. The first is the libretto. As we have already seen, he invited Jutta Bell to make contributions to the story and characterisation. While the finished text is to all intents and purposes his work, along the way he had taken on board valuable suggestions from her, and he manages to avoid both the worst literary flaws of *Irmelin* and its conflict of musical styles. Musically, *The Magic Fountain* hangs together well, thanks to the composer's intense work over a short period and his introduction of a Wagnerian set of leitmotifs. The few leitmotifs in Irmelin had functioned purely as name badges or shadows attached to the characters. Here, in his second opera, the composer explored the potential that a motif system gave him to breathe dramatic subtext into his stage music. Underpinning the scenes and texts are not only motifs for places and characters but also motifs suggesting abstract ideas and ideals motivating the characters. For the love duet that brings *The Magic Fountain* towards its close, Delius again moved his intense, lyrical and flowing music onto another level. It is a genuine offspring of Wagner's operatic language at its most fluid. From Wagner he had also learned a lesson about the intensification of the love drama at the dénouement of the opera: that it added great power to the narrative to let the lovers' passion remain unresolved. One definition of passion points out that it is 'deepened and releases its energies only in proportion to the resistance it meets'.[45] While Wagner had developed his music dramas towards conclusions fashioned round this dynamic, Delius – despite being an admirer of *Tristan und Isolde* since his student days – had let Nils and Irmelin disappear hand-in-hand into the sunset. Not Watawa and Solano. Their love

---

[44] Letter from Delius to Jutta Bell, 29 July 1894 (JUL).
[45] 'Love' in Philip P. Weiner (ed.), *The Dictionary of the History of Ideas*, III (New York, Charles Scribner's Sons: 1973), 101.

reaches its emotional climax when they sacrifice themselves for each other in the death-bringing water of the magic fountain. In his next two operas, Delius would again insist on happiness being unattainable for his lovers here on earth, and opening the doors of death to them.

In Berlin at the close of 1895, Delius seems to have been reassured by his wealthy aunt that he could rely on some financial assistance from her. On his way back to Paris he stopped off in Leipzig, where Grieg was wintering, and his Norwegian friend sat down to peruse the score of *The Magic Fountain*. He discovered much of which he could approve; certainly the staging of the work would pose huge problems, commented Grieg, but the music contained 'wonderful things, simply ingenious and full of character'.[46]

Perhaps the two also discussed over a glass of champagne how the gods of love were playing them for fools. Grieg, now fifty-two years old, had just come from Copenhagen where he had nurtured an infatuation with the young Anglo-Danish pianist Bella Edwards. From his covert letters to her it is clearly evident how one-sided the emotions were, and by the end of the year Grieg had realised his mistake.[47] In a cogitative New Year letter to Frants Beyer he recalled an anecdote from his student days in Leipzig. His harmony professor had corrected the work of another student, criticising him for having forgotten to put a double bar line at the end: 'Und so machen wir denn den Schweinstall zu!' ('And this is how we lock the pigsty!'). The professor had then drawn a double bar line, locking the 'pigsty'. Grieg assured Beyer: 'Here and now, as he did, I take my pen and lock away with two hefty // [pen strokes] all the stupidity of the past year. Fortunately without any repeat sign!'[48]

Delius would have been no less happy than Grieg to round off 1895 with a double bar line and direct his gaze forward. He had confidence in Glünicke's extracts; he had managed to steer his personal finances away from the rocks; he has also found inspiring source material for a new opera: a story of an African prince shipped to America as a slave. It was now over two years since he had been to Norway and his longing once again activated his creative powers. It was probably at the end of 1895 that ideas for a new orchestral work brimming with Mountain Music began to take form: the overture *Over the Hills and Far Away*.

Most significant of all in the process of imposing discipline and direction on his art – although he did not know it yet – was the fact that, just after the turn of the year, he would meet the woman who was to become his life partner.

---

[46] Letter from Grieg to Iver Holter, 12 January 1896 (EG1).
[47] Grieg's letters to Edwards have been published online by the Edvard Grieg Archives of Bergen Public Library.
[48] Letter from Grieg to Frants Beyer, 31 December 1895 (RA).

6

1896
Norway regained

'I am leading a life quite Adam like'

Letter from Delius to Jelka Rosen, 15 June 1896

I first met Delius in January 1896 in Paris at the house of a Swedish sculptress, Mme Benedix-Bruce; her husband was a Canadian painter.[1] Knowing how much I loved the songs of Grieg which I sang so often, she always said: 'You must know a young Englishman, a friend of ours. He also loves Grieg and composes music himself' [...] I did not wish to see this young man she always spoke of. But once when I dined there with my mother who was living with me in Paris, he was there too.[2]

Helene Rosen was born in 1868. Known to all as Jelka, she was a painter from a Schleswig-Holstein family with distinguished figures in music and diplomacy. After this dinner, the hostess implored Jelka to sing for the company:

I sang the 'Swan' and 'Solveig's Song' of Grieg – with a naïveté I have often marvelled at later on, for I had but a small soprano voice and had only had just a few singing and breathing lessons. [...] Anyhow Delius seemed to like my singing, for he told me he would come to my studio and bring me a book of his own songs.[3]

Delius brought his *Seven Songs from the Norwegian* and played for her one of the songs that Grieg had also set, probably 'Twilight Fancies', and informed Jelka that he considered his version the superior one.[4] If it was through Grieg's music they had made their introductions, it was an author who bound them together: 'At that time I was full of enthusiasm for Nietzsche's Zarathustra', she

---

[1] Carolina Benedicks-Bruce, married to William Blair Bruce.
[2] 'Jelka Delius' (Gerhardi/Steinweg collection), published in LC1, 408.
[3] *Ibid.*, 408–9.
[4] Eric Fenby, 'Jelka Delius: A recollection' in *Journal of The Delius Society*, No. 79 (April 1983), 8.

11. Painter Jelka Rosen got to know Delius early in 1896 in Paris. Here she poses for her painter friend, Ida Gerhardi.

related, 'and I was greatly surprised when this young Englishman said he knew and loved Zarathustra'.[5]

Jelka frequently entertained Delius at her studio and as winter turned to spring in Paris she enjoyed 'a happy, wonderful time'.[6] They would sometimes take the train out from the city and go for long walks in the countryside. After submitting her latest canvas to the spring Salon des Indépendants, Jelka indulged herself with a few days of holiday in the village of Grez-sur-Loing, near Fontainebleau. Delius arranged to be visiting at the same time the neighbouring village of Bourron, where his friend Charles F. Keary was staying. Keary had assumed the task of writing the libretto to Delius's third opera, *Koanga*. Jelka met Delius several times in Bourron and then, when he came to Grez, they rowed out on the river Loing, which was in spring flood.

> We managed to get thro' under the old stone bridge of Grez with great difficulty and struggled on until we got to the landing place of an old deserted but lovely garden belonging to the Marquis de Carzeaux, with an old rambling, but very cosy looking house at the top, facing the street. I had permission for several summers to go and paint in this glorious garden. [...] Fred said: 'A place like that one could work in, it is so beautiful and quiet and unspoilt.' These words proved to be prophetic – but neither of us thought of that at all at that time.[7]

Edvard Munch and the Molard circle

In February 1896, Edvard Munch returned to Paris and quickly rejoined Delius's artistic circle, writing home: 'I spend my time with Delius and Vilhelm Krag'.[8] Many years later, the artist, now rich and famous, reminisced about this period in a letter to Delius:

> I recalled that impoverished but lovely period when I had my studio on Rue de la Santé – At that time – I recall how I determined to sell empty wine bottles to make enough to buy food – And I couldn't make as much as 10 centimes – And then, do you remember, that I often came to eat with you – drank splendid wine and you raised my spirits with your good humour – It was also then that you took me along to Molard where they were so friendly to me.[9]

The reason for Munch returning to Paris for an extended stay (until the summer of 1897) was his desire to specialise in prints, the French capital attracting the most experimental artists in the medium. In a biographical note, again from

---

[5] 'Jelka Delius' (Gerhardi/Steinweg collection), published in LC1, 408. Friedrich Nietzsche's *Also sprach Zarathustra* was published in 1883–85.

[6] *Ibid.*, 409.

[7] *Ibid.*, 411.

[8] Letter from Munch to Karen Bjølstad, 27 March 1896 (MM).

[9] Letter draft from Munch to Delius, undated, probably late 1926 (MM). It is not known whether the letter was actually sent, but it is likely.

near the end of his life, Munch gives us an overview of the network of artists with which Delius helped to connect him:

> I was constantly with Delius during my 2-year stay in Paris 1895–1897 [...] He lived in a small street near Rue Lion de Belfort. Strindberg was there then and our circle consisted of friends of Gauguin who at that time was in Tahiti and also friends of van Gogh. Our circle also included friends of Verlaine who was dead and Malarmé and the Mercure de France circle. Merrill was there too. Oscar Wilde came sometimes.[10] [...] We frequented the Café Lilas [La Closerie de Lilas] and Harcourt [Café d'Harcourt]. We were often to be found along the Boulevard S Michel or at Bullier.[11] I had a studio then on Rue de Santé. Delius was a fine person. It was around that time that Delius got the germ of his disease.[12]

While he was in Paris, Munch rekindled a friendship with a young female painter he had pursued in Kristiania a couple of years earlier. Tupsy (actually Martha) Jebe, born in Trondheim in 1871, was the younger sister of violinist Halfdan Jebe, Delius's close friend. In Paris she fell seriously in love with Munch, while he gradually felt it more and more necessary to keep her at a distance. This was a recurring pattern in Munch's life, as Atle Næss notes: 'He finds it problematic to give clear signals to those women who make it clear that they want him.'[13]

These are words which Jelka Rosen might also have applied to Delius at this stage of their relationship. Early in June 1896, he left Paris for Norway, a stay that would last almost three months. Already in love with Delius, but unsure how important she was in his life, Jelka feared that this break in their close contact might douse the flame of intimacy. She wrote to him in Norway, starting her first letter with a sigh from the heart: 'Of course you did not write; I thought you weren't going to so I was not very disappointed.'[14] She was mistaken. Their letters had crossed in the post.

Summer 1896: Haugen in Bagn

Three years had passed since Delius was last in Norway. He was now thirty-four, and a combination of experiences, not least his serious illness, had altered his needs and priorities, giving him a changed perspective on where he stood

---

[10] No sources have been found that confirm American poet Stuart Merrill and Oscar Wilde as members of Delius's circle in Paris. In 1899, Norwegian painter Alfred Hauge wrote home and told his family that both men were part of *his* circle, and this at a time when Hauge and Delius spent a lot of time together (see p. 178). Wilde and Delius had indeed met each other in London in February 1892 after the première of Wilde's *Lady Windermere's Fan*.

[11] Bal Bullier was a popular ballroom. The second act of Puccini's opera *La Rondine* (1917) takes place there.

[12] Undated note by Munch (MM N 222) (MM).

[13] Næss, *Munch*, 159.

[14] Letter from Jelka to Delius, undated, c.20 June 1896 (GM).

in his life. The man who on earlier visits had desired to enjoy a Bohemian life-style with artist friends by the Kristiania Fjord and had preferred the sensual pleasures of sailing and bathing to walking in the mountains, now sought out a peaceful environment in clear mountain air where he could work, before he went trekking in the hills for days on end. In 1891, he had derided Grieg's *Sturmmärsche* through the mountains; this summer he would traverse Jotun-heimen and Rondane in daily stages of twelve to fourteen hours. With his visit to Norway in 1896, Delius was entering a new phase of his life.

He disembarked in Kristiania on one of the first days of June and began to plan a stay in the valleys of Valdres. It was an established procedure that tour-ists would register with Bennett's Tourist Office, which drew up an itinerary that included all necessary transport and accommodation. Delius may well have availed himself of Bennett's service this summer. While he waited for the last pieces to fall into place he wrote, seemingly on an impulse, to Trold-haugen. It was probably the first contact between the two composers for six months: 'I arrived here a couple of days ago – and intend to travel to Valdres and work quietly there. Shall we go to Jotunheimen together? It would give me great pleasure to make this trip with you again.'[15] Grieg had to decline, this time because of Nina's poor health. Instead, Grieg invited Delius to Western Norway and, poking fun at his flirtatious episodes with Petra Vogt and Anne Mohn in 1889 (see p. 60), reminded him that 'there are young ladies in the neighbourhood, – however from this simple fact no children arise!'[16] Had Delius and Grieg again wandered in the mountains this summer, it might have inaugurated a renewed intimacy between them. As it turned out, this exchange of letters was probably their last before 1903, nor is there any evidence that they would meet again before Grieg died in 1907.

Grieg was no doubt unaware of it when he joked about his English friend's attraction to the fairer sex, but during Delius's stay in Kristiania it would seem that his reputation as a womaniser had created something of a scandal. What we know, can be read between the lines of two letters he sent to Randi Blehr. The first was penned from Valdres, probably in late June, thanking her for the hospitality she and her family had shown him on his way through Kristiania – he had perhaps stayed with them. In addition he wrote: 'I hope […] you are no longer vexed about this silly Arvesen business – I have forgotten the whole thing and now find it highly amusing.'[17] We get a hint of what this 'business' was in his Christmas letter to Blehr at the close of 1896, in which Delius was looking forward to his next visit to Norway, 'where I am sure', he added, 'a couple of new "seducer stories" await me'.[18] We have already noted that Delius's

---

[15] Letter from Delius to Grieg, undated, early June 1896 (BOB).
[16] Letter from Grieg to Delius, 18 June 1896 (BOB).
[17] Letter from Delius to Randi Blehr, undated, late June or July 1896 (RA).
[18] Letter from Delius to Randi Blehr, 6 December 1896 (RA).

12. Delius stayed at Haugen, a farm and post house in Bagn, Valdres, for much of his summer holiday in 1896. Here he worked on *Koanga*. The full name of the post house is Gjestgiverhaugen ('The Hostelry Hill').

violinist friend from Hamar, Arve Arvesen, could be rather free-speaking – even creative – in his evaluation of other people's morals. Whether he is the Arvesen in question here, and whether he perhaps had spread rumours about Blehr and Delius, has not been possible to corroborate.

For the next two months, Delius's address was that of a farm called Gjest-giverhaugen (literally, the Hostelry Hill) on the east side of the valley above the village of Bagn, in the district of Sør-Aurdal. Gjestgiverhaugen, or just Haugen, was – like most post houses – both a component in the local transport network and a busy farm. On the north side of the farmyard a two-floor annex had been erected to accommodate travellers. When a survey of the farm was carried out in 1866, there were registered nine acres of cultivated fields and twenty-one acres of hay fields, as well as forest and scrubland.[19] The owner when Delius was a guest, Erik Steingrimson, ran a post house with long tradi-tions. Since the seventeenth century, travellers had found a meal and a bed here. The main road between Eastern and Western Norway followed the Etna

---

[19] Jon Ola Gjermundsen, *Gard og bygd i Sør-Aurdal, Bind B* (*Farms and Villages of Sør-Aurdal, Vol. B*) (Sør-Aurdal: Valdres Bygdeboks forlag, 1988), 102.

valley a few kilometres further east, then climbed the Tonsåsen hill and followed the ridge north to Fagernes. Many travellers chose, however, to come
down from Tonsåsen, passing Haugen, to the sheltered valley of the Begna
river and follow it through Sør-Aurdal north to Fagernes. After the opening in
1906 of the Valdres railway, which followed the main route, traffic past Haugen
dried up.

Delius occupied a corner room on the upper floor of the main farmhouse
and had a magnificent view across the valley, along which the Begna river
curved its way past high hills. He had 'a really terrible piano, but good enough
for my needs',[20] and could work in peace on his opera *Koanga*; he was orches-
trating the first act and planning the second. Parts of the Louisiana opera were
indeed brought to life on a hillside in Valdres. It is striking, the disparity that
existed this summer between the composer's inner creative life and the landscape and culture that surrounded him. The area around Bagn was renowned
for its clean mountain air and attracted large numbers of tubercular refugees
fleeing the pollution of the capital city; the Tonsåsen Sanatorium lay just a few
kilometres away on the hill behind Haugen. With a view of one of the loveliest
valleys in Valdres, Delius sat and composed music that almost steams with
Mississippi atmosphere; he set to music dances and songs he had learned from
black workers in Florida and Virginia; he fashioned a music drama from a
narrative of cruel plantation slavery; if a cowbell tinkled from the hillside, it
would blend with the sound in the composer's head of banjo strumming; when
he wrote in July to Jelka that the farmhands 'are now making hay & the smell
is delicious',[21] his thoughts were simultaneously filled with images of black
workers cutting cane or picking cotton. This duality might even be said to be
a characteristic of his personality: his longing both for the chill mountains of
Norway and the climate and nature of the southern United States. Thomas
Beecham wrote of the composer's twin loves:

> The impression created within him by an exotic landscape and the simple Negro
> life with its songs and dances lingered for long years in his memory. If his spirit
> was attuned to hyperborean regions, snow-clad mountains where no birds sang,
> and mighty fjords, his senses were captured by and remained in willing bondage
> to the antithetical opulence of the tropical South.[22]

From letters Delius sent to Jelka Rosen we can gain insights into the mind
of a man who had found some peace within himself:

> The nights are *grand*: light all night & the color of the atmosphere, the hills &
> the woods & the water is most beautiful – The sun sets at about 8-30 behind

---

[20] Letter from Delius to Randi Blehr, undated, late June or early July 1896 (RA). The piano on
which he worked is still in existence.
[21] Letter from Delius to Jelka, 8 July 1896 (GM).
[22] Beecham, *Frederick Delius*, 34.

the mountain, and immense shadows begin to creep across the great valley – at 10-30 only the tops of the hills, covered with fur [sic] trees are lighted by the sun's rays – and stand out as if in gold. Then the whole disappears in a mystic half-light, a very dreamy and mysterious effect – It is light enough to read & distinguish every detail at the other end of the valley and on the mountain tops – [23]

In the same letter to Jelka, Delius told her that he was living cheaply on the farm, his days simple and unsophisticated: 'I am leading a life quite Adam like'. He joked that he was in the process of becoming 'too country like', and was therefore grateful that she had let him borrow her copy of *Also sprach Zarathustra* – 'invaluable for my present state'. Nietzsche's philosophical and poetic novel about a man who, to gather his life wisdom, forsakes society in favour of an isolated existence in the mountains would have chimed deeply with the composer after three years in the tumult of artistic life in Paris. Jelka sent also poems by Nietzsche that Delius promised to set to music.[24] He was embraced by the daily life of the farm in various ways, not least a large family gathering that took place the week after his arrival:

> The other day we had a funeral here and had an immense time. It was the old grandmother[25] who had just died before my arrival. Just fancy they keep their dead here 8 or 10 days in a cold place – They take death in a most natural & charming way – Nobody seems to care much & they all do as if nothing had occurred – 50 people came for the funeral & it more resembled a feast than anything else – [...] They have a pretty custom here of building a little house of fur [sic] trees and placing the coffin underneath it – before they take it to church to be buried.[26]

Summer 1896: Hamsun, Delius and Jebe

In the first days of August, one of the most remarkable concert troupes ever to entertain a Norwegian audience was to be heard in Valdres. Fritz Delius, Knut Hamsun and Halfdan Jebe combined their talents in a programme of words and music, travelling between hotels and guesthouses, their visits characterised by an abundance of good humour and strong drink. In the Rabelaisian narrative that makes up the friendship of Delius and Jebe, this is one more chapter. Although Knut Hamsun's participation is not conclusively confirmed in any of the primary sources, the circumstantial evidence is overwhelming.

---

[23] Letter from Delius to Jelka, 15 June 1896 (GM).
[24] Apart from the poem *Venedig* (*Venice*) it is unknown which she sent. Two years later, however, Delius had composed four *Lieder nach Gedichten von Friedrich Nietzsche*, perhaps to verses he had received from Jelka in Valdres. *Venedig* was not among them.
[25] Hanna Lovise Helgesdotter (b. 1835), the owner's mother, not grandmother.
[26] Letter from Delius to Jelka, undated, c.26 June 1896 (GM).

Whether by chance or planning, Hamsun and Delius were drawn from the Continent to the same Valdres village at the same time.

Hamsun first came to Aurdal in the autumn of 1884 to recover his health. Then newly returned from the United States, he was ordered by Kristiania doctors to make a retreat to a mountain area where the climate would help him overcome a life-threatening bronchitis. He was then twenty-five years old and had published some articles and short stories. For a year and a half he lived at the Frydenlund post house in Nord-Aurdal (sixteen kilometres north of Bagn). As soon as he was strong enough he engaged in rural society, singing in a choir and travelling to the valley's institutions to give talks on literature. When he returned in the summer of 1896, Hamsun had the successes of *Sult* (*Hunger*, 1890) and *Pan* (1894) behind him and was acknowledged as a leading light in Norwegian letters. He travelled from Munich in the middle of June, and in the first week of July, just as Delius was settling in at Haugen, Hamsun checked in at Tonsåsen Sanatorium. These two artists who, with a high degree of probability, had got to know each other in Paris were now living nine kilometres apart on the same stretch of rural road. With Tonsåsen as his base, Hamsun spent much of the summer travelling around, meeting old friends. In a letter of 24 June, he related: 'I've been up in Slidre visiting acquaintances. I know the whole Valdres valley, although children from my previous time here have grown up and got married.'[27] In the same week that Hamsun was in Slidre, Delius too was on an excursion away from Haugen. It is possible that he first visited the parliamentarian and historian Ole Knutsen Ødegaard at the Løken post house in the western part of Slidre – a visit that had been recommended to him by Randi Blehr before he left Kristiania. However, his main plan, according to a letter to Jelka of 8 July, had been to visit Halfdan Jebe, who was summering with his family in Trondheim; it is likely that around 20 July Delius travelled north to meet him, probably taking the train up Østerdalen from Hamar.[28]

Tupsy, Halfdan's painter sister, was also at the Jebe home in Trondheim. She shot off letter after letter to her beloved Edvard Munch, complaining that she felt suffocated by having to assume a bourgeois lifestyle under her father's roof. Around 23 July, she accompanied her parents to Røros, a picturesque mining village, where they checked in at Fahlstrøm's Hotel. Painter Johannes Müller had a summer house there, but when he had to go away for some days, he left the house – and the keys to the wine cabinet – in the hands of Tupsy. 'I drank a silent toast to you', she wrote to Munch, 'and balanced along his finest

---

[27] Letter from Knut Hamsun to Bolette and Ole Johan Larsen, 24 July 1896. Harald S. Næss (ed.), *Knut Hamsuns brev, II: 1896–1907* (Oslo: Gyldendal, 1995), 31. Slidre is a district in the north of the Valdres region.

[28] Today's branch line from Hamar to Trondheim via Røros was in 1896 the only railway line north. The main line over Dovre opened in 1921.

furniture [and] smoked cigarettes stretched out on his chaise longue'.[29] She soon had company. 'Halfdan and Delius have arrived', she related in a new letter of 26 July, 'they are planning to give concerts and are rehearsing for all they are worth'.[30] On 30 July, she could inform Munch that 'Halfdan and Delius left this aft. for Valdres, where they are planning to give concerts'.[31]

Delius's plans had, it seems, undergone some revision. As late as 8 July (letter to Jelka), he had intended to return directly to Kristiania from Trondheim. A plan for a much livelier alternative had now been hatched and he returned to Valdres with Jebe and a freshly rehearsed concert programme. It seems plausible that a meeting with Knut Hamsun in the weeks prior to his Trondheim/Røros excursion had been the decisive factor, and that they together had hit on the amusing notion of a concert troupe of three performers. From around the first to the fourth of August they may have visited, for example, Tonsåsen Sanatorium, Gjestgiverhaugen, and the post houses at Frydenlund and Løken. Many years later, Jelka noted down her memories of this summer, the details of the concert party no doubt based on letters she had received from Delius or his own recollections:

> On this trip Fred also made a concert tour together with his friend Jebe and with Knut Hamsun. The latter is the well-known Norwegian author. He had quite an imposing appearance and always went about with a grey top-hat and frock coat altho' the tour took place in all sorts of mountain resorts.[32]

Jelka narrated that Hamsun and Jebe were generally drunk: 'On one occasion Hamsun entered an hotel where they were to perform rather pompously as was his wont. Suddenly he fell down full length on the steps of the veranda where all the guests were assembled, shouting: "Jeg trænger Luften!" (I need air).' Delius accompanied Jebe's violin solos and performed some piano pieces. From Thomas Beecham's biography of the composer we have an insight into the breadth of his repertoire on this tour:

> I once asked him what he had played, and he answered, 'All Chopin.' As at that time I had heard him occasionally strumming on the keyboard in a way that in no wise suggested overfamiliarity with the character and capacities of that instrument, I gazed at him incredulously for several moments. But he smiled somewhat mysteriously, and assured me that in very truth he had essayed this courageous task. I remained for quite a while undecided as to which of two possible explanations of the mystery could satisfy my curiosity: his own unbounded

---

[29] Letter from Tupsy Jebe to Munch, 30 July 1896 (MM).

[30] Letter from Tupsy Jebe to Munch, 26 July 1896 (MM).

[31] Letter from Tupsy Jebe to Munch, 30 July 1896 (MM). In this letter, Tupsy also suggested that from time to time Delius overestimated his ability to evaluate other arts than music: 'Delius criticised my work, but I don't have much confidence in him. He painted a sketch himself which was beyond all criticism, but with which he was really pleased.'

[32] 'Jelka Delius' (Gerhardi/Steinweg collection), published in LC1, 412.

assurance, or the undeveloped state of musical culture in Norwegian provincial audiences.[33]

Neither Jelka nor Beecham offered any hint as to what Hamsun's contribution to the programme might have been.[34]

After this diverting episode with Hamsun and Jebe, which had followed six weeks of disciplined work on *Koanga*, Delius was ready to pack his knapsack and trek up into the mountains. He left his music things in safe storage at Haugen and for ten days walked through Jotunheimen and Rondane. It is likely that Jebe returned to Trondheim.

> I, together with a guide tramped for several days across these mountains. [...]
> The feeling is really exquisite up so high & tramping all day – 12 or 14 hours –
> in that invigorating mountain air & I enjoyed it thoroughly. I then cut across
> to Vågå, a lovely & smiling valley on the other side of Jotunheimen, & thence
> over to Gudbrandsdalen where I again cut up into another wild range of hills
> – 'The Rondane' – & tramped for several days over to Folldalen on the other
> side – staying at nights at Seters in a very primitive style – On the top of the
> Rondane group we were overtaken by a tremendous thunder storm – in fact we
> were up so high that we were in it literally, lightning flashing all about us – it
> looked awfully dangerous – but I don't suppose it really was – we lay down in the
> drenching rain & waited until the Lightning became less lively – A few scared
> reindeer rushed by a short distance from us at a tremendous pace – [35]

Delius travelled down Østerdalen to Mjøsa lake and from there on to Gjøvik and so back to Sør-Aurdal and Haugen. After a couple more days on the farm he was itching for the mountains again. Haugen owned at this time a *seter* at Haltkinn in the Ølnessæter hills between Hallingdal and Valdres, and it is probably here that he spent the last days of this long and reinvigorating visit to Norway before returning south to Kristiania.[36]

---

[33] Beecham, *Frederick Delius*, 84.

[34] Hamsun's biographers, if they mention this tour at all, leave the author's participation open to doubt, because it is mentioned in the correspondence neither of Delius nor of Hamsun. (In correspondence with the present author, Hamsun's son and biographer Tore Hamsun also stressed this point.) The fact that neither of them actually wrote any letters in this period might rather be thought to support the argument that they were busy with some other activity that demanded their full attention. Jelka's account has shown itself to be reliable in every other detail.

[35] Letter from Delius to Jelka, 15 August 1896 (GM).

[36] For information about Gjestgiverhaugen I am indebted to its owner, Anne Karine Haugsrud. Thanks to her efforts, the farm buildings and the beautiful surroundings are much as they were in Delius's day.

Koanga: The first opera about African-Americans

The story of *Koanga* was adapted by Delius from the chapter 'The Story of Bras-Coupé', a self-contained episode in the novel *The Grandissimes* (1880) by George W. Cable. Delius and his librettist, Charles F. Keary, took the legend of the escaped slave who had led a guerilla struggle against cruel slave owners, upgraded the slave to be an imposing prince of Africa's Dahomey people, then marinated the whole in arcane voodoo magic. Purely as music drama, *Koanga* is the most conventional of Delius's operas, with dances, ensembles, arias and choral songs. In other ways it is an extraordinarily innovative and bold project, well before its time. African-Americans on stage were far from being a novelty in the 1890s; they performed, however, mostly as comic figures or in popular melodramas. There had also been black opera companies since 1872, but they trod a conservative line, staging standard repertoire or new works based on European and African mythology.[37] To create a serious music drama that not only had African-American roles at its core, but also dealt with the harsh working and living conditions of the blacks, was groundbreaking. Particularly uncompromising were the portrayals of a cynical plantation owner and his brutal, whip-happy henchman.[38] Scott Joplin's 1910 opera *Treemonisha* has some similarities with *Koanga*. He, too, was concerned with black life on a plantation, and emulated folk songs and dances for his ensemble numbers. Unlike Delius, however, he was motivated by a desire to show the liberated blacks intent on improving themselves, setting his moralising tale in 1884 in post-Reconstruction Arkansas.

There are also many infusions of exotic colour in the soundscape of *Koanga*. From his own knowledge of African-American music Delius plucked a bouquet of folk songs and dances, including the brilliant 'La Calinda' in Act 2, and he added two banjos to the orchestra. The composer goes a long way to succeeding, as did Bizet with *Carmen* twenty years earlier, in letting exotic rhythms and melodic nuances establish a distinct tone for the opera. In spite of the Wagnerian recitatives given to the white characters, the composer's striking mix of energetic work songs and underlying melancholy ensures that the whole remains fresh, original and powerful.

Delius's choice of librettist on this occasion was the Englishman Charles F. Keary, with whom he shared a fascination with all things Norwegian. Keary was a historian and novelist, and before advancing to the novel genre had published several works on Viking culture and Old Norse literature. He

---

[37] See Elise K. Kirk, *American Opera* (Champaign: University of Illinois Press, 2001), 186–90.

[38] One precedent for a brutal slave-owner character was to be found in Donizetti's *Il furioso all'isola di San Domingo* (1832) (revived in an English version in 2015 with the title *The Wild Man of the West Indies*). A secondary character, Kaidamà, is a slave who is beaten by his master for having run away. He is, however, a *buffo* character. The opera was hugely popular in the middle of the century.

had obviously researched far less into the sort of daily language that might adequately befit a libretto narrative on a Mississippi plantation. He gave the slaves poetic phrases that would have been better suited to a lyric entertainment in a Victorian drawing room than to cotton fields in the years after the Louisiana Purchase. The American *Koanga* belongs to the periphery of this study. It is, however, worth noting that Delius, when he wished to clothe in music the majestic and maligned African prince, again opened the toolbox he had previously reserved for his most noble Mountain Music. *Koanga*'s plastic leitmotif is flexed and turned in many ways by Delius to convey a spectrum of emotions, but when he represents the slave at his most princely, the motif might have been lifted from one of the composer's *Paa Vidderne* scores (see, for example, the motif in the low strings in Act 1, fig. 17, bars 9–12).

Over the Hills and Far Away: A Norwegian fantasy

Over the Hills and Far Away was described by Delius variously as a fantasia and as a fantasy overture. Precisely when it was written is unclear. An early version was probably begun in the winter of 1895–96 when the composer was longing to be back in the Norwegian highlands after an absence of three years. In the following winter of 1897, Delius was back in Florida and, perhaps once more ridden with nostalgia for Norway, continued to work on the score. He may have borrowed the title from an ancient and popular English folk ballad. It is possible, however, that it had got into his imagination by way of the publication in 1892 of a poetry collection by William E. Henley, in which one poem is called 'Over the Hills and Far Away':[39]

> Out of the sound of the ebb-and-flow,
> Out of the sight of lamp and star,
> It calls you where the good winds blow,
> And the unchanging meadows are;
> From faded hopes and hopes agleam,
> It calls you, calls you night and day
> Beyond the dark into the dream
> Over the hills and far away.[40]

The poetic English title of the composition has to a certain degree masked the fact that *Over the Hills and Far Away* is one of Delius's quintessentially Norwegian mountain works. As were *Paa Vidderne* and *On the Mountains*, this is an exploration of a part of his personality that he wished to express through metaphors of the mountainscape and mountain journey. If the Violin Sonata

---

[39] Delius would go on to set Henley verses to music on two occasions: *The Nightingale Has a Lyre of Gold* (1910) and *A Late Lark* (1924).

[40] William E. Henley, 'Over the Hills and Far Away', verse 3, from the collection *The Song of Swords and Other Verses* (London: David Nutt, 1892).

in B Major is included in the sequence, then *Over the Hills and Far Away* is a fourth stage in the composer's ongoing refinement of the idiomatic language he had fashioned for such works: Mountain Music (see Table 2, p. 45).

In this instance, the material is developed almost exclusively from horn calls that correspond to the two categories 'Peak'-music and 'Plateau'-music, and to four of their six idiomatic types. It has an episodic structure, a sequence of reflections on Mountain Music motifs:

Bar	Section	Category
0	A	Plateau B
40	B	Peak A
87	C	Plateau C
109	D	Peak C
160	C2	Plateau C
183	A2	Plateau B
225	B2	Peak A
259	Coda	Peak C

Gone are the energetic and dynamic openings that propelled both *Paa Vidderne* and *On the Mountains* out into the wilderness. Instead, the fantasy overture has a prelude of reflective wonderment (*andante molto tranquillo*), the mood formed from two simple herding calls. The second of them, a rolling call (Example 6.2) is similar to others Delius had used to convey the reflective and naked spirit, the wanderer in a wide, open landscape (type 'Plateau B'):

Example 6.1 *Over the Hills and Far Away*, 1–6

Example 6.2 *Over the Hills and Far Away*, 7–10

When we arrive at the B-section's *allegro*, a variant of Example 6.1 bursts in with springing, rising rhythms (type 'Peak A') before the motif finally divests itself of all introversion and is sounded boldly as a brass fanfare. The C-section, however, introduces a melody soaked in the melancholic modality of type 'Plateau C':

Example 6.3 *Over the Hills and Far Away*, 87–8

The central D-section of the work consists of a sequence of small variations on Example 6.4, a pentatonic herding call:

Example 6.4 *Over the Hills and Far Away*, 109–12

Among them is a variant for strings (117–24) that is the most chromatic music Delius had written up to that point. Finally – as did Example 6.1 earlier – Example 6.4 throws off its shepherd fleece and reveals itself capable of heroic majesty (141–55).

Over the Hills and Far Away is less musically adventurous than most other scores Delius created in this period, particularly parts of *The Magic Fountain* and *Koanga*. The constant generation of melodic material from a few simple motifs that typified the violin sonata and the love duets of the operas is almost absent here. At the same time, the overture is rich in captivating mountain melody, has well-turned, distinct episodes, and has been spared any of the overblown climaxes of the composer's previous mountain work for orchestra, *On the Mountains*. Memories of, and longing for, the highlands had stimulated Delius's creative imagination and his responses were never anything other than genuine. The duality of the mountain experience – both solitude and majesty – is present already in the raw material of Examples 6.1 and 6.2; from those two motifs grow both reflective wonder and strident fanfares. So satisfied was Delius with the uplifted mood he built from these themes that he would call on them again for exalted moments in his two masterpieces of the early twentieth century: *A Village Romeo and Juliet* (1900–02) and *A Mass of Life* (1904–05) (see pp. 189, 190 and 200).

Several times in *Over the Hills and Far Away* Delius also acknowledges his fundamental attraction to the highlands with a familiar signature. As a closing gesture at the end of each episode (74, 104, 255) and again as a valedictory motif at the close (262, 272), the *Paa Vidderne* fanfare is called across the texture, just as it was in the melodrama (Example 3.5) and at the close of *On the Mountains*. At work on the score through dark days in Paris, and then later in the subtropical forest of Florida, this signal perhaps resounded in the composer as a resolution to return to Norway at the first opportunity.

A time for decisions

On his way home to France from his long summer in Norway in 1896, Delius made visits to opera impresarios in Copenhagen and Karlsruhe, without waking any enthusiasm for his work. 'I hope something will come from somewhere shortly', he sighed in a letter to Jelka Rosen. 'I am getting sick of all my futile efforts to get heard.'[41] He hoped to make enough to live on from the sale of songs, producing a handful of settings of J. P. Jacobsen verses and several beautiful songs to French texts. These latter were published in Paris in 1896, probably sponsored by one of the composer's more devoted aristocratic female admirers. The breakthrough, however, seemed as far off as ever. Delius worked on with undiminished energy on *Koanga* and for a whole year memories of his years in America had stimulated his creative work, inspiring some of the finest music he had written. This strong flood of exotic Americana overflowed at the close of 1896 into a small orchestral work, *Appalachia: American Rhapsody for Orchestra*.[42] No less motivating for him was the fact that, in the late summer, he had resolved to escape the European winter and spend some months in the United States. Once again, Jelka Rosen interpreted his decision as a forewarning that their intimate friendship was coming to an end. In December, she was invited to his apartment in Rue Ducouëdic:

> His Norwegian friend, the violinist Halfdan Jebe was there too, and they intended to go back to the orange grove in Florida for some months. Fred wanted to see the place as the negro in charge pocketed all the gains. I was miserable about Fred's going so far away, and the terrible fear – a kind of obsession – clutched at my heart that all would [be] over, that he would have forgotten our friendship on his return. He was so fascinating and had so many women friends, lovely Scandinavians, English and French.[43]

It seems that the decision to travel to Florida was one link in a comprehensive financial, artistic and personal process that had been going on in Delius's life throughout 1896 in the wake of his health crisis. The purely financial aspect was represented by his wish to tidy his affairs on the plantation and, if possible, make it a secure source of income. In addition, an American impresario, Victor Thrane (grandson of the Norwegian socialist leader Marcus Thrane), had taken an interest in Delius's music and encouraged him to test it out on the

---

[41] Letter from Delius to Jelka, undated, c.26 June 1896 (GM).
[42] This first *Appalachia* has little in common with the masterly *Appalachia* of 1902–03, apart from some themes and moods. The Indian name Appalachia was originally that of a village in Florida, but in the sixteenth century was applied by the Spanish to the whole region.
[43] 'Jelka Delius' (Gerhardi/Steinweg collection), published in LC1, 412.

American concert scene. As for his music, he had now resolved that he would no longer squander invaluable time trying to sell himself to opera producers. He wrote to Jutta Bell: 'I have neither wish nor energy enough to go kicking around the ante chambers of well known Conductors & as I feel quite certain that one of these days they will be kicking their heels in my ante chamber I give myself no trouble about them.'[44] He added that he washed his hands of publishers who had so little faith in him that they would not forward an advance: 'I am not going to publish anything more gratis, even if I die of starvation.'

On a more personal level, the trip to Solana Grove in 1897 may have been made with a particular goal. After Delius's death, his close friend Percy Grainger disseminated the story that the main reason for the Florida visit was to try and find the black lover he had there in 1885, perhaps also to bring her and their son back to Europe. Grainger being the only source of this version of events, Delius commentators have been divided as to how much veracity it contains. Considering the fact that Grainger was deeply committed to notions of racial purity, it seems unlikely he would invent such an anecdote about one his closest friends. If it is correct, it strongly nuances the impression often given of Delius as an inveterate egoist – a picture that dominated early biographies, but which is based for most part on the testimony of people who knew the composer late in life when his disease had hardened his personality. While a shake-up of the plantation was intended to secure a steady income, this search for his lover – if it happened – may have been an attempt to secure his peace of mind.

He and Jebe spent Christmas and New Year in Bradford and with Delius's sister Clare in her old house at Stone Gappe on the wild Yorkshire moorlands. She recalled them all enjoying a long hike, and as they tramped across the heather the men 'sang the Norwegian National Anthem in Norwegian at the top of their voices. [...] Fred tall, handsome, aloof – Jebe, a medieval troubadour born out of his time, gloriously indifferent to material things, and letting the morrow take care of itself.'[45]

On 9 January, Delius sailed from his troubles in Europe. At just the same time, a Norwegian moved to Paris as correspondent for the Kristiania daily, *Verdens Gang*. Gunnar Heiberg and the Norwegian national anthem would be waiting for Delius when he returned from his American adventure.

---

[44] Letter from Delius to Jutta Bell, undated, late December 1896 (JUL).
[45] Clare Delius, *Frederick Delius*, 119.

7

1897
Front page news

'the most unpopular man in Norway'

        Delius, as described in *Verdens Gang*, 23 October 1897

For a whole month in October and November 1897, Delius would be front page news in Norway on account of the scandal he caused with his music for the theatre comedy *Folkeraadet*. At the start of the year he had also kept the gossip columnists and headline writers of the New York press busy.

For several years, the composer had indulged in an affair with one of the most beautiful of Parisian aristocrats. Born Marie Léonie Mortier de Trévise in 1866, she had been married since 1888 to the Prince of Cystria, Baron de Faucigny-Lucinge. A child of the *Belle Époque*, she was more attracted to the cultural life of the great city than to her family's grand estate, which she was destined to inherit. A proficient singer herself, the Princesse de Cystria attracted the leading musicians of Paris to her salons, including Ravel and Debussy. Her love for Delius seems to have been genuine and enduring and it led to her accompanying him and Halfdan Jebe on their journey to Florida in 1897. In his 1959 biography of the composer, Thomas Beecham relates that for Delius the expedition was in part a way for him to flee the princess's obsessive attentions, and that she disguised herself as a man, stole on to the ship, and only disclosed her identity '[four] hundred miles out at sea, and six full days to run before reaching the haven of New York'.[1] It is a beguiling version of the events that has been repeated in Delius biographies since. Nevertheless, it is a narrative that more than likely was invented by Delius at some later date to make the participation of the princess in the America trip easier to swallow for Jelka. The sources reveal a different course of events which – for elements of farce, masquerade and prankish mischief – trounces the invented version by a good margin.

---

[1] Beecham, *Frederick Delius*, 87.

Far from being a disguised and secret passenger, the Princesse de Cystria boarded the liner *New York* in Southampton together with Delius and Jebe.[2] It is true that she diverted attention by using one of her less dazzling titles, Mme de Faucigny, but a covert operation it was not. Delius, on the other hand, did travel under a false name: Cyril Grey. As it turned out, the party was unsuccessful in avoiding the attention of their fellow passengers. A maid of Marie Léonie let slip that she was serving a princess, and on the ship's arrival in New York early on 16 January a number of newspapers sent reporters to interview the princess and the mysterious Mr Grey. That same day, *The Evening Telegraph* announced in bold headlines:

PREFERS TO BE
KNOWN AS BARONESS

But Fellow Passengers on the New
York Think She Is a Princess Incog.

SHE IS SURROUNDED BY MYSTERY.
Attentive Mr Grey, Who Seems to Know All About Her.

In paragraph after paragraph the newspaper related for its readers the gossip concerning the behaviour of the baroness during the crossing, and all the time the equally enigmatic Cyril Grey orbited the baroness, trying to keep journalists at arm's length. 'Mr Grey appeared to be a well-to-do Frenchman', conjectured the paper. 'He was stylishly attired in English cut clothes, has dark complexion and dark hair and a small black mustache, twisted at the ends.'[3] *The New York Herald* noted Mr Grey's protective manner in regard to the baroness: 'Here her guide, philosopher and friend appeared upon the scene and protested against any questions being put to the woman. He would tell them all they wanted to know.'[4] Delius then fed the reporters disinformation that succeeded in both obscuring the reality and further piquing their curiosity. The baroness intended to travel to Brazil, he informed them. Or was it Puerto Rico?

The next day, journalists set up camp at the Metropolitan Hotel in an attempt to solve the riddle. The scent of mystery made for good copy and the New York papers hungrily hunted this story. *The World* was on the trail:

About 7 P. M. he came down from his room, where he had been all day, and hurried through the hotel office. He was buttonholed by half a dozen reporters who had been waiting for him. After a few protests and shrugs he finally consented to be interviewed.

'Yes,' he said, 'my name is Cyril Grey. That is to say, that is the name on the passenger list, and that is enough of a name for anybody. I am an Englishman. I

---

[2] Passenger lists accessed 14 November 2015 at www.nationalarchives.gov.uk.
[3] *The Evening Telegram*, 16 January 1897.
[4] *The New York Herald*, 17 January 1897.

am nobody. Who I am or what my business is here concerns nobody but myself. I am travelling for pleasure and shall probably go West to find it.'

'And the Princess?' asked the reporter.

'Ah, you mean Madame, the lady. I do not see why her name as it is on the passenger list does not content you. It is most indelicate to say more about her in the papers. But then Americans have strange ways of doing things, anyway. Princess? Of course she is a princess. Any woman who holds the position she does in the De Faucigny family would be entitled to be called princess.

[...]

With a deprecating curl of his mustache, 'Cyril Grey' turned on his heel and walked away.[5]

When the papers discovered the party's connection to impresario Victor Thrane, there was fresh speculation that the princess was merely an actress and that the travelling party was a spectacular publicity stunt for some theatrical tour. *The World* cornered Thrane and the publicist in him could not resist a bit of a flourish: "'Yes, she is a princess,' said Victor Thrane, "and the heiress to a throne. She and her party are passing through this country on a mission quite as strange and interesting as any that has been hinted at in the newspapers.'"[6] By the time the party was ready to leave New York, the media had enrolled both the princess and Halfdan Jebe in the Brazilian aristocracy. One newspaper reported:

> The Princess incognita left the Metropolitan yesterday, and, accompanied by her maid and Balfedein Jebe [sic], boarded a train for the South. Cyril Grey remains. He announced his intention yesterday of leaving for the West the latter part of the week. It is thought that Balfedein Jebe is the son of Comte D'Eu [Imperial consort of Brazil], and that the Princess is a member of the Brazilian Imperial family.[7]

It is possible that Delius travelled with Thrane to meet the impresario's family in Eau Claire, Wisconsin, before again meeting up with Jebe and the princess. The trio was certainly reunited by the end of January in Danville, Virginia, the town where Delius had been a music teacher in 1885–86. Now among old friends, Delius of course let the mask drop, while the disguises of his companions became even more far-fetched. Now the princess had become a renowned Russian diva and Jebe had been promoted to a professor of the violin by the name of Mr Lemmanoff. On 30 January they gave a concert, which was reviewed by the local newspaper:

> Madame Donodossola gave delightful rendition to several choice selections, and was heartily encored. Mr Lemmanoff, by his brilliant technique, charmed his audience in his violin numbers. Mr Delius was very happy in his

---

[5] *The World*, 18 January 1897.
[6] *Ibid.*
[7] *The World*, 22 January 1897.

accompaniments and his old friends in the city were pleased to hear the evidence of his talent as a composer in the composition of his which Madame Donodossola so faithfully rendered.[8]

Exactly why the three travellers should devote so much energy to this hoax is uncertain. For Delius and the princess, their affair demanded a degree of discretion. The masquerade seems, however, equally likely to be an expression of Delius's sense of humour. And this bubbled to the surface again in May when he and Jebe, returning home from New York, entered their names in the passenger list of the liner *Orinoco* as C. Grey and C. J. Grey – Delius and Jebe, blithe brothers happily defying the norms of society.[9] For Delius there may also have been an element of 'stag party' exuberance to his various ruses, for he was determined to lead a disciplined life on his return to France. This was in fact the last journey he would undertake with his restless Norwegian friend.

The trio finally arrived in Jacksonville and took the paddle steamer up the St Johns River to Delius's plantation, Solana Grove. Delius and Jebe stayed there from February until the end of April; the princess was also at the grove for a period before continuing her journey, probably south to Guadeloupe.

Neither the personal nor the financial goals Delius had set himself for the journey were achieved. According to Percy Grainger, the black woman who – in this version of events – had been Delius's lover was warned of his visit and 'thinking he might want to take the child away from her, fled […] & he never heard what became of her & the child'.[10] On the business side of things, there were initially grounds for optimism. Delius leased out the plantation to tobacco growers and the prospects were good for some regular income. Shortly after his return to Europe, however, the deal fell through.

During his first stay in the subtropical climate of the St Johns River, 1884–85, Delius had cooled himself with fantasies of Norway and, with Jutta Bell as guide, had explored treasures of Norwegian song. In the spring of 1897, he again had ample time to compose and once more it seems that his longing for the chill and expansive plateaus of Norway influenced much that he wrote. We have already seen that he wrote parts of *Over the Hills and Far Away* while on the plantation. In the main, however, he worked on the first version of his Piano Concerto in C Minor, and also here elements of his Mountain Music insinuated themselves into the material.

---

[8] 'The Delius Concert' in *Danville Register*, 31 January 1897.
[9] Jebe had perhaps a more moderate sense of humour. In 1905, he tried to tempt Delius to accompany him on a tour of Pacific countries, but stipulated a few conditions: 'Well prepared, no idiocies, no princesses, and no false names, – ours are good enough.' Letter from Halfdan Jebe to Delius, 24 April 1905 (DT).
[10] Letter from Percy Grainger to Richard Muller, 5 October 1941 (GM).

The first version of the piano concerto on which Delius worked at Solana Grove bears the title 'Fantasy for Orchestra and Pianoforte' and was constructed as a one-movement work in a sequence of episodes. When the work finally arrived on the concert platform in 1904 it had been revised and expanded into a larger opus with three movements. Before its publication in 1907, however, it had undergone a new revision: the composer had forged his material into yet another version in one movement. The majority of the musical material was already present in the early Florida manuscript.

Suggestions of his Mountain Music mark some of the melodic material, although less stridently than in the mountain works for orchestra such as *Paa Vidderne* and *Over the Hills and Far Away*. We recognise the first cell of the opening melody (Example 7.1, *x*), presented by the strings, as a typical 'horn call', and indeed this motif will reappear later in the work as a call for solo horn:

Example 7.1 Piano Concerto, 1–5

Energetic dotted rhythms (type 'Peak A') lift the music forward (fig. 1). It is however in the character of the concerto's large and majestic climaxes that we most clearly discern traits that have typified the composer's mountain scores. The brief, soft theme that introduces the work's central section is suddenly infused with muscular energy and is lifted by upward-striving triplets to new heights; finally, after fig. 9, it is transferred to the horn section and lifted high into clearer air.

The piano concerto was among the earliest works by Delius to gain international acclaim. Throughout the first decades of the twentieth century, piano virtuosi performed it in Europe and North America. Paradoxically, its popularity can to a large extent be ascribed to the composer's backward gaze in the construction of the work, with stylistic traits similar to Romantic concertos by Schumann and Grieg.

Jelka Rosen heard nothing from Delius during the first months after his departure; only in April did he deign to send her a letter from Solana Grove. She resigned herself again to the inevitability of her dream of a permanent relationship turning to dust. However, around the same time as 'C. Grey' was boarding the *Orinoco* in New York for his return voyage, Jelka's life was taking an unexpected turn. When he finally arrived back in the Rue Ducouëdic at the end of May, Delius found a letter from her that contained surprising news.

The owner of the beautiful house and garden in Grez-sur-Loing had got into financial difficulties and Jelka had managed with the help of her mother to scrape enough cash together to purchase the house. She had just moved in, together with a painter friend, Ida Gerhardi. If she could not match princesses and other fine ladies for their wealth or beauty, she was now in possession of a property that offered an ideal environment for creative work. Shortly after, she received a postcard from Paris: 'that fateful postcard that almost made my heart cease beating: it was from Fred and said that he was back from Florida and coming to see me the next day'.[11] Delius arrived in the quiet village of Grez with a small suitcase, checked into a local hotel for a few weeks, then later moved into Jelka's house, a guest who never again moved out.

> From the outset Fred worked there most contentedly. In the afternoon we had beautiful walks. [Ida and I] painted in the garden and [we] had our evening meal in the yard with the gorgeous summer-evening sun glowing on the big trees near the river that made the background of our vista. Talking of all those inexhaustible subjects until the sun faded and the moon rose over the river and came up to shine on the simple, white old house and the purplish-brown roofs and grey walls.[12]

During most of his adventure in America, Delius had not taken the trouble to keep in touch with Jelka, and now he was suddenly living under her roof. From our distance, he seems undoubtedly to be exploiting the situation to his advantage. To Jelka, it remained always 'the apogee of my life, Delius's coming to Grez'.[13] A close friend, the German journalist and publisher Heinrich Simon, would later sum up this aspect of their relationship:

> Very often some instinct tells a man of this kind what is best. It is not selfishness in the ordinary sense; it is an economy of nature, which seeks to get the utmost out of what it meets. Creative genius must be selfish. Delius was no exception and in that sense he was an egoist. He must surely have felt that this woman would become his best friend and most devoted friend and yet would not lose her own personality – a thought abhorrent to Delius, who hated colourless people and loved the beauty and variety of life.[14]

Gunnar Heiberg: from Paris to paradise

Forty years after the scandal surrounding *Folkeraadet*, the theatre critic of Bergen's leading newspaper would look back and evaluate it as 'the most significant

---

[11] 'Jelka Delius' (Gerhardi/Steinweg collection), published in LC1, 413.
[12] *Ibid.*, 414.
[13] *Ibid.*, 415.
[14] Heinrich Simon, 'Jelka Delius' in *The Monthly Musical Record* (December 1935), reprinted in Redwood, *A Delius Companion*, 132.

theatrical event of the 90s'.[15] The seeds of this momentous event were sown far from the streets of Kristiania, in an idyllic country garden south of Paris. In mid-July, the Norwegian dramatist and journalist Gunnar Heiberg entered the house at Grez, one of the first guests to seek out Delius in his new retreat. Just when Heiberg got to know Delius is unknown; they had many acquaintances in common in both Kristiania and Paris. Since the start of the year, Heiberg had been Paris correspondent for the left-wing Kristiania paper *Verdens Gang*, a position that left him plenty of time for creative work. His newest comedy had been accepted by Norway's then principal theatre, the Christiania Theater, and Heiberg wished to commission from Delius entertaining incidental music. Jelka showed him proudly round her property and in later correspondence Heiberg would sigh about her 'paradise garden in Grez'[16] and 'le beau, faux paradis'.[17] There, under the midsummer sun, with insects buzzing around the wine glasses, composer and author reached an agreement. Heiberg and Delius were harnessed together in a project that barely three months later would cause one of the fiercest protests in the history of Norwegian theatre. The most poisonous invective would be poured onto their heads by the press and cultural elite of Kristiania. Some would accuse them of grievous sins that were committed as far back as this first evening around a table in Jelka's living room or on the terrace of her overgrown garden: that Gunnar Heiberg, for so deeply Norwegian a play, should ask a foreigner to supply music, and that Fritz Delius should have been so insensitive as to accept the commission.

'Everyone noticed Gunnar Heiberg straight away', writes Einar Skavlan in his Heiberg biography. 'His appearance was unusual. He had light red hair, cut short, intense blue eyes behind his pince-nez, a broad, meaty face and a large sensual mouth with large lips. He had an almost greedy appearance.'[18] Heiberg was born in Kristiania in 1857. His father, a lawyer, was interested in the theatre and sat for some years on Christiania Theater's board of directors. On his mother's side he was a cousin of Helge Rode, Delius's poet friend in Copenhagen. The young Heiberg entered the law faculty at the University of Kristiania, but abhorred the fact that the institution – still governed by some of the most conservative forces in Norwegian society – had banned any teaching in the theory of evolution. He changed tack, choosing instead to devote himself to poetry and drama and drawing his inspiration from two contemporary springs. In Copenhagen, Georg Brandes had become a vociferous opponent of the traditional power of the church and the bourgeois system. And much closer to home, the Norwegian theatre had provided the most radical thinkers

---

[15] Christen Gran Bøgh, 'Studenterliv i nittiårene. Små erindringer' ('Student Life in the 90s. Brief Recollections') in *Bergens Tidende*, 5 August 1941, 5.

[16] Letter from Gunnar Heiberg to Delius, 22 September 1897 (DT).

[17] Letter from Gunnar Heiberg to Delius, undated, late summer 1897 (DT).

[18] Einar Skavlan, *Gunnar Heiberg* (Oslo: H. Aschehoug & Co., 1950), 7.

13. Caricature of dramatist Gunnar Heiberg by Olaf Gulbransson.

of the day with a cultural arena. In his study of Heiberg, Knut Nygaard points out that in his most receptive years as a young man,

> the contemporary dramas of Bjørnson and Ibsen came thick and fast, each one more likely to disturb the status quo than the last, and turning the theatre into a battleground where one could argue about ideas and proclaim the truth. And it was in this phalanx of poets he wanted to march, in order to prepare the way for a new age.[19]

Not that the capital city's theatres were always open to radical texts. One in particular had a conservatively-minded management that preferred to shy away from anything with an aroma of sedition or immorality: Christiania Theater, the city's principal theatre.[20] In Norway, the customary form of protest was not to boo, but to whistle, and in 1881 Heiberg had whistled with the best of them his dissatisfaction when Christiania Theater had refused to stage Ibsen's *Gengangere* (*Ghosts*). In 1884, Heiberg's first play, *Tante Ulrikke* (*Aunt*

---

[19] Knut Nygaard, *Gunnar Heiberg: Teatermannen* (Bergen: Universitetsforlaget, 1975), 11.
[20] Christiania Theater was situated at the corner of Bankplassen and Kirkegate. In 1899, its functions having been transferred to the new Nationaltheater, it was demolished to make way for Norges Bank, a building that today houses the Museum of Contemporary Art. The entrance to the theatre lay some forty yards east of the entrance to today's museum.

Ulrikke), was published in Copenhagen – but rejected by Christiania Theater. His two most important texts of the early 1890s, *Kong Midas* and *Balkonen* (*The Balcony*), were also both rejected by Christiania Theater, the first because it was thought to parody the character of Bjørnstjerne Bjørnson, and the second because it propounded a liberal attitude to sexual morals. The theatre's reputation as a bastion of conservatism was further reinforced when *Kong Midas* was accepted by Det Kongelige Teater (Royal Danish Theatre) in Copenhagen.

Kong Midas established Heiberg as a bold and innovative voice in the cultural life of Scandinavia, and he quickly became known for his characteristic blend of genuine engagement with social and political issues and a biting irony. The sheer force of his revolt against the conservatism of church and state ensured that his plays inflamed and enthused audiences in equal measure. It became, therefore, a typical feature of a Heiberg first night that the final curtain set off a competition for supremacy between those applauding and those whistling. As a dramatic artist, Heiberg was also credited in Norway with developing naturalistic styles of dialogue.[21] It seems surprising that a dramatist who could set alight a theatre audience a hundred years ago is so completely absent from today's repertoire, even in Norway – a fate he shares with Bjørnstjerne Bjørnson. The issues that defined and inspired his creative identity, including the struggle for national independence, were social concerns that to all intents and purposes have passed into history.

Faced with Heiberg's position as the most talented dramatist of his generation, the obduracy of Christiania Theater's board members in keeping him from their stage became untenable. They were subjected to constant pressure by the radical press, and finally in 1897, when the manuscript of *Folkeraadet* was submitted, they relented. Heiberg's political comedy would have its première at the nation's foremost theatre.

To Kristiania during the general election

Gunnar Heiberg's principal reason for accepting the position of journalist in Paris was the opportunity it gave him to pursue his long-standing affair with painter Oda Krohg, wife of Christian Krohg. In the summer, artists swarmed from Paris to the picturesque village of Grez-sur-Loing, and it also worked its charm on Oda. On his trips from the capital to visit her there, Heiberg would have had plenty of opportunity to clarify for Delius exactly what he required in the way of incidental music to *Folkeraadet*: a prelude to Act I – a pithy, lively overture – and interludes before Acts II, III and V, where there were scenery

---

[21] See Ivo de Figueiredo, *ord/kjøtt: Norsk scenedramatikk 1890–2000* (*word/flesh: Norwegian theatre drama 1890–2000*) (Oslo: Cappelen Damm, 2014), 55.

changes.[22] Throughout the composition period, Delius worked to verbal information supplied by the dramatist, and may not have seen the text before arriving in Kristiania. The mere thought of an Aristophanic comedy poking fun
at the bourgeoisie and the inflated conceit of politicians would have appealed
instinctively to 'Cyril Grey' – to the part of Delius that played astrologer and
palmist in the salons of Parisian aristocrats and laughed behind a fictional
identity in the salons of ocean liners.

Just when the notion of employing the Norwegian national anthem sur-
faced, and whose idea it was, is unknown. In an undated letter, probably from
Kristiania in mid-September, Heiberg wrote to Delius that he was enclosing
'the melody'. This may have been the national anthem or the folk song 'Kjerringa med staven', as both turn up in the incidental music. Heiberg also seemed
concerned about slow progress on the musical front: 'The play will likely be
staged in the very near future, so you really must hurry.'[23] Late in September,
Heiberg was about to direct the first rehearsals of *Folkeraadet*. When he wrote
to Delius on the twenty-second, the opening date had not been fixed, but he
warned that it could not be more than three or four weeks away. (This remarkable situation is explained by the fact that in a low-technological age, works
that performed poorly could be pulled pretty much overnight and plays rarely
ran for more than a week.) Heiberg was looking forward to seeing Delius again
and expected this to be in Paris, an indication that Delius initially had no plans
to break off a period of intense creativity to travel to Kristiania. In the same
letter, however, Heiberg also provided Delius with a rundown of the available
brass instruments in the theatre orchestra: only two horns, two trumpets and
one trombone. It was perhaps this sobering information that tipped the balance. A couple of days later, Delius packed his trunk and rushed north from
Paris, travelling day and night by train through Germany and Denmark to
arrive in the Norwegian capital as speedily as possible.

On 1 October he was installed, and could follow and influence rehearsals
right up to the first performance on Monday 18 October. The days were inten-
sive, the production process demanding all of Delius's energies; a good deal
of the music was also written in Kristiania. Nevertheless, it would have been
impossible for him to ignore the febrile atmosphere in the city. He had arrived
in Kristiania when the campaign for the approaching parliamentary election
was at its most belligerent, and the newspapers were full of party propaganda.
During breaks in theatre rehearsals and round the dinner table everyone was
talking politics. A couple of days before the première, Delius wrote to Jelka a
letter that suggests he had gained some inkling of the consequences that might
ensue from his use of the national anthem:

---

[22] A couple of melodramatic moments in the action were also enlivened with a few bars of musical accompaniment. These were most likely composed at short notice during the rehearsals.
[23] Letter from Gunnar Heiberg to Delius, undated, probably mid-September 1897 (DT).

14. For nearly four weeks in October and November 1897 Delius's music to *Folkeraadet* was the focus of ferocious protest at Christiania Theater. This photo is from 1899, the theatre decorated for its final performance before demolition.

Kristiania is in suspense and there will very probably be a 'manifestation'. At the theatre they are afraid that my music will cause trouble as I have employed the *National hymn*. […] On the whole I am *very, very glad* I came; I know now where I am: and this affair is of the greatest importance for my future work. As long as they don't lynch me or stone me too badly I don't mind.[24]

No rehearsals were held on the actual election day in Kristiania, 14 October – just four days before the first night. This gave Delius the opportunity to spend several hours at the same table as Henrik Ibsen, probably at the dramatist's customary watering hole, the Grand Hotel. The aging radical, who no doubt relished the thought of a theatre scandal, pronounced himself 'very much interested' and 'promised to be there'.[25] By an extraordinary coincidence, Edvard and Nina Grieg arrived at the Grand Hotel on this same day. They were on their way from Bergen to England by way of Copenhagen, continuing their journey next day by the night train. Grieg had arranged to meet conductor Iver Holter at the Grand to discuss their plans for a Norsk Musikkfest (Norwegian Music Festival) in 1898. It would be something of an anomaly if Delius and Grieg were in the same hotel but did not meet. The sources offer,

[24] Letter from Delius to Jelka, 16 October 1897 (GM).
[25] *Ibid.*

however, no hint of a reunion between the old friends. Both Edvard and Nina were struggling with health problems just then, and perhaps found it expedient to keep a low profile. Nevertheless, it might still be taken as a sign that the overflowing warmth they had previously found in each other's friendship had cooled somewhat.

A reunion would certainly have taken place between Delius and Edvard Munch. The artist was in Kristiania in connection with an exhibition of his works and Delius would no doubt have made every effort to see the show before it was taken down on 18 October, the same day as *Folkeraadet's* first night. The exhibition was a comprehensive presentation of old and new works – eighty-five paintings, sixty-five prints and thirty drawings.

The 1897 election: a watershed moment in Norwegian history

Folkeraadet was destined to become 'the most significant theatrical event of the 90s', to quote again the theatre critic of *Bergens Tidende*. The combination of text and music alone go only part of the way to explaining why it should have won this accolade. Only when the timing of the first night is also taken into account can we begin to comprehend the uproar caused by the event. The première took place at the climax of a general election; and not any general election, but one of the most decisive votes in the struggle for national independence. On both sides, therefore, the dominant issues went far beyond questions of social rights or taxation. The prime concern was about the identity of the nation, perhaps even its very existence.[26]

The general election of October 1897 was fought, directly and indirectly, on the question of dissolution of the union. In the party programme for the right-wing Høyre the electorate was warned that the radical alternative would force on the country this dissolution. Emphasis was placed on the damage that would be wreaked on commerce by war rhetoric and by the shadows of superpowers lurking offstage. For its part the left-wing Venstre was aiming for a sweeping victory. With a constitutional majority (two-thirds of parliament, seventy-six seats), the party would have a mandate to enact the two pillars of its political programme: suffrage for men over the age of twenty-five and a 'clean' Norwegian flag.[27] This extension of the franchise would empower sections of the population that could not be expected to feel the pull of conservatism as did the ruling bourgeois class. At subsequent elections an enlarged electorate would therefore ensure stronger demands for independence.

---

[26] The story and statistics of the 1897 election related in this chapter have for most part been drawn from the leading Norwegian newspapers of the day: *Morgenbladet*, *Aftenposten*, *Verdens Gang*, *Norske Intelligenssedler*, *Ørebladet* and *Social-Demokraten*.

[27] The Norwegian flag was considered by nationalists to be sullied by the union mark in one corner, a mishmash of the two countries' colours popularly known as 'the herring salad'.

If the conservative right wing lost the election, it fully expected the eventual, but unavoidable, consequence to be war with Sweden. If the left wing could win the election, it expected the country to unite behind it in loosening the ties of union that bound Norway to Sweden and hampered its independent growth. And for supporters of both camps the national anthem, 'Ja, vi elsker dette landet' ('Yes, We Love This Country'), was the emblem of what they were campaigning for.

The election took place over several weeks across the length and breadth of Norway. Already at the end of the first week, Venstre had secured fifty-seven representatives, passing its result from the previous election in 1894. As election day in Kristiania approached, eighty-six seats had been won, sixty-nine of them by Venstre. There were still twenty-eight seats to contest and the growing probability of the left securing the constitutional majority of seventy-six galvanised both fronts to renewed efforts in what was dubbed 'The Battle of Kristiania'. A provisional result was published in the press on the morning of Saturday 16 October and confirmed on Monday 18 October – the day of the *Folkeraadet* première. Venstre took Kristiania with a small margin and the party's constitutional majority was now all but secure. The final result of the general election would eventually show a landslide for the left wing, Venstre taking seventy-nine seats to Høyre's twenty-five, and smaller parties securing ten.

It is difficult to imagine a moment during Norway's march towards independence when it would have been less favourable for a foreigner to be suspected of making fun of the national anthem. Long before the first night of *Folkeraadet*, news had spread that Delius had written variations on 'Ja, vi elsker' for comic effect. Passionately interested in all things Norwegian, he should perhaps have been fully capable of reading the writing on the wall. Indeed, as late as the summer of 1896 he had enjoyed close contact with leading figures in the country's political life, such as Randi and Otto Blehr. We have noted, however, that he struggled to grasp the complexities of Norwegian–Swedish politics (see p. 99). On the day he arrived in Kristiania, he sighed in a letter to Jelka: 'As soon as I come out of your garden at Grez, everything appears to me to be in an uproar.'[28] Five weeks of uproar were to follow.

It was mentioned above that Christiania Theater strove to keep Norway's pre-eminent, but troublesome, dramatist from its hallowed stage. In retrospect, it seems even more astonishing that the theatre would choose *this* opportunity to open its doors to Gunnar Heiberg, offering his *Folkeraadet* – an impudent political satire – as an epilogue to a parliamentary election that would determine the fate of the nation. The first night took place as the election results were being announced for Kristiania, yet 'before demobilisation after The

---

[28] Letter from Delius to Jelka, 1 October 1897 (GM).

Battle for Kristiania was completed', as one critic phrased it.[29] It would be a highly volatile moment in any important general election, but in 1897 the usual powerful sweep of deep disappointment and bruised sensibilities on one side, high intoxication and hubris on the other, had additional and extraordinary perspectives. Nevertheless, it was on this night that the theatre audience was invited to laugh at Heiberg's parody of Norwegian parliamentarianism. Was this a declaration of confidence by the theatre in Norwegians' growing sense of security in their national identity and maturing democracy? It is much more likely, considering the parlous state of the theatre's finances, that *Folkeraadet* was timed to capitalise on election fever. With this text and this music the management had got the whiff of a *succès de scandale* in their noses.

Folkeraadet: Title, synopsis and background

The title of the play translates literally as *The Council of the People*. It was intended by Heiberg to be a metaphor for the parliamentary system adopted by the Norwegian elected body, the Storting. As such, the title of the play might be simply translated as *Parliament*.

In Act I, Parliament is assembled in Parliament Square, discussing whether war should be declared on 'the neighbour'. Leaders of Right, Left and Centre are all equally vociferous in their patriotism; when the Moderates suggest that the debate might actually be turned to the agenda, the motion is carried unanimously. The Poet and Ella enter – he is a man who only acts through words, she demands action. There is also a hotel bellboy, Rype, an entertaining figure who represents the common sense of the people.

In Act II, the city is excited because Parliament is discussing the vital (but undefined) 'paragraph 739' of a bill concerning the country's right to self-determination. When a foreign tourist enters he mistakenly takes it to be a national holiday, but is corrected by the people, who assure him there are more important things to think about, namely paragraph 739. Parliament is in heated discussion, and when a courier delivers the message that the enemy has crossed the border, it is regarded as a joke. When the dispatch turns out to be reliable, The Poet suggests that Parliament, very much to blame for the crisis, should form the front line with the equipment they have procured for the defence of the country: two cannon, a hundred army capes and a keg of dynamite.

In Act III, the bellboy Rype leads these defenders of the nation to the unfortunately named Shit Bridge, the only thing separating them from the enemy. The parliamentarians, concerned that their noble deed might become known as 'The Battle of Shit Bridge', quarrel about a more suitable

---

[29] *Aftenposten*, 19 October 1897.

alternative. It degrades into a fist-fight which results in the deaths of the parliamentarians, every last one shouting 'Long Live the Fatherland' with his dying breath. Rype blows the bridge with the dynamite and thereby saves his country.

In Act IV, the populace arrives at the scene and, discovering the fallen, believes them to have shed their blood for the country. Their corpses are carried away in solemn procession.

In Act V, the coffins of the fallen are displayed on Parliament Square and The Poet gives the eulogy. When Ella explains to him the truth of the situation he angrily informs the people of the facts. A strong man is needed, he proclaims, and Rype only just manages to avoid being sworn in as leader of the masses. 'But we must have a parliament', a voice shouts, and on this sceptical note the play comes to an end.

The background for Heiberg's satirical attack on parliamentarianism was provided by Norway's humiliating retreat from conflict with Sweden in 1895 (see p. 11). For nationalists, it was one lost battle in the long political struggle for an independent Norway. However, every Norwegian suffered this climb-down as if a personal humiliation. It came at a time when national identity had been vigorously bolstered: nationalist historians had rekindled a vision of cultural affinity with the old Viking greatness, and Norwegian figures such as Ibsen, Grieg and Nansen were prominently visible on their international stages. It stung badly to be given a bloody nose by a bully in the form of a Swedish big brother. No one in 1897 who saw the play was in any doubt that Heiberg's *folkeraad* was the Storting, that the fatherland was Norway and that the neighbouring country was Sweden – all in parodic representations. Nevertheless, Norway is never mentioned in the text. It was the audience's ability to draw parallels between their own lives and that of the fairytale democracy of the play that provided them with much of the humour and entertainment. In ignoring the comedic genre to which the play belonged – in lifting the thin veil Heiberg had draped over the country of origin – Delius perhaps made a mistake. With the Norwegian national anthem constantly bubbling to the surface of the music, the play's comic contract with its audience became difficult to sustain.

Monday 18 October: First night and an interview with Christian Krohg

The theatre was filled to the last seat, the tension before the performance was incredible – having been raised for weeks.[30]

There was a vigorous reaction on the first night to Delius's use of 'Ja, vi elsker'. According to *Ørebladet*, the perceived insult was received with intense

---

[30] *Norske Intelligenssedler*, 19 October 1897.

whistling and hissing, as well as blasts from toy trumpets. There was, however, also a good deal of applause: 'An evening which in its stormy character reminded one of the long-gone *Ghosts* days – with the theatre in two camps, one applauding wildly, the other whistling ferociously'.[31] Delius sat quietly throughout in his seat in one of the front rows. At curtain fall, Heiberg was called to the stage three times, the audience in uproar:

> His entrance and exit gave us the finest performance of the evening. The controlled, arrogant smile with which his rather pale face greeted the whistlers was worthy of unanimous applause. A more convincing embodiment on stage of a self-confident, modern super-human with contemptuous indifference to the braying masses would be difficult to imagine.[32]

After the performance, a reception was held for the participants, and here Delius was interviewed. In the mid-1890s, the renowned painter Christian Krohg had introduced in *Verdens Gang* a new journalistic form, the portrait interview, and now he attended the *Folkeraadet* reception to engage the composer in conversation. Delius's Norwegian was far from perfect, and spread among his replies was a handful of grammatical errors. It would, of course, have been a common courtesy to have corrected these in print, but they are included in the newspaper. Krohg had his reasons for preserving the inadvertently comic tone of the composer's speech.[33] As the guests arrived, they were greeted with applause and whistling:

> The worst was however reserved for the moment Delius crossed the threshold, elegant and smiling. [...]
> 'What impression has it made, the way you have been received?'
> 'I am the most astonished man. I will answer you as The Tourist in *Folkeraadet*: "I'm not feeling well. My poor head! I really must get away from here."'
> 'I rather think that at the moment you are the most unpopular man in Norway.'
> 'I think so too. It pains me, for I am very fond of Norway.'
> 'But perhaps not so fond of Kristiania.'
> 'I enjoy the mountains, but not all the nonsense in which one indulges in this town.'

When Delius explained his use of the national anthem, it is clear that the composer had chosen to overlook Heiberg's initial intention of depicting a fictitious country:

> 'In itself, a rendering of the national anthem can hardly be regarded as scornful. It is necessary in a political play. Since it is national sentiment that is affected

---

[31] *Ørebladet*, 19 October 1897.
[32] *Morgenbladet*, 19 October 1897.
[33] No attempt has been made in the extracts to suggest in English the grammatical errors Delius made in his Norwegian.

15. 'Two of the Homeless'. A policeman stops the author and composer of *Folkeraadet* in Kristiania's main street, after they have been ejected from their hotels. 'It's best you accompany me to the station. You can't wander about 'ere all night!'

by the death of Parliament, the strongest national symbol must be used in a sorrowful manner, for it is a sorrowful event. I mean, one has to use it in a *minor* key. Minor is beautiful. If Bjørnson died, I am sure one would find it beautiful to play "Ja, vi elsker" in the *minor* at his grave.'

Delius was still unhappy with the provincial quality of the orchestra:

'But the whistlers provided you with an extra instrument.'

'Yes, that was not in my score. But, comically enough, it was actually quite effective in a couple of places. It matched the trumpets, either by accident or perhaps they were led by a musical man.'

[…]

Delius got up to leave. The assembled company struck up 'God Save the Queen'. Delius bowed with a smile and said: 'As far as I'm concerned you can sing it in the minor key.'[34]

---

[34] *Verdens Gang*, 23 October 1897.

Tuesday 19 October: The critics pass judgement

The Kristiania and regional papers of the time consisted – excluding advertisements – of only two or three pages. This notwithstanding, a staggering amount of printer's ink was expended on *Folkeraadet* in all of them. For some critics the dramatist had failed to rise to the soaring expectations of him prior to the first night, both on the right wing –

> The play's significance as a metaphor for our political life must be set much lower than the author's undeniable talent – and let us add: the grateful theme – had given us reason to expect.[35]

– and on the left:

> If only the play had been able to kick up a storm! If only it had rebuked and scolded and demonstrated the laziness of this parliament – from which all these problems arise! If only it had been able to make us laugh so heartily that all chains were sundered.[36]

Heiberg did, however, have his supporters in the corps of critics: 'I know no bolder comedy than this; none that is more bounteously conceived, more surely constructed, more inexorably carried through; none with higher aims, none with wider horizons; none that reaches further into our time and our lives.'[37] The music of Delius divided the critics too:

> It is quite simply an abomination. In four long interludes which – considered purely as music – are without substance, the foreign composer has indulged in parody and ridicule of our national anthem in every conceivable fashion.[38]

> To Heiberg's comedy, Fritz Delius has fashioned music that adheres to the comic content, a music as sharp and cutting as the comedy itself. […] In particular it was the 'ridicule' of 'Ja, vi elsker' that was the cause of this storm of ill will. There has however been a serious misunderstanding; there was no ridicule, no scorn, everything was done with the utmost seriousness.[39]

The music critic of Norway's largest newspaper, *Aftenposten*, was the highly respected – and highly conservative – Otto Winther-Hjelm:

> If a play of this sort is to be illustrated with music, a sharper wit and a far more professional approach is needed than composer Fritz Delius has at his disposal. There are a couple of good ideas in the preludes to Acts 1 and 3; but for most part the music consists of cacophonies, the result of an undigested Grieg/Svendsen style and poor melodic writing.[40]

---

[35] *Aftenposten*, 19 October 1897.
[36] *Social-Demokraten*, 19 October 1897.
[37] *Verdens Gang*, 19 October 1897.
[38] *Ørebladet*, 19 October 1897.
[39] *Eidsvold*, 19 October 1897.
[40] *Aftenposten*, 20 October 1897.

There was a 'postscript' to the portrait interview Christian Krohg conducted with Delius after the first night. On Tuesday, he visited the composer in his hotel room to complete his portrait drawing and Delius, once again describing himself as 'the most astonished man', asked:

> 'But why is Høyre so angry with Heiberg? They are themselves opposed to the excesses of parliamentarianism.'
>
> 'Well, this I can tell you. They have lost the election, principally because they were so foolish as to adopt a non-nationalist position. Now they realise their mistake and will do anything to avoid Venstre becoming the party of patriotism. What I don't understand, however, is the reaction of the socialists. The play is after all an attack on the bourgeoisie.'

Delius could also inform his interviewer that the hotel in which they were sitting had asked him to leave. Krohg asked if it was because of the first night scandal:

> Yes, I presume so. For I took this room two days ago and booked it for the length of my stay. But my booking was terminated this morning and I have to be out today. The girl gave me a sympathetic look when she told me, and a critic has been shown the door at another hotel for praising the play. They told him the reason to his face.[41]

Heiberg's publisher in Copenhagen, Gyldendal, had now published the text and the morning papers could assure their readers that a shipment of books would be arriving later in the day. Not that the public's opportunity to immerse itself in Heiberg's play would have any effect on the fate of *Folkeraadet* at Christiania Theater. During the second performance, it was abundantly clear that the whistling protest had caught on. Delius was no doubt happy that he had attended the rehearsals – from now on he was not going to hear much of his music during performances.

> But then the curtain fell. All hell broke loose. A storm of applause above which the whistlers screamed their whining protest. For 5 minutes this deafening racket continued. Then we heard a loud voice: 'Three cheers for Heiberg!' – 'No!' – 'Yes!' – Another storm of applause and whistling. But Heiberg did not show himself. He felt he had acquitted himself adequately on the opening night, and that was sufficient. The gas was turned down, but nobody wanted to leave. 'Heiberg! Heiberg!' No, still no Heiberg. But perhaps Delius would make an appearance. 'Three cheers for Delius!' No Delius.[42]

---

[41] *Verdens Gang*, 23 October 1897.
[42] *Eidsvold*, 20 October 1897.

Wednesday 20 October: On hearing the last cuckoo in autumn

After the second performance, Delius wrote to Jelka that it had been a 'furious evening' and that he now felt he had people on the left wing on his side. 'All artists were for me and all the other bourgeois were furious.'[43] He had, however, underestimated just how effective *Folkeraadet* had become for the release of accumulated pressure after weeks of social tension. Theatre-goers across the political spectrum were happy for some comic relief, even if they had to provide it themselves. For this evening's performance the whistlers had organised themselves and

> came in precisely each time the orchestra began to play 'Ja, vi elsker'; at times the struggle between the two bands was quite exciting, the melodic performance was pretty evenly matched inside and outside the pit, and the two bands could boast an equal number of virtuosi.[44]

A cuckoo call from an ocarina up in 'the gods' was especially enthusiastically received.[45]

Thursday 21 October: The commentators rouse themselves

After a couple of days of convalescence, the newspapers' political commentators showed signs of life. In *Morgenbladet*, the leading organ of the right wing, the theory was put forward in an editorial that the ill will the public felt towards the music of Delius was in fact transferred indignation from prolonged abuse of the national anthem for political advantage. One of the readers of *Norske Intelligenssedler* was in an ironic frame of mind when commenting on the composer's juxtaposition of two songs, one a popular ditty, the other an object of patriotic veneration:

> Thank you for your sublime idea of placing 'Kjerringen med staven' as a pendant to that stinkingly patriotic 'Ja, vi elsker'. [...] I hope Norway, though unworthy of this magnificent gift, might in gratitude immediately foster a musician who might at least go part of the way to achieving with the same spiritual superiority a juxtaposition of your country's 'Daisy Bell' and 'God Save the Queen'.[46]

At the evening's performance, the fourth with a full house, the protests were worse than ever.

---

[43] Letter from Delius to Jelka, undated, probably 20 October 1897 (GM).
[44] *Dagbladet*, 21 October 1897.
[45] *Aftenposten*, 21 October 1897.
[46] *Norske Intelligenssedler*, 21 October 1897.

Friday 22 October: The police step in

Dear Editor! The undersigned has 3 times attended Gunnar Heiberg's *Folke-raadet* at Christiania Theater. Despite this fact I have yet to hear the music composed for the play by Mr Delius.[47]

For reader 'P.' in *Aftenposten* and for other members of the public who wished to judge for themselves whether the music constituted such a horrendous insult, help arrived at the end of the first week from two quarters. On Friday, in what seems to be a coordinated campaign, two colleagues of Delius wrote letters of support to the Kristiania newspapers. One of them was Per Winge, the conductor of the theatre orchestra, who assured readers that the music 'contains no parody or mockery whatsoever of "Ja, vi elsker dette landet"; the use made by the composer of the national anthem seems to me wholly justified artistically and, musically speaking, is both characterful and effective'.[48] The other supporter was composer Johan Selmer, who, 'bound by duties of hospitality and collegiality',[49] felt compelled to protest at the way the visitor had been treated. The last time Selmer had figured in Delius's story was in 1890 when he hijacked the orchestra in Leipzig with which Delius had hired rehearsal time. This new intervention may have been well-meant, but also smacked of self-aggrandisement. Having first excused Delius by arguing that he had merely followed Heiberg's instructions, Selmer pointed out: 'It is possible that I myself, had I been appointed to rise to this challenge, would have preferred "Sønner av Norge", as this – in my opinion – would have better lent itself to comic effect. But this is a refinement one could hardly expect of an outsider.'[50]

Rather more muscular assistance came in the form of the Kristiania police force. Constables had in fact been scattered around the seating areas of the theatre since the second night, but without the opportunity to step in; the signal that this was necessary had to be given by the theatre. According to the civic ordinances, 'audible expressions of opinion during or after public performances must not continue after a signal that they should desist has been sounded 3 times'.[51] This signal was three strokes of a gong. After the uproar on Thursday, the theatre was left with no choice and an announcement was placed

---

[47] *Ibid.*

[48] Several newpapers, including *Morgenbladet*, 23 October 1897.

[49] *Ibid.*

[50] 'Sønner av Norge' ('Sons of Norway') was a patriotic march that had been the official national anthem until 'Ja, vi elsker' was adopted in 1864.

[51] *Kristiania bys politivedtægt og sundhedsforskrifter med tilhørende bestemmelser* (*The City of Kristiania's Police Directives for Law and Order with Associated Ordinances*) (Kristiania: J. Chr. Gundersen, 1899), par. 69.

in Friday's papers that 'precautionary measures have been taken for the use of the gong at the theatre this evening'.[52]

In a letter to Jelka on Friday, Delius assured her that he found the whole scandal amusing, even though he had been threatened with violence: 'as yet no one has yet dared to attack me in the street. I am too big and Englishmen have the "renommée de pouvoir boxer" here!'[53] He had also spent time with Henrik Ibsen, who was 'delighted and congratulated me most heartily'. This was the last day Delius planned to spend in Kristiania. At the evening's performance, the orchestra had struggled manfully on

> until Police Inspector Jelstrup rose quietly and majestically from his seat in the first row of the stalls. This was evidently a pre-arranged signal, for at that moment Mr Winge put his baton down on his music stand and stepped calmly down from his podium, while the curtain was again raised. The stage was now open, but devoid of any of the actors. From the pit one then heard the three muffled strokes of the so-called gong, which more resembles an old battered saucepan. Order was immediately restored.[54]

Saturday 23 October: Unprecedented mayhem in the Students' Union

Folkeraadet. The gong is sounded. – Delius has withdrawn his music.[55]

This and similar headlines dominated the Saturday papers, which also published a press release from the theatre informing readers of the latest developments:

> The composer of the incidental music to *Folkeraadet*, Englishman Fritz Delius – who has been greatly offended by the reception his music has received from certain quarters, and who has suffered personal affronts on the same account – has requested that the Management withdraw his music, a request to which the Management in the prevailing situation has decided to accede, while in no way adopting a position as to the justifiability of the complaints. For Mr Delius the whole uproar seems wholly inexplicable, as he maintains that the music was composed in all seriousness and exclusively with artistic propriety in mind.[56]

Although he had written to Jelka that he found the whole thing 'very amusing', Delius now found himself at the centre of a storm partly of his own making, and his wavering actions on the Saturday seem to speak of an artist exposed to considerable pressure from different sectors of society. He cancelled his plan to leave Norway that day, most likely because he wished to attend the evening's

---

[52] *Aftenposten*, 22 October 1897.
[53] Letter from Delius to Jelka, undated, probably 22 October 1897 (GM).
[54] *Aftenposten*, 23 October, 1897.
[55] *Eidsvold*, 23 October 1897.
[56] Several newspapers, including *Verdens Gang*, 23 October 1897.

16. The Large Hall of the Students' Union in Kristiania in 1903, much as it would have looked on the night of the debate about *Folkeraadet* six years earlier.

meeting of the Students' Union at which his music was to be debated. Several of the city's finest orators had also accepted the students' invitation, as had the press. There was plenty of steam left in the *Folkeraadet* boiler. By the end of the night the composer would decide to return his score to Christiana Theater and the scandal would keep headline writers busy for a couple more weeks.

The main hall of the Students' Union was filled to overflowing for a debate described by *Aftenposten* as 'quite unique even in the eventful annals of the Union. [...] As the evening progressed, the meeting assumed such a lively character that one would struggle to find its match, even taking into consideration the debates about the Norwegian flag, renowned for their ferocity.'[57] *Ørebladet* related that 'the mayhem was unrivalled', the debate conducted in an atmosphere 'reminiscent of the great spiritual battles in the Students' Union in the 80s'.[58] According to the minutes of the meeting, the motion being debated was initially: 'The Students' Union protests at the mockery of the national anthem of which Christiania Theater is guilty through its performance of the

---

[57] *Aftenposten*, 24 October 1897.
[58] *Ørebladet*, 25 October 1897.

incidental music to *Folkeraadet*.[59] *It was proposed by Just Bing, a literature scholar, who was obliged by the composer's withdrawal of the music to adopt a fresh approach:*

> [Mr Bing] proposes therefore that his motion is withdrawn and, under certain conditions, that the following resolution is adopted: 'The Students' Union has arrived at the following resolution: Since the music has been withdrawn and since one expects that a similar affront to our national feeling never more will confront us at Christiania Theater or on any other Norwegian stage, the original motion is not subject to debate.'
> [...]
> The speaker does not doubt that the composer is indeed as innocent as the driven snow. [...] Delius was an overgrown child. In pure ignorance he has managed to mock the national anthem. But the national anthem is one of our roots, it is a part of us, and no mockery whatsoever is to be tolerated.

Intended as a powerful closing statement, the effect was deflated by Bing's use of the words 'part of us' – in Norwegian *del i oss*, pronounced almost identically to *Delius*.[60] Once the explosion of mirth had died down, the next speaker, student Christen Gran Bøgh, took the floor:

> One must not abstract the music from the play itself. Delius had merely illustrated the content of the drama and that was his task. It was cowardly not to whistle at the play and instead direct one's protest at the music. He then put forward the following motion: 'The students invite Mr Delius to return his manuscript of the *Folkeraadet* music to Christiania Theater.'

The floor was open and some of the foremost voices in the cultural and political life of the capital made known their opinions, including Christian Krohg. Gran Bøgh, who had opposed the motion, was the same writer who many years later would record his memories of the occasion for *Bergens Tidende*:

> The discussion lasted until 2 in the morning. The following statement from the composer, who was present, was then read out: 'In light of the discussion, which has shown that the ill will to a large degree is caused by the play or wholly extraneous circumstances, and since experts in the field have stated that my music contains no mockery of the national anthem, I am willing to return the score of my music to Christiania Theater.' [...] When the votes were counted around 3 o'clock, it turned out that Just Bing's resolution had gained 78 votes – Gran Bøgh's 158.
>
> After the meetings, beef and onion was usually served with beer and spirits in the boardroom for the speakers and participants, – a tradition that could not be disregarded merely because it was an advanced time of night.

---

[59] Minutes of the meeting of Det norske studentersamfund (The Norwegian Students' Union), 23 October 1897 (RA).
[60] Fredrik B. Wallem, *Det norske studentersamfund gjennem hundrede aar* (*A Hundred Years of the Norwegian Students' Union*) (Kristiania: Aschehoug, 1916), 986.

It was a lively gathering. – The chairman, Johannes Irgens, gave an excellent speech in French for Delius. It was met with intense whistling. The merry gathering was worried that Delius would feel out of place if he did not hear the now familiar sound. And so whistling was adopted for the night as the general form of applause.[61]

The first scandalous week with *Folkeraadet* on the billboards was rounded off on Sunday with a performance that was 'denuded of – or liberated from, if you prefer – the incidental music of the English composer', as *Aftenposten* put it.[62] The orchestra selected in its place other intermezzi from its repertoire and 'a peaceful decorum' accompanied the comedy to its final curtain.

This decorum was merely the eye of the storm.

Week two: The commentators come out fighting

On Tuesday 26 October the music was back in place. And the protesters? *Eidsvold* left its readers in no doubt:

> If our municipal grandees in their wisdom were to drive a steam-roller over the tail of every cat in town, it would not sound more infernal – and yet they were far from unmusical, the people volunteering to assist the orchestra, which time and again showed its gratitude by suspending its efforts and letting the gong player beat the time, – for no matter how cunningly Mr Delius had hidden 'Ja, vi elsker' under his awful music, these irrepressible amateurs found its familiar tones and greeted them with their *katzenjammer*.[63]

The beating of the gong was no longer sufficient to dampen the enthusiasm of young men determined to make their dissatisfaction known. At every performance this week there were several who defied the ban on protests after the signal had been sounded. Their names were taken by the police and they were ordered to pay a stinging fine of twenty crowns, the punishment for an unpaid fine being three days in jail. It made little difference. In fact the protests, until now confined to spectators in the circles and balcony, spread to the expensive rows of stall seats. They spread also from the music to the text, certain lines now setting off howls of derision. On some evenings, there was still an element of competition between those who applauded and those who whistled, and after two weeks there had not been an empty seat at any performance.

Also in the press there was a sharper tone to the debate. Political commentators on the right were particularly aggressive this week, filling column after column with their attacks on the *Folkeraadet* monstrosity. In *Morgenbladet*, literary historian – and anglophile – Christen Collin expressed his opinion

---

[61] Christen Gran Bøgh, 'Studenterliv i nittiårene', *Bergens Tidende*, 6 August 1941.
[62] *Aftenposten*, 24 October 1897.
[63] *Eidsvold*, 27 October 1897.

that Delius had brought shame down on his nation: 'It is simply a loss for us all when an Englishman, through thoughtlessness or lack of tact, strengthens the conviction that Englishmen look down on the national sentiment of all other peoples from the lofty height of their own national pride.'[64]

National sentiment, as *Folkeraadet* had amply demonstrated, was not the exclusive property of any political faction. On Saturday 30 October, Norway's most outspoken radical ideologue launched an attack on *Folkeraadet* and its creators. Arne Garborg, also a distinguished author, had known Delius at least since the year before, when the Englishman after a dinner in Paris had entertained the guests with a demonstration of his astrology skills, enlightening Garborg with the sobering news that in 1911 his days would be at an end. (It was a reading of the celestial bodies by Delius that in the course of time would be premature by thirteen years.) In an editorial in his periodical *Den 17de Mai* it was now Garborg's turn to pass a death sentence – on *Folkeraadet* and the music of Delius:

It was this music that really knocked me off balance. I felt the anger rise up in me; sorrow stirred and woke, hate too. I hated Fritz Delius, that splendid young man; I hated Heiberg even more: but most of all I hated the burghers who sat there and lapped it all up. And then suddenly I *understood* Gunnar Heiberg. At just such a moment was born the inspiration for this play. He has considered these people without nationality; without love for a fatherland, without a living national pride, and he has said to himself: these people really are there to be mocked. So he sat down and wrote *Folkeraadet*. And he asked a composer to write some mocking music that might suit *Folkeraadet*; he gave himself a particularly jaundiced pleasure by asking a *foreigner* to compose this mocking music; and from all of this came a work full of scorn and ridicule, but without joviality or merriment, without celebration.[65]

Monday 1 November: Mock assassination

Verdens Gang: **Shots in the theatre**
Dagbladet: ***Folkeraadet* protests now taking on terrible forms**

Two weeks after the curtain had been raised, the narrative had reached a dénouement, a turning point in the plot imbued with so much pathos and melodrama that ladies on the first rows fainted into the arms of strangers: a new character entered the stage, lifting the drama to its momentous climax. His name was Albert Tønnesen. After his astonishing solo performance, pretty

[64] *Morgenbladet*, 28 October 1897. The general 'conviction' among Norwegians of English arrogance was cemented at the end of the Napoleonic Wars when Britain supported Sweden's claim on Norway.
[65] *Den 17de Mai*, 30 October 1897.

much everyone was ready for the finale to bring down the curtain on Delius's music. *Eidsvold*'s reporter was at the scene:

> It gets worse and worse. Up to now, protesters have confined themselves to whistling and hissing Mr Delius's music, but now they have started shooting at the conductor – we will soon all be Americans.
>
> It happened yesterday evening. The audience sat and enjoyed the widely discussed and delightful funeral march which opens Act V of *Folkeraadet*. Suddenly a pale, but determined, young man rose from his seat in the first row of stalls, pulls a shiny six-shooter from his pocket, takes cold-blooded aim at the broad back of conductor Winge, and pulls the trigger – 3 shots, if we include the one that didn't fire.
>
> Mayhem ensued. Many leapt to their feet in shock and rushed with unsure steps towards the exits, my young girlfriend fainted with a sigh into my arms, and everyone expected to see Winge collapse bleeding onto the floor, murdered treacherously from behind.
>
> But wait – he did not! On the contrary he seemed to be in the best of health, and that with two bullets in his back! That's our boy!
>
> How was one to explain all this? Well, it turned out that the young man had used blanks. He fell many per cent in my respect straight away.
>
> But why did he bother shooting if it was not his intention to draw blood from Mr Winge? Well, there were three reasons.
>
> First, because he wanted to get his name in the papers, and that satisfaction we can give him. He is called Tønnesen and is a 25-year-old scenery painter – who would have guessed that he was even an adult! – and the town on which the honour falls for having fostered this fine specimen is called Flekkefjord.[66]
>
> Secondly, because he wanted to go one better than his brother, who was among the protesters who recently were fined 20 crowns for not obeying the rule of the gong.
>
> And thirdly, because he thought he had too much money and wanted to lighten his load, and I have no doubt the police will gladly liberate him from some of it. In fact, no sooner had he fired his shots than Police Inspector Ramm sank his claws into him and dragged him off to the station.[67]

By the time the evening papers were on the street the next day, Tønnesen had given his deed a heroic slant: 'I felt it was shameful for every Norwegian that this music should be performed night after night […] It struck me that, to bring the monstrosity to a close, only one single man was necessary, if he applied himself with a little energy to the matter.'[68] Several newspapers called

---

[66] Although often belittled in the contemporary accounts, Albert Tønnesen was a respected young craftsman. He would later study under Harriet Backer and at the Academy of Art, he would be represented at several Autumn Exhibitions in Kristiania, and would become one of the artists entrusted with the restoration of the interior of Norway's old churches. See 'Albert Tønnesen' in *Norsk kunstnerleksikon* (*Norwegian Art Lexicon*), https://nkl.snl.no/Albert_Tønnesen, accessed 10 April 2016.

[67] *Eidsvold*, 2 November 1897.

[68] *Dagbladet*, 2 November 1897.

him the modern Herostratus, while at the same time expressing a degree of sympathy with his actions. The swingeing fine of 200 crowns was no doubt more than a scenery painter was able to pay, and Tønnesen made a virtue of necessity by declaring that his political convictions prevented him from accepting the fine. 'Herostratus-Tønnesen from Flekkefjord seems determined to hold on by hook or by crook to the laurel wreath he won with his heroic blank shots at Christiania Theater', *Morgenbladet* wrote[69] – with poorly disguised sarcasm, and failing to capture the popular sentiment sweeping the city. There were in fact reports emanating from the police station that Tønnesen's cell was overflowing with floral tributes. Editor Arne Garborg in *Den 17de Mai* gauged better the temperature, putting in motion a fundraising drive with the aim of paying off Tønnesen's fine.

On Wednesday 3 November, Delius went to the theatre and again withdrew his music, releasing a flood of irony and humour in the press, both in the daily papers and the weekly satirical magazines. And the pistol-toting Tønnesen was awarded his part of the glory:

> O, Tønnesen! handsome Tønnesen from Flekkefjord! What the voices of the people in the radical and conservative press were unable to achieve, despite their unified and most strenuous efforts, you have realised with a slight twitch of the index finger of your right hand! You have cleansed Thalia's temple![70]

'Have you ever seen such fuss / as that made by this Delius!'

In all probability it was Tønnesen's action during Monday's performance that was the last straw for Delius. If, however, the faintest embers of hope still glowed within him that his music might 'catch on', they would have been extinguished by signals coming from the orchestra. In the course of Wednesday, the theatre manager received a request from all the musicians in the orchestra, apart from two, that they be spared the discomfort of playing Delius's music; the situation had become unpleasant and combustible. Delius packed his trunk and left for Copenhagen that afternoon. When the press release was published the next day, it was in the form of a letter from the conductor to the theatre manager:

> Mr Delius, who yesterday left the country, has asked me to convey to the management his wish that the music he has composed for *Folkeraadet* be definitively withdrawn. When the music was returned to Christiania Theater it was on condition that the professional support for his music would have removed what he regards as a mistaken interpretation of it.

---

[69] *Morgenbladet*, 3 November 1897.
[70] *Vikingen*, 13 November 1897.

He does not however wish to be the cause of unrest and disorder in the theatre and will therefore entreat the management to comply with his request.[71]

The following day, Thursday 4 November, there was no performance of *Folkeraadet*. It was in fact Union Day, marking the fraternal collaboration between
Norway and Sweden – hardly an appropriate day for Heiberg's appeal for a
strong leader to lead the nation to independence. On Friday, the comedy was
back on the billboard, but demand for tickets vanished with Delius's music;
in the newspapers for 26 November the final performance was advertised for
the following evening. In these same papers it was announced that the general
election had now formally been concluded. It was an election which, according to *Aftenposten*, had brought changes 'of such a magnitude that one must
go back many years to find anything similar'.[72] They had followed each other
pretty much from start to finish, this historic election in Kristiania and its
court jester, *Folkeraadet*.

In due course it became clear that the parliamentary system in Norway
was not as toothless as Gunnar Heiberg had supposed. The election gave Venstre a mandate to extend the franchise to all men over the age of twenty-five,
and with this augmented electorate – revitalised by farmhands and industrial
workers – the writing was on the wall for the union with Sweden. The will of
the people had been heard, and it insisted that wise Norwegian heads were
fully capable of steering the nation to independence from Sweden. They finally
did so in 1905.

It was Delius's misfortune that at exactly the same moment that Norwegians,
as an electorate, defined their distinctive identity and their will to achieve
independence, he should have raised his head and suggested some humorous
ways in which their national anthem might be parodied. In the end, it was he
who became the object of ridicule. In the newspaper interviews with Christian
Krohg, the foreigner's small grammatical slips were left uncorrected so that his
statements lost their authority and he seemed rather to be a comic interloper.
Around the derisible figure of the outsider all shades of the political spectrum
could unite and, in an unexpected manner, consolidate their opinions regarding the inviolability of Norwegian sovereignty. It was not least for this reason
that Christen Gran Bøgh could write forty years later that *Folkeraadet* had
been 'the most significant theatrical event of the 90s'.

Several attempts were made in the wake of Christiania Theater's *succès de scandale* to cash in on the infamy of the production. A few weeks after it closed in
the capital, *Folkeraadet* was staged in several other towns. First came Bergen's
important theatre, Den Nationale Scene – though here the incidental music

---

[71] Several newspapers, including *Morgenbladet*, 4 November 1897.
[72] *Aftenposten*, 26 November 1897.

was not included, and the play flopped; then the touring ensemble Det norske Theaterselskab (The Norwegian Theatre Company) brought the play for one evening to several eastern Norwegian towns, including Halden (5 December) and Moss (7 December). For this production Heiberg had again directed the play himself. The ticket prices, inflated for the event, did not deter people from filling the provincial theatres to capacity. Unaccompanied by election fever, however, the excitement had dissipated. When it also transpired that Delius's notorious music was served up in an anaemic arrangement for piano and solo violin, the critics made no bones about expressing the general disappointment felt by the audience:

> Of the highly controversial music of Delius, it was impossible to gather any impression. A piano and violin cannot in any manner function as a substitute for a large orchestra, which would have been necessary for the music to have any effect. It was rather astonishing, therefore, that this harmless arrangement for piano and violin could provoke one whistle – short, but penetrating – from the gallery, accompanied by a torrent of verbal garbage.[73]

As the last days of 1897 were counting down, it was only the satirists who refused to let the old year pass without enjoying one last laugh at the expense of Heiberg, Christiania Theater and the unfortunate Englishman who gate-crashed a strictly private party. The author Hans Aanrud published as a pamphlet his own parody, *Selvraaden* (*Self-Help*), and for its Christmas edition the satirical magazine *Tyrihans* concocted a lengthy mock-*Folkeraadet* pillorying the greed of the Christiania Theater management:

Refrain
O, Delius, my darling
I need your music now
the press's slings and arrows
we'll battle through somehow!

The Author.
Has he pinched his score again?
Why, it was just restored again!

Theatre Manager.
Yes, have you ever seen such fuss
as that made by this Delius![74]

[73] *Moss Tilskuer*, 9 December 1897.
[74] *Tyrihans*, Christmas 1897, 7.

Grieg, Holter – and the long shadow of *Folkeraadet*

> Delius has really had quite a success in Norway and given the newspapers plenty
> to write about, it will no doubt be providential, for there has been so much focus
> on his name up there, and that can never be a bad thing.[75]

These words of William Molard, in a letter to Edvard Munch, would prove
far from prophetic. Heiberg's *Folkeraadet* was pushed out of the news and
opinion columns by a new scandal: the Dreyfus affair in France, which was
made public in November. One might, however, have expected, as Molard did,
that the period of fame that the composer had enjoyed would bring with it
long-term advantages. Here also, the opposite was true. Although Delius had
felt that he had the support of most artists, this did not extend to the most
influential leaders of opinion among *musicians*. In a letter to Grieg, Johan
Selmer commented that 'quite a storm was blowing around the music of Delius
and Norwegian=Kristianian chauvinism'.[76] To Selmer and other friends Grieg
expressed his dismay at Delius having taken the Heiberg commission in the
first place:

> The whole Delius story seems to me clear evidence of the low level of musical
> life at home. People manage to make a musical issue out of something that, at its
> core, has nothing to do with music; I mean, no one can tell me that people are
> *musically* indignant. All the necessary insight is lacking, for that to happen. It is
> only when chauvinism is at its root that an issue can assume such proportions.
> I regret that Delius has used his beautiful gift on this work. I don't know it, but
> judging by the contents of the play it seems to me a misconception on his part to
> have had anything to do with it. [...] What is the point of playing 'Ja, vi elsker' in
> the minor key? No, I just don't get it. I would certainly not like to see Bjørnson
> buried to the tones of 'Ja, vi elsker' in the minor![77]

With this last retort Grieg is harking back to Delius's bold statement in his
interview with Christian Krohg (see p. 149) that, if Bjørnson died, Norwegians
'would find it beautiful to play "Ja, vi elsker" in the *minor* at his grave'. That
the melody of the national anthem was written by Rikard Nordraak, whose
memory Grieg held sacred throughout his life, would have compounded his
sense of disappointment. He shared some of his opinions with conductor Iver
Holter, who replied:

> Delius has really done something very stupid in my opinion. His music was not
> without a certain charm [...] but it was run-of-the-mill stuff, there really wasn't
> much in it at all, certainly nothing of genius. He will not be able to present

[75] Letter from William Molard to Munch, 7 March 1898 (MM).
[76] Letter from Johan Selmer to Grieg, 22 November 1897 (BOB).
[77] Letter from Grieg to Johan Selmer, 11 November 1897 (NB).

himself as a composer here for a long time to come; in my opinion it is no more than he deserves.[78]

From our standpoint, it is easy to see that Holter was correct. Delius did disappear from Norwegian theatres and concert halls. It is, however, important to see Holter's words as much more than an inspired guess, for it was in his power to ensure that Delius never would be able 'to present himself as a composer here'. As the leader of the capital's symphony orchestra until 1911, and also as editor of Scandinavia's foremost music magazine (*Nordisk Musikrevue*) from 1900 to 1906, Holter helped to define the parameters of Norwegian musical taste during the most crucial phase of nation building. Even *with* the support of opinion, it is possible that the tide of independence would in any case have worked against Delius finding an audience in Norway. For this generation of Norwegians, which would be entrusted with the momentous task of bringing their country to independence, it was in fact inopportune to see too much of the larger picture, to listen to too many and diverse voices.

There was a third man who, from the turn of the century, was as important in defining the parameters of musical taste as Grieg and Holter. Johan Halvorsen conducted the orchestra of the Nationaltheater from 1899 to 1929, also leading the ensemble in more than two hundred concert programmes. Only once was a work of Delius ever conducted by his friend from Leipzig – the Piano Concerto in C Minor, at the University Concert Hall on 15 October 1918.[79] In a strange twist, it would be Halvorsen who would finally demonstrate that, to mark the passing of Bjørnstjerne Bjørnson, and contrary to Grieg's opinion above, the national anthem might indeed be played in a minor key to great effect. Bjørnson died in 1910 and the Nationatheater organised in his honour a memorial event, a programme that concluded with a funeral march composed for the occasion by Johan Halvorsen and entitled 'Bjørnstjerne Bjørnson in memoriam'. After two bars of solemn brass chords to the beat of a ponderous march, the melody of 'Ja, vi elsker' enters – in the minor. The similarity to the scandalous Interlude in *Folkeraadet* is striking. What an upstart Englishman could permit himself in 1897 and a trusted Norwegian could permit himself in 1910 were two entirely different things.

For Delius personally, there is no doubt that the events in Kristiania in 1897 were a turning point in his attitude to Norway – or, rather, to the new, militantly jingoistic mood in Norway's cultural life. He continued to visit the

---

[78] Letter from Iver Holter to Grieg, 13 November 1897 (BOB).

[79] Øyvin Dybsand, 'Johan Halvorsen', Appendix II, 'Kronologisk oversikt over Halvorsens kon-sertvirksomhet' ('Chronological Overview of Halvorsen's Concert Programmes'). What Halvorsen felt about the Delius scandal of 1897 is unknown, but when *Folkeraadet* was revived in 1924 at the Nationaltheater, Halvorsen – as house composer – had the task of writing new incidental music. This was the first time since 1897 that the dust had been blown off Heiberg's comedy and the performances were greeted with a complete absence of whistling and toy trumpets.

country roughly every other year. His music would remain as inspired as ever by what he had seen and felt in Norwegian mountains and by Norwegian fjords. As for Norway's capital city and the leading actors on its political and cultural stages – these were now of scant interest to him. And Norway stopped enquiring about his music. When travelling in the country, Delius spent as little time in Kristiania as possible. Figures such as Iver Holter and Randi Blehr – the latter married to one of the pioneers of Norwegian parliamentarianism – disappeared from his story.

Con spirito: The music to *Folkeraadet*

We have already read many opinions about the *Folkeraadet* music, most penned by people who gathered their impressions through a blanket of whistling, hissing and toy trumpets. To anyone listening to the music today who has not studied the political background, it seems astonishing that such jovial, playful and friendly pieces were able to project such a horrendous shadow on the wall and be mistaken for such a mocking monstrosity.

Only three months separated Delius's acceptance of the commission from the first orchestra rehearsal. Judging by the happy result, the work must have gone *con spirito*, to borrow one of its musical expressions. So smiling is the *Folkeraadet* music that it is easy to see that most of it was written during a happy summer in beautiful Grez far from the political maelstrom of an intense general election. Iver Holter remarked that the music had no spark of genius to it; the commission was, however, for incidental music to a farcical and feathery satire with political undertones and, instructed by Heiberg as to the character of the text, the composer delivered theatre music that fitted the bill. Indeed, his treatment of well-known melodies would in normal circumstances have been regarded as winning in its ingenuity, his flirtation with the national anthem as joyfully witty and never without a pointed parallel in the text. Here are the opening bars of the Norwegian national anthem, 'Ja, vi elsker dette landet':

Example 7.2 'Ja, vi elsker dette landet'

Some of the variants of 'Ja, vi elsker' are so integrated into the composer's fluid thought processes that they will hardly have registered on the antennae of the whistlers, and the first of these come with the music's opening. One *forte* chord sounds on the whole orchestra to fix the attention of the audience, and the 'Prelude to Act I' is off on an energetic, striding theme (Example 7.3) which coaxes a small reply from the oboe – both themes alluding to the opening tones of the national anthem (marked *x*):

Example 7.3 *Folkeraadet*, Prelude to Act I, 1–2

The 'Interlude between Acts I and II' is a joyous 6/8 march into which a variant of 'Ja, vi elsker' is introduced as a countermelody (bar 33), the first warning of a gradual development of the theme:

Example 7.4 *Folkeraadet*, Interlude between Acts I and II, 33–9

Before we get that far, however, there are hints (bar 65, bassoon and horn) of something altogether different and, while the audience would have been sitting and wondering – *Did I really hear that?* – Delius drops the muted approach and lets loose, *fortissimo* on the full orchestra, the exuberant folk song 'Kjerringa med staven' ('The Old Women with the Staff'):

Example 7.5 *Folkeraadet*, Interlude between Acts I and II, 79–84

When this playful folk song, much loved by children, is converted into a hunting or herding call (from bar 110), it seems almost that Delius is mocking himself for his own love of distant horns as a metaphor for the wild Norway. After a reprise of the Interlude's march, and just before the curtain rises on Act II and the parliamentarians' pompous debate of 'paragraph 739', the composer puts his toys to one side and presents the national anthem in its full splendour, first as a brass choir (from bar 186), then majestically for the whole ensemble.

During a long change of scenery between Acts II and III, Delius weaves together different themes representing the politicians and the blossoming relationship between The Poet and Ella. At times we are teased with phrases from the national anthem and then, as a tone picture of the bickering parliamentarians, he presents a contrapuntal squabble, again with the opening notes of 'Ja, vi elsker':

Example 7.6 *Folkeraadet*, Interlude between Acts II and III, 105–8

When the curtain rises on Act V, we see the coffins of the politicians laid out on Parliament Square. The Interlude that prepares this scene begins with a funeral march, at first barely audible in the distance (muted drum beats), which then approaches with quiet brass fanfares, before finally passing in procession to the tones of the national anthem in the minor key. It is this sequence that provoked the most violent protests at Christiania Theater:

Example 7.7 *Folkeraadet*, Interlude between Acts IV and V, 32–5

In the second half of the Interlude, Delius gathers the threads together – leaving room for a reminder (from bar 106) that there are much finer qualities to the Norwegian spirit than displayed by these vacillating politicians: a quotation from a dance melody Grieg used in the first of his *25 norske folkeviser og danser* (25 Norwegian Folk Songs and Dances) (op. 17, no. 1).

Ridiculed in Kristiania – noticed in Germany

If the way things turned out in Kristiania was dispiriting for the composer, 1897 was actually rounded off in style and optimism thanks to the première in Germany of his fantasy overture *Over the Hills and Far Away*. The event came about through the selfless advocacy of Jelka Rosen's painter friend, Ida

Gerhardi. She had grown up near Elberfeld and now used her connections with musicians there to put Delius's score on the desk of the city's conductor, Hans Haym. Delius arrived on 10 November and followed the rehearsals of *Über die Berge in die Ferne*, as it was called there, through to performance. On the evening of 13 November an audience heard for the first time the atmospheric opening with its quiet herd calls rising from the silent horizon, a picture of the solitude and oneness with nature Delius associated with his journeys in Norway and looking out across endless mountain plateaus.

Initially, it seemed to be as much a local 'flash in the pan' event as had the isolated performances of *On the Mountains* in 1891 and 1894. It opened no floodgates. What makes this date an especially significant milestone in the composer's career is that in Hans Haym he had finally found a conductor who understood him and who was greatly enthused by his music. Even more important, early in the new century Haym would burn with a fervent desire to spread the music of Delius as widely as he could. The composer had acquired a champion. From 1901 to the outbreak of war in 1914, Haym promoted Delius's music as often as possible, giving the first performances of several of the composer's most significant works. Lionel Carley has remarked: 'How strange that this unique music, with all its complex beauties, should come to first flower in Elberfeld. And how easy it has perhaps been to forget that it was in fact in this grimy industrial town to the south of the Ruhr that a performing tradition for Delius's music was first established.'[80] While the Norwegian satirical magazines were still making fun of Delius and his music, his Norwegian mountain overture was being played in Elberfeld. Even though Hans Haym's decisive intervention in Delius's career lay some years in the future, it is justified to let the simultaneous ridicule he met in Norway and warm welcome in Germany stand as a symbol of the approaching shift in the direction of his life. At the close of 1896, Delius had brushed the dust of impresarios and publishers from his coat. At the close of 1897, he was equally convinced that his interests were better served far from the capital city of Norway and – as he expressed it in his interview with Krohg – 'all the nonsense in which one indulges in this town'.

Before the composer's story is moved on, a small postscript to *Folkeraadet* must be attached, a few words about an event that took place in Kristiania five months later. Once more it involved a Gunnar Heiberg play with music by Delius, but this time the composer's contribution went almost unnoticed. In November 1897, the theatrical husband-and-wife team Alma and Johan Fahlström had managed to curb Halfdan Jebe's wanderlust, at least for a period, by engaging him as leader of the orchestra of their newly started company, Centralteatret. ('Farewell Paris and Montrouge', he sighed in a letter to Delius.

---

[80] Lionel Carley, 'Hans Haym: Delius's Prophet and Pioneer' in Redwood, *A Delius Companion*, 187.

'One day you wake up and discover that you are dead.'[81]) No doubt motivated by the publicity that had attached itself to Heiberg's name at the end of 1897, the Fahlstrøms decided to give in March 1898 the Norwegian première of the dramatist's *Balkonen* (*The Balcony*), with Heiberg himself as director. And it was not long before orchestra leader Jebe was in touch with Delius to propose 'a hilarious idea' – that he should write incidental music for the production. Or, at the very least, an overture.

If Jebe had expected a new sheaf of cameos capable of putting the noses of the bourgeoisie out of joint, he would have been disappointed to receive at the end of January 1898 one of his friend's old compositions, a small serenade.[82] During the performance the piece was played as the last of four intermezzi, following compositions by Gade, Mendelssohn and Grieg. While the first night of the play was received with acclaim, the presence of Delius's music was ignored by most critics. *Morgenposten*'s reviewer, however, could not resist a dig at the infamous composer of *Folkeraadet*, offering him a dubious compliment, namely that his Serenade was 'far too original not to have been borrowed from somebody else.'[83]

---

[81] Letter from Halfdan Jebe to Delius, undated, probably January 1898 (DT).
[82] This Serenade seems not to have survived.
[83] *Morgenposten*, 3 March 1898.

8

1898–1902
Unshakeable self-belief

'Snow-mountains in the distance'

Stage direction in *A Village Romeo and Juliet*

In the year following *Folkeraadet*, Delius's career stagnated. He nurtured a dream of finding the key that would open the musical life of London, in particular an opera house that would stage *Koanga*. For the time being he lacked the resources that a prolonged promotional campaign in London would cost him. A new opera project based on the short story 'Romeo und Julia auf dem Dorfe' by Gottfried Keller had ground to a halt because Keary, his librettist for *Koanga*, could not work up any enthusiasm for it. In a period with little direction or continuity in his career, and still encouraged by the publicity *Folkeraadet* had brought to his name, it is unsurprising that Delius should have sought new theatre commissions.

In the spring of 1898, the book of Helge Rode's new theatrical piece, *Dansen gaar* (*The Dance Goes On*), was published in Copenhagen. It was a study of the struggle for genuine love and art and of the obstacles placed by daily life in the way of these ideals. The drama is played out around the figure of Aage Volmer, a painter, and Klara, the daughter of an industrialist, who secretly get engaged, despite Klara's father having negotiated for her a union with a *nouveau riche* aristocrat. Volmer's speeches about love and art seem to float on a cloud of aestheticism, distanced from the world. Shortly after its publication, two of Helge Rode's closest friends found much in it that spoke directly to their sensibilities: Edvard Munch and Fritz Delius. Indeed, Rode had mirrored a metaphysical ideal that was a common denominator in the creative lives of all three friends – poet, painter and composer. Volmer tells Klara:

I envisaged a beauty – I mean a sort of clear, transparent, spiritually aware beauty that rendered people larger, higher, so that they despised all things base. Yes, I really believe that if one could collect beauty – all sorts of beauty from the whole wide world, all the sounds and colours of love – then it would create a collective feeling, – it could open for us a life of greatness – [1]

When Aage Volmer describes the work he intends to paint, he depicts love as a state of ecstasy binding the lovers both to nature and to death:

> The Dance of Life. My painting shall be called The Dance of Life! There will be a couple dressed in flowing clothes dancing one light summer night down an avenue of dark cypresses and red rose bushes. The roses offer glimpses and flashes of the delicious blood of the earth [...] He holds her in an embrace so tight that she is half absorbed by him. She is afraid. Afraid – and yet something wakes in her. Strength floods into her from him. And before them is the abyss.[2]

These are lines that gripped both Delius and Munch. In her study of the dramatist, Hanne Engberg points out that Rode with this work seemed 'to express in words all the loneliness and anxiety of summer nights that were to be found in Munch's contemporary paintings'.[3] On reading the play Munch had immediately made his first sketch of a tightly dancing couple, and later the motif would be developed as *The Dance of Life*, a key work in his series *The Frieze of Life*.

Helge Rode was as ardent an admirer of Nietzsche as was Delius, and in Aage Volmer's fusion of artist and nature, as well as in his cultivation of a spiritual force that would lead people to 'despise all things base', we hear echoes of Zarathustra. Hanne Engberg suggests that the influence of the German poet-philosopher is easiest to identify in Rode's early works in their 'ecstatic lust for life'.[4] It is a phrase that might equally be applied to some of the finest music by Delius. Even in the *Paa Vidderne* scores his most exalted passages were inspired by poetry suffused with poetic-philosophic conviction, transferred from the hunter in Ibsen's epic poem, a proto-Zarathustra figure.

As soon as he had read *Dansen gaar*, Delius wrote to Helge Rode suggesting that he compose an overture and incidental music to the play, which was scheduled to have its première in Copenhagen the coming winter. Rode's first response was disappointing; he believed that music was completely out of place in a psychological drama. Delius was exasperated by the off-hand manner in which Rode brushed aside the suggestion, and the dramatist had to write again to his friend, pouring oil on the troubled waters, partly by alluding to the *Folkeraadet* debacle in Kristiania: 'Probably the Theatre would say: We want no Music, it is unnecessary. More Work and more Money. And if it was a Foreigner who has made the Music, perhaps they would further say: "Why not at all Events a Dane. We have young Komposers, who want to try

---

[1] Helge Rode, *Dansen gaar* (Copenhagen: Gyldendalske boghandels forlag, 1898), 55–6.
[2] *Ibid.*, 110.
[3] Hanne Engberg, *En digters historie* (*History of a Poet*), 65.
[4] *Ibid.*, 85.

their Power".[5] Rode could not make any promises, but in the end concluded that, if Delius was burning to write something for *Dansen gaar*, he might go ahead and compose a prelude. When the work was completed in the summer of 1899, now expanded into a symphonic poem with the French title *La Ronde se déroule*, the title page was adorned with just those lines about The Dance of Life from Aage Volmer's speech. As far as is known, the work was never performed in conjunction with Rode's drama, but the composer was pleased with much of the music he had written. On two occasions, in 1901 and 1912, he would blow the dust off it and make revised versions, now with a new title coined directly from Volmer: *Lebenstanz* (*The Dance of Life*). It was the same title that Edvard Munch had borrowed for his most Rode-inspired paintings.

While writing *La Ronde se déroule*, Delius had also been studiously developing ideas for a new opera, and the closing scene of Rode's drama would be significant for his work on *A Village Romeo and Juliet*. The lovers Aage and Klara turn their backs on the world and walk hand in hand towards an exalted and erotic death. Volmer exclaims:

> It is beautiful to die in a state of exalted happiness. [...] I don't think any more that – that I am human. – I think – there is something that is opening itself for us. Now we can embrace all of life's greatness.[6]

On Delius, a passionate admirer of *Tristan und Isolde* since his student days, Aage Volmer's *Liebestod* would have made a deep impression. (Rode's Klara belongs, however, to the world in a way that Wagner's Isolde did not, and at the decisive moment changes her mind, crawling away from the cliff edge on all fours.) In Volmer's longing for an ideal union with his beloved in the bosom of nature before dissolving in death, there are clear contact points with the suicide pact of Sali and Vrenchen in *A Village Romeo and Juliet*. There, the young couple walk to the Paradise Garden and then on towards death.

1898: A first visit to Norway with Jelka

Among the documents that came to light during the preparation of this book is a letter that offers circumstantial evidence that Delius returned to Norway in the summer of 1898. Also that Jelka Rosen got her first taste of the country. On a later visit, in 1906 (see p. 210), Delius and Jelka stay in Munch's summer retreat of Åsgårdstrand, but are disappointed to find that the painter is staying in Germany. Munch's Aunt Karen writes to tell him of Delius's presence in Åsgårdstrand, adding: 'He really likes being here and told me that he had been present when you bought the house'.[7] It is this statement that strongly indicates

---

[5] Letter from Helge Rode to Delius, 14 September 1898 (DT).
[6] Helge Rode, *Dansen gaar*, 226.
[7] Letter from Karen Bjølstad to Munch, 9 July 1906 (MM).

that the composer was in Norway in 1898, and likely on a visit to Munch in Åsgårdstrand. (Jelka Rosen's presence on this trip to Norway is inferred from the lack of surviving correspondence between the couple in these summer months. On all his travels abroad without her, Delius wrote frequently.)

Edvard Munch stayed most of August and September 1898 in the fishing village, but when necessary travelled back and forth to Kristiania on the fjord steamer. It was while on one of these trips that he fell into conversation with an Åsgårdstrand fisherman who wanted to sell a small house close by the fjord edge.[8] Munch was immediately interested. Whether Delius was present on the ferry trip, at a subsequent viewing of the property, or at the contract signing in Kristiania on 25 August is unknown. The tiny house would become a retreat for the painter in summers up to 1905, more sporadically in later years. After Munch's death in 1947 it was purchased with public funds and opened as a museum in 1949.

Helge Rode was evidently also in Åsgårdstrand at the same time as Delius and Jelka. Many years later, most likely in 1929, Munch drafted a letter to Delius:

> Do you remember when we – you Helge Rode and I in Åsgårdstrand more than 30 years ago discussed things that were to come. We talked about the transparency of the body and telepathy – That is just what we have now, X-rays and radio and the wonderful waves that bind us all to the whole world and the cosmos – [9]

In the autumn of 1898, the becalmed composer suddenly got fresh wind in his sails. His loyal supporter throughout the 1890s in Paris, Uncle Theodor, died and Delius inherited a tidy 25,000 francs that could immediately be invested in his career. He quickly relocated to London and embarked on rounds of dispiriting visits to wealthy patrons of the arts in the hope of finding a sponsor for *Koanga*.[10] With him he had letters of introduction from influential acquaintances, including Gabriel Fauré. The door-opener for Delius, however, turned out to be his Norwegian friend from Florida. Jutta Bell was now working in London as a voice teacher and in all likelihood it was she who introduced Delius to her agent at the Concorde Concert Control. Plans were soon in motion for a wide-ranging presentation of the music of Delius, including much of *Koanga*, at a prestigious London concert in May 1899.

Mr Grey in hardback

Delius invariably left an impression on people he met, and his strong personality was often commented upon. On at least two occasions around the

[8] Næss, *Munch*, 188.
[9] Letter draft from Munch to Delius, undated, probably March 1929 (MM).
[10] London's polluted air was also depressing for Delius. 'Everything fine & free must wither here', he wrote to Jelka (undated letter, probably 5 January 1899) (GM).

turn of the century he also served as a role model for different authors. We have already witnessed that the exalted proclamations of Helge Rode's Aage Volmer may have been sublimated from conversations he had with Delius and Munch. In two other literary works the composer made an appearance in an even lighter disguise.

Under her professional name of Jutta Bell-Ranske, his Florida friend had her first book published in London in 1901, a collection of short stories about Norwegian country life entitled *Peasant Lassies: Tales of Norway*. Here, the insatiable English appetite for books on Norway was fed with seven independent stories of peasant girls, tales of irresistible love among meadow flowers and at barn dances, sprinkled with songs and folk tales Jutta would have learnt as a young girl. The longest story in the collection is about Asta, not a 'peasant lassie' but a young woman from a well-to-do Kristiania family, as was Jutta. Asta is sent on a summer holiday to a Gudbrandsdal farm and camouflages her breeding in a country dialect and simple attire so that she might take part in the daily workings of the farm. Asta's father sends an emissary with letters for her, a young, tall and charismatic Englishman with a weakness for good cigars. Well disguised, she succeeds in deceiving Mr Grey into believing that she is a peasant girl. Yes, Mr Grey – the name Delius had himself chosen when wishing to deceive the world. As people often did when they met Delius, Asta comments on Mr Grey's blue eyes:

> For Grey had a knack of looking at women as if the one he spoke with was 'the one' in all the world. He had beautiful, dreamy blue eyes, like the mountain mere, that seemed to reflect all things from such depths that you would think they really lingered there.[11]

Asta falls for Mr Grey's charms, despite being aware that he is the sort of man who abuses the trust of gullible girls. He has, after all, a certain talent for explaining away his actions:

> 'I wish I could chuck my stupid impulses away with you! But what will you have? I am not responsible for my thoughts and moods; my surroundings are. I am a "Stimmungsmensch", a decided "Stimmungsmensch"!'[12]

Stimmung was something of a catchword in Delius's language, one of many German words that leaked into his English and French.[13]

If Grey was modelled on what Jutta knew of Delius, then it is reasonable to read into Asta's situation what we know of Jutta in Florida and Paris. Asta

---

[11] Jutta Bell-Ranske, *Peasant Lassies: Tales from Norway* (London: Freemantle & Co., 1901), 13.
[12] *Ibid.*, 34.
[13] Here is a typical example from a letter to Jelka (5 January 1899) in which Delius asks how a couple of her paintings are progressing: 'How is my poppy garden getting along? & the moonlight Stimmung?' (GM).

stands by her respectable morals, perhaps much as Jutta had done when resist-
ing the passionate approaches of the young Delius in Florida (see p. 19):

> Why had he spoken so sneeringly of love as an ennobling influence to keep one
> good and pure? Why had he laughed when she said she would rather die than
> see her ideal soiled by an unworthy lowering desire?[14]

When Jutta had looked up Delius in Paris in 1893, she had found a man no
longer in love with her. He appreciated Jutta as a 'sister nature' to his own (see
p. 108). Is it this cool detachment Jutta is deriding when she has Asta warn Mr
Grey that

> 'you will find your gain turning to loss if you play with love.' There was a sweet
> dignity about her as she said it, and he could not help feeling it. He would have
> liked to have had a sister like that, he thought; but about another fellow's sister
> he had less compunction.[15]

Asta's infatuation with the charismatic English emissary ends tragically when
she takes her own life.

It is unknown whether Delius ever read *Peasant Lassies*. He devoured, however, the novel *The Journalist*, written by his librettist Charles F. Keary and
published in London in 1898. 'Keary's book is very good', he noted in a letter
to Jelka a week after coming to England in November, commenting that for
the character of Sophus Jonsen, an Anglo-Danish playwright, the author had
'taken an awful lot of sayings out of my mouth'.[16] Lionel Carley has detailed
Keary's debt to the free-speaking composer, pointing out that Sophus Jonsen
'dabbles in alchemy, and is a disciple of Nietzsche. He is equally at home in
England, France or Germany [...] His ingrained cynicism is usually turned
to the mockery of the bourgeoisie and of philistinism in general – especially
when manifested in England.'[17] At least one other person in Delius's circle can
be identified in the novel. An itinerant musician strolls in and out of the life of
Sophus Jonsen, a man known for 'his enchanting fiddle and his squalid loves'.[18]
His name is Hauch, and Keary describes him as 'an extraordinary man! Where
had he not wandered and on foot, paying his way mostly by playing on his
violin, a little fiddle which he kept specially for such journeys, and carried
in its case strapped on his back?' Keary would have become acquainted with
Halfdan Jebe in France in 1896 while working with Delius on the libretto for
Koanga.

At the start of 1899, the itinerant Norwegian strolled back into the life of
Delius. Jebe had tried to cage his wanderlust and live a more conventional life

---

[14] Jutta Bell-Ranske, *Peasant Lassies*, 76.
[15] *Ibid.*, 82.
[16] Letter from Delius to Jelka, 28 November 1898 (GM).
[17] *The Journalist*, Appendix VIII, LC1, 416.
[18] Charles F. Keary, *The Journalist* (London: Methuen, 1898), 260.

as conductor of the Centralteater orchestra in Kristiania. There he had fallen in love with one of the actresses, Sofie Bernhoft, and they had got married in secret. Several small compositions by Jebe were also published in Kristiania in 1898. He was trying to settle down, but it was all to no avail. After only one season at the theatre – a period of incessant argument with the theatre management – Jebe was desperate to shake the city dust from his jacket and stride out into the world again. He wrote to Delius:

> And now I am on a journey to the world beyond, as befits an old entertainer. Always onwards, always onwards! it is still far to the land of the holy madness. Well, have you not taught me, you my only good teacher in the world, to skim the cream off the milk and to pluck the flower of youth? And you will see that I have understood you, because I have killed myself to ensure that joy lives forever.[19]

In the middle of January, Delius travelled home to Grez from London, taking Jebe with him. When the important Delius Concert was held in London in May, it was Jebe who led the orchestra. Although Delius's network of Norwegian contacts shrivelled after *Folkeraadet*, two men remained among his dearest friends until the end of his life. Halfdan Jebe was one of them, Edvard Munch the other. In the spring and summer of 1899, the threads of Delius's and Munch's lives were to be spun ever closer together.

1899: Tulla Larsen in Grez and Paris

Munch's relationships with women followed a pattern. Once the first fascination had worn off, he felt suffocated and threatened. Thus ran his affair with Jebe's sister, Tupsy. And thus ran his relationship with Mathilde Larsen, the woman who suffered most from this poor treatment and who endured it longest. Tulla, as she was known, was the daughter of a vintner who had died in 1875, leaving her a substantial private fortune. She was twenty-nine when Munch got to know her in Kristiania in August 1898 and around Christmas they were drawn into an intimate relationship. To escape the censure of the provincial chattering classes they fled in March 1899 first to Paris, then on to Florence. These days were, in the words of Atle Næss, 'both a honeymoon period and an end station for the affair between Tulla Larsen and Munch – seen from his angle. It would however take three and a half years for him to bring it to a close, and the rest of his life to process the after-effects.'[20] In Florence, Munch had a breakdown, both physical and mental, and insisted on Tulla returning alone to Paris. By coincidence, Helge Rode was in the Renaissance city with his mother Margrethe Vullum and, to aid his recovery, she

---

[19] Letter from Halfdan Jebe to Delius, undated, probably autumn 1898 (DT).
[20] Næss, *Munch*, 192–3.

contrived to move Munch up to the quiet mountain village of Fiesole. For her part, Tulla – in despair at being separated and on the brink of her own breakdown – threw herself into the nightlife of Paris with other Norwegian artists, and with Munch's composer friend, Fritz Delius. Through her letters to Munch we catch glimpses of Delius's life, split between the pulsating city and the quiet garden of Jelka Rosen. It seems that 13 April is the date Tulla Larsen first met the composer:

> Together with the Segelckes, Obstfelder, Delius, Gunnar Heiberg, Miss Arnesen [I visited] all sorts of places and came home at 5 o'clock. What do you think. But I promise to better my ways. Travel next week out to Marlotte to Hauge and Delius at least for a few days. [...] I really like Delius, he has promised to play some music for me when I go down to the country.[21]

On another evening, Tulla went from restaurant to restaurant in the company of Oda Krohg, Gunnar Heiberg, Edvard Diriks, Hans Werner Jacobsen and the Segelckes and, having danced at Bal Bullier, arrived home at six in the morning. Her letter suggested that Halfdan Jebe was also a member of the Norwegian colony:

> I'm often together with Delius. He is nice – travels on the 20th to London to lead the rehearsals for his big concert there on 30th of May. Yesterday I looked through some of his J. P. Jacobsen and Drachmann settings, the translations for which he has done himself. [...] Is Helge Rode still in F[lorence] now? Is Miss Jebe there, her brother asked me to find out yesterday?[22]

Ten years after moving to Paris, Delius still favoured the company of artists from the Norwegian colony. Of this group we already know dramatist Gunnar Heiberg well, and artist Edvard Diriks had been acquainted with Delius at least since 1893 (see p. 102). What of the others?

Sigbjørn Obstfelder: Tulla Larsen's letter is one of two known sources connecting Delius with the Norwegian poet in Paris. The other is a letter Delius wrote to Rode in September 1900: 'I was extremely sorry to hear of Obstfelder's death – Mrs Krogh [sic] told me of it. I did not know him well but he always struck me as being very refined & delicate.'[23]

Alfred Hauge: A close friend of Munch – they had shared a studio in Kristiania in 1895 and Åsgårdstrand in 1898. The ailing and impoverished Hauge had influential sponsors in Norway to thank for his being able to travel to Paris in March 1899 and in April to move out to the artist colony in the village of Marlotte, just a few kilometres from Delius's home in Grez-sur-Loing. Art historian Tone Skedsmo has suggested it was Obstfelder who introduced them, and also that Delius proposed that Hauge accompany him on a restorative

---

[21] Letter from Tulla Larsen to Munch, undated, probably 14 April 1899 (MM).
[22] Letter from Tulla Larsen to Munch, undated, probably mid-April 1899 (MM).
[23] Letter from Delius to Helge Rode, 22 September 1900 (DT).

trip to Florida, presumably the one taken in early 1897. Hauge's constant lack of resources prevented him from travelling.[24] In the same way as he did for Munch's art, Delius left no stone unturned in promoting Hauge among Parisian gallerists.

The lyrical moods of the paintings of **Oda Krohg** are seen as a foreshadowing of neo-romanticism. Her affair with Gunnar Heiberg had started in 1893 and since 1897 they had been more or less living together in Paris. Oda was also looking after her son Per,[25] born to her and Christian Krohg in 1889. **Hans Werner Jacobsen** was a painter from Kristiania. How much contact he and Delius had is uncertain, but they had known each other since the summer of 1887 when the composer had stayed with Jacobsen's family on Malmøya in the Kristiania Fjord: Hans Werner was the brother of Delius's friend from his Leipzig days, Camilla Jacobsen. **Severin Segelcke** was an artist and military officer. He and his wife arrived in Paris together with Hauge in March 1899. **Borghild Arnesen** was attached in this period to the artist colony gathered around the French painter Armand Point in Marlotte.

From Alfred Hauge's letters home to his family we know that two other significant literary figures were occasionally part of the Norwegian group in Paris: American poet Stuart Merrill and Anglo-Irish dramatist Oscar Wilde. We have previously seen that Edvard Munch regarded both as being members of the artist group in Paris to which he and Delius belonged (see p. 119). Merrill had lived in Paris for so many years that Hauge took him to be French. Wilde had spent two years in prison for sodomy from 1895 to 1897, and would experience relatively isolated years in Paris with deteriorating health until his death in 1900. Whether or not they spent any time with Delius is uncertain, but it is highly likely. Hauge relates:

> I have met all sorts of strange people in Paris [...] Merrill, brilliant, French – modern poet. – Oscar Wilde, the great poet and infamous criminal (he has however had no influence on my morals). – Gunnar Heiberg, one of the few large-spirited Norwegians, Mrs Krohg, our finest Norwegian female painter.[26]

It is clear from Tulla's correspondence with Munch that her intention was partly to arouse his jealousy in the hope of hastening his arrival in Paris, and to that end she fed him stories of Heiberg and Jacobsen flirting with her. Delius, too, gets short shrift after his departure for England: 'He has now left to prepare

---

[24] Tone Skedsmo. 'Alfred Hauge' in *Norsk kunstnerleksikon* (*Norwegian Art Lexicon*), accessed 14 November 2015 at https://nkl.snl.no/Alfred_Hauge.

[25] It was perhaps inevitable that Per Krohg should grow up to be an artist. Today he is best known for his majestic mural that dominates the chamber of the Security Council in the United Nations building.

[26] Letter from Alfred Hauge to Ester Fett, 24 June 1899 (NB).

17. Though taken early in their relationship, c.1900, this photograph seems to capture some of the persistent tension between Edvard Munch and Tulla Larsen.

his big concert in London, we are almost glad to see the back of him. I sort of like him, but all his flirting can get on your nerves.'[27]

Artists were now preparing to leave for their summer colonies in the idyllic villages south of Paris, including Grez and Marlotte. On 24 April, Tulla Larsen took up residence in the Hôtel Chevillon in Grez, along with another figure from the periphery of the Norwegian colony, Alexandra Mowinckel.[28] Four days later, Oda Krohg and Per arrived. For the next six weeks, Tulla Larsen's address was in Grez and, in between drawing and painting and lively evenings with Norwegian friends, she penned despairing letters to Edvard Munch. She had been allowed by Delius the use of his piano, but her presence and that of the other Norwegians quickly became an irritant for Jelka. Delius wrote from London: 'I can't stand Mrs Mowinckel – she is tactless & stupid (almost) – it was all I could do not to be rude to her in Paris […] Miss Larsen is better & more natural – If you don't like them send them to Hell! – not much in either of them […] Hauge is very nice –'[29] Alfred Hauge, who cycled over from Marlotte most evenings, was also useful to Jelka, sitting as her model.[30] From London, Delius invited Gunnar Heiberg to his concert, at which excerpts from the *Folkeraadet* music were to be performed. Heiberg declined, blaming work commitments for the *Verdens Gang* newspaper, but was no doubt also reluctant to be too far away from Oda Krohg, with their relationship now going through a bad patch.

Around 15 May, Edvard Munch had recovered sufficiently to travel to Paris on his way home to Norway. His nerves were, however, so fragile that he avoided socialising and demanded of Tulla that she keep her distance. After a few days he relented and the couple had a short, strained reunion in the capital before she was again packed off on a train for Grez.

Immediately after his concert in London on 30 May, an exhausted Delius travelled back to France, stopping in Paris to visit friends. He brought with him the concert's conductor, Alfred Hertz. 'On Saturday evening Delius and I were at the Molards' for a while. They were so nice to me', Tulla wrote to Munch, informing him that she had made his excuses: 'I told them that you would have so much liked to have been there – but were too ill to move.'[31] By the following evening, Delius and Hertz had arrived in Grez and Tulla was invited round:

---

[27] Letter from Tulla Larsen to Munch, 24 April 1899 (MM).
[28] She was the sister of Charlotte Bødtker, the Kristiania woman with whom Delius spent some time during his Norway trip of 1891 (see p. 78). Alexandra Mowinckel had also met Delius in Kristiania during the run of *Folkeraadet*.
[29] Letter from Delius to Jelka, undated, c.4 May 1899 (GM).
[30] Letter from Tulla Larsen to Munch, 12 May 1899 (MM).
[31] Letter from Tulla Larsen to Munch, undated, probably 5 June 1899 (MM).

Delius is living here now – as is his orchestra conductor from Breslau – to whom the credit for Delius's success in London should probably go. Yesterday I was invited to the house – you know he is now living with Miss Rosen – Later Hauge also came – poor fellow – he really hasn't got two sous to rub together now – and is completely at a loss for ideas.[32]

Both Munch and Delius were now longing for the Norwegian summer. On 5 June, Munch travelled home to the small house he had purchased in Åsgård-strand. Tulla Larsen remained in Paris a couple more weeks to take care of some business for the artist, including the printing of several lithographs and woodcuts. Oda Krohg and Gunnar Heiberg had also left Grez. So a semblance of rural peace returned and Delius could devote himself to a couple of months of creative work before he and Jelka also took the ferry to Norway.

Delius Orchestral Concert in London

In St James's Hall in London on 30 May an audience in Delius's homeland heard for the first time his orchestral music. The sounds that introduced him were the quiet, rising herding calls of *Over the Hills and Far Away* – an exploration of the part of his personality that was stimulated by the Norwegian mountain landscape. With two intermezzi from *Folkeraadet* also on the programme, along with five Danish songs and the newly completed prelude to Helge Rode's *Dansen gaar* (here presented as *The Dance Goes On*), it is hardly surprising that some reviewers wrongly deduced that the composer was of Scandinavian descent. Advertised as the Delius Orchestral Concert, the extensive programme also placed before its audience abundant evidence both for the wide horizons of the composer's inspirations and for his talents as a writer for music theatre. This was not least due to the extracts from *Koanga* – parts of the first and third acts and the whole of the second – which were performed in concert version with a choir of over a hundred and fifty voices.

All expenses were met by Delius from the money he had inherited, and with this courageous investment of resources he 'presented his card' to the London musical establishment. To Jutta Bell, who had helped him with the concert preparations, he wrote: 'The Concert of course has done me an immense amount of good & has placed me amongst the first composers of today – The german papers also have long articles.'[33] As far as the English musical world was concerned, the optimism was poorly founded. Eight more years would pass before his homeland would press its exiled son to its bosom with any warmth.

---

[32] *Ibid.*
[33] Letter from Delius to Jutta Bell, undated, probably mid-June 1899 (JUL).

Through much of the winter and spring of 1899, Delius worked on the orchestral composition that was performed in London with the title *The Dance Goes On* and which on the title page of the score is called *La Ronde se déroule*. It is therefore strange that, a month after returning to Grez, he should have written to Helge Rode: 'My "Vorspiel" to "Dansen Gaar" will be quite completed in a week – I hope I am not too late for the first performance.'[34] It is possible that Delius wished to revise the work after hearing it in London. Even more peculiar, however, is the fact that he was unaware that the theatrical première of *Dansen gaar* had taken place at Det Kongelige Teater in Copenhagen on 6 April. It did not enjoy much critical success and had a run of only six performances.

The whirlwind energy of the symphonic poem, a life-affirming dance in waltz rhythm, seems to have remained in his creative mind throughout 1899. On his return from Norway in August, he threw himself into creating a closely related work, *Paris: A Nocturne (The Song of a Great City)*. This too was a symphonic poem, this too had exuberant and glittering dance episodes, and the motor of this new work was a waltz melody almost identical to that driving *La Ronde se déroule*. With the refinement of his art represented by these two works, Delius lifted his skills to a level he had never previously attained. The outer influences working on him are not difficult to trace. In London he had enjoyed days of listening to his orchestral music in rehearsal. At the same time, he was a studious admirer of the symphonic poems of Richard Strauss from the 1880s and 1890s; they were potent and inspirational. In the course of 1899, Delius managed through *La Ronde se déroule* and *Paris* to hone his skills as a master of the nuances of orchestral colour.

1899: By the coast with Edvard Munch, to the mountains with Ole Olsen

Edvard Munch left Paris on 5 June. When Tulla Larsen returned to Norway two weeks later she had with her a letter from Delius – the first between Munch and Delius that has survived: 'I intend to come to Norway at the end of July to do some walking in the mountains – Would you like to come along with me into Jotunheimen or on Hardangervidda? I could be a pretty good guide – How are the etchings of the sick girl coming along?'[35] Munch replied from Åsgårdstrand on 24 June, complaining that work and poor health prevented him making any commitment:

> At the very least I hope we will meet – there is a possibility I might be able to join you – if not up to the mountains then part of the way –

---

[34] Letter from Delius to Helge Rode, 29 June 1899 (DT).
[35] Letter from Delius to Munch, 12 June 1899 (MM).

> I am living in my small house in Åsgårdstrand. Unfortunately the guestroom has not been fitted out yet – otherwise you could have stayed there for a while – before you left for the mountains – In any case you must come down here for a few days.[36]

Delius travelled to Åsgårdstrand in early July – again with Jelka, so we are bereft of the detailed information that was habitually contained in letters home to her when he travelled alone. It is only from two letters from Tulla Larsen to Munch that we know of the time they spent in Munch's summer paradise. Forbidden by Munch to come near him, she wrote from her place of exile on the other side of the fjord, filling her letters with the anguish of the spurned lover:

> Today at last I got a small sign that you are alive – the postcard from E. M.! – Delius and Rosen – So you have got those two to come down and I suppose you will see a lot of them – how I envy them – if only I had the easy conversational talent of Delius, always pleasant to be with, even for you – yes, him you like a lot![37]

In reply to the query in Delius's letter about *Det syke barn* (*The Sick Child*), Munch wrote in his reply: 'Do you think we could organise that plan with etchings and music – and J. P. Jacobsen?' When these two artists had discussed this joint venture, and what it would entail – about this we unfortunately have no further information. John Boulton Smith, who made a study of the friendship of Munch and Delius, pointed out that this was 'a period when synthesis between the arts was a common aim and innumerable examples could be instanced'.[38] Many commentators have pointed out the musical expressivity of Munch's paintings and both the Schwarzen Ferkel group in Berlin and the Molard circle in Paris brought together the talents of painters, poets and musicians. Munch and Delius were equally enthusiastic admirers of the poetry of Jens P. Jacobsen. In the mid-1890s, the artist was fascinated with Jacobsen's novel *Niels Lyhne* (1880) and Munch historians have suggested that the proposed collaboration would have been Delius settings of texts from the book with Munch scenography[39] – an intriguing thought in the light of the fact that Delius would draw the material for his final opera, *Fennimore and Gerda* (1908–10), from Jacobsen's novel. Boulton Smith, however, was of the opinion that Delius's Jacobsen songs would have been a more likely starting point. It has to remain speculation. Even if the tantalising project was further discussed while Delius and Jelka were at Åsgårdstrand in July 1899, nothing seems to have resulted from it.

---

[36] Letter from Munch to Delius, 24 June 1899 (DT).
[37] Letter from Tulla Larsen to Munch, undated, probably second week of July 1899 (MM).
[38] John Boulton Smith, *Frederick Delius and Edvard Munch: Their friendship and their correspondence* (Rickmansworth: Triad Press, 1983), 51.
[39] See Arne Eggum, *Edvard Munch: Livsfrisen fra maleri til grafikk* (*Edvard Munch: The Frieze of Life from painting to print*) (Oslo: J. M. Stenersens forlag A. S., 1990), 15.

'Well imagine that, Delius and Miss R. have moved on already', exclaimed Tulla Larsen in a letter to Munch on 11 August.[40] In fact, Delius had left Åsgårdstrand for the mountains in mid-July, while Jelka travelled to Germany to be with Ida Gerhardi. For two to three weeks he toured in Jotunheimen with Norwegian composer Ole Olsen. On 21 July they ascended with the aid of a guide from the valley floor of Visdalen to the mountain lodge of Juvvasshytta, ready to conquer Galdhøpiggen the following day. Their signatures in the lodge guestbook are the only evidence we have of their trip and, indeed, of Delius's friendship with Olsen. Twelve years older than Delius, Olsen has been described as 'one of the most famous and popular personalities' in Norway at the turn of the century. His music fell out of fashion after his death in 1927.

In mid-August, Delius continued south to Copenhagen, writing to Jelka: 'I saw Jebe just before leaving Christiania, he is vegetating – or waiting for something to turn up'.[41] He closed the letter to her with the words: 'Believe me, your sincere friend'. In the coming years, however, their friendship would be put under severe pressure.

1900–1901: Storm at home

With resolute conviction in his abilities, Delius entered the 1900s with focus on *A Village Romeo and Juliet*: 'I want to begin the century with a work absolutely, entirely modern & new – the basis of the next century so to speak as far as dramatic art goes.'[42] He was painfully aware of his lack of ability as a poet, but at the same time he had been frustrated by several attempts to stimulate his librettist Charles F. Keary to explore modern solutions, with the sensibilities of Italian *verismo* as his model. In the end, however, Delius once again felt he was best equipped to produce the text he desired and set about writing it himself.

On every occasion in 1900 and 1901 when he could clear for himself a period for undisturbed work, he sat and worked at the opera. Such periods were few and far between. He had approached the new century with optimism, but soon discovered that he was still ensnared in the problems of the old one. With regard to his health, his financial situation and his stagnant career, the period of 1900–01 is not dissimilar to the dark year of 1895. Delius began to notice that his eyesight quickly tired, another warning of the disabling disease that was to blight his life. With most of his inheritance swallowed by the London concert, he now found his relatives in England and Germany even less interested in offering him assistance. For a period of six months from October 1900 he made a demoralising tour of conductors and producers in Germany. With him he had many new scores, as well as positive reviews of his London concert. To

[40] Letter from Tulla Larsen to Munch, 11 August 1899 (MM).
[41] Letter from Delius to Jelka, 14 August 1899 (GM).
[42] Letter from Delius to Charles F. Keary, undated, early 1900 (DT).

Delius it seemed, however, that the barrier he faced was as impenetrable as ever: 'as far as I can see before I am also catalogued & stamped I have not the slightest earthly chance – not the slightest – only a miracle can push me thro'.[43]

In the first years of the 1900s, he also had to cope with a crisis in his private life that added further knots of anxiety to his mind. Jelka Rosen, thirty-two years old at the turn of the century, slid into a depression. The principal reason seems to have been either that she had become deeply insecure about her relationship with him, or that she was struggling to accept the consequences of the choices she had made. Jelka was as free-thinking a spirit as Delius, as lightly bound by convention. When, however, she had invited him into her house it was an act of genuine love, a passion that would mature and become richer the better she understood his music. In return, Delius offered only an affectionate friendship and genuine admiration for her art; for several years after moving to Grez, he continued to have affairs. The first serious signs of discontent are evident in letters from the first half of 1899. While he was in Paris, he received from her a letter – now lost – in which she apparently questioned his behaviour. He replied:

> Don't ever think that I don't understand you – I do – and that's why I hate myself so much sometimes. The truth however is – that my artistic aspiration has drowned & smothered everything else in me – Am I going to the devil or not? I don't know, but I must go after my art & I know you understand it & want it so.[44]

In mid-1900, Delius sent in secret a plea for help to Ida Gerhardi, at the time working in Germany, begging her to come to Grez: 'She is terribly depressed & out of sorts – She keeps saying she thinks she is going mad. […] I think I was rather foolish to move into the house here.'[45] Travelling in Germany six months later, he wrote to Jelka: 'I am not affectionate – and regret it also. […] Please follow me thro' your friendship eyes where I am always to be found – Thro' love's eyes, no doubt, I become hazy and indistinct.'[46] And a little later:

> I am trying to live so that I can accomplish something in art – *that is all* – The mere fact of my being able to work so well in your home ought to speak for itself – When I suddenly wake up to the fact that you are suffering a sort of hell, then only have I ever thought of leaving.[47]

Few of Jelka's letters from this period survive, but from his we get the impression of a man trying to handle the situation to the best of his ability. The ability to understand or feel empathy with the needs of others was, however, not among his most developed talents. In 1900, Jelka got to know Auguste Rodin

---

[43] Letter from Delius to Jelka, undated, probably 9 November 1900 (GM).
[44] Letter from Delius to Jelka, undated, probably March 1899 (GM).
[45] Letter from Delius to Ida Gerhardi, undated, probably 28 July 1900 (DT).
[46] Letter from Delius to Jelka, 14 January 1901 (GM).
[47] Letter from Delius to Jelka, 24 January 1901 (GM).

in Paris, and the inspiration and support she found in the sculptor's work, as well as his close interest in her as an artist and a person, were invaluable to her in this testing period.

Jelka evidently found herself on the horns of a dilemma. She longed for a child, but feared it would lead to her losing Delius. It is almost certain that he regarded his artistic ambitions as irreconcilable with family life; and there was the added, perturbing possibility that any offspring might inherit his syphilis – so the couple may even have refrained from sexual intimacy.[48] The conflict reached its crisis point in 1902 when Jelka was further burdened with the task of caring for her dying mother in Paris. 'You know that I care for you immensely and am your real friend', he wrote. 'But you really ought to have somebody to love you in the way you desire – A real strong man who could entirely absorb your nature.'[49] In the summer of 1902, the couple undertook an extensive tour of Norway; as we shall see below, a new depth was opened in their relationship and they put the crisis behind them.

On his self-promotional tour in Germany, Delius was offered friendly support by Halfdan Jebe. In the spring of 1901, Jebe arrived in Berlin on the first leg of a meandering, summer-long trip through Europe with his actress wife Sofie. On leaving Berlin, the couple travelled to Dresden, Vienna and Budapest, then into Serbia and Romania, before turning west again and enjoying Venice for a month. Jebe cajoled money for this trip from friends and relatives or earned some along the way with his violin. By the middle of June, they had moved on to Naples and were keen to see Delius and Jelka join them on the final leg of their journey. 'Are you coming or are you not coming with us to Cairo? That is the big question', proclaimed Jebe.[50] An exotic summer holiday? No, for Jebe the dream of escaping Europe for an extended period had become an obsession and he suggested that the two couples should stay in Egypt at least a year. 'What do you think, and when would you like to go? That will be fine for me, or as soon as possible.' What Delius replied is unknown, but a month later Jebe was back in Paris and soliciting his friend for money. In return he could offer a souvenir from Egypt: 'you shall have an account of my travels and a little "hashish". I hereby invite you to let your hair down next time you are in Paris. And without women!'[51] Newly returned, Jebe's wanderlust was already itching: 'A new summer will no doubt come along [...] when are we going to the Pacific Ocean, will I also have to do that on my own?'

---

[48] From October 1901, however, a fragment of a letter survives (GM), though Delius had urged Jelka to destroy it, in which he warmly praised the way she had tackled a personal crisis. Although his language was deliberately guarded, the traumatic event was most likely a miscarriage or an abortion.

[49] Letter from Delius to Jelka, undated, probably spring 1902 (GM).

[50] Letter from Halfdan Jebe to Delius, 15 June, probably 1901 (DT).

[51] Letter from Halfdan Jebe to Delius, 26 July 1901 (DT).

From our privileged position, with an overview of the direction in Delius's life towards an eventual breakthrough early in the last century, it seems absurd that Jebe would expect Delius to abandon musical Europe for a year of carefree living in Cairo. We should keep in mind, therefore, that no one knew the 'Cyril Grey' side of Delius's personality better than Jebe. During their Bohemian years in Paris, during their alcohol-fuelled tour of Norwegian mountain hotels in 1896 and of course during their escapades with false names in America in 1897, the Norwegian had observed the pull exerted on Delius by the exotic, unsullied and genuine, and his friend's need to kick over the traces in polite society. If ever was a real danger that these forces in Delius would define his course, it had passed by the time he returned from Florida in 1897. Jebe would continue for some years to tempt him with visions of a Pacific tour, to poke the slumbering 'Cyril Grey', but without ever again waking more than a powerful longing in his friend. Some years later, Delius would pertinently sum up the difference between himself and the wandering Norwegian troubadour: 'He seems to be making a reality of his life & living all the music that he has in him – With me it is just the contrary, I am putting everything into my music – all my poetry & all my adventures.' [52]

Delius was not to be found in Cairo that summer; Jebe can, however, be found in the large composition that occupied him, *A Village Romeo and Juliet*. The figure of The Dark Fiddler comes and goes throughout the story, embodying an alternative lifestyle to that of the village and its censorious morality. And in the words Delius penned for The Dark Fiddler we hear Jebe's constant maxim, that the whole rotten society was worthless.

A Village Romeo and Juliet: a mountain opera

At the end of 1900, Delius felt that 'only a miracle could push me thro''. One year later there were signs that perseverance, hard work, good friends and resolute self-confidence might also get the job done. In March 1901, two of his Jacobsen songs for soloist and orchestra were performed in Paris under the baton of Vincent d'Indy. Throughout the spring, Ferruccio Busoni nurtured plans to give the premières in April of both *Paris* and the Piano Concerto with the Berlin Philharmonic. To Delius's bitter disappointment Busoni fell ill shortly before the concert, but the *Folkeraadet* music was performed instead. Then, in December 1901, Ida Gerhardi's unstinting promotion of the composer in Elberfeld bore fruit, conductor Hans Haym seizing the chance that Busoni had let slip. 'Paris will be done!',[53] he wrote enthusiastically to Delius a week before giving the first performance of the colourful symphonic poem.

---

[52] Letter from Delius to Adey Brunel, 27 April 1913 (CB).
[53] Postcard from Hans Haym to Delius, undated, but 6 December 1901 (DT).

The wind had begun to turn and also in his new creative work Delius seemed to be supremely confident of his powers. He had wished to meet the new century with a composition that would be 'entirely modern & new' in the history of music drama. With *A Village Romeo and Juliet* Delius went a long way to realising his ambition. For his theme he went to a source that was closer to Mascagni's *verismo* in *Cavalleria rusticana* than to the valiant derring-do of Koanga and Solano – extensions of an earlier period's mythical gods and noble heroes: this was a short story by Gottfried Keller, 'Romeo und Julia auf dem Dorfe', from the collection *Die Leute von Seldwyla* (1856). It relates the increasingly thorny dilemma encountered by two young lovers, Sali and Vrenchen. Their fathers are impetuous and proud farmers, forbidding them to see each other, and the lovers' displays of affection also go against the grain of village morals. Delius attempted to remove all elements extraneous to the central narrative, fixing his focus on the young couple's emotional drama. Writing in 1959, Thomas Beecham noted just how appropriate the lyrical and poetic music is to the story, clothing it in 'a recurring strain of tenderness more fully present than in any other operatic score of the past fifty years'.[54]

A Village Romeo and Juliet is the composer's most successful opera and of his six music dramas the one that is most frequently staged. In one important respect it can also be described as Delius's most 'Norwegian' opera (even after taking into account the purported Norwegian fairy tale backdrop to *Irmelin*) – in the sense that the Mountain Music developed in his Norwegian orchestral scores is here brought into play. At its most intense the drama is played out in an overgrown field, beside a river and in a beautiful garden by a dilapidated rural inn. Nature at its most intimate folds the lovers into sanctuaries without wider geographical contours. If, however, we allow our camera eye to draw back from the most emotionally charged situations, we discover that two vital components of *A Village Romeo and Juliet* rest on the set of stylistic traits, Mountain Music, that Delius crafted to express the metaphoric content of the mountainscape:

1. Principal leitmotifs of the opera are fashioned with Mountain Music characteristics;
2. Where nature is expansive in the opera, Delius uses horn calls to suggest mountain landscapes.

These landscape scenes constitute the frame of the opera and he has devoted much of his resources, both musical and dramatic, to establishing it; in productions it is, however, usually neglected by the director or scenic designer.

A Village Romeo and Juliet opens with broad melodic brushstrokes, suggesting a wide and open vista. The simple melody consists of two cells, one falling, one rising:

---

[54] Thomas Beecham, *A Mingled Chime* (G. P. Putnam's Sons: New York, 1943), 299.

Example 8.1 *A Village Romeo and Juliet*, opening

Both cells come to dominate much of the opera's leitmotif material. The phrase's rising cell, marked *x*, is closely related to rising herding calls we have seen in the composer's mountain scores, including Example 4.6 from the early Violin Sonata (the 'mountain sonata') and Example 6.1, the call that opens *Over the Hills and Far Away*. The falling phrase is also frequently rounded off with a lingering variant, similar to pentatonic calls in Delius's mountain works:

Example 8.2 *A Village Romeo and Juliet*, fig. 2, 1–4

A new element is soon added to the opening melody: Example 8.3. The upward-striving triplet is familiar from several themes in the two *Paa Vidderne* scores, such as Examples 3.3 and 4.3.

Example 8.3 *A Village Romeo and Juliet*, fig. 1, 3–5

This rising phrase will come to drive much of the love music in *A Village Romeo and Juliet*. There occurs, in other words, a re-envisaging or transference of certain types of Mountain Music: the striving, onward-driving force that Delius earlier associated with the mountain journey is here used to capture young love's upward rush of heart blood. Our initial reaction may be that mountaineers and lovers belong to different spheres, urge themselves towards different goals. In the creative mind of Delius, however, they were evidently linked in their pull upwards towards the ecstatic, towards an exalted sphere far from the confusion and pollution of everyday life. Just how closely coupled Mountain Music was to love music in his sensibilities in this period will be demonstrated later, when we consider the next phase of its re-envisaging – in two masterful compositions from the years 1905–06: *A Mass of Life* and the opera intermezzo 'The Walk to the Paradise Garden' (a later addition to *A Village Romeo and Juliet*).

At the rise of the curtain it is the wild land between the ploughed fields of Sali's and Vrenchen's fathers that is to the fore. As to what might be in the background, the stage directions here give no hint. We can, however, sketch in the missing details from the opening of Scene III, which takes place in the same wasteland – the young couple have secretly planned a tryst there:

> *The wild land overgrown with red poppies in full bloom, surrounded by cornfields; in the background fields and small villages perched here and there in the hills. Snow-mountains in the distance.*

The horizon is a mountainscape. As Scene III commences, the broad brush-strokes that started the opera, Example 8.1, open up the vista once more, but now the close relationship of this melody to Mountain Music is fully revealed. During the scene change a miniature tone-poem is played out, evoking for the listener a mountain landscape through the use of six onstage horns instructed to play several series of herding calls 'as if in the distance':

Example 8.4 *A Village Romeo and Juliet*, Scene III, opening, 3–4

The two rolling calls, marked *y* and *z*, we have met previously. Motif *y* we saw, for example, in *Paa Vidderne* (see Example 3.6), and motif *z* in *Over the Hills and Far Away* (Example 6.2). As we noted during the discussion of the melodrama, Delius may well have borrowed the rolling triplet call from Grieg, who, for his part, heard it sung by the herd girl Susanne. Versions of the calls echo in high woodwind, as if they are carried up into thin mountain air. All of these elements will be further developed in sequences of *The Song of the High Hills* twelve years later, in which the opera's compact tone poem is expanded to evoke the spiritual grandeur we associate with endless mountain panoramas.

After twenty-eight bars of calls the curtain rises and Sali and Vrenchen come into view. A new horn call is introduced; it is motif *x* from Example 8.1, now transformed into an upward-striving fanfare. Once more, mountain energy is being reassociated with young love.

If we refer to the overview of Mountain Music presented in Table 2 (p. 45) we see that the herding calls of the opera's opening belong in category 1, 'Peak'-music – associated with striving and energy. The horns' tone-poem at the opening of Scene III belongs instead to category 2, 'Plateau'-music – associated with solitude and oneness with nature. The same applies to the horn calls shortly after the opening of the opera's finale, Scene VI. In this passage we see clearly that the mountains framing the narrative are far more important than theatrical scenery. Sali and Vrenchen have fled from the eyes of the village to a place where society's outcasts gather – a run-down inn with a beautiful, over-grown garden – and here they meet again The Dark Fiddler and his vagabond friends. These are the stage directions:

> *In the distance the snow-mountains. [...] The dark fiddler stands with his back towards the audience and his hands on his back at the back of the stage and looks at the high mountains with the last glow upon them.*

From afar, the horns sound a pentatonic call, this time over a whispered tim-pani roll, an effect like the distant haze across the mountain horizon. To our sensibilities this whole tableau, with the 'outsider' looking to the horizon, can perhaps feel contrived, with a too rich taste of Romantic sentimentality. For this reason the mountains generally form no part of modern productions. Instead of seeking some way to renew the mountain metaphor, its imagery is usually jettisoned. In his transference of Mountain Music to love music, Delius is implying through The Dark Fiddler that the mountain plateau is an ideal-ised sanctuary for which all outsiders and all lovers long, exalted and secluded above the polluted paths of the world. For Sali and Vrenchen, banished from society, the perfect retreat of the uplands might embrace and hide them. The other vagabonds, however, are more down to earth; they point out that love will cool and then the couple can share partners with others in the group. Young love cannot endure such sentiments; the thought of losing each other is not to be endured. Sali and Vrenchen resolve on a suicide pact and push out into the river in a hay barge.

It is thought that the fictional Seldwyla around which Keller placed the story of Sali and Vrenchen is based on the borderland along the Rhine north of Zurich, more precisely in the riverside villages of Glattfelden and Kaiserstuhl in which his parents had their roots. It is an area of ancient villages and fertile, rolling hills, and may well have enchanted Delius as he travelled the Rhine valley via Basel on his way from France to Germany and back. The nearest 'snow-moun-tains', however, are very distant. And when uplands are mentioned by Keller at all, they are densely wooded slopes, not snow-topped summits. The proximity of Alpine mountainscapes suggested by Delius both in motif material, stage directions and in the horn call episodes – the weaving colloquy that opens Scene III, the sunset mood of Scene VI – is his own invention. A transferral

of the mountain aesthetic of his Norwegian orchestral scores to operatic narrative. At key moments he suggests that there is always a way out of social
conformity, always something beyond. It was a belief he sustained personally
through his constant visits to the remote uplands of Norway.

1902: Frederick and Jelka towards Galdhøpiggen

Delius's adventure in America in 1897 under the pseudonym Cyril Grey indicates that he was not averse to toying with his name under special circumstances. One of his principal goals in the early years of the century was to break
through in London, and this may have been motivation enough for him to
begin using, from 1902 onwards, an anglicised version of his Christian name.
Fritz, now forty years old, became Frederick.

In January and February 1902, Delius was back in Berlin for another circuit
of influential conductors and impresarios. Edvard Munch was also in the city
and, although a meeting is not documented, they almost certainly spent time
together. The artist had been invited to exhibit the twenty-two paintings that
made up his *Frieze of Life* series at the Berlin Secession in March and April, 'the
high point of his career so far and, for that matter, a not insignificant event in
the history of art', to borrow the words of Atle Næss.[55] By the time the exhibition opened, Delius was back in Grez. Much of the spring was devoted to composing an opera in one act, *Margot la Rouge*, a *verismo* treatment of a seedy
tale set in a Parisian café. Writing specifically for an Italian opera composition
(which he failed to win), the composer took some uncharacteristic stylistic
steps sideways and ended up with a work that was luridly melodramatic – and
has largely been ignored. Due to its extensive passages of high-quality writing,
however, the short opera has been going through a process of reappraisal in
recent years. In this same period he was working on a composition that speaks
of his constant affection for North America. The magnificent variations on a
slave song, *Appalachia*, now in a version for orchestra and choir, were begun
this year and demonstrate a sustained innovative imagination fired by his
reminiscences of Florida and Virginia.

Undated sketches for a composition for piano and orchestra with the working title *Mountain Solitude* may also date from this period.[56] It was now three
years since Delius had been in Norway and the pull of the mountains was
irresistible. Jelka had to spend much of the spring of 1902 at the bedside of
her dying mother in Paris and, while there, received letters from Frederick
outlining plans for a summer tour of the Jotunheim and Dovre mountains and
the Kristiania Fjord. With seemingly scant concern for her onerous duty, and
with enthusiasm mounting, he sent her lists of all the things they would need

---

[55] Næss, *Munch*, 237.
[56] See Threlfall, *Frederick Delius: A supplementary catalogue*, 217.

and other travel trivia – all at a time when Jelka was seriously weighing up her choice of life partner. In another light, his letters can also be seen as revealing that the prospect of showing Jelka the mountain landscapes that meant so much to him gave him an irrepressible pleasure. In May, he sought advice from Norwegian friends as to where he might hire cabins, and soon he could write from Grez to Jelka: 'I have just received news from Milly Bergh – She has the "hytte" [cabin] in the Dovre Fjeld – 75 Kroners for the whole summer – and also a boat – (near a lake) 2 rooms & an Alcove – Fine, Eh! We can get eggs & milk & butter from a Saeter near by and also a girl to clean up!'[57]

After Nina Grieg, Milly Bergh was the Norwegian woman with whom Delius maintained the longest friendship. They had known each other at least since 1897, when her husband Ludvig Bergh had had a role in *Folkeraadet*, and the friendship seems to have lasted until 1919 or perhaps longer. In Norwegian cultural history she is best remembered for her part in the early adult life of Edvard Munch. In 1885, already married for the first time to a brother of painter Frits Thaulow, Milly spent the summer at home in Borre and got to know the 21-year-old Munch, whose family was staying at nearby Åsgårdstrand. The erotic atmosphere that charged their long walks in the beech wood and by the edge of the fjord can be sensed in many of the artist's most sensual summer canvases. The mutual attraction turned into an affair that continued for a few months in Kristiania. Milly married for a second time in 1891, now to actor Ludvig Bergh, and in the early 1890s acquired for herself a name as an actress. In his book covering the artistic life of Norway's capital in this period, Mentz Schulerud writes: 'Milly Bergh was recognised as the leading beauty of Kristiania at that time, and her actor husband the most handsome man in town'.[58]

On 11 June 1902, Jelka's mother died. A little over a week later, Frederick left France, having arranged that Jelka would follow on as soon as possible. Nothing was to get in the way of his first visit to Norway in three years. Around 23 June, he disembarked from the fjord steamer at Fredriksværn and continued by road along the coast to the little fishing community of Nevlunghavn. Here he had rented accommodation with the owner of the general store, but after a couple of nights the simple standard compelled him to remove to the house of harbour pilot Nikolai Edvardsen. 'I take enormous sun & sea baths', he wrote home to Jelka. 'No work as yet – too lazy'.[59] At this point, the couple's plan had been to travel to the Dovre mountain cabin around mid-July and stay there until mid-September. Once Jelka arrived in Nevlunghavn in early July,

[57] Letter from Delius to Jelka, 14 May 1902 (GM).
[58] Mentz Schulerud, *Norsk kunstnerliv* (*Artistic Life in Norway*) (Oslo: J. W. Cappelens forlag, 1960), 314.
[59] Letter from Delius to Jelka, undated, c.25 June 1902 (GM).

they altered their arrangements; their Norwegian stay would be curtailed by a month so that Jelka could get home all the sooner and keep a watchful eye on the execution of her mother's testament.

Just as they had in 1898 and 1899, Jelka and Frederick spent some days in Åsgårdstrand, where Edvard Munch was spending the whole summer. American friends of Delius also enlarged the artistic colony – the wife and five children of his New York impresario friend, Victor Thrane. Thrane's daughter Irma has left a small memoir in which she writes:

> We spent several weeks at Åsgårdstrand, where there was quite a colony of artists among whom were *Edvard Munch, Dörnberger* [Carl Dørnberger] and the English composer *Delius*, besides other artists of different nationalities. We derived both great pleasure and profit from the intercourse with these interesting and prominent people of the artistic world.[60]

The summer of 1902 developed into one of the most eventful of Munch's life. Early in August an old conflict flared up with another painter living in Åsgård-strand, Johannes von Ditten, and their enmity ended in a fist-fight outside the village council offices. Worse was to follow later in August when Tulla Larsen, banished by Munch and sick from longing for him, made a half-hearted attempt to take her own life with an overdose of morphine. When Munch, a few weeks later, brought her to Åsgårdstrand to discuss their predicament, a revolver shot was fired and two fingers on the artist's right hand were injured. 'She maintains that I wanted to shoot her', he protested later. 'I had grabbed the revolver in a rage and was toying with it [...] and it just went off.'[61] Frederick and Jelka had moved on before these developments.

His Åsgårdstrand stay may also have given Delius the opportunity to renew old friendships with other Norwegians. Although no meeting is documented, Johan Halvorsen was also in the tiny fishing village all summer, and for most summers of this period Christian Sinding hired a fisherman's cottage just south of the village. A reunion of the three old card-playing companions from Leipzig seems highly likely.

For much of July, Frederick and Jelka were in the Dovre mountains. The cabin lay close to the Vålåsjøen lake, north of Fokstuen mountain lodge. Cold and damp weather would have limited their movements, but it seems they took trips to other places in Dovre, including the Drivstuen lodge further north in Drivdalen, and both this and the cabin at Vålåsjøen were excellent points from which to start a two or three-day round trip to the majestic Snøhetta (2,286m), Norway's highest mountain outside of Jotunheimen. Frederick also wanted to show Jelka the Jotunheim mountains, perhaps to help her better understand

---

[60] Irma Schmertz, *My Grandfather Marcus Thrane*, handwritten memoir, December 1949 (NB). She implies that her visit to Åsgårdstrand took place in 1903. She seems to have erred by a year, as neither Delius nor Munch were in Norway that summer.
[61] Quoted in Ludvig Ravensberg's diary (MM).

him and his art. Around 30 July, the bad weather breaking, they arrived in Dombås and from there hiked across the mountain plateau to Vågå. At the post house Sve Gard they were served a late dinner which they remembered for many years afterwards, and their host lent them a horse and carriage in order to get back to Dombås. Next day, 2 August, they returned to Sve and added their names to the guestbook in a peculiar fashion, maintaining the illusion that they were independent tourists rather than an unmarried couple:

Name	Home city	Previous stop	Next stop
Frederick Delius	Paris	Domaas [Dombås]	Juvasshytten [Juvvasshytta]
Jelka Rosen	Belgrad, Serbien	Voolasjøen [Vålåsjøen]	Galdhøpigen [Galdhøpiggen]

Before leaving Vågå, they visited the stave church and admired one of its medieval treasures, a large crucifix with an expressively carved figure of the suffering Christ.

On 3 August, they continued further up Bøverdalen to the Røisheim post house at the foot of the Galdhø massif. Their journey – 'our memorable trip', as

18. Røisheim post house in the heart of Jotunheimen, c.1885. From here tourists began their ascent of the Galdhøpiggen massif. Delius was at Røisheim several times, notably with Jelka in 1902 and Beecham in 1908.

Delius later described it[62] – was approaching its ultimate goal. Before turning in early to bed, the couple enjoyed a stroll in the light summer night along the banks of the Bøvra, grey-green with meltwater from Jotunheim glaciers. Early next morning, probably around five o'clock, they were accompanied by a guide up to the Juvvasshytta[63] mountain lodge at 1,841 metres. Their movements from here on are unknown. The weather on 4 August was fine and they perhaps continued with their guide across the Juvflye plateau and its glacier, Styggebreen, and made the ascent of Norway's highest peak. For only a few days a year is there good visibility from the summit of Galdhøpiggen (2,469m), and already the next day there was mist and rain. They may equally likely have stayed at Juvvasshytta and missed the window of good weather. The travellers soon turned south again, making their way down to Kristiania, and a week later were back in France.

After the emotional chaos that had marked their relationship for several years, this tour of Norway seems to have helped them rediscover each other and to resolve the question of their future. Shortly after returning home, Frederick informed his relatives that it was his intention to marry Jelka.

The year 1902 had begun in turmoil for Delius on account of the strains in their relationship. Before the year was out, however, he had taken large strides forward in his life. The couple had agreed on a form of partnership within the bonds of marriage. Then, in October and November, his music was programmed by two influential conductors. In Berlin, *Paris* was performed under Ferruccio Busoni's direction, while in Elberfeld *Mitternachtslied Zarathustras* was conducted by Hans Haym. The composer's German name was now dormant, but Germany was waking up to the music of Frederick Delius.

---

[62] Letter from Delius to Jelka, 18 August 1908 (GM).
[63] The official spelling of the lodge is now Juvvasshytta. For much of its history, however, Juvasshytta/Juvasshytten have been widely used alternatives.

9

1903–1907
Breakthrough in Germany and England

'You "hear away into distances" which others have not yet heard'
Letter from Julius Buths to Delius, 26 July 1903

As early as 1896, Delius had promised himself that he would never again 'go kicking around the ante chambers of well known Conductors' in the hope of igniting some interest in his work. In the ensuing years he was left with no option but to swallow his pride; without unlimited resources there was really no alternative. He continued, therefore, to send his scores and to make personal visits to music's power brokers, especially those in Germany; but felt that 'only a miracle can push me thro'. To call the breakthrough that he finally enjoyed in Germany between 1903 and 1906 a miraculous act would be to rob the composer of the credit he deserved. Delius and his closest supporters, in particular Ida Gerhardi, never stopped promoting his music. It is, however, clear that the decisive factor was the extraordinary maturing, around the turn of the century, of his creative identity and technical processes. When, at last, the dam was breached, it was because the sheer weight of artistic mastery in his music had become irresistible. Leading conductors such as Hans Haym in Elberfeld, Julius Buths in Düsseldorf, Fritz Cassirer in Berlin and Hermann Suter in Basel, as well as Max Schillings and Carl Schuricht, all experienced the same intoxicating feeling that they were discovering a hidden treasure, a unique musical genius who with every new score broke more new ground. German festivals began to compete for the prestige of giving Delius works.

Having acquainted himself with the scores of *Paris*, *Lebenstanz* and *Appalachia*, Julius Buths, musical director at Düsseldorf, wrote to the composer that his compositions demonstrated

> that for you everything in the world which you have seen and experienced with emotion is capable of becoming music, that the world surrounds you in terms of 'sound' and that these sounds you carry in your very being. You 'hear away into distances' which others have not yet heard.[1]

---

[1] Letter from Julius Buths to Delius, 26 July 1903 (DT).

One of Delius's finest scores, *Sea Drift*, was composed in 1903 to words by Walt Whitman. After conducting the work in Dortmund, Carl Schuricht assured Delius that he found in his music 'a new flowering of the purest, *most spiritual and most perfect art*'.[2] Fritz Cassirer 'could have howled with delight' on getting the same score in his hands: 'You are now so glorious in your maturity. Sitting comfortably and plucking the fruits from the tree. Round and ripe and sweet, it says everything that one simply forgets the artist.'[3] In the opera conductor Cassirer, Delius had finally found an enthusiast for his music dramas. The music of *Koanga* attained an 'absolutely original level',[4] Cassirer discovered, and it inspired him to have it staged. *Koanga* was performed three times at the Stadttheater in Elberfeld at the end of March 1904 under Cassirer's baton, the first staging of a Delius opera. He preferred the slave opera to *A Village Romeo and Juliet*, but also here Cassirer could identify the workings of an important innovator: 'All in all – this repressed ardour, this near-chaste anxiety of the modern soul, this deep, passionate stillness – you are the first who has dared on the operatic stage to speak so softly.'[5] Fritz Cassirer used all his influence to bring *A Village Romeo and Juliet* to Berlin's Komische Oper in February 1907, and also conducted this première.

All the old obstacles standing in Delius's way were falling, one by one. Early in 1906, he received a letter from the Berlin music publisher Harmonie: 'We take the liberty of bringing our publishing house to your notice ...'[6] The days of kicking his heels in the antechambers of a publisher were finally over. Frederick Delius had become a sought-after composer, even if, for now, only in Germany.

'Con elevazione': *A Mass of Life* and Nietzsche

The resistance to Delius's music in German musical life was finally broken down by works inspired by Delius's American experiences – *Koanga*, *Appalachia* and *Sea Drift* – rather than those with a Norwegian or German background. Yes, his passion for Scandinavian nature and culture was present in *Lebenstanz*, *A Village Romeo and Juliet* and the Piano Concerto, but not overtly. Germanic culture at a rural level had of course been present in the Swiss tale used in *A Village Romeo and Juliet*, but due to its inadequate staging in Berlin the work had contributed little to the composer's success. However, one German work from 1898, *Mitternachtslied Zarathustras* (*Zarathustra's Midnight Song*) – a setting for baritone soloist, choir and orchestra of a passage from Nietzsche's *Also sprach Zarathustra* – was regularly performed. This piece would turn out to

---

[2] Letter from Carl Schuricht to Delius, 3 October 1910 (DT).
[3] Letter from Fritz Cassirer to Delius, 6 October 1906 (DT).
[4] Letter from Fritz Cassirer to Delius, 13 May 1904 (DT).
[5] *Ibid.*
[6] Letter from Harmonie Verlag to Delius, undated, early 1906 (DT).

be the harbinger of a much more ambitious score that came to occupy Delius throughout 1904 and 1905, a composition that fuses in extraordinary ways the elements he had drawn into his creative chemistry from German culture and Norwegian nature.

A Mass of Life is huge in every way; it is the composer's largest non-dramatic work and is scored for double choir, soloists and an orchestra of over a hundred musicians. Eleven movements are arranged in two parts and the texts, selected by Delius in collaboration with Fritz Cassirer, are from the more poetical sections of *Also sprach Zarathustra*. The large forces he musters are used sparingly, and really only fully unleashed in the two heaven-storming movements that open Part I and Part II. It is these that are of particular interest for this study. Here, when his technique and creative personality had attained full maturity, Delius composed two muscular and driving movements that were the culmination of more than fifteen years of attempts to capture the exalted emotions for which the metaphor of the mountain journey was his chosen poetic 'vehicle'. From the magnificent climaxes of the *Paa Vidderne* melodrama of 1888 there runs a direct line to these movements, passing through all the other works uplifted by his Mountain Music: *On the Mountains*, the Violin Sonata in B Major, *Over the Hills and Far Away* and *A Village Romeo and Juliet*.

Already in the virile energy that announces the work – 'O Du mein Wille!' (*animato*) – we recognise the rhythmic impulsion that typifies Mountain Music of category 1, 'Peak'-music (see Table 2, p. 45). The chromatic choral lines are more neutral, the writing similar to the choral treatment in other of his works after the turn of the century. Soon, however, the attributes of Mountain Music make their presence felt, first with a theme fuelled by the familiar upward-striving triplets (type 'Peak B'):

Example 9.1 *A Mass of Life*, Part I, 1st movement, fig. 1, 16–17

Thereafter with a theme, initially pentatonic, that is as majestic and noble as any he composed for the two *Paa Vidderne* scores or *Over the Hills and Far Away*:

Example 9.2 *A Mass of Life*, Part I, 1st movement, fig. 3, 1–4

Although the composer has tapped into the stylistic traits of his resolute Mountain Music, the text makes no mention of mountain nature, but is rather a fervent paean to the Will. When we turn to the movement that opens Part II of *A Mass of Life*, we see from the text here that the similarly exalted character of the treatment is associated directly with the metaphor of airy heights where one is neighbour to snow peaks and nests of eagles:

> Vorbei die zögernde Trübsal meines Frühlings. Sommer wurde ich ganz und Sommermittag! Ein Sommer im Höchsten mit kalten Quellen und seliger Stille: O! kommt, meine Freunde, daß die Stille noch seliger werde! Denn dies ist unsre Höhe und unsre Heimat; Nachbarn den Adlern, Nachbarn dem Schnee, Nachbarn der Sonne![7]

> ('Tis gone, the lingering sorrow of my springtide! Summer am I become, yea, Summer's Midday! On mountains' high summits, by cooling waters, 'mid rapturous stillness O! come my companions, and the silence our soul shall enrapture! For this is now our home: snow-clad mountain summit's dwellers with eagles, dwellers 'mid the snows, neighbours of the Sun we.)[8]

Different types of Mountain Music (category 1, 'Peak'-music) lift and propel the whole movement, which also has the direction *Con elevazione e vigore*. The double choir introduces at once a theme bristling with purposeful energy to the words 'Herauf! nun herauf, du grosser Mittag!', passing the melody on to the horns and trumpets (type 'Peak A'). When the soloists assume the leading role and further elevate the music, Delius adds two horn calls – simple phrases, but for him highly charged. He borrows from *Over the Hills and Far Away* the two opening calls, one rising, one rolling (Examples 6.1 and 6.2). But we are still ascending to the summit, and now Example 9.1 from the first movement of *A Mass of Life* returns in an extended form:

Example 9.3 *A Mass of Life*, Part II, 1st movement, fig. 63, 1–4

In the discussion of Mountain Music in *A Village Romeo and Juliet* (p. 189) it was mentioned that the striving, rising motifs that Delius initially associated with the mountain journey were later often transferred to depictions of young love. This is never clearer than in the partly new intermezzo he wrote for the opera in 1906, shortly after completing *A Mass of Life*. The intermezzo is now

---

[7] From *A Mass of Life*, Part II, 1st movement, extracted from *Also sprach Zarathustra*, Zweiter Teil, 'Vom Gesindel' and 'Von den Taranteln'.

[8] English translation by John Bernhoff, in the reprint of the original 1907 score from Harmonie (London: Boosey & Hawkes, 1952) 94–9.

known as 'The Walk to the Paradise Garden' and represents the moment when the two lovers turn their backs on society and abandon themselves to the love that binds them. The piece has won enormous popularity due to its lyrical and passionate love music. And its principal theme is Example 9.3, lifted from the mountain vista of the *Mass*. Music that in 1905 was suitable for an exalted state as 'neighbours of eagles' was equally suitable in 1906 for a state of exalted love. To Delius, they were both expressions of the ecstatic.

The intense choral movement 'Herauf! nun herauf' is numbered as the first movement of Part II. Before the full orchestra and choir break in, however, an extraordinary prelude is played – the most contemplative Mountain Music Delius ever penned.[9] In the manuscript, he gave it the title 'Auf den Bergen'. In these sixty-seven almost static bars is distilled the essence of his other Mountain Music category: 'Plateau'-music – that is to say, an emotional quietude and oneness with nature, for which he employed the poetic visual metaphor of the endless mountain moorland. Solo horns sound and echo repeatedly a simple call against a background tone (cello and bass, whispered timpani roll), and eventually we also hear the call through a haze of long, hanging string chords. And that is all. No rhythmic pulse moves the music forward. There is barely any movement in the pedal tones supporting the horn calls.

While the two euphoric choral movements are a logical culmination of all the Mountain Music Delius had written since 1888 in category 1 – 'Peak'-music – 'Auf den Bergen' is a radical reimagining of category 2 – 'Plateau'-music. For this prelude the horn call is stripped almost naked of its programmatic content, the poetic force of the metaphor distanced as far as possible from Romantic images of shepherd boys and herd girls. Distanced, but not removed; the power of emotional transference in the metaphor is still necessary if we are to understand that, before they were sublimated, the rolling and diminishing horn calls once had their home among unending vistas and mountain ridges. Delius has moved the *ranz des vaches* to an extreme limit where the call has almost nothing to do with either animal herding or mountain tourism, but represents rather the human element, meditative and reflective, in a landscape stretching towards infinity. What landscape? The emotions the composer attempts to recreate with 'Auf den Bergen' are ones he no doubt experienced many times in the Norwegian mountains. Nevertheless, this miniature tone-poem is not about specific geography, but rather a spiritual state that may be attained and cultivated while looking out across the mountain wilderness. It is a landscape where external circumstances have fallen away or fallen quiet, and humans can contemplate their place in nature and the cosmos.

---

[9] Having studied the manuscript of *A Mass of Life*, Robert Threlfall pointed out that this prelude to Part II seems to be an afterthought, inserted at a late date in the composition process. He published his observations in 'Delius: A fresh glance at two famous scores' in *The Musical Times*, Vol. 125, No. 1696 (June 1984), 318.

Cassirer saluted Delius for being, with *A Village Romeo and Juliet*, 'the first who has dared on the operatic stage to speak so softly'. With 'Auf den Bergen' he was also among the first to allow music to be so minimalistic, the structure of the prelude sustained by the listener's ability to activate a musical metaphor and thereafter to turn his or her inner eye out over an endless landscape. Both of these achievements are worth remembering when the composer is cited – as he so often is by people who know only a sliver of his catalogue – as a purveyor of excessively laden textures. Written by Delius as the most understated of 'curtain-raisers', the prelude performs almost a music-dramatic function, suggesting an emotional landscape in advance of the dramatic mountain-paean that is to follow with the entry of the full orchestra and voices. As such, 'Auf den Bergen' can be seen as following in an operatic tradition, where so-called *Klangfläche* (or sound-sheets) were utilised by composers from Wagner onwards to suggest – by means of static harmony and self-contained themes – the character of landscape. This is a subject we will return to with *The Song of the High Hills*.

In the two vibrant choral movements of *A Mass of Life* Delius had for the last time employed a heroic Wagnerian language to express youthful energy and resolve in the mountains. 'Auf den Bergen' speaks rather of reflection, of maturity, of ruminative self-knowledge. After this, Mountain Music became a much less frequent feature of his compositions; indeed he never again had recourse to the music types of category 1, 'Peak'-music. Only one more large canvas is still to be stretched in his attempts to depict the feelings he associated with Norwegian mountain nature. With *The Song of the High Hills* (1911–12) the inner landscape of the *Mass* prelude will be expanded into an all-encompassing spiritual panorama.

When Delius set Nietzsche's words with Mountain Music inspired by Norway, it was as a metaphor for exalted emotion. Could this music, by extension, also be regarded as an interpretation of the Zarathustra doctrine of the *Übermensch*? We have earlier seen that Delius was enthralled by Nietzsche's works, also that they were an important link between himself and Jelka Rosen. Halfdan Jebe teased his friend because of his admiration for the German poet-philosopher. He would ask: 'What are you up to now? Übermensch!',[10] and on another occasion wrote of himself: 'I have taken Bohemianism to its logical extreme, to Über-Bohemianism (in your language)'.[11] When, however, Delius later in life felt obliged to explain to others what Nietzsche had meant for his personal development, he was at pains to accentuate: 'It is not Nietzsche's philosophical

---

[10] Letter from Halfdan Jebe to Delius, 15 June 1901 (DT).
[11] Letter from Halfdan Jebe to Delius, November 1903 (DT).

side that I love, but the poetic one'.[12] It was a theme on which he was often willing to expand:

> I consider Nietzsche the only free thinker of modern times & for me the most sympathetic one – He is at the same time such a poet. He feels nature. I believe, myself, in no doctrine whatever – & in nothing but in Nature & the great forces of Nature – I believe in complete annihilation as far as our personal consciousness goes.[13]

Thomas Beecham suggested that for the individualist Delius, the cultivation of Nietzsche was first and foremost a confirmation of his own self-image:

> After a while I discovered that his entire philosophy of life was based upon an ultra-Nietzschean conception of the individual. The individual was all in all, a sovereign creature who perhaps owed certain perfunctory duties to the State in return for mere protection and security, but certainly nothing more to anyone but himself and the vital needs of his task.[14]

In the final decade of his life, when disease blighted his days and made him dependent on others, Delius – despite the emphasis he placed on the poetic rather the philosophic qualities of Nietzsche – found in the author's doctrine of the sovereignty of the strong individual support for a moral arrogance that let him behave in a hard and authoritarian manner to those closest to him.

1903–1906: Contact with Norway through friends

Success in Germany meant that Delius's life for a period was divided between Grez-sur-Loing and music trips to German cities. In the summer, he and Jelka took short holidays in Holland and Brittany, and a further three years would pass before he could return to Norway, the longest break in the chain of visits that continued to 1923. Through Norwegian friends such as Edvard Munch and Halfdan Jebe, as well as Gunnar Heiberg, whom he occasionally met in Paris, Delius could keep up to date with the dramatic and tense developments in relations between neighbours Norway and Sweden before the dénouement in 1905. And finally, Edvard Grieg was back in his life.

Since 1899, Grieg had refused to perform in France in protest over the Dreyfus affair. He eventually returned to Paris in April 1903, but Delius chose to keep a low profile in Grez during his visit. When, a couple of months later, the Norwegian's sixtieth birthday was celebrated at Troldhaugen in regal style, Delius seized the opportunity to send greetings: 'We have not heard anything from each other for such a long time, which is certainly my fault.'[15] With these

---

[12] Letter from Delius to Ernest Newman, 13 December 1933 (DT).
[13] Letter from Delius to Philip Heseltine, 23 June 1912 (BL).
[14] Thomas Beecham, *A Mingled Chime*, 118.
[15] Letter from Delius to Grieg, undated, mid-June 1903 (BOB).

words Delius re-established contact with Grieg. Some letters may have been lost, but it seems likely that this was the first time they had been in touch since the summer of 1896. Between the lines in this initial letter there seems to be a rather chill tone. Delius was at pains to tell Grieg of his successes in Germany, yet had to admit that he was still working towards securing a publisher. The discomfiture Delius felt on this point – no doubt compounded by Grieg's involvement in the rejection by Edition Peters of his Violin Sonata in B Major ten years earlier (see p. 102) – may indeed have contributed to the long interruption in their correspondence. Grieg's warm and sympathetic reply quickly revived the embers and Delius expressed the hope that they would see each other in the coming winter in order to experience 'alten & neuen Stimmung'.[16] With a weary quip about Delius's *Lebenstanz*, Grieg pointed out that his health would most likely be an obstacle to any reunion, for he had now 'reached that point in life when I would no longer be able to write "A Dance of Life". Instead, "Fatigue of Life", also a theme worthy of a symphonic poem.'[17] In late September 1903, Delius wrote to inform the Griegs that he and Jelka had just married in the Grez town hall, and that he now answered to the name Frederick. Grieg replied:

> Many years ago I found a certain *Fritz* Delius very likeable. Whether the same will be the case with this *Frederick* Delius, I really don't know. What harm did 'the old Fritz' do? Both my wife and I ask: Will we never more see that same man? We had become very fond of him.[18]

A further break in correspondence occurred before they got back in touch again in 1906. Delius was in Norway (see p. 211) and wrote to Troldhaugen to invite Grieg on a hiking trip in the mountains. Unfortunately we have only Grieg's side of the correspondence, but everything suggests that Delius failed to grasp how reduced the Norwegian's health now was. Grieg replied at the end of June 1906: 'An old man, so worn down by bodily woes that he can hardly go on, wishes you a warm welcome to Norway. Are you not coming to Western Norway? Please try! It would probably be our only opportunity to see each other again.'[19] This heartfelt and direct appeal seems to have gone over Delius's head. Not only did the chance slip for the two friends to meet before it was too late, but a month later Grieg was again politely declining another invitation from Delius to accompany him on a trek into the wilderness:

> I am very ill and cannot meet you anywhere, much as I would like to. Yes, I was always a weakling. Now however, with the onset of age, my life has become more

---

[16] Letter from Delius to Grieg, 28 September 1903 (BOB).
[17] Letter from Grieg to Delius, 23 October 1903 (DT).
[18] *Ibid.*
[19] Letter from Grieg to Delius, 30 June 1906 (DT).

and more a burden. My abysmal health keeps me from working, even though I still feel that I have it in me. It is this that makes life intolerable for me.[20]

From this extraordinary friendship, arguably the most important of Delius's life, there remains but one more letter. It was written from Delius to Grieg in October 1906, and he was finally able to send his old mentor a printed score, first fruit of his collaboration with the Harmonie publishing house in Berlin: the piano reduction of *Sea Drift*. 'I hope this letter finds you relatively well & cheerful & perhaps working on something new.'[21] Again, there is little sign of Delius having understood how close to the end of his life Grieg was.

Edvard Munch, like Delius, had cultivated German connections rather than French. From 1903, however, he decided he would exhibit annually at the large spring show in Paris at the Salon des Indépendants. There seems to have been a good deal of correspondence between Munch and Delius during this period that has now been lost; from surviving letters it is evident that they must have met relatively frequently in France and Germany. In early March, Munch accepted an invitation from Delius to stay with him in Grez and use his home as a base until the Indépendants exhibition opened on 20 March. Jelka, who was also showing five paintings, was pleased to have the artist under her roof, and Munch was generous in his professional encouragement of her work. In a letter to Rodin, Jelka warmly recommended the 'very, very interesting Norwegian painter'[22] and sent the master an admission ticket to the Salon des Indépendants in case he wished to acquaint himself with Munch's work. After Munch left France, Delius continued to look after his interests, arranging the sale of some pictures and offering advice on pricing. In his study of the friendship between the men, John Boulton Smith notes that their correspondence 'shows the trouble that Delius would go to to help his friends'.[23] Indeed, Delius wrote some years later that 'when I believe in anything I am capable of putting forward considerable energy & persuasive powers – Especially when it is someone else's work'.[24] In subsequent years, it was unusual for Munch to come to Paris for the Indépendants, but thanks to his friend in Grez he was still able to exhibit. Delius would pay the advance fee for him, receive and deliver his pictures, then collect and forward them after the exhibition.

In the spring of 1902, Munch got to know the English violinist Eva Mudocci in Berlin. A year later, they ran into each other again while he was preparing for the Paris exhibition and the friendship ignited into a love affair. In accordance with the typical Munch pattern, he recoiled from making any

[20] Letter from Grieg to Delius, 21 July 1907 (DT).
[21] Letter from Delius to Grieg, 11 October 1906 (BOB).
[22] Letter from Jelka to Auguste Rodin, 12 March 1903 (RM).
[23] Boulton Smith, *Frederick Delius and Edvard Munch*, 69.
[24] Letter from Delius to Philip Heseltine, undated, but 3 July 1918 (BL).

commitment to Mudocci, believing they 'had met under inauspicious circumstances'[25] – that is to say, while his anxiety about women was intense following
the Tulla Larsen drama of the previous summer. They were together again in
Hamburg at the end of the year and the artist sought advice from Delius, who
also knew Mudocci: 'Eva Mudocci and Bella Edvards – They are here – Miss
Mudocci is wonderfully beautiful and I almost fear I have taken a fancy (one
of thousands) to her – What do you think? After the last affair with T I am
madly apprehensive – '[26] Despite long intervals while they worked in different countries, Mudocci and Munch kept their relationship alive, and it proved
to be one of the most equally matched the artist ever enjoyed. However, the
deep wounds left by the Tulla crisis were far from healed, and in the course of
1905 the couple drifted apart, staying in touch by post. In December, Mudocci
answered a query from Munch about their common acquaintance:

> You asked about Delius – Yes – we have seen him – last spring he visited us
> together with his wife, & a few weeks ago they were here again – I like her very
> much – she is so calm & good-natured & shrewd in her own way – she has also
> I feel a kind heart – he is as always; a little older – a little more Mephistophelian!
> – [27]

Halfdan Jebe, now in his mid-thirties, had tried to settle down for a while with
his wife in Kristiania. In 1902, he entered into a creative partnership with Norwegian author Peter Egge and artist-author Christian Krohg with the goal of
creating a full-scale opera, *Vesle Kari Rud*, based on a folk legend (see Illustration 10). He became, however, ever more disillusioned with the corruption he
saw everywhere in society. In 1906, he would in fact turn his back on Europe
for good. A warning of his final break came in 1903, all of which he spent
on a vagabond journey through East and South Asia. When Delius first got
word from him, roughly halfway through the voyage, Jebe had arrived in Japan
from China, where he had visited Shanghai and Guangzhou. In November,
Delius received a second long letter from Colombo, in today's Sri Lanka; Jebe's
unquiet spirit had kept him moving through lands of the South China Sea –
Vietnam, Malaysia, Sumatra – before he sailed further west to Calcutta and
finally Sri Lanka. To pay his way, he performed on his violin, and on ships he
travelled as a stowaway ('it costs nothing and is very exciting'). In Colombo he
received a letter from Delius and replied:

---

[25] Letter draft from Munch to Eva Mudocci, undated, probably May 1903 (MM).
[26] Letter draft from Munch to Delius, undated, probably January 1904 (MM); it is unknown
    whether it was sent. Bella Edwards, Mudocci's accompanist, is the same woman with whom
    Grieg was infatuated at the end of 1895 (see p. 115).
[27] Letter from Eva Mudocci to Munch, 12 December, probably 1905 (MM).

[Rarely] in my life have I been so happy about a letter. Now, to understand this you would have to have experienced how it is to smell land again, when your journey has lasted forever. [...] But the long adventure poem which I have now completed – not on paper, but with bleeding footsteps across the world, through previously unimagined depths of Bohemian living conditions – this wonderful adventure I bring home alive, – not for the children and not for the adults, only for the few who do not get tired of playing the Game. [...] I have quite simply travelled towards the horizon; I have carried an idea to its logical extreme, I am dead, all done – it is the transmigration of the soul.[28]

Wherever possible, he lived among the native population; out in the Japan countryside he dressed in the Japanese manner and learnt the language. And everywhere he went, it seems that Jebe's 'squalid loves', as Keary had dubbed them, were a vital element of his vagabond journeys: 'Only in Japan can one purchase young girls very cheaply.'

After several months alone, he was now ready to return to Europe, and he longed for Norway. 'I must live quietly at home for a couple of years, and then later perhaps you will come and visit some beautiful places with me and for a year live a life as idyllic, as ideal, as your peaceful life in Grez.' His return journey brought him to Paris and on 6 January 1904 he arrived by train in Grez. The reunion was less hearty than expected, for in some way or other he managed to offend Jelka. ('I regret enormously that I angered her', he later wrote.) It is easy to imagine that Jelka's protection of her husband's talent and Jebe's wish to sign him up as a travelling companion put them on a collision course. Or that his daily use of a 'universal medicine'[29] – opium he brought with him from Asia – made him a difficult guest.

Settled again outside Kristiania, he managed to cage his restlessness for a year and a half. He slipped once more into the role of Sofie's husband and renewed his efforts to write his opera *Vesle Kari Rud*. His wanderlust was, however, bubbling just below the surface: 'Sometimes I burn with fever to see again those lands where I felt reborn.'[30] In his letters to Delius he never let the opportunity pass to arouse his friend's desire to free himself of convention. A voyage to the Pacific? Perhaps a world tour with selected female musicians? Jebe constantly hoped to strike the spark that would set Delius alight: 'My dear friend, how quickly time flies. Action! Action! Movement! The great sleep is approaching. Then we will dream about what we are now living, our dreams will dissolve into eternal primitive music.'[31] Political tensions in Norway and the threat of war frightened him, but he also longed to see the country independent of Sweden. Extreme expressions of jingoism helped to confirm for

---

[28] Letter from Halfdan Jebe to Delius, November 1903 (DT).
[29] Letter from Halfdan Jebe to Delius, January 1905 (DT).
[30] Letter from Halfdan Jebe to Delius, 21 June 1904 (DT).
[31] Letter from Halfdan Jebe to Delius, 22 July 1905 (DT).

him, however, that most people belonged on the 'Inside', a place in which he could never feel at home. In his last surviving letter to Delius, he put into words the feeling of alienation that drove him on:

> It depends on this: that there is an 'Outside' – then I don't care how things go on the inside. I have lived for so long on the outside, I now know large tracts of this endless country, to which no one has given a name. But I never meet another person here, not since meeting you, and you went back again. […] I am not Norwegian. I come from 'Outside'.[32]

In the autumn of 1905, he abandoned the pretence that a provincial life in Kristiania could ever satisfy his desires. He travelled first to Paris, then in 1906 on to America, working first as a violin teacher at a school in Kansas, then as an itinerant soloist (see pp. 241–2). Eventually his movements would become so erratic that he would disappear for years from Delius's story.

In 1905, Christian Sinding re-entered Delius's life. The announcement of marriage between Jelka and Frederick had been sent to him at the end of 1903, along with an open invitation to come to Grez. When Delius heard nothing he renewed the invitation in March 1905 and received from Sinding a reply explaining that his gravely ill stepson had absorbed much of his time and resources. Just one month later, Augusta lost her son and Delius received a new letter from Sinding:

> We shall stay here for some time yet, but definitely not another winter. My native country is certainly very fine and beautiful, but it is not good to stay too long there. You become too readily 'Troll be thyself – enough'. […] I want to get out into the world again and I should like to announce myself at your home as soon as possible.[33]

Christian and Augusta Sinding did indeed come to Grez, probably in the spring of 1906, and around this time Delius also organised a meeting with Sinding and Busoni in Paris, together with their spouses. The Norwegian's compositions were, however, beginning to bring him considerable international recognition, particularly in Sweden and Germany, drawing him ever further away from old friends. Considering how dim it is today, it seems astonishing that Sinding's name should have shone so brightly in European music in the years between the two world wars. Johan Halvorsen, in a memoir written late in his life, put forward one explanation: '[We thought Sinding] would develop our national music even further than Svendsen and Grieg. In the fullness of time, however, his admiration for Wagner has led him far from everything that was personal

---

[32] *Ibid.*
[33] Letter from Sinding to Delius, 24 April 1905 (DT). The troll quotation is from Ibsen's *Peer Gynt.*

and characteristic in his early works.'[34] In Norway there is a further reason for his diminished position. During World War II the occupying Nazi forces exploited the love that Sinding – old and enfeebled – had for German culture; his apparent sympathy for the occupying forces would cast a long shadow over his reputation.

By a strange coincidence, three of Delius's closest Norwegian friends – Jebe, Sinding and Munch – all fled Norway for a period after 1905, repelled by the exaggerated nationalism stimulated by the struggle for independence. To Delius, victim as he was in 1897 of a wave of collective jingoism, their decision would have come as no surprise.

We can also record here Delius's friendship with Mons Lie, the son of Jonas Lie, the latter being the famous Norwegian author around whose person and Paris home the Norwegian colony had coalesced since his move to the city in 1882. Mons, a couple of years younger than Delius, had come to Paris to study violin at the Conservatory. He would, however, become a thorn in the side of his father, abandoning his musical career in the 1890s to try his hand – with little success – as an author, and making a marriage in 1894 of which his parents disapproved. Exactly when Delius and Mons Lie became acquainted is unknown. Still told by Lie's descendants today, however, is an anecdote from 1904, shortly after the birth of Mons's first son, christened Mons Michael:

> One day the famous English composer Frederick Delius came to visit. He was a good friend of the family. The conversation turned on the need for children to have their musicality stimulated from a very early age. So tiny Mons Michael was placed under the grand piano and [Delius and Mons Lie] played with great enthusiasm the Kreutzer Sonata for the poor child, to properly stimulate its musicality. Fortunately the child's hearing was not damaged. In fact, perhaps just the opposite.[35]

The baby would, indeed, grow up to be an acclaimed violinist, who was said to have perfect pitch!

1906: A summer by the fjord

Frederick and Jelka spent the summer of 1906 in Norway. With the exception of a couple of weeks in July, when Delius was in the mountains, the couple seem to have spent almost three months by the Kristiania Fjord – although not necessarily together. Early in June, Jelka was quartered at the Hotel Victoria in Åsgårdstrand, while her husband had travelled further down the coast to Fredriksværn. Whether this reflects their individual needs for differing

---

[34] Quoted in Øyvin Dybsand, 'Johan Halvorsen', 142.
[35] Mona Lie Thommessen, 'Fiolinisten Mons Michael Lie', offprint of an article first published in *Fåberg historielags årbok (Yearbook of Fåberg Historical Society)*, No. 22 (2003), 5.

environments, or some other cause, is unknown. Jelka had transported her painting equipment and was looking forward to a creative summer in a colony of artists with Edvard Munch at its centre. There had either been a misunderstanding or a change in his plans: he had commissions in Germany and would not be visiting his Åsgårdstrand house, and though Jelka and Frederick each sent an appeal to him to return, he could not be enticed home.

Events the previous summer, in 1905, had culminated in Munch breaking not only with Åsgårdstrand, but with Norway. Ever since the Tulla Larsen drama, it did not take much to tip his usual delusions over the edge into an obsessive persecution complex. The political atmosphere was intense and threatening, a war with Sweden seemed likely and from Åsgårdstrand one could see warships patrolling the fjord. 'This tension is really not good for my health', Munch admitted to a friend, 'when all is quiet here I'm fine, but the least excitement makes me ill'.[36] The last straw was a shameful incident when, with many witnesses, an intoxicated Munch disciplined a 21-year-old admirer by laying her across his knee and spanking her. Apart from one short visit, Munch stayed away from his homeland for four years.

From Fredriksværn, Delius sought a vacancy at a number of mountain hotels, without any luck. When he was finally on his way north, it was first to Kristiania to visit Milly Bergh, and then once again to a cabin that Bergh seems to have recommended or procured. On 9 July, he arrived at the enchanting Storfjellseter mountain lodge, eighteen kilometres west of Atna Station in the Ringebu hills, where the old *seter* buildings had been supplemented by lodge accommodation built from huge timber logs. It seems that he hired a cabin near the lodge, and a week later wrote to Jelka in Åsgårdstrand:

> I am sorry that you are in low spirits – it must be the bad weather. Buy a good pair of boots & walk more. The weather here today has been fine & I took a lovely walk up Skarvvola, a high mountain with a lovely view of Rondane & Jotunheimen. On the way I found a lot of yellow violets with a lovely scent. I also found some white heather which is quite rare. Enclosed I send you some of both – Mrs B. arrived last night, her husband follows in a few days. [...] I fish a great deal & am going off with one of my boys this afternoon to catch some trout. Every day I take a shower bath which is delicious with water from a mountain stream.[37]

It does not seem unreasonable to wonder whether Jelka's low spirits were connected with the fact that her husband and Milly Bergh were alone in the mountains. In 1906, Bergh's marriage was in serious trouble; three years later she would write openly to Delius about her longing for him (see p. 229).

It was his intention that Storfjellseter should only be a halfway house on his way to Jotunheimen and, as we saw earlier (see p. 204), Delius hoped to tempt

---

[36] Letter from Munch to Gustav Schiefler, probably June 1905 (MM).
[37] Letter from Delius to Jelka, 18 July 1906 (GM).

Edvard Grieg to join him there. It was just as well that the ailing Norwegian turned down the offer, for rain clouds rolled in across mountain-Norway, forcing Delius to change his plan, and by 24 July he was back in Åsgårdstrand. Almost nothing is known of what or who may have occupied Frederick and Jelka or of where they may have travelled in the month before they left Norway. One blink of light in the darkness was, however, provided by the Norwegian painter Torstein Torsteinson, who, in a letter to Delius a couple of years later, reminded him that they had met at the Konnerudkollen Tourist Hotel outside Drammen, while the Deliuses were waiting for their North Sea ferry home.[38]

1907: Delius becomes an English composer

The musical life of Great Britain around 1900 was characterised by a large degree of isolation from movements on the Continent. Had Delius stayed on in London after the success of his concert in 1899, his compositions might have stood a chance of being adopted into the English repertoire. Instead, he had fled the hubbub of the city for Grez and the flicker of fascination detected among Englishmen with their exotic compatriot had quickly faded. Between 1905 and 1907, however, the curiosity of every devoted follower of music would have been piqued by reports coming out of Germany of Delius successes. In April 1907, conductor Henry Wood enticed Delius to England to discuss a performance of the Piano Concerto, and the composer was astonished to find that he was in demand for musical soirées and dinners, that his courting of soloists and impresarios was welcomed, and that the publishing house of Breitkopf & Härtel had secured the rights to publish his music in England. 'Everyone wants me to come and live in London', he wrote with wonderment to Jelka.[39] Just as in Germany two or three years earlier, leading figures of English musical life experienced a sort of revelation – the sensation that they had stumbled across a priceless treasure that everyone else had overlooked. Two events in 1907 can be said to mark when Delius 'came home' and, at the age of forty-five, was finally accepted by his compatriots. On 22 October, the Piano Concerto was performed under the baton of Henry Wood and on 22 November *Appalachia* received its English première under Fritz Cassirer.

The young Thomas Beecham was in the hall for *Appalachia* and late in his life would describe the performance as 'one of the half-dozen momentous occasions'[40] of his career: 'Like every other musician under thirty years of age who was present at the performance of *Appalachia* in November, I was startled

---

[38] Torsteinson reappeared in Delius's life in 1908 when he was awarded a Norwegian state bursary. He moved to Paris and came to Grez to visit Delius and see his Gauguin painting *Nevermore*, which the composer had bought in 1898.
[39] Letter from Delius to Jelka, 21 April 1907 (GM).
[40] Beecham, *Frederick Delius*, 146.

and electrified.'[41] In the ensuing weeks, the most ardent musicians wished to become acquainted with the composer. Granville Bantock wrote to Delius: 'Your music has struck a fibre in my being, which is beyond analysis, but which I feel is the truest and noblest chord that has yet been sounded in our art.'[42] A similar tone was adopted by Havergal Brian: 'English musicians are very proud of you [...] We have so few men of *sincerity* in our midst – & you have won for yourself the position of greatest among them.'[43]

To the cluster of enthusiastic admirers belonged, among many others, Percy Grainger, Robin Legge, Percy Pitt, Cyril Scott, Balfour Gardiner, Norman O'Neill, Philip Heseltine, Ernest Newman, Roger Quilter and Ethel Smyth. While many of them became lifelong friends of Delius, none was to have greater significance for his reputation than the dynamic and charismatic conductor Thomas Beecham, who, in the weeks after the shock of hearing *Appalachia*, was already in full swing preparing performances of works by this bright 'new' English sun in the musical sky.

One year earlier, at the end of an extensive European tour in the spring of 1906, Grieg arrived in London. He was nearly exhausted after a month of performances in six cities and challenging journeys between them. The dark clouds in London were, however, dispelled by one lustrous personality who succeeded in alleviating Grieg's depression – the young Australian composer and piano virtuoso Percy Grainger. A huge admirer of Nordic culture in general and saga literature in particular, Grainger astounded Grieg with his knowledge of Norway and his insightful interpretations of the Norwegian's music.

A year on, and it was Delius who was in London and, with their common love for both Norway and Grieg, it was inevitable that he and Grainger would discover a similar magnetic attraction. The friendship that blossomed after their first meeting in April 1907 was not only warm, it was also creatively enriching for both. Grainger's harmonic style, in particular his chromatic voice writing, owes much to the older man. For his part, Delius was captivated by the folk melodies Grainger showed him. On the evening of their first meeting, Grainger played him Grieg's op. 66, no. 14, a piano interpretation of 'I Ola-dalom, i Ola-tjønn' ('In Ola Valley, in Ola Lake'), a folk tune from Valdres. Delius would incorporate the melody some years later into his *On Hearing the First Cuckoo in Spring*. He was also greatly stimulated by Grainger's choral setting of the traditional English song 'Unto Brigg Fair' and only three months later had completed his brilliant orchestral variations on the same theme.

Grainger could inform Delius that he was expected at Troldhaugen at the end of July to work on his interpretation of Grieg's Piano Concerto with the

---

[41] *Ibid.*, 146.
[42] Letter from Granville Bantock to Delius, 22 November 1907 (DT).
[43] Letter from Havergal Brian to Delius, 24 November 1907 (DT).

19. There was an immediate rapport between Delius and Percy Grainger when they met in 1907. It was due to the Australian's athleticism that the ailing Delius could be carried to the summit of Liahovdane in 1923.

composer. Grieg had in fact agreed to conduct the work at the Leeds Festival in October on the condition that Grainger was the soloist. This was interesting news for Delius and at the end of May, back home in Grez, he wrote to Grainger: 'I send you "Appalachia" which *please take with* you to Grieg when you go as he knows nothing of my music & it will put us in touch again as I really like him so much.'[44]As the day of Grainger's departure approached, Delius wrote again:

> In the summer I have always a great longing to go to Norway & live among the Mountains. I love the light nights so. Which way will you go? Let me know also when. The feeling of nature I think is what I like so much in Grieg's best things. You have it too & I think we all 3 have something in common. I won't swear that I shan't turn up on the steamer when you go to Bergen. If Grieg were only young & well enough to go into the hills we might have a lovely time.[45]

[44] Letter from Delius to Percy Grainger, undated, 31 May 1907 (GM).
[45] Letter from Delius to Percy Grainger, 10 June 1907 (PG).

Grainger arrived at Troldhaugen on 25 July and discovered that Grieg, though seriously ill, was playing host also to the Dutch composer Julius Röntgen, and opened his house daily to the visits of musical friends. There was even organised an outing to Blåmannen, one of the seven hills collaring Bergen, a venture that took Grieg to his physical limits. Grainger left Bergen again on 4 August. A month later, on 5 September, Delius read in the newspaper of Grieg's death the previous day and wrote immediately to the Australian: 'I am *very very* sorry. Have you any particulars. Please write me all you know.'[46] Grainger's reply would have brought Delius comfort: 'He was always talking of you, affectionately & admiringly, & told me lots of jolly anecdotes of your trips together in the High Hills. I showed him Appalachia & played him bits & he studied often in the score, & was *keenly interested*.' [47]

Twenty years earlier, Grieg had observed that with this 'English-American, musically deep, marvellous Hardangervidda Man […] we've got nothing in common except our feeling! But in the end, of course, that's everything!' Finally, just before it was too late, Edvard Grieg had in his hands the evidence confirming the wisdom of placing so much confidence in Delius. In *Appalachia*, he had powerfully demonstrated his mastery of orchestral colour, structure and nature evocation. In short, that here was an artist who had worked through the influences of Grieg and other masters and found his own identity.

---

[46] Postcard from Delius to Percy Grainger, undated, 5 September 1907 (PG).
[47] Letter from Percy Grainger to Delius, 9 September 1907 (DT).

10

1908–1912
Changes of direction

'Et je m'en vais / Au vent mauvais'

from 'Chanson d'Automne', Paul Verlaine

In the life of Frederick Delius, 1907 was a momentous year. It has been called his *annus mirabilis* on account of the explosion of interest his music enjoyed in England.[1] Also seen in the light of his connections to Norway, it was for the composer a transitional period, but for very different reasons. Norwegian friends such as Halfdan Jebe and Christian Sinding were moving out of his life and now Edvard Grieg, the artist whose music represented for Delius the irresistible pull of Norway, was gone. For the development of his career in the foreseeable future, only Germany and England mattered. With his success in England, the process that had been going on since *Folkeraadet* of redefining his relationship to Norwegian society was at an end. Hereafter, Delius would look to Norway for neither a professional network nor an audience.

This notwithstanding, Norway's place at the core of his creative life would become more secure than ever, through the persistent importance to him of Norwegian nature, and of the Norwegian folk character that thrived between the mountains. Indeed, in 1908 – the year after the English breakthrough – we see him driven by a compulsion to show his new English friends exactly where he found much of the inspiration for his works, where his creative spirit was renewed: in the light of Norway's summer nights, and in the loneliness of Jotunheimen's mountain plateaus.

Delius devoted the first half of 1908 to composition and to trips to England and Germany to hear his works, including the première of *A Mass of Life* in Munich. It was probably while in London in March that Delius spent some time with the renowned Norwegian cabaret singer Bokken Lasson. At the end of April she sent him tickets for her upcoming London concert and hoped that

---

[1] See GD, 185.

'you have not quite forgotten me'.[2] By then, Delius was back in Grez and could not make use of them. It is unknown whether or not this was the first time they had met; Lasson was the sister of Oda Krohg and could therefore have met Delius through their many common acquaintances in Paris and Kristiania. Around the time of their meeting in London, Lasson was being courted by the Norwegian lawyer and dramatist Vilhelm Dybwad, husband of Norway's leading actress Johanne Dybwad, who had played Ella in *Folkeraadet*. Vilhelm Dybwad and Bokken Lasson would marry in 1916 and a few years later Delius, experiencing trouble selling his cottage in Lesjaskog, would avail himself of Dybwad's expertise in Norwegian law (see p. 297).

A summer tour in Norway had been on the drawing board all winter. Percy Grainger had mentioned several times to Delius how much he was looking forward to accompanying him and envisaged that they would go collecting folk songs in remote villages. Around New Year, Nina Grieg had also implored Delius to plan their route so that it led him and Grainger past the door of Troldhaugen. In the end, Grainger had to give priority to a concert tour of Australia, and Delius tried instead to tempt his English champions Balfour Gardiner and Thomas Beecham. At the end of July, just a couple of days before Delius was to leave for Norway, Gardiner also made his excuses. Beecham, however, had cleared his busy schedule for the summer and was ready for the challenge.[3]

Both the invitation to Beecham and its acceptance reflect the status of the relationship the two men were building. Beecham was twenty-nine. He had made his conducting debut in London at the end of 1905 and with his New Symphony Orchestra was quickly making a name for himself. Delius would have warmed to the genuine enthusiasm Beecham expressed for his music after *Appalachia* in November 1907, and by his promotion of *Paris* in January 1908. If he was to trust his music to the young man, time spent together in Norway would let him gauge Beecham's mettle. And we can conclude that the conductor passed with flying colours. In each of the six long letters Delius sent from Norway to Jelka, he heaped praises on his travelling companion: 'Beecham is enjoying himself immensely & the more I see of him – the more I like him';[4] 'He does nothing that I do not like as, often, people one travels with do';[5] 'B has an eye for Nature & likes the sort of thing that I do'.[6]

---

[2] Letter from Bokken Lasson to Delius, 23 April 1908 (DT).
[3] Beecham had seemingly widened his horizons since 1897 when, to mark the end of his schooling, he had taken a friend on a cruise of Norway. The friend recalled that: 'I used to land, and climb the mountains alone, while he stayed on the ship all the time, playing the piano non-stop to admiring audiences of ladies'. John Lucas, *Thomas Beecham: An obsession with music* (Woodbridge: Boydell Press, 2008), 10.
[4] Letter from Delius to Jelka, 30 July 1908 (GM).
[5] Letter from Delius to Jelka, 6 August 1908 (GM).
[6] Letter from Delius to Jelka, 10 August 1908 (GM).

Summer 1908: A month in the mountains with Beecham

Only to Jelka did Delius ever write with openness about his travels, so for those summers in which the couple travelled together in Norway we have, at best, only a bare outline of their movements. His letters home to her in 1908 are among some of the last substantial descriptions we have of how he experienced the country and for this reason alone they are worth quoting in some detail below. They give us, however, also vivid insights into the extraordinary energy that typified Delius in his best years. 'It was lucky for me that I was in pretty good physical condition at that time', Beecham would write later, 'for Delius proved to be a first-class mountaineer and a pedestrian of untiring energy'.[7]

First week. Whether or not he planned it that way to break Beecham softly into the programme, Delius had scheduled a first week with little walking, but considerable distances covered by carriage and steamer.

27 July	Delius sails from Antwerp, Beecham from Hull
28 July	Delius arrives in Arendal, sails to Kristiania
29 July	Delius and Beecham meet in Kristiania, take train to Lillehammer
30 July	Lillehammer – Otta – Vågå
31 July	Vågå – Grotli
1 August	Grotli – Djupvatnet
2 August	Djupvatnet – Merok [Geiranger]

After a first day of transit (30 July), Beecham and Delius stopped in the mountain heart of Southern Norway at the village of Vågå. As Delius and Jelka had done on their stop in Vågå in 1902, they visited the small medieval church: 'Went to visit the old church, which is wonderful – That Jesus on the cross – is remarkable', he wrote to Jelka.[8] Climbing steadily higher on the road to Merok (today's Geiranger), they spent an afternoon fishing in a mountain lake at Grotli. After a detour to take in a panorama of the western mountains from a vantage point in Stryn (probably Videsœter), they continued north. Their road rose to well over a thousand metres, threading its way across dramatic and naked mountain-top passes, before falling in spectacular hairpin bends to sea level at the Geiranger Fjord:

> [The] finest scenery I have ever seen – fantastic – Of course you must see this –
> We passed one lake hemmed in by a gigantic black, blue & green Cliff of solid
> rock with patches of snow on the quite perpendicular side – perhaps a clear

---

[7] Beecham, *A Mingled Chime*, 126–7.
[8] Letter from Delius to Jelka, 30 July 1908 (GM).

1000 ft from the lake – The sides were reflected exactly into the entirely dark blue water & formed an extraordinary reflection.[9]

More than was his practice when travelling alone, Delius had chosen well-trodden tourist routes, no doubt to please his companion. The reverse side of the jaw-droppingly beautiful scenery was represented by the tourists; as today, the spectacular fjord and mountain landscape around Geiranger was the principal goal for many travellers in Southern Norway. At one lodge, Delius and Beecham stayed on an extra night 'to get rid of some unpleasant french tourists with a priest!',[10] only to endure instead a caravan of Germans who 'take entire possession of the sitting room & begin to play the piano & sing in chorus german Folksongs & student songs – they are all fat & ugly! […] wherever we arrive – people are playing the piano & never stop – I am trying to write, but really I must stop, they are hammering away at the damned instrument.'[11]

Second week. During the next days, Delius and Beecham took in the wide fjords and snow-capped mountains of Sunnmøre from the decks of fjord steamers, going briefly ashore at small coastal towns.

3 August	Merok – Vestnes
4 August	Vestnes – Molde
5 August	Molde – Ålesund
6 August	Ålesund – Volda – Sæbø
7 August	Sæbø – Øye – Grodås
8 August	Grodås – Loen
9 August	Loen – Kjenndal Glacier – Mindresunde

Looking across the fjord from Molde to the Sunnmøre Alps, Delius wrote to Jelka: 'This is the place where you would like to stay some time & paint – The sun sets just opposite a wonderful range of mountains throwing its rays right upon them, just like in Grez with the trees.'[12] The companions enjoyed sea bathing and climbing the hills around the town. On Thursday 6 August they turned south again, crossing fjord arms, moving steadily inland towards the great goal Delius had set for their third week, the Jotunheim mountains. *En route* to Sæbø, they stopped at the idyllic Vatne lake, 'beautifully situated between enormous mountains but with a very wide & lovely view – We stayed here 6 hours to fish – A peasant lent us his boat & we rowed about the lake but got no fish.'[13] Arriving for the night at the fishing hamlet of Sæbø, out of which ferries plied the Hjørund Fjord, Delius was enchanted by the 'wonderfully

---

[9] Letter from Delius to Jelka, 2 August 1908 (GM). The lake is probably Djupvatnet.
[10] *Ibid.*
[11] *Ibid.*
[12] Letter from Delius to Jelka, 4 August 1908 (GM).
[13] Letter from Delius to Jelka, 6 August 1908 (GM).

formed mountains overhanging the fjord'.[14] Here his thoughts of Jelka led him to buy her some gifts:

> I saw some lovely old silver buttons, a fine old silver brooch, gilded & with red stones, & also another little silver brooch which I bought for you & hope you will like – The brooch is 300 years old – I had to buy these things, firstly as I know you will like them & secondly because one can scarcely get such things any more – They will just suit you – [15]

By Saturday they had arrived at Loen, the furthest point inland reached by the salt waters of the Nordfjord. The curse of the tourists was still upon them. This time it was the English who were a 'great nuisance & hold divine service on Sundays – When I came down on Sunday morning a priest & another man were on their knees in the drawing room praying – Beecham & I fled instantly.'[16] They made their escape on a day-long hike up the narrow Lodal to the foot of the Kjenndal Glacier, a branch of the Jostedal Glacier – and for Beecham a first view of the ice barrier he would soon have to overcome. The towering valley sides had hidden dangers; three years earlier fifty-nine people had been drowned when a cliff face had crashed to the fjord, causing a wave that flooded the farms. The second week of the tour was finished off at Mindresunde, a spit of land between two great lakes: 'Lovely view over the fjord from both sides & magnificent hills & Mountains'.[17]

Third week. Delius had acclimatised Beecham; for the third week there would be no holds barred. Their journey would take them from sea level to the summit of Norway's highest peak, across some of the least hospitable terrain in Norway.

10 August	Mindresunde – Stryn – Hjelle
11 August	Hjelle – Skora
12 August	Skora – Sunndalssætra
13 August	Sunndalssætra – Jostedal Glacier – Mysubytta *seter*
14 August	Mysubytta *seter* – Sota *seter* – Skjåk
15 August	Skjåk – Røisheim – Juvvasshytta
16 August	Juvvasshytta – Galdhøpiggen – Spiterstulen

The charming Hjelle Hotel, preserved today much as it was a hundred years ago, was their last fjord refuge before the inland mountains, and here on Monday Delius and Beecham entered their names in the guestbook. Between them and Jotunheimen was the great white barrier, the Jostedal Glacier lying atop eighty kilometres of mountain plateau. There were good roads going

---

[14] *Ibid.*
[15] *Ibid.*
[16] Letter from Delius to Jelka, 10 August 1908 (GM).
[17] *Ibid.*

20. During their 1908 tour of Norway, Delius and Beecham spent a night here at Sunndalssætra, high in the Sunndal valley, before crossing the Jostedal Glacier the next day.

round, but Delius had chosen a challenging experience for the midpoint of their tour. To traverse the ice cap they had to wait for a local guide, and finally on Wednesday they trekked up the wild and lovely Sunndal to a mountain *seter* at the foot of the glacier. They spent the night in 'a dirty little hut [with] nothing to eat & we had to sleep on some dry twigs with only a dirty cover'.[18] The next two days would, however, provide them with anecdotes and memories that would enliven conversations for the rest of their lives:

> [Next] day we left at 6 am for our big walk up to the glacier. 5 hours almost as steep as a house – Beecham seemed quite done up & faint & I thought we should have to turn back – he pulled together however very pluckily – I carried his knapsack & the guide carried mine – The walk over the glacier was grandiose & nothing but snow in sight & snow covered peaks – after we crossed the glacier we descended gradually to Mysubytta seter which was a frightful distance – We were 14 hours walking – with only a couple of sandwiches each – B could scarcely walk any more – we had to wade a stream which took me almost up to the waist. The man carried B across.[19]

---

[18] Letter from Delius to Jelka, 18 August 1908 (GM).
[19] *Ibid.* According to Eric Fenby, Delius never forgave Beecham 'for forgetting his sandwiches the day they lunched on a glacier'. See *Delius* (London: Faber & Faber, 1971), 66.

There were other perils on the trip – bears, which were known to have 'an unpleasant habit of appearing suddenly on the glacier', as Beecham recalled in his autobiography. He forgot his anxiety 'in the contemplation of this marvellous sea of ice [...] taking on gradually a richer hue of gold as the sun sank lower and its rays grew longer'. On arriving next day at Skjåk, however, they were startled to discover in front of the post house 'a huge specimen of the tribe, which had wandered down only an hour or two earlier from the glacier in search of food, and had been shot by one of the farmers who had been on the lookout for it'.[20]

Delius had planned several stops at mountain huts, but now changed the route, probably to get Beecham back on his feet, staying in Skjåk at the well-equipped Ånstad Farm. Already the next day, their route took them from Bøverdalen and Røisheim, the famous post house in the heart of Jotunheimen (see Illustration 18), up to one of the most extreme mountain lodges in Norway, Juvvasshytta, arriving late at night. It is a climb of some 1,340 metres. Even though they took a porter with them, Delius was now asking a lot of his companion, but Beecham was up for the challenge. Juvvasshytta (1,841m) lies in a desert of glacial moraine almost a kilometre above the tree line, and is a morning's march across moraine and glaciers away from Norway's highest mountain, Galdhøpiggen (2,469m). Blessed with good weather, Beecham and Delius made the ascent together with two other tourists – led to the summit by a legendary figure in Norwegian mountain lore, the Juvvasshytta guide Knut O. Vole. In the afternoon they continued their journey, down into Visdalen to the remote Spiterstulen lodge where they nevertheless still had the company of Germans: 'The other guests were 4 german women of the ugliest kind – Even the guides hanging around began to laugh as they came trudging in – Something fearful to look at.'[21]

Fourth week. The pair spent another four days among the Jotunheim mountains before returning south.

17 August	Spiterstulen – Gjendebu
18 August	Gjendebu
19 August	Gjendebu – Gjendesheim
20 August	Gjendesheim
21 August	Gjendesheim – Fagernes
22 August	Fagernes – Kristiania
23 August	Kristiania – Fredriksværn [Stavern]

---

[20] Beecham, *A Mingled Chime*, 127.
[21] Letter from Delius to Jelka, 18 August 1908 (GM).

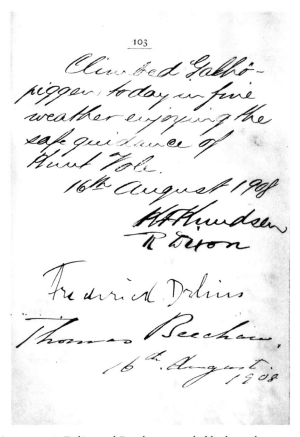

21. On 16 August 1908, Delius and Beecham were led by legendary mountain guide Knut O. Vole to the summit of Galdhøpiggen, afterwards signing Vole's Guide Protocol. Two other tourists were on the climb, one of them noting that they had enjoyed 'fine weather'.

On Monday evening they had 'a most glorious trip thro' one of the wildest valleys of Jotunheimen'[22] to arrive at the western end of Gjende, the eighteen-kilometre proglacial lake famous for its aquamarine colour, caused by glacial sediment. Delius had also stayed at the Gjendebu lodge with Grieg and Sinding in 1889, and now, finding it 'so nice and clean',[23] he and Beecham stayed on for a couple of days to fish in the lake and give their feet a rest. To reach the Gjendesheim lodge at the lake's eastern end, they had to traverse the airy knife-edge of Besseggen to the north of the water, well-known to theatre-goers as the cliff along whose rim Peer Gynt imagines being carried by a careering reindeer in the opening of Ibsen's eponymous verse play. Delius was concise in his letter to Jelka: 'Very

[22] *Ibid.*
[23] *Ibid.*

exciting & lovely view'.[24] Despite the few words, the view would undoubtedly have stirred many memories for him; from the rim of Besseggen, Delius could gaze down and across to the far side of the lake and point out for Beecham the cabin in which he had spent the summer of 1889 with Grieg and Sinding.

They had crossed Jotunheimen from north-west to south-east, and finished the week making their way back to Kristiania. Neither on the way to the mountains nor on the way back did Delius tarry in the capital. Since the *Folkeraadet* debacle, the city had held little of interest for him, and this year there was also an outbreak of smallpox there. Instead, he took Beecham with him to his favourite coastal village on the Kristiania Fjord, Fredriksværn, for a few days of bathing and fishing.

Fifth and sixth weeks. On Thursday of the fifth week Delius and Beecham parted company.

24 August	Fredriksværn
25 August	Fredriksværn
26 August	Fredriksværn
27 August	Beecham sails to Kristiania and then home, Delius to Kragerø
28 August	Kragerø – Arendal – Tromøya
29 August	Tromøya – Fevik
30 August	Fevik
31 August	Fevik
1 September	Fevik
2 September	Fevik
3 September	Fevik – Kristiansand
4 September	Delius sails from Kristiansand for Antwerp

Delius took the coastal steamer west towards Arendal, intending to leave next day for Antwerp. Half way there, however, the swell made him seasick and he disembarked at the fishing village of Kragerø. He completed his journey to Arendal the following day, but, alarmed by forecasts of an approaching storm, delayed his homeward voyage, spending another week bathing in hamlets along the south coast. Accommodation was found for him in the houses of local sea captains. When he got bored, Delius sat in the cottages and practised conducting his *In a Summer Garden*, having agreed to conduct its first performance in December at the Queen's Hall in London.

Any intention Delius might have had of visiting Nina Grieg in Bergen seemed to have been abandoned once Percy Grainger's participation in the summer tour was out of the picture. A year later, however, she wrote Delius a letter intimating that he had perhaps kept the option open during his travels

---

[24] Postcard from Delius to Jelka, 23 August 1908 (GM).

with Beecham: 'You didn't come to Troldhaugen last summer', she sighed, 'I expected you so often.'[25] It would not be the last time Delius disappointed his old friend.

At the summit: *Brigg Fair* and *In a Summer Garden*

The years 1907–09 constitute a brief and intense period in Delius's life when his spiritual well-being, physical health and creative strength were all firing in a splendid unison. On a personal level, he had achieved many of the goals to which his life had been directed for twenty years. That he simultaneously was at the peak of his creative powers is evidenced by two orchestral works written between spring 1907 and spring 1908: *Brigg Fair* and *In a Summer Garden*. They mark a capstone of his life, a period of contentment with the world and his place in it.

In a Summer Garden is a masterpiece of mood painting, alternating between drowsy reverie in a garden with birdsong and insect noises, and an exalted lyrical outpouring occasioned by love and happiness – these lyrical sections, depicted against a backdrop of flowing figuration, are perhaps to be associated with a boat trip on the river. If this was a composition that expressed Delius's delight in his environment at Grez, then the energy and mastery of *Brigg Fair* (subtitled 'An English Rhapsody') tells us much about what it meant to him to have conquered his homeland. Paul Guinery has written of *Brigg Fair* that it is 'one of the most satisfying and characteristic works of Delius's maturity, its form convincingly structured, its ideas fertile and memorable, its sense of direction and flow impeccable and its orchestration of the utmost imagination and sensitivity. [...] He had by now unquestionably found his own true voice.'[26] Both of these works are bursting with melodic fecundity allied with sustained expressivity. These are characteristics worthy of particular notice, for captivating melodies were about to disappear from his language for some five or six years; it was a gift he came to set less store by, or maybe even lost for a period.

Apart from a notably Griegian turn of phrase at the start of *In a Summer Garden* (flute, 9–10), there is nothing that would lead one to connect the work to any place Delius loved, other than his home at Grez. In two episodes of mood painting in *Brigg Fair*, however, it is possible to trace the material to stylistic traits of his Norway-related Mountain Music. At the close of two slower sections between lively dance variations, quiet and repeating horn calls are introduced, soothing from the music its propellant energy, bringing it finally to moments of rest. The first of these, Example 10.1 – an extended horn solo

---

[25] Letter from Nina Grieg to Delius, 22 May 1909 (DT).
[26] Paul Guinery and Martin Lee-Browne, *Delius and His Music* (Woodbridge: The Boydell Press, 2014), 250.

that begins four bars after fig. 18 – takes up the melodic variation of the folk song introduced by strings after fig. 15. Its dying phrase is constantly repeated by the horn like a distant call:

Example 10.1 *Brigg Fair*, fig. 18, 4–17

Even more remarkable is the second passage, for which Delius puts to good use a variant of the rolling horn call he had first used in *Paa Vidderne* twenty years earlier (see Example 3.6), there associated with the wide horizons of the mountain plateau:

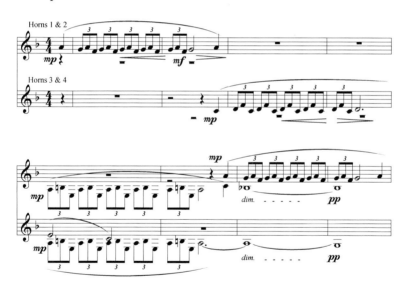

Example 10.2 *Brigg Fair*, fig. 28, 3–7

These horn calls are children of his 'Mountain Music', but here, in a work anchored firmly in the composer's rekindled affection for England, they may be intended to evoke pastoral associations: a dialogue of shepherd calls. It is equally likely that they are not intended to transport the listener to a geographical place at all, but to a place in the spirit – to a mood, an emotional latitude. As we saw in the previous chapter, Delius had begun to consider the emotions he associated with his Mountain Music transferable to music unrelated to mountains, most notably to love's otherworldly detachment or passion, as exemplified by *A Village Romeo and Juliet*. In coming works, similar horn calls will be associated variously with the human life energy (*Requiem*), the hope of morning light (*Fennimore and Gerda*) and oneness with great nature (*The Song of the High Hills*). And what, then, do these two calls, initially inspired by emotions experienced in Norwegian mountains, carry with them to *Brigg Fair*? A sense of repose and acquiescence in an open, natural landscape, and oneness with this landscape; solitude is, however, also part of the emotional mix.

At this high point in his life, Delius found that *Brigg Fair* and *In a Summer Garden* flowed easily from his pen. Shortly after completing them, a further brilliantly coloured orchestral work burst from him that not only continued the sequence of works marked with vivid instrumentation and melodic lyricism, but was a throwback to the youthful exuberance of a period that lay ten to twenty years in his past. *Dance Rhapsody* (later numbered No. 1) is an astonishing hotchpotch of stylistic elements. It opens with low reed instruments playing pastoral calls, but with an oriental twist that looks forward to his incidental music to *Hassan* (1921). Then follows a folk dance theme suggestive of both a Scottish jig and a Norwegian fiddle dance. As the music becomes more boisterous, brass and percussion are added on off-beats in a conventional fashion that takes us back to the 'Calinda' dance of *Florida* and the war dance of *Hiawatha*. The jaunty and happy melodies throughout are among the last Delius wrote that are 'catchy' and easy to recall. Coming in 1908–09, and therefore bordering on the composer's first period of chill Nordic writing, the *Dance Rhapsody* seems a rather baffling, if delightful, anachronism.

He could not, of course, see what was round the next corner. In 1907 and 1908 he had revelled in his English breakthrough, then a wonderful summer in Norway with Beecham; he had almost spewed forth *Brigg Fair* and *In a Summer Garden*. There seemed to be no clouds in the noontide sky. It would be banal to state that, once at this summit, the only way forward for Delius was downwards, but, at least in the relatively narrow sense of his physical health, this would turn out to be the case. In his creative life, the trajectory was much more nuanced. His musical language moved sideways, away from sensuous summer into a less clement season; in the principal works of 1908–11 the sun rarely broke through. There would be towering achievements in this coming period, *The Song of the High Hills* above them all, but never again a work suffused with the same ease and happiness. Was this move sideways a sign of the composer absorbing changes in his life, or deliberately seeking a new language? Above, Paul Guinery identified the language of *Brigg Fair* as the composer's 'true voice'. Having found this voice, however, the composer soon after regarded it as one with which he no longer could truthfully speak. There is a possibility that Delius demanded of himself stylistic development, that he – having achieved the peak of *Brigg Fair* and *In a Summer Garden* – actively sought a new direction. It is more likely, however, that the personal trials of the next years, which made him abundantly aware of the frailty of his health, applied existential pressure to his worldview, remoulding his creative vision into new expressions.

The work that signposted his change of direction was written at the same time as the 'noontide' compositions. Stylistically, it is simply extraordinary that *Brigg Fair* and *Dance Rhapsody* can belong to the same period as the *Songs of Sunset*. For this uneven work for orchestra, chorus and two soloists, Delius took poems by Ernest Dowson which may at that time have seemed redolent of contemporary culture, of a *fin de siècle* melancholy. Taken on their own merit, the *Songs of Sunset* do offer many sensuous, glowing textures, albeit for short passages. Compared, however, with the passionate energy of *Brigg Fair* and the *joie de vivre* of the *Dance Rhapsody*, this was a work concerned with the slow burn of middle age, these were songs of the fading light. The composer, so recently magnanimous with melodic gifts, was now cultivating a non-melodic style where texture was all. And there was a further element creeping into his writing for the first time that it is less easy to come to terms with: he allowed himself to be self-indulgent.

This is a different composer from the one who wrote *Brigg Fair*. The summer of the spirit was over, the wind was turning. The gust that was approaching from the north was the *vent mauvais* of Verlaine's 'Chanson d'Automne' – a poem the composer would set in 1911:

Les sanglots longs	(The long sobs
Des violons	Of the violins
De l'automne	Of autumn
Blessent mon coeur	Wound my heart
D'une langueur	With monotonous
Monotone.	Languor.
Tout suffocant	All suffocating
Et blême, quand	And pale, when
Sonne l'heure,	The hour strikes
Je me souviens	I recall
Des jours anciens	The old days
Et je pleure;	And I cry.
Et je m'en vais	And go away
Au vent mauvais	On an ill wind
Qui m'emporte	That carries me off
Deçà, delà,	Here, there,
Pareil à la	Just like the
Feuille morte.	Dead leaf.)

22. Delius sent Nina Grieg this portrait in 1909, recalling a walk he had taken with her on the Haukeli mountain plateau in 1891 (see p. 80).

1909–1910: Tertiary syphilis diagnosed

Delius's works were being embraced all over Germany and England. Thomas Beecham and Hans Haym both gave important performances of *A Mass of Life* in 1909 and at the end of the year *Paris* was given in Boston, the first time his orchestral music was heard in America. Early in the year, he turned his attention to a new music-dramatic work, an adaptation of Jens P. Jacobsen's novel from 1880, *Niels Lyhne*. A summer holiday was spent walking in the Black Forest with a friend from England, composer and conductor Norman O'Neill. The countryside was pleasant enough, but Delius lacked the stimulating drama of Scandinavia's fjords and mountains, writing to Jelka: 'All this is nothing to

Denmark & Norway'.[27] It was to the first of these that he and Jelka travelled in August 1909 at the invitation of Danish friends they had made in London, the industrialist Einar Schou and wife Elisabeth. The Schous had recently purchased Palsgaard Slot, a manor house outside Juelsminde on the east coast south of Aarhus. Delius was also in correspondence with Milly Bergh a couple of times this year and it is clear that his intention had been to visit Norway in the summer. From Palsgaard he wrote to inform her that he would not after all be coming further north. It was a disappointment for Bergh; evidently smitten with the composer and newly divorced from Ludvig Bergh, she wrote back to Delius from Kristiania: 'Tonight I should have played the piano and done some translation work and made coffee and eaten supper, but I long for you'.[28]

In England in September, Delius's health took a turn for the worse, and he blamed his 'bilious attacks' on having to put up with London society for far longer than his nerves could stand. The English bourgeoisie could not, however, be blamed for a further worsening of his condition after a trip to Germany in December. Having enjoyed a performance of *A Mass of Life* under Hans Haym in Elberfeld, he and Jelka continued to Berlin where he engaged solicitors to represent him in an increasingly acrimonious battle with his publishers, Harmonie. The stress caused by the conflict – regarding lost scores, late proofs and general incompetence – coincided with a sudden and grave weakening of his constitution. Attempting a diagnosis a year later, his doctor registered: 'About 1 year ago (after an attack of influenza and excitement after legal proceedings) he collapsed, i.e. there was a noticeable loss of strength; about the same time other pains occurred: arms, shoulders and in the area of the thorax, toes, repeated gastric crises'.[29]

Despite his deepening health concerns, Delius travelled widely in 1910 to hear his music. In May, he was in Zurich to hear *Brigg Fair* and had the pleasure of befriending Zoltán Kodály and Béla Bartók, respectively twenty-seven and twenty-nine years old. It seems that, once again on making new artistic friends, Delius wasted no time in regaling them with accounts of Norway's light summer nights and great mountain wildernesses and inviting them to join him on a trek there at the first opportunity. Bartók in particular seems to have been enchanted by his tales of the north, but wrote in early June to Delius: 'Now you are going to your Norway again or are already there – unfortunately I cannot leave the city this summer – and all I can do is yearn for the wild regions you told me about'.[30]

Whatever plans Delius may have hatched for a journey north, they came to nothing. While in Zurich, he had consulted a specialist about his condition,

---

[27] Letter from Delius to Jelka, undated, mid-July 1909 (DT).
[28] Letter from Milly Bergh to Delius, 3 September 1909 (DT).
[29] Report by Dr W. Bothe, quoted in Philip Jones and J. R. Heron, 'A Fever Diluted by Time' in *Journal of The Delius Society*, No. 98 (Autumn 1988), 5.
[30] Letter from Bartók to Delius, 7 June 1910 (DT).

and was strongly urged to take a hydropathic cure in the Swiss mountains. 'Unfortunately I cannot go this summer to my beloved Norway', he replied to Bartók, 'as I have to start in eight days on a sanatorium treatment'.[31] While undergoing a month of cures at the establishment in Mammern, Delius was given a diagnosis by the medical staff to which he afforded little credence, writing to Jelka: 'My trouble comes from the Central Nerven [sic] System & may have something to do with my old Syphilis – I don't believe this at all'.[32] When news arrived from Milly Bergh that the weather in Norway was set fair for the coming weeks, Delius took the manner of his restitution in his own hands. He sent off a postcard to Jelka: 'Let us go to Norway & shut up the house'.[33] The wheels were put in motion for a rapid decampment to northern climes, but on his way back to Grez in mid-July Delius suffered a relapse and all plans were again put on hold.

It is remarkable to note his absolute faith in the restorative powers of Norwegian nature. As far back as 1888 he had written to Grieg, declaring his intention of moving to Norway: 'Streets and smoke distort our ideas. One has to breathe pure air before one can think purely. I feel so well in mind & body when nature is beautiful.' Now in 1910 and, as we shall see, repeatedly up to his final visit to Norway in 1923, he seemed to hold the conviction that, if only he could get up into the mountains again, his vigour would be restored. This gives us a clearer insight than any letter describing the scenery could, into what constituted the pull of the country on Delius. Yes, his travels there were as holidays anywhere – breaks from routine and an opportunity to recharge physical and mental batteries. However, this recourse to the Norwegian mountain wilderness at a time of crisis, when he felt physical decay and disorder threatening the core of his life, tells us that he sought there something more substantial, more spiritual, than recreation or alleviation of routine.

From early December 1910 to early March 1911 he was again under the supervision of medical teams, first at a sanatorium in Dresden, then in Wiesbaden. Onerous and heavy duties were now placed on Jelka's shoulders, and in a letter from Dresden to a relative she told of Delius's dependency on her, a chilling harbinger of even darker days to come: 'I have to conduct all the correspondence, to nurse him, walk with him, read to him – There is not much time left over to myself – '.[34] It was while he was at this institution that a thorough diagnosis of his condition was recorded, leaving no doubt as to the cause of its deterioration. In addition to the symptoms noted from his collapse a year earlier, the physicians also remarked on his 'uneven yet reactive pupils, and indeed increased knee reflexes, reduced pain sensation in the lower extremi-

[31] Letter from Delius to Bartók, 11 June 1910 (BB).
[32] Letter from Delius to Jelka, 17 June 1910 (GM).
[33] Postcard from Delius to Jelka, 9 July 1910 (GM).
[34] Letter from Jelka to unidentified family member ('Liebste Leni'), 4 January 1911 (GM).

ties' and on Delius's upper left thigh there was 'a tertiary syphilid' – a skin lesion caused by syphilis. The Wassermann blood test for syphilis, introduced in 1906, was then taken. It showed positive. His neurosyphilitic condition was indeed a typical late development of the disease at its tertiary stage. Although the effective medication Salvarsan was being introduced around this time, it is believed that Delius staunchly upheld his faith in homeopathic remedies. Ida Gerhardi recorded a visit by the composer in mid-1910:

> [He] had hardly been in my Paris studio for 5 minutes before he looked out of the window and said: 'It's my spinal cord' – he said it so wretchedly and thus sounded so in need of comfort that I felt an indescribable pity. He then said he believed after all that it was quite possible to heal his condition as long as one had the correct prescription from the correct doctors. He was like a child.[35]

Fennimore and Gerda and An Arabesque: Texts

Whenever his condition allowed in the years 1909–10, Delius was at work, creating from Jacobsen's *Niels Lyhne* a new opera. Yet another significant work to words by Jacobsen, *An Arabesque*, would follow in the autumn of 1911. In Chapter One we saw that Norway and Denmark shared a common literary culture in the nineteenth century, and for this reason the most significant Danish works composed by Delius can be seen as an inevitable extension of his knowledge of Norwegian culture and ties to Norwegian artists. These two Jacobsen works also belong squarely in a study of Delius and Norway on account of their narrative and musical content, both of which are intimately connected to the composer's Norwegian affinities. Once more it must be emphasised that it is not the present author's intention to diminish the significance of Danish authors in Delius's story or in any sense to redefine them as 'pseudo-Norwegian', but rather to point out that the particular Danish texts to which he was drawn shared that same aesthetic of nature symbolism that had drawn him to musicians, authors and painters of Norway, and which he associated with Norwegian nature. We can look first at the texts selected for these important compositions.

Rather than being in any sense specifically Danish, the nature symbolism of Jacobsen's text for *An Arabesque* (1868), where the brevity of summer is equated with the brevity of love and life, can be regarded as pan-Scandinavian.

Har du faret vild i dunkle Skove?	(Have you lost your way in dark forests?
Kender du Pan?	Do you know Pan?
Jeg har følt ham,	I have felt him,
Ikke i de dunkle Skove,	Not in the dark forests,

---

[35] Letter from Ida Gerhardi to her mother, 15 July 1910, quoted in Jones and Heron, 'A Fever Diluted by Time', 6.

Medens alt Tiende talte,   When everything quiet, spoke,
Nej! den Pan har jeg aldrig kendt,   No! I have never known that Pan,
Men Kærlighedens Pan har jeg følt, –   But I have felt the Pan of love, –
Da tav alt Talende.   Then all speech fell silent.

I solvarme Egne   In warmer climes
Vokser en sælsom Urt,   Grows a strange herb,
Kun i dybeste Tavshed,   Only in the deepest silence,
Under tusende Solstraalers Brand,   Warmed by a thousand sunbeams
Aabner den sin Blomst   Does it open its flower
I et flygtigt Sekund.   For a fleeting moment.
Den ser ud som en gal Mands Øje,   It looks like the eye of a madman,
Som et Ligs røde Kinder :   Like the red cheeks of a corpse:
Den har jeg set   I have seen it
I min Kærlighed.   In my love.
[…]
Alt er forbi!   All is past!
Paa den snedække Slette   In a snow-covered glade
I den brune Skov   In the brown forest
Vokser en enlig Tjørn,   Grows a single hawthorn,
Vindene eje dens Løv.   Its leaves scattered by winds.
Et for et,   One by one,
Et for et   One by one
Drypper den de blodrøde Bær   It lets its blood-red berries
Ned i den hvide Sne;   Drip down on the white snow;
De glødende Bær   The glowing berries
I den kolde Sne. –   In the cold snow. –

Kender du Pan?   Do you know Pan?)

In an analysis of the poem made by Jelka Delius in 1929, she was at pains to point out just how generally northern it was in spirit, particularly in its first section:

> This is one of the finest Scandinavian poems and to me it does not seem obscure. Think of the endless Scandinavian winter and the marvellous all too short summer. It is a lover's rhapsodic recital of his love. First he describes the so typically northern summer-feeling – Pan – the sensual love, destructive, unreasonable, under the spell of a short moment of bliss only.[36]

At the time of writing *An Arabesque* in 1911, Delius had experienced the brief and intense northern summer many times, but only once in Denmark – the visit to Palsgaard in 1909. It was by the Kristiania Fjord his summer associations had been formed.

---

[36] Attachment to a letter from Jelka to Thomas Beecham, 14 August 1929, quoted in John White, 'The Hidden Meanings of *An Arabesque*' in *Journal of the Delius Society*, No. 142 (Autumn 2007), 69–70.

In a remarkable way, the text of *An Arabesque* also captures the essence of that idiosyncratic blend of nature symbolism and anxiety caused by the liberated woman that so typified the work of male artists of the age. Erik A. Nielsen writes that in the poem we are tempted into the depths of the forest 'where a wonderful and heartless woman has attracted to herself all the longings and desires a man can possess – and then she lets him fall, so that he is poisoned by the sheer lack of direction to his passion'.[37] In no other artist's works is this mix of life, death and sexual anxiety more clearly defined than in those of the greatest Norwegian artist of the time, Edvard Munch. John Boulton Smith has identified in *An Arabesque* and *Fennimore and Gerda* 'similarities in mood and imagery to works of Munch', and points out: 'The words of *An Arabesque*, with their association of love, death and flowers, use images which we find in such Munch works as the Baudelaire *Fleurs de Mal* drawings (1896) or the lithograph *The Flower of Love*, and Delius's brilliantly appropriate setting is full of this fin-de-siecle pessimism'.[38]

An Arabesque was pan-Scandinavian in its essence, and for *Fennimore and Gerda*, too, the composer selected none of the scenes from Jacobsen's *Niels Lyhne* that connected the novel to specifically Danish events (such as the Battle of Dybbøl) or those set in urban Copenhagen. The operatic action takes place in and near three houses, one in the country and two by the edge of fjords. Played for most part against the backdrop of these fjords, the opera is more likely to have been coloured and inspired by the ten summers Delius had spent by the Kristiania Fjord than by his weeks by the Kattegat in 1909 as a guest of the Schous. As in *An Arabesque*, Boulton Smith sees in the opera musical similarities to the Nordic expressionism associated with Munch – both the highly strung psyche of the characters, and the natural settings: 'the acting out of the tragedy against the background of fjords and trees recalls so many of the artist's *Life Frieze* subjects' – this sequence of paintings being of Kristiania Fjord motifs.

Delius had been enthralled by the symbolism of Jacobsen's poetry and the naturalism of his prose since the mid-1880s. When he read his *Bildungsroman* from 1876, *Marie Grubbe*, he described it as: 'One of the best books I have ever read'.[39] Just when he first read *Niels Lyhne* is unknown, but it was probably soon after the German translation appeared in 1889. It had fired debate and enthusiasm among Delius's contemporaries. Gunnar Heiberg wrote that no book had ever left him 'so dejected and inspired'.[40] Edvard Munch was captivated by *Niels Lyhne* in the mid-1890s. As we have seen, Munch took an

---

[37] Quoted by Jan Thielke in 'J. P. Jacobsens Pan-manifest – en læsning' in *Graf*, Vol. 5, No. 1 (2007), 68.
[38] Boulton Smith, *Frederick Delius and Edvard Munch*, 104.
[39] Letter from Delius to Jelka, undated, 4 January 1901 (GM).
[40] Letter from Gunnar Heiberg to Edvard Brandes, 13 December 1880 (KB).

initiative in 1899 to collaborate on a work with Delius based on Jacobsen texts, and the project may indeed have been visualised as a musical version of this novel (see p. 183).

The great Danish critic Georg Brandes summed up the central theme of *Niels Lyhne* soon after its publication as being

> how the book's hero and other characters deal with religion in their lives, or to be more precise, with the direction of their thoughts and feelings – partly in relationship to religious beliefs they have inherited, partly in relationship to reality (in so far as it is defined by science). Here there is something new and deep, that we see just how impossibly difficult it is for an individual in a society steeped in fantasy [...] to 'endure life as it is and be formed by life according to life's own laws.'[41]

The narrative of the novel follows the life of Niels Lyhne from childhood to death, a period from 1828 to 1864. There are four main sections, each of them dominated by a strong female figure – and it was from the last two, revolving around the worldly Fennimore and the innocent Gerda, that Delius chose his material. Born on a farm, Niels inherits from his parents conflicting qualities; his mother was poetic and creative, his father a hard-nosed realist. During his student days, he comes into contact with free-thinking radicals, but also discovers his own talents as a poet. His childhood friend, Erik, has become an artist, and together they visit and both fall in love with the beautiful Fennimore. She chooses Erik, but after three years the marriage falters and Fennimore and Niels rekindle their feelings for each other, while Erik finds distraction with drinking friends. When he is killed in an accident, Fennimore is filled with remorse and angrily cuts Niels from her life. With little to hold onto apart from his atheism, Niels returns to the family farm. Here, he falls in love and marries the young Gerda, who bears him a son. When first the child dies, and then Gerda, Niels's atheism is sorely tested, and continues to be so, right up to his own demise at the Battle of Dybbøl.

Throughout 1909 and 1910, Delius referred to his opera as *Niels Lyhne*. There can be little doubt that the theme of Niels's fight to remain a free-thinking atheist in the face of great vicissitudes would have gripped Delius, who had undergone similar struggles as a young man. Much more doubtful is the suitability for operatic treatment of a novel in which burning existential dilemmas are thrashed out. During early stages of composition he fully intended to expose his Niels to such challenges, including the death of Gerda. As work progressed, however, the composer vacillated between different ways of handling the issues, finally throwing out the whole Gerda sequence and most references to the main character's battle with religious belief. On its completion in 1910, the

---

[41] Georg Brandes, 'J. P. Jacobsen', reprinted in *Georg Brandes: Essays* (Copenhagen: Gyldendalske Boghandel, 1963), 555.

opera *Niels Lyhne* was a tragic, almost Ibsenesque, triangular drama between Niels, Erik and Fennimore. As the prospects for a first performance in 1914 in Germany played on Delius's mind (the production was eventually cancelled), he began to doubt 'the gloomy and inconclusive ending'[42] and retrieved once more the sketches for his Gerda music. New scenes were welded to the end of the opera, depicting Niels's return to the countryside and engagement to the young daughter of his neighbour – and it was given a new title, *Fennimore and Gerda*. Shadows of death or existential crisis were removed from the conclusion of the work, which now ended happily. Although he had ditched essentials of Jacobsen's text, Delius's version of the Fennimore story had been concise and self-contained; now with its new scenes, the whole became unwieldy and unbalanced, bleak realism and *fin de siècle* weariness (Fennimore) relieved at the close by bucolic idyll (Gerda).

Perhaps even more so than his *Requiem* (1913–16), *Fennimore and Gerda* is the work that most often divides both the critics and lovers of Delius's music, not least because of these late scenes. Philip Heseltine, writing in 1923 the first biography of the composer, felt it was the 'disproportion and psychological falsity' of the Gerda section that most jarred.[43] Delius's fierce advocate, Thomas Beecham, could never warm to the work and wondered whether the composer, with his sweeping elimination both of the novel's psychological conflict and of operatic conventions – including lyrical melody – had 'carried a step too far' his drive for realism. The variable quality of the libretto, once again sewn together by the composer, must also be mentioned. All of this notwithstanding, *Fennimore and Gerda* exerts an influence on its many advocates that constantly draws them back to it, the orchestral score overflowing with extraordinary passages of writing.

The appeal for Delius of Jacobsen's *An Arabesque* and *Niels Lyhne* was, then, their reflection of a *zeitgeist* that he – and perhaps non-Scandinavians in general – regarded as characteristically Nordic or North Scandinavian rather than intrinsically Danish. Indeed, the poignance of a nature symbolism representing the brevity of life and love might be said to increase incrementally the further north one travelled. For Delius it would have interlinked both with his own longing for the short, glowing summers by the Kristiania Fjord and with the potent expression of existential and sexual angst captured in the paintings of his close friend, Edvard Munch. With these works his musical language, too, would be affected by a Nordic chill.

---

[42] Letter from Delius to Universal Edition, 24 January 1913 (UE).
[43] Heseltine, *Frederick Delius*, 96.

Fennimore and Gerda and *An Arabesque*: Music

Around 1910, Delius's tonal language suddenly moved off at an acute angle to other recent scores such as *Brigg Fair* and *In a Summer Garden*. Taut and chill textures, few and brittle melodies – this was music seemingly redolent of a Nordic aesthetic. The laboratory in which this language evolved was *Fennimore and Gerda*. Radically, Delius divided the action into what he dubbed eleven 'pictures', describing some years later his method as a blueprint others might follow: 'Long dialogues and wearisome narrations must go, and will be replaced by short, strong emotional impressions given in a series of terse scenes. [...] Suggestion will replace masses of detail in the opera, as in modern painting.'[44] By 'modern painting', Delius was perhaps thinking of Edvard Munch, whose expressionist style was gaining wider acceptance, particularly in Germany. Equally interesting is that much of the 'terse' psychological drama was to be carried by the orchestra, for on stage there would only be a 'suggestion' of it. Far more than in *A Village Romeo and Juliet*, the orchestra of *Fennimore and Gerda* is a dynamic body: as the characters sing, it is lithe and responsive to small nuances – each rumination, each longing – and stormfully evocative at moments of emotional eruption. These restless movements of the human psyche are, however, framed and relieved by small orchestral tone-poems, mood pictures against backdrops of natural symbolism.

A typical example of the terse drama is found at the opening of the Fourth Picture, where Erik bares his soul to his old friend Niels, who is on an extended visit. The searching lines of the orchestra – constantly in movement, highly chromatic and with only fleeting tonal centres – capture perfectly the nervous tension that is driving Erik. In the Seventh Picture it is autumn, and Fennimore and Niels have stolen away into the beech forest. Under the existential pressure of natural symbolism – falling leaves, an empty nest – they reach out for something more, for each other. A declaration of love! But in the next moment Fennimore is contorted with anxiety (fig. 71–72). Compared with the love duets that had poured from the composer's pen up to and including *Margot la Rouge*, this is the most fleeting of lyrical outbursts, wing-clipped before it has taken flight. One moment, then the angularity of the singing line returns, and in the orchestra the chromatic angst has never let up for a moment. Such textures are frequent in the Fennimore section of the score (Pictures 1–9). The abiding impression is unrest, a mental disquietude that in its musical expression never finds the relief of a tonal centre or diatonic melody, always turning in sinewy movement, casting around it for repose without ever finding it. Knowing what we do about the life crisis Delius went though at the same time as he was writing the opera, it is impossible not to see in this bleak language a remoulding, if

---

[44] Interview with Delius in *Evening News*, 1919, quoted by Clare Delius, *Frederick Delius*, 199.

hardly a refreshing, of his creative philosophy. Put in its simplest terms: there was no time to waste, no optimism to waste, no love to waste.

Admirably well-judged is the balance between the Ibsenesque scenes – the characters struggling with inner turmoil – and the connecting instrumental passages, the small tone-poems heavy with natural symbolism. The most beautiful of several strikingly evocative intermezzi comes early, moving the characters from the interior of Consul Claudi's house in the First Picture and out on to the fjord for the Second Picture. The stage instructions tell us that it is late evening, there are glowing insects on the water, and Fennimore and Erik sit in a boat by the landing jetty. Across the fjord comes the song of an unseen boatman:

Example 10.3 *Fennimore and Gerda*, Second Picture, 3–6

The disembodied voices of boatmen are also heard at the close of *A Village Romeo and Juliet*. There, however, their role is to introduce an element of river symbolism (transience); here Delius has transposed his horn calls from the mountain plateau to the fjord to effect – through a sense of distance and depth – a oneness with nature. (A variant of this same call is used in *The Song of the High Hills*; see Example 11.5). Wordless and modal, the floating theme binds the whole world of the loving couple; it stands for their oneness with their natural surroundings. As such, it is as highly expressive of summer eroticism as Munch's most famous paintings of evenings by the Kristiania Fjord – works such as *Moonlight*, *The Voice/Summer Night* and *Kiss on the Shore*. The voice across the fjord also brings to mind again the Romantic poem by Bjørnson, Det første møde (see p. 49), in which both 'sang på vågen' ('a song across the fjord') and 'horn i uren' ('horns between the mountains') unite the listener with greater nature. Distant horn calls are actually introduced into the instrumental opening of the Sixth Picture, twilight turning to dawn as Fennimore awaits the return of Erik. A symbol of the return of light, the calls embody Fennimore's returning hope of starting life anew with Erik. For his preludes to the Seventh and Eighth Pictures, where the symbolism is of autumn and winter respectively, Delius gradually draws the warmth out of his music, ending up with icy textures that chill the listener.

The two short scenes that constitute the Tenth and Eleventh Pictures – the happy Gerda 'coda' to the Fennimore drama – are each introduced by smiling summer pastorals. The song of the boatman (Example 10.3) had transported to the opera one response to Norwegian nature that would carry over to further works, most notably *The Song of the High Hills*; these Gerda-preludes also have a Norwegian coloration, but are instead backward-looking to an early period in Delius's career when Grieg's folkloristic traits occasionally coloured his music. This is the opening of the Tenth Picture:

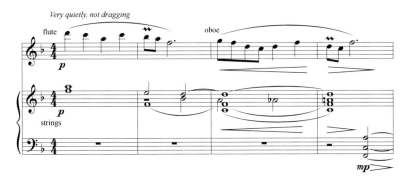

Example 10.4 *Fennimore and Gerda*, Tenth Picture, 1–4

The second prelude is an extended colloquy of herding calls between flute and oboe. We have met these rolling, repeating, distant calls several times in the composer's mountain scores, but here the intention was to paint a scene of bucolic tranquillity. The preludes are lovingly executed but, with their idiom from an earlier period of his development, contribute to the impression that the Gerda appendix belongs to a different sphere entirely.

With a month in Norway behind him, Delius sat down again in the autumn of 1911 with Jens P. Jacobsen's words in front of him, now exchanging his own reduction of Jacobsen's prose for the full-on symbolism of Jacobsen's poetry. His health was seemingly restored for the time being, but there was no way back for his musical language to the unbridled lyricism of *Brigg Fair* and *In a Summer Garden*. His setting of *An Arabesque* for baritone solo, choir and orchestra did, however, combine the nervous textures of *Fennimore and Gerda* – its winding chromatic lines and restless harmony around fleeting tonal centres – with a late flowering of intoxicating passion. While the intense, passionate bursts are brief, the high level of creative inspiration is sustained throughout. The effect is utterly compelling, at times mesmerising, and after its customary thirteen or so minutes *An Arabesque* often leaves the listener grasping for a first deep breath. At the first entry of the soloist, the texture could have come straight from the opera:

Example 10.5 *An Arabesque*, fig. 1, 1–4

Jacobsen asks, 'Har du faret vild i dunkle Skove? Kender du Pan?' ('Have you lost your way in dark forests? Do you know Pan?'), but then proceeds to tell of the Pan he knows, not the woodland faun so much as the god of fertile eroticism, and that he was introduced to the deity by a woman who seduced him as she had many others. In her analysis of the poem, Jelka Delius suggested that she had first-hand knowledge of the influence such Nordic temptresses had on their lovers: '[She] wielded her power over them, so that they gladly drank to her out of the poisonous […] chalice (their undoing). This is also typical of the Scandinavian woman. […] Then all is past. Winter storm – the red berries, last vestige of the mad summertime, drop one by one into the snow.'[45] For this conclusion, Delius chills us to the marrow with musical symbolism at its deeply penetrative best. Against a frost of high chords, the falling berries are picked out one by one in pizzicato:

---

[45] Attachment to a letter from Jelka to Thomas Beecham, 14 August 1929, quoted in White, 'The Hidden Meanings of *An Arabesque*', 70.

Example 10.6 *An Arabesque*, fig. 16, 2–5

In October 1912, Delius attended the UK première in Birmingham of Sibelius's fourth symphony, spending time with the composer before and after the concert. He noted that Sibelius 'is trying to do something new & has a fine feeling for nature & he is also unconventional'.[46] It is fascinating that Delius recognised in the Finn a kindred spirit, for there are interesting parallels at work in their musical aesthetics. There are also similarities in the way the reductive drive of musical history has packaged the two composers: Delius – the English pastoralist; Sibelius – the tone-painter of the North. In his edition of Sibelius essays, Daniel Grimley has pointed out that the idealised Nordic landscape – 'an exotic realm of icy wastes, somnolent lakes, endless spruce forests and untouched wilderness' – is problematic, for it 'has exerted a powerful influence on Sibelius reception'.[47] In Delius's case, a small handful of works associated with summer has led reception of his music to be too strongly biased towards an image of him as a singer and dreamer of idylls, an even more damning

---

[46] Letter from Delius to Jelka, 2 October 1912 (GM).
[47] Daniel Grimley (ed.), 'Sibelius, Finland, and the Idea of Landscape' in *Jean Sibelius and his World* (Princeton: Princeton University Press, 2011), xii.

'packaging' than that of Sibelius. Far from summer idylls, the Nordic character we have seen in *Fennimore and Gerda* and *An Arabesque* came to dominate many works of his maturity.

Emotional tension, sparse melody, nervous and fragmented rhythms – these represented a development in his creative life that mirrored developments in his daily life. They might be said to typify a move away from the folkloric wistfulness of Grieg towards Nordic expressionism, with a kinship to Sibelius. The brevity of the Nordic summer became a metaphor for the frailty of life; the human struggle in a sun-starved environment a metaphor for the leaner creative powers of middle age. Just as his new musical language was a response to his feelings of mortality, so was Delius's fascination with the sobering attributes of Scandinavian nature – its brevity, its cold waters, its fruits falling into snow – a response to the loss of his youth. In the new language that emerged from the laboratory of *Fennimore and Gerda* we understand that he had taken a farewell from the sunny fjord landscape where he had spent youthful and sensuous summers. Equipped with this new music, he was ready for his next great work, *The Song of the High Hills*; and here Delius would, musically speaking, take his leave of the Norwegian mountains.

Before leaving *An Arabesque* it has to be noted that Delius dedicated the work to his close Norwegian friend, Halfdan Jebe. It is unlikely that Delius had heard anything of him since he had turned his back on his homeland in 1905. Propelled by his restlessness and a deepening dislike of Kristiania's petty bourgeoisie, he had started a new life in the United States. He was invited to come by his uncle, Alf Klingenberg, who was only slightly older than his nephew.[48] Klingenberg had also pursued a musical career as a composer and pianist and since 1902 had been professor of piano at the Washburn College in Topeka, Kansas. On being asked to lead a new music faculty there in 1906, he invited Jebe to join him, and the new violin professor from Norway was presented to college and community at a concert in October. His performance was reviewed by a local journalist and between the lines we can read that – even if his wanderlust was temporarily deflected – the restlessness of his spirit was never fully doused: 'Mr Jebe has all the physical and professional idiosyncrasies of genius. He needs no label to distinguish him, and after seeing him walk upon the stage, one is prepared for his mastery of the violin and his temperamental gifts.'[49] In early 1907, Sofie, Jebe's actress wife, left her career in Norwegian theatre to join him. For a couple of years it seems that Jebe performed his teaching duties at the college then, during vacations, travelled America giving recitals, with

[48] It is unknown whether Klingenberg met Delius, but he was an intimate friend of Camilla Jacobsen at the same time as Delius, and in 1902 married Alexandra Mowinckel – the friend of Tulla Larsen, whom Delius so abhorred (see p. 180). Klingenberg would go on to found the Eastman School of Music in New York.

[49] *The Topeka Daily Capital*, 16 October 1906, 5.

Sofie declaiming passages from Ibsen and Bjørnson. By 1908, however, the ties to Kansas had been broken. In the spring they were performing in San Francisco and, according to the local newspapers, Jebe was of a mind to return to Europe. Instead, the autumn found the couple on a major tour of American cities, from California to Minneapolis in the Midwest. After that, their movements become less clear for some years.

It pained Delius to have lost contact with his bosom friend. Around the turn of the year 1910–11, Jelka made enquiries among Jebe's acquaintances, including the writer Adey Brunel in London: 'Alas! dear Mrs Delius I do not know where Jebe is […] it is strange that he does not write to either Delius or me.'[50] Contact would be restored in 1913, but Jebe continued to avoid Norway, because of what he then called 'Eisklumpen in seinem Herzen' – the lumps of ice in its heart.[51] What he would have made of *An Arabesque* we can only surmise, but he would no doubt have been surprised also to hear in the music of his English friend that there now flowed some ice in his veins.

1911–1912: The distant hills

In early March 1911, Delius returned home to Grez after his extended periods of treatment in sanatoriums and, with the onset of fine spring weather, found his condition continually improving. The frailty of his constitution was, however, underlined in June when he undertook a Channel crossing to hear Beecham give a concert of his works, arriving in London in a state of near exhaustion. Illness had prevented him from visiting Norway in 1910. He was determined that nothing would stop him in 1911, and as early as April he was busy arranging with Nina Grieg dates when he and Jelka could visit her at Troldhaugen. On 11 July he wrote to Percy Grainger that they were 'on the point of leaving for dear old Norway',[52] and a week later the Deliuses were ensconced at Lauvåsen Sanatorium in the hills west of Gudbrandsdalen between Fåvang and Ringebu.[53] They probably stayed in the area for a month, moving after a couple of weeks just a little further north to the Golå Høyfjellssanatorium (Mountain Sanatorium).

This summer differs from all Delius's previous visits to Norway in the choices he made both of area and type of accommodation. Previously known as Gausdal Vestfjell (The Hills West of Gausdal), the region was given in 2005 the more marketable title of Huldreheimen (The Home of the Huldre, seductive female forest creatures of Norwegian folklore). Though far less dramatic

---

[50] Letter from Adey Brunel to Jelka, undated, probably late 1910 (DT).
[51] Letter from Jelka to Delius, 8 July 1913 (GM).
[52] Letter from Delius to Percy Grainger, 11 July 1911 (GM).
[53] They left for Norway on 14 July, delaying their departure as long as possible to accommodate a proposed visit from Bartók. As it was, the Hungarian arrived in France just too late to meet Delius.

than its northerly neighbour, Jotunheimen, the attractions of Huldreheimen were abundantly clear to the various consortia of medical experts and entre-preneurs who a century earlier had established sizeable health retreats beyond the timberline of Gudbrandsdalen. Here were to be found quiet lakes, clean air and a relatively flat terrain extending into a far horizon. Pleasant and invigor-ating upland country, but not a mountain wilderness. While the landscape was ideal for the recuperating Delius, it is doubtful whether the sanatorium clien-tele suited him so well. The market for these thin-air hotels was the well-off middle class who wished to flee city pollution. Golå Høyfjellssanatorium, for example, listed its attractions as: '3000 foot above sea level – excellent kitchen – 90 beds – 2 lawn tennis courts – extensive trout fishing – splendid view across the Golå Lake to the ice peaks of Jotunheimen – doctor in attendance – patients with lung disease not admitted'. Not *that* kind of sanatorium, in other words. (It should be noted that the many Norwegian mountain 'sanatoriums' patronised by Delius were not clinics, but to all intents and purposes fashion-able hotels, with one or two doctors in attendance.)

Accompanied by Jelka, Delius had little need to write letters during this stay, and details are therefore few and far between; what we know comes from a couple of letters to Nina Grieg. In a letter of 26 July he assured her that, while Jelka painted the vista of the Rondane mountain range (off to the north-east) 'in every possible light', he was taking 'long walks paa Vidderne' and found it wonderful.[54] It would, however, not have satisfied this lover of the Jotun-heim mountains to wander these gentle uplands, all the while looking north to the white peaks. Sure enough, there was soon mention of plans for a 'small tour of Jotunheimen'. Once again, Delius's promises to Nina that he and Jelka would visit her at Troldhaugen came to nothing. 'The thing is', he wrote in early August, 'my friend Thomas Beecham – the London conductor – will be visiting me here in the next few days to discuss an autumn performance of the "Mass of Life" in London. […] It is naturally of the greatest importance!'[55] This pompous cancellation received from Nina the disdain it deserved. Though Delius wrote that he was sorry, Nina replied: 'Not half as sorry as I am, rest assured, and I might wish Mr Beecham and your "Mass of Life" gone over the hills, although – joking aside – I would rather like to hear it'.[56] She had always found the abrupt manner in which he framed his letters hard to swallow and, not for the first time (see p. 98), interpreted it as a desire to end the friend-ship. She concluded her letter: 'Out of the blue I suddenly cried out: Goodbye!' There is no record of whether Delius subsequently dared to inform Nina that

---

[54] Letter from Delius to Nina Grieg, 26 July 1911 (BOB).
[55] Letter from Delius to Nina Grieg, undated, early August 1911 (BOB).
[56] Letter from Nina Grieg to Delius, 7 August 1911 (DT).

Beecham altered his plans again and was not coming after all.[57] Nor of whether he and Jelka made their 'small tour' of Jotunheimen.

Delius performances were now being given in many large musical centres throughout Europe. Health permitting, he would regularly travel to prestigious concerts of his music. In the winter of 1911–12, however, nothing could tempt him away from his music room; he was working on a new work for choir and orchestra, a task that absorbed him utterly. Finally, in the spring, pressing business matters disrupted his creative focus. The old matter of the inadequacies of his German publisher, Harmonie, was still unresolved, and he and Jelka made two trips to Munich – separated by a holiday in Venice – to bring the matter to a head. In the end, he had to put his grievances in the hands of lawyers, and the matter would drag on for several more years before his rights were transferred to Universal Edition.

Back home in April, Delius became once more consumed by the composition on his writing desk. Many years later, Eric Fenby recalled the composer telling him: 'Passages eluded me; one in particular, the eight-part chorus that wouldn't come right!'[58] Delius remarked, too, that this was the only occasion on which he had 'not been able to bring himself to put a work aside'. In early December he wrote to his young admirer Philip Heseltine, apologising for leaving his letters unanswered: 'I am working hard on a new Choral & Orchestral work & am already far advanced.'[59] *The Song of the High Hills* was taking form.

As others before him whom Delius trusted, Heseltine was given the stamp of approval: an invitation to see the source of his inspiration. 'At the end of next month', Delius wrote to him in the summer of 1912, 'I intend going to Norway for a 3 weeks walking tour in the mountains – Doesn't it tempt you? I love Norway & the Norwegian peasants.'[60] A month later he had to concede that he had too much work on his hands, and cancelled the proposed trip. Fortunately, he had not on this occasion forewarned Nina Grieg of his plans to visit Norway. On the contrary, it was Nina who had written to him in May to say that she was coming to London in the autumn and hoped to meet up with him and Jelka.[61] She had also touched him by sending a photograph of Grieg,

---

[57] He did, however, inform her that he planned to travel through Copenhagen and Kristiania the coming winter. It would have been Delius's first winter visit to Norway, but eventually also this plan failed to come to fruition. Both the winter journey to Norway and a proposed trip to Jacobsen's birthplace were perhaps conceived as 'research' for the decor for the wintry Eighth and Ninth Pictures of *Fennimore and Gerda*.

[58] Fenby, *Delius*, 66.

[59] Letter from Delius to Philip Heseltine, 4 December 1911 (BL).

[60] Letter from Delius to Philip Heseltine, 23 June 1912 (BL).

[61] Indeed, Nina would attend, with Delius, performances in October of his *Dance Rhapsody* and Piano Concerto.

Delius for once responding with words that would have warmed her: 'I often think of Grieg & all the lovely times we spent together – I loved him greatly.'[62]

Norway was as important to Delius as it ever had been and, in this period of existential insecurity, perhaps more important. (He even brought Norway into the house at Grez, hiring Norwegian maids.) Since the restoration of his health in Norway the summer before, his love of the country was working on his creative mind in several ways: his affectionate memories of Grieg, his desire to walk the high uplands, his need for the spiritual peace he found there. The result was a composition without parallel in the classical repertoire, and the final summit in the sequence of Delius mountain works that had begun with *Paa Vidderne* in 1888.

---

[62] Postcard from Delius to Nina Grieg, 31 May 1912 (DT).

11

1912–1918
High hills, dark forests

'all the poetry & melancholy of the Northern summer & the high mountain plateaus'

Letter from Delius to Henry Clews, 20 June 1918

The Song of the High Hills can be regarded as a true culmination – a 'crowning peak' – of over a hundred years of musical attempts to associate or equate musical expressions with mountain nature, as interpreted in a Romantic aesthetic. For Delius's work to rise to this height, three different timelines had to cross at the right moment:

- He was at a moment in his life, marked by the vicissitudes of ill health and middle age, when his personal outlook seems to have magnified for him the frailty of human existence and the intransience of nature;
- He was at a moment in Western music when it was becoming easier for composers to distance themselves from Austro-German traditions;
- He was at a moment in Western civilisation when scientific enquiry had given individuals new understanding of their place in historical time and the eternity of the cosmos.

Before we turn to look in some detail at the score, it will be useful to trace how these three timelines come together.

In the *Paa Vidderne* melodrama of 1888 we saw Delius for the first time experimenting with effects of distance. His striking attempts here to equate musical expressions of majesty and bleakness with the high moorlands were replaced in *On the Mountains* with Wagnerian heroics and Lisztian drama. A sense of wonderment and introspection returned with *Over the Hills and Far Away*, then in parts of *A Village Romeo and Juliet* there followed a refinement of the Alpine *ranz des vaches* trope to suggest an escape route for the trapped lovers into timeless, nameless mountains. For *A Mass of Life* Delius adopted for the last time a Wagnerian language to extol the heights – in this case the metaphorical heights of Nietzsche's spiritual aristocrat, Zarathustra. Even then, with his 'Auf den Bergen' prelude to Part II of the *Mass*, the metaphorical landscape was changing character. For a pointer to what caused this new climate, it is not to Nietzsche, but rather to Schopenhauer we might turn to find some insight:

> The cheerfulness and buoyancy of our youth are due partly to the fact that we are climbing the hill of life and do not see death that lies at the foot of the other side. But when we have crossed the summit, we actually catch sight of death that was hitherto known only from hearsay.[1]

If the seriousness of middle age pressed itself upon the composer as he penned the meditative 'Auf den Bergen', then his physical collapse in 1910–11, when he did 'actually catch sight of death', is indivisible from his actions in the year that followed. His first reaction was a need to get up into the Norwegian mountains to take stock of his life, seemingly motivated by a longing for places that harmonised with the existential nakedness of his own spiritual landscape. And then he composed *The Song of the High Hills*, swept along by a compulsion he was unwilling to ignore until the composition lay finished on his writing desk. With *The Song of the High Hills* we follow to their climax the composer's responses to his experiences of Norwegian mountains.

The second timeline concerns a peculiarity of Romantic music in the nineteenth century. At the outset of written history, mountains were widely taken to represent the lofty seats of deities, or a cloud-piercing interface with the supernatural. Over time, however, the metaphor of the mountain as the stairway to heaven's forecourt, as divine altitude, came into conflict with other readings of what it might represent. The sheer inaccessibility of their slopes and heights turned the mountains of folk culture into nightmares – lairs of the wild, the unnatural and the otherworldly. Before modern communication, the mountain range might also represent a strategic line of defence or a barrier to progress. In the course of fifty years, starting in the late eighteenth century, a further *volte face* took place, and Romantics came to embrace the emotions stimulated by the wild regions, the mountain serving as metaphor both for the grandeur of nature and its violence, as well as a cradle and shelter for the rustic farmer untainted by industrial blight or urbanity. In her seminal study, *Mountain Gloom and Mountain Glory*, Marjorie Hope Nicolson went so far as to describe this paradigm shift as 'one of the most profound revolutions in thought that has ever occurred', and expanded thus:

> The change in human attitudes about mountains involved a reversal of many basic attitudes. [...] Before the 'Mountain Glory' could shine, men were forced to change radically their ideas of the structure of the earth on which they lived and the structure of the universe of which that earth is only a part. Theology,

---

[1] Arthur Schopenhauer, *Parerga and Paralipomena*, trans. E. F. J. Payne (Oxford: Clarendon, 1974), 483.

philosophy, geology, astronomy – basic and radical changes in all these occurred before the 'Mountain Gloom' gave way to 'Mountain Glory'.[2]

Composers of the Romantic era were as fascinated as other artists by everything that mountains represented in the art and literature of their age. In Western music of the nineteenth century, however, those wishing to convey emotions stirred by contemplation of mountain vistas had inherited a language poorly suited to the task. The Romantic movement came at a time when instrumental music was coupled to a governing principle of constantly changing and developing thematic argument. At composers' disposal was an Austro-Germanic toolbox with highly refined equipment for creating cohesive and intellectually satisfying structures from logical sequences of harmonic/thematic events. One might say it was a language intrinsically geared to *negating* the inert and empty – for bridging the void, but not for contemplating it. There is, therefore, something of a contradiction in terms, an aesthetic illogicality, when the Austro-Germanic symphonic language is employed to evoke the mountainscape. Composers indentured to a Germanic aesthetic of art music experienced this contradiction any time they tried to weave into the flow of their harmonic shifts and motivic textures a response to nature at its least transient. The contradiction is already present in the final movement of Beethoven's *Pastoral* symphony, where a spatial indicator – a shepherd's horn theme – binds together a sonata rondo structure. And it is carried to its most colourful extreme a century later in Strauss's *An Alpine Symphony*. With this overtly programmatic, almost filmic, tour of the sights and sounds of a day on the hills from sunrise to sunset the contradiction arising from symphonic treatment of mountain metaphors is conspicuous.

Many nineteenth-century composers inspired by 'Mountain Glory' explored, therefore, ways around this contradiction. The most obvious detour was in opera, where the *modus operandi* governing symphonic treatment of themes operated far more loosely. Audiences were thrilled by small, experimental tone-poems that drew on emotions associated with magic and mood, and not least the emotions invoked by tropes of Romantic distance. Rossini in *William Tell* (1829), for example, halted the action with a *ranz des vaches*, once as an alarm in Act I, then in bucolic contentment for the Act IV finale. Innovative composers transferred the same principle to their instrumental music. In the pastoral movement of the *Symphonie fantastique* (1830), Berlioz slowed the musical narrative, introducing elements of loneliness and solitude into the pastoral idyll. Schumann's music for *Manfred* (1848), too, comes to peaceful rest as the eponymous hero, atop the Jungfrau, hears the call of a distant shepherd ('My soul would drink these echoes'). The freedom of the tone-poem

[2] Marjorie Hope Nicolson, *Mountain Gloom and Mountain Glory: The development of the aesthetics of the infinite* (Seattle: University of Washington Press, 1997; first published Ithaca: Cornell University Press, 1959), 2.

or the programmatic overture allowed composers to infuse their mountain-inspired works with mood, drama and majesty, while retaining the energy of motivic treatment: for example, Liszt's *Ce qu'on entend sur la montagne* (1854), and the first movement of Raff's Symphony No. 7, *In the Alps* (1875) – entitled 'Wandering in the High Mountains'.

This was a development that reached its climax in the works of Gustav Mahler. Mahler had been as inspired as Delius by the effect of distant horns in Act II of *Tristan und Isolde*, and was the only composer of the time to go further than Delius in exploring the Romantic trope of distance in music through the spatial effects of seemingly distant instruments – including shepherds' horns, post horns and village bands. Most interesting in the present context are perhaps the calls '*in der Ferne*' that open Mahler's Symphony No. 1, the first part of Mahler's Symphony No. 3 – original title 'What the Stony Mountains Told Me' – with its powerful horn-call passages, and the call and echo of two shepherds' or watchmen's horns with which the first 'Nachtmusik' of the Seventh Symphony begins.[3] While Mahler never indulged in tone-painting as blatant as that of the *Alpine Symphony*, it is impossible to ignore in his work (and many would regard it as a characteristic quality) the tension of two aesthetics pulling in different directions: the programmatic and the absolute. To accommodate programmatic elements associated with the ever-monumental, never-changing mountainscape, the progress of symphonic argument often had to be temporarily suspended.

It was Bartók, we noted in an earlier chapter, who rebuked a musician who did not take Grieg seriously: 'Don't you know that he was one of the first of us who threw away the German yoke?' Arguably, a masterpiece of mountain music that succeeded in conveying something of the essential unchanging nature of the mountainscape could not come from composers under that yoke. Frederick Delius, inspired and mentored by Edvard Grieg, was able to distance himself from the strictures of Austro-German musical art further than these predecessors. *The Song of the High Hills* uses thematic argument and development only in so far as it frames episodes devoid of the same; the driven, striving human arrives at places beyond the temporal weave.

The third timeline is that of scientific enquiry and what understanding it offered the individual of his/her place in the world. As we saw in an earlier chapter (see p. 50), Delius was born into an era of iconoclasm and scientific breakthroughs. He became an artist in a post-Darwinian and Nietzschean world where geologists had disclosed the timeless strata of history, cosmologists had suggested the endless depths of the universe, and God, if not dead, was evidently insubstantial, indifferent and operating on timescales beyond man's comprehension. Above, we registered (in Nicolson's words) that Romantics

---

[3] For an extensive examination of these aspects of Mahler's music, see Thomas Peattie, *Gustav Mahler's Symphonic Landscapes* (Cambridge: Cambridge University Press, 2015).

'were forced to change radically their ideas of the structure of the earth on which they lived and the structure of the universe of which that earth is only a part'. It took time for this existential revolution to filter through to music. Even as late as the works of Mahler and Strauss, mountains are still an expression of superior and heroic Man. It was Delius who broke with this Germanic tradition. Instead of extolling the superiority of immense height (with the Alps as its metaphor), Delius turned his vision to the wonder of immense space (with the *vidde*, the high plateau, as its metaphor). In *The Song of the High Hills* he lets man dwell on his oneness with the greatness of nature, yet also the insignificance of his part in its narrative.

Other composers, also freeing themselves from the constraints of Austro-Germanic musical traditions, would find their own metaphors for the contemplation of man's place in incomprehensible and eternal nature: we might mention Gustav Holst, who looked to the night sky with his 'Neptune, the Mystic' movement of *The Planets* (1914–16), and Ralph Vaughan Williams, who meditated on the struggle in the ice wilderness of *Scott of the Antarctic*, first with music to the film of this title (1947) and subsequently in his use of the material in his *Sinfonia antartica*. In both of these instances the composers employed ethereal wordless choruses in a similar fashion to Delius in *The Song of the High Hills*.

The Song of the High Hills

As he worked on his sketches, Delius toyed with a variety of titles: *Songs of Nature*, *Mountain Sounds*, *Poem of the Mountains*, *the Song of the Mountains*, *Mountain Song*, *Hill Song*. Common to almost all was that the work would be a 'song', an expression of his most intimate self, and that the metaphor of the highland would best represent what he needed to say. He took steps to make his vision accessible and comprehensible, steps he did not repeat for any other work. At its still, contemplative core – when the voices are introduced into the texture – he wrote above the score: *The wide far distance – The great solitude*. It is unclear whether 'solitude' here is the state of being alone or the poetic use of the noun, employed in his letters when writing of Norwegian mountains, to describe a lonely, unpeopled place. Either way, the annotation is a signpost that leaves us in no doubt that we are far from the tourist trail, that we are on a spiritual expedition. Shortly before the first performance of the work – delayed until 1920 – the composer was asked to provide some insight into his composition for the programme notes. He offered a few lines, this time employing the term 'solitude' unambiguously:

> I have tried to express the joy & exhilaration one feels in the Mountains & also
> the loneliness & melancholy of the high Solitudes & the grandeur of the wide

Table 3 Structural scheme of *The Song of the High Hills*

		Bars	**Figure in score**
Part 1: 'Out of Mists'			
A1	Theme 1a [Example 11.1]	0	
	Theme 1b [Example 11.2]	19	2
	Theme 2a	39	4
	Theme 2b [Example 11.3]	65	6^{+9}
	Horn call bridge	73	7^{+8}
Part 2: 'Wide Horizons'			
B	**'Plateau I'**		
	Theme 3	82	8^{+7}
	Theme 4	108	11
	Bridge (incl. Theme 2b)	132	14^{+1}
	Horn call bridge	156	16^{+8}
C1	**'Man in Nature I'**		
	(Variations on theme: *'The wide far distance – The great solitude'*)		
	Theme 5 [Example 11.4]	164	17^{+7}
	Var. I	183	18^{+5}
	Var. II	194	20^{+5}
	Bridge	204	21^{+7}
D	**'Plateau II'**		
	Theme 6 [Example 11.5]	219	23^{+4}
	Bridge	248	26^{+7}
C2	**'Man in Nature II'**		
	Var. III	256	27^{+7}
	Var. IV	280	30
Part 3: 'Mists and Approaching Darkness'			
A2	Theme 1a	321	35
	Theme 2a variant	339	37^{+3}
	Theme 2b variant	382	42^{+4}
	Horn call bridge (extended)	406	45^{+4}
	Theme 1a	414	46^{+5}
Coda	Theme 6 from **'Plateau II'**	432	49

With quiet easy movement

Example 11.1 Opening

Example 11.2 fig. 2, 1–4

Example 11.3 fig. 6, 9–fig. 7, 1

Very slow

Example 11.4 'The wide far distance – The great solitude', fig. 17, 7–fig. 18, 2

Example 11.5 fig. 23, 4–7

far distances. The human voices represent man in Nature; an episode, which becomes fainter & then disappears altogether.[4]

With this second sentence his intentions with the work to explore parts of his personal philosophy are made clear.

In the structural scheme on p. 251 and the following analysis of *The Song of the High Hills* I have suggested subtitles for groups of material that may help to elucidate further what is represented by the mountain metaphors that are in play here. (They are, of course, subjective interpretations; only the motto *The wide far distance – The great solitude* is the composer's.) The work is written for a large orchestra and choir, and performances usually vary between twenty-six and thirty minutes. Delius imposes onto his material a superstructure of three parts:

1. 'Out of Mists'. Bars 1–81. For orchestra alone.
2. 'Wide Horizons'. Bars 82–320. Four distinct sections: two with dialogues between horn calls, two with variations on the theme Delius called *The wide far distance – The great solitude*. Into these latter sections the wordless voices of the choir are introduced.
3. 'Mists and Approaching Darkness'. Bars 321–447. Largely a reprise of the opening section, as the voices die away.

Part 1: 'Out of Mists'. In the opening, a falling, sighing phrase in the violins is answered with wisps of melodic motif in the viola (Example 11.1). Philip Heseltine referred once to the eerie mood created in these bars as that of 'wandering mists'. More generally, commentators have hit on the notion of the whole of Part 1 being an 'ascent' to the highland, despite the fact that for the closing Part 3 of the work – which they of course call the 'descent' – Delius reprises the selfsame material. In so far as we might look for any programmatic structure to the work, it may be helpful to regard Part 1 as expressing not so much an 'ascent' as a movement of mists or a traverse into clearer air.[5]

At bar 19 (fig. 2) a new theme is introduced by flutes and trumpet (Example 11.2), containing a motif (marked *x*) that comes to generate the rhythm and shape of much of the material of Part 1. While Delius eschews motif development for the inner plateaus of *The Song of the High Hills*, the outer parts (Parts 1 and 3) are powered by conventional symphonic 'fuel'. Equally significant for the rest of Part 1 is the falling tuplet quaver-movement introduced here by the bassoons. For the remaining fifty bars this motif is ever-present, leaning on the

---

[4] Letter from Delius to Norman O'Neill, 10 February 1920 (DT).
[5] The mood here brings to mind some lines from Delius's 1887 Norway diary, as he crosses a ridge between Etne and Skånevik: 'The view down towards Etne is magnificent. The sun for a moment flashes a few rays over the long valley, I from amongst the clouds look now on almost a fairy like scene. The light & shade effects I never saw before, but only for a few minutes, & then all is again bleak & misty.' See p. 25.

texture, pushing it onwards. The sparse, astringent chromatic textures Delius had explored and evolved in the pages of *An Arabesque* and *Fennimore and Gerda*, with their characteristic 'Nordic' chill, come fully into their own here.

At bar 65 (just before fig. 7) another new theme is introduced, but it is the underpinning provided by bass instruments (Example 11.3) that Delius is to reuse several times throughout the score. A muscular, climbing motif that thrusts its way up into the complex texture, it is a device intended to both create mounting expectation and symbolise a final push towards the first clearing in the clouds.

Suddenly, we are there. Out of chromatic murk, we burst into the brilliance of E major, held as a pedal in the strings (over six octaves) against rolling herding calls in the high woodwind and a falling-scale call on all six horns: B-A#-G#-F#-E. The adrenalin rush of achievement subsides quickly during this horn call bridge, which carries us to B major at bar 82 (three bars before fig. 9) and the beautiful textures of Delius's spiritual uplands in Part 2.

The introduction of the raised fourth – the A# in the E major bridge – activates the distinctive 'two-tier' metaphor of folk music and landscape – or rather 'folk music = landscape' – that was a staple of Romantic nationalist composers, and none more so than Edvard Grieg. (Two-tier – because the association is first with folk music, and then by extension with the geographical areas where folk music is played.) The raised fourth is a characteristic of the Lydian scale that prevailed in much of Norway's folk music. Some researchers believe the raised fourth to be the natural outcome of the harmonic series of natural instruments, such as the willow pipe. 'But a more plausible (and more prosaic) explanation may be offered', suggests Chris Goertzen in his book on Norwegian fiddle music. 'When the fiddle is in its commonest tuning, A D A E, pitches in the scale of the commonest key, D major, issue from the lowest three strings when each is fingered precisely the same.' If the fiddler also 'casually' fingers the top string, it would be a G# – a raised fourth in D major.[6] In other words, the characteristic folk sound of the raised fourth may owe as much to amateur lack of dexterity as exotic modality.

For classical composers, including Grieg and Delius, the origins of the raised fourth in Norwegian folk music were immaterial. What mattered was how it was received by the listener: the association woken by the raised fourth was with unsophisticated music-making and, by extension, the sort of landscape in which this might occur: rural, unspoilt, far from urban engineering. Carl Dahlhaus was among the first to point out that composers from Weber to Smetana, Glinka to Grieg all employed folkloristic elements in the same way – against a backdrop of pedal notes, or bourdons – to suggest a rural setting:

---

[6] Chris Goertzen, *Fiddling for Norway: Revival and identity* (Chicago, University of Chicago Press, 1997), 137.

The combination of a 'static' acoustic backdrop and a non-functional, coloristic additive, whether a dissonance or a chromatic note, is a structural principle that links musical landscape painting with exoticism and folklorism, placing both of them outside the classical-romantic norm of harmony as consisting of chord progressions set in motion and directed towards a goal by dissonance and chromaticism.[7]

The static backdrop has been termed a *Klangfläche*, or sound-sheet: non-developing textures built up as layers of sound. It arose in nineteenth-century opera as a technique for halting the narrative drama, for taking in the metaphorical significance of landscape and scenery – for example the 'Forest Murmurs' scene in *Siegfried* and the Nile scene in *Aïda*. Orchestral masters at the turn of the century, including Debussy and Sibelius, transferred the use of extensive, static sound-sheets into non-operatic works. For the next 240 bars of *The Song of the High Hills*, over half of the work, Delius conjures up one sound-sheet after another, evoking associations with the mountain landscape. And at the bridge to Part 2, sounding out from the six horns, the raised fourth is Delius's motto to indicate in music – as he soon would in words with his 'great solitude' motto – that there now lies before us a metaphorical vista of wide and endless horizons.

Part 2: 'Wide Horizons'. Delius invites us to remove ourselves from the world and inhabit a sphere of contemplation. He links together four sections – 'a magical sequence of sounds and echoes, both vocal and instrumental, all culminating in a great outburst of tone that seems to flood the entire landscape', to quote Thomas Beecham.[8]

'Plateau I' is the first of two sections for which Delius constructs a multi-layered texture from a colloquy of different herding calls. Against a backdrop of long pedal notes in cello and bass and a haze of slowly-moving high-string harmony, a pair of horns sound their calls and echoing replies. Rolling calls in flutes and clarinets add their input to the discussion.

Across Norway and Sweden in pre-electronic times, shepherds, milkmaids and goatherds conversed in ritualised calls, and their sounds and echoes would have been a familiar and riveting experience for the walker and climber. They might be played or sung. When sung, the voice's falsetto range was used to carry the sound far into the mountains, with various inflections to denote differing messages. The same calls were transferred to and from folk instruments, such as a ram's horn or the long, trumpet-like *lur*. The Swedish researcher Susanne Rosenberg has studied the phenomenon in her country, where the art of sending a signal by a musical call is to *kula*:

---

[7] Carl Dahlhaus, *Nineteenth-Century Music*, trans. J. Bradford Robinson (Berkeley and Los Angeles, University of California Press, 1989), 309.
[8] Beecham, *Frederick Delius*, 168.

The melodic line is spun further through its phrases, like a continuing story in the herding call. There is no obvious ending – to be able to spin further is an important part of the herding call itself; after all, it is not up to yourself to decide when to finish – it depends upon whether somebody hears your call and answers back. It is because of this that the improvisatory part of the call is important, the theme serving as a base which can be varied upon.[9]

The dialogue of calls sounding from different places, such as it is employed by Delius, is a potent spatial metaphor: it suggests not only distance, but also height and space. At bar 108 (fig. 11) the conversation changes its topic, with new calls on the same instruments – as if a different signal is being transmitted, perhaps of impending storm, as suggested by the distant rolling of three timpani notes. From this point the music of 'Plateau I' gains in momentum and chromatic intensity, the calls edged out by the busy orchestra – we are again being moved onwards, away from mists to an even higher opening in the low cloud cover. At bar 142 (three after fig. 15) the muscular motif of Example 11.3 is reprised, providing the energy a second time to bring us out into the clearest mountain air, as the herding calls are heard echoing from the hills. As they die away, we are left in an exalted place of complete tranquillity.

'Man in Nature I'. Above his score at bar 164 (seven after fig. 17) Delius has written: *The wide far distance – The great solitude.* The section ushers in the first entry of the choral voices, adding an ethereal curtain of high, slowly turning chords, *ppp*. To each entry of the vocal groups he has also appended the instruction: *To sound as if in the far distance.* 'The first entrance of the full choir singing as softly as is possible', wrote Beecham, 'is surely a stroke of genius, and of its kind without equal, either in him or any other composer'.[10] As we have seen, the composer himself informed the audience at the first performance that 'the human voices represent man in Nature'.[11] For Daniel Grimley, the entry of the choir

> suggests an increase in depth of acoustic field or the opening out of auditory range as much as a widening of prospect or vision. Whether we interpret the voices as nature sounds or traces from a barely remembered past, their half-heard state suggests a sense of the supernatural, of sensuous memory rather than actualized presence.[12]

---

[9] Susanne Rosenberg, 'Kulning – an Ornamentation of the Surrounding Emptiness: About the unique Scandinavian herding calls' in *Voice and Speech Review*, Vol. 8, No. 1 (February 2014), 101.

[10] Beecham, *Frederick Delius*, 168.

[11] The use of a wordless chorus was still highly innovative in 1911. One of few earlier occurrences with which Delius might have been familiar was the sensual texture created by Debussy with wordless female voices in the 'Sirènes' movement of *Nocturnes* (1899).

[12] Daniel M. Grimley, 'Music, Landscape, and the Sound of Place: On hearing Delius's *Song of the High Hills*' in *The Journal of Musicology*, Vol. 33, No. 1 (2016), 32.

It is not to the choir, but to muted violins, that he entrusts the theme for this section, a modal melody similar to a folk song (Example 11.4) that will undergo in the rest of this section two further variations in the orchestra. An extraordinary bridge passage ensues at bar 204 (seven after fig. 21), an unworldly and hauntingly beautiful *Klangfläche*. Edged with high celesta chords and brittle harp scales, a curtain of slow chords in flutes and strings is slowly lowered – as if icy air is gradually warming as we return to a lower vantage point.

So on to '**Plateau II**'. We can again hear the shepherd calls, now a discussion among high reeds with occasional deep responses in bass instruments. Example 11.5 is passed around the slopes, all the while blown by a chilling ostinato of high violins.

Soon the notes of any call from the hillsides and valleys will be beyond our hearing. To the tones of a final duet between oboe and flute, the fourth section of Part 2, '**Man in Nature II**', commences at bar 256 (seven after fig. 27). A solo tenor reintroduces the mountain song, Example 11.4, and as the last vestiges of herding call die away, the choir takes up the theme *a cappella*. The place for wonderment *at* nature is now behind us; Delius quickly expands the choral treatment into an eight-voice outpouring, a rapturous statement of being at one *with* nature. It is an episode, he informed us, 'which becomes fainter & then disappears altogether' as the music from the opening bars returns and the choral voices fade from the texture.

Part 3: 'Mists and Approaching Darkness'. The joy at the summit is curtailed as mists again drift across the panorama. Delius reprises most of his material from Part 1, but themes are given darker timbres, and the composer withholds also the coaxing power of the falling tuplet quaver-theme of Example 11.2 until much later in the scheme (bar 371, fig. 41). For a last time, the low clouds part for us and we enjoy again the splendour of the high hills (bar 406, four after fig. 45) with horn calls rolling around the slopes. Then the wandering mists obliterate all and the mood becomes darker.

Finally, for an evocative coda (from bar 432, fig. 49), the failing twilight is represented in banks of string chords slowly fading to nothing, as the shepherd calls are 'dying away to the end'. The ritual of singing herding calls at twilight was, indeed, practised in many Alpine regions. 'The effect of the magic power', wrote ethnologist Fritz Frauchiger, 'lay in bringing about a continuation of the day into night [...] The transition between the two was considered dangerous, and only continued sound (by the alphorn) was regarded as capable of bridging this perilous gap [...] [The] human voice would gain the same power if it imitated the instrument and its tone.'[13]

---

[13] Fritz Frauchiger, 'The Swiss Kuhreihen' in *The Journal of American Folk-lore*, Vol. 54 (1941), 126.

Works like *Over the Hills and Far Away* and 'Auf den Bergen' have shown us that Delius's herding calls had become ever more disembodied, until they now had as little to do with Alpine farming as his Lydian 'raised fourth' had to do with fiddle dances. *The Song of the High Hills* is a wholly symbolic landscape. Written while the physical breakdown of 1910–11 was still fresh in Delius's psyche, it employs the metaphor of a mountain journey to express his personal philosophy. We are asked to reconcile 'the loneliness & melancholy' of a frail and cursory life-span and the 'joy & exhilaration' that is possible to the free spirit aspiring to the blissfulness and lack of ego that is the goal of contemplation. The work is also the culmination of a period that included *Fennimore and Gerda* and *An Arabesque*, in which Delius exploited the short Nordic summer as an overriding metaphor for the ephemeral happiness of both love and life.

Delius had wandered far from the classical tropes that informed pastoral music by Mozart, Haydn and Beethoven, far from the mythical Edens where the bond between man and nature, loosened in daily society, still held. The horns sounding from Delius's Alpine pastures evoke no less mythological a state than that of Beethoven's *Pastoral* symphony, but it is not an idyll of dignified toil and nature's bounty they call us to contemplate. In *The Song of the High Hills* we traverse a state of existential nakedness and experience the loneliness and melancholy of the searching atheist. Beethoven's shepherds are thankful to their beneficent God for the passing of the storm, and would never have the slightest urge to scale a mountaintop above their pastures. With Delius, however, we continue beyond the reach of herding calls, up beyond the last suggestion of society to a solitude where we, without the confusion of worldly distractions, might consider our place in the grand scheme of nature, both worldly and cosmic. Marjorie Hope Nicolson has pointed out that many eighteenth-century Englishmen who discovered the Sublime in the external world resorted to exaggeration and extravagant hyperbole in their writings. 'To express their experience, new in the history of the human race, there was neither speech nor language.'[14] In his mountain song – in the exaggeration of the near-motionless soundscapes and the hyperbole of the chorus's great eight-part outpouring – we might also recognise a composer reaching for a new language of Man in his Cosmos.

For some, the lack of comfort during this mountain visit will already make *The Song of the High Hills* forbidding, and they will decline Delius's invitation to join him. In a real sense, there are also a couple of reasons why we might feel justified in asking the question: is *anyone* fully able to join him anymore? Reception of the work has been considerably altered by cultural changes in the past century. Essentially a mystic work, it may instead seem mystifying because of its reliance on the metaphorical muscle of two signifiers that have lost much of their meaning: folk music modality and the horn call.

---

[14] Marjorie Hope Nicolson, *Mountain Gloom and Mountain Glory*, 33.

The formula that equates folk traits with landscape may still hold true in many regions, but those traits favoured by Romantic composers – particularly raised fourths in the melody above a pedal bass – have become too widespread, too watered down, to retain their power of metaphoric transmission. With the horn call, it is the other way round. In Delius's day, the sound of herding calls would have been common and, as metaphor, it could embody universalities of human experience, in the first instance a spatial experience, but by extension an emotional one. Today it has disappeared; we have no longer first-hand experience of distant vocal calls echoing in an otherwise tranquil mountain landscape.[15] Fading cultural references are, of course, the *raison d'être* of the cultural historian and the programme writer. It falls upon them to mediate something of the historical context, if reception of the work today is not to lack a vital element: the significance for the composer of horn calls and herding songs heard in the highlands of Norway.

Many years later, Delius would say of *The Song of the High Hills*: 'I think it is one of my works in which I have expressed myself most completely'.[16] No further mountain works came from his pen. Following his physical breakdown and the subsequent exploration in *The Song of the High Hills* of his philosophical stance, he was, however, clearer than ever in his own mind of the importance to his well-being of returning regularly to the mountains. It was in 1918 that Delius wrote to a friend that he might consider travelling to Tahiti – but it would only be for a brief visit:

> I should never think of settling [...] too far from my beloved Norway & the light summer nights & all the poetry & melancholy of the Northern summer & the high mountain plateaus where humans are rare & more individual than in any other country in the world.[17]

The Song of the High Hills is an extraordinary achievement. Nevertheless, as this book was being written, it was still awaiting a first performance in Norway, more than a hundred years after its composition. If it has lacked a champion in Norway, it found several in English-speaking countries, and none more vociferous than Percy Grainger. Not only did he in 1924 give, at personal expense, the first performances of the work in the United States, but during his return voyage to Australia he penned a lengthy letter 'TO MY

---

[15] The debate about how universal a metaphor the herding call could be is not a new one. From the middle of the eighteenth century onwards, it had exercised commentators such as Rousseau, Senancour, Goethe and Schiller, who were fascinated by anecdotes regarding the fits of nostalgia that affected Swiss soldiers on hearing their country's *ranz des vaches* while on campaign. Wordsworth took up the debate in 1820 with his poem 'On Hearing the "Ranz Des Vaches" on the Top of the Pass of St Gothard'. The poet concluded that a lonely sound in a lonely place could ignite anyone's longing for the society of their home life.
[16] Letter from Delius to Percy Grainger, 16 December 1922 (GM).
[17] Letter from Delius to Henry Clews, 20 June 1918 (DT).

FELLOW-COMPOSERS' with the express purpose of informing them that he
had discovered a timeless masterpiece:

> No words can tell the elation I feel about Delius's 'Song of the High Hills'. For
> 25 years I have been waiting for an Anglosaxon work that should not be merely
> gifted & original, not merely part of the musical tide-stream of the moment, but
> that should strike me, on mature association, as being GREAT, IMMORTAL,
> UNIVERSAL – a work to be placed beside Bach, Walt Whitman, Wagner. At
> last I have it.[18]

Cuckoos in spring: 'Spring always means for me a longing for Norway'

Delius had written three major scores – *Fennimore and Gerda*, *An Arabesque*
and *The Song of the High Hills* – characterised by a language of chill textures
and sinewy chromatic harmony. It was a development that, at least in part,
reflected a response to a life crisis. Likewise, as the health scare receded, the
nervous intensity in his music seemed to ease again. We have already seen
that, in the years after completing the opera *Niels Lyhne*, he began to regard
the mood of the opera as too bleak, extending it with the blithe, melodious and
bucolic Gerda-ending – and giving it a new title. In 1912, he also blew the dust
off one of his most life-affirming scores, his Helge Rode-inspired tone-poem
A Life's Dance, to make a second and final revision, now giving it the German
title *Lebenstanz*. To this same optimistic, post-crisis period belong two smil-
ingly melodic miniatures, the Two Pieces for Small Orchestra: *On Hearing the
First Cuckoo in Spring* and *Summer Night on the River*.

As we noted earlier (see p. 87), several generations of Delius commentators
have claimed *On Hearing the First Cuckoo in Spring* 'for England' – though
conceding that any early cuckoo heard by Delius would likely have been in
Grez.[19] For them the work is – to borrow Robert Threlfall's phrase – 'quintessentially English'. In its melancholic tone English commentators have heard
regret for the lost pastoral idyll of England's innocence – all well and good as a
subjective reception of the work. This notwithstanding, the short piece is one
of the most thoroughly Norwegian works Delius ever composed. One of the
two main themes is a Norwegian folk tune, as indeed is made clear by the composer's explanatory subtitle: *Introducing a Norwegian Folk Song*. And the work
came into being as an expression of his desire to be deep in Norwegian nature,
as evidenced by a postcard Delius wrote to Grainger in January 1914: 'If you
are in London go & hear my 2 pieces for small Orchestra at the Philharmonic.

---

[18] Letter from Percy Grainger to 'My Fellow Composers', 25 May 1924 (GM).
[19] Letters suggest that Delius discussed the work with Percy Grainger while in London in June
      1911. Preliminary work seems then to have been done in the flush of spring in Grez after his
      hard winter in diverse sanatoriums. Robert Threlfall offers insights into the work in 'Delius: A
      fresh glance at two famous scores' in *The Musical Times*, Vol. 125, No. 1696 (June 1984), 315–19.

I hear Mengelberg is doing them on the 20th or 21st? I have introduced "I ola Dalom" in the 1st one – Spring always means for me a longing for Norway.'[20]

The earliest we know of Delius travelling to Norway in any year was the beginning of June, so he never experienced spring there, nor the year's first cuckoo. He would, however, have heard the bird everywhere on his Norwegian travels, also in the mountain valleys. While any and every manner of reception of the music is, of course, equally valid, we can assume that the composer's actual intention was to project his personal longing for 'the light summer nights & all the poetry & melancholy of the Northern summer' – a longing ignited by the year's first cuckoo at Grez or wherever he was at that moment.

Percy Grainger may have been instrumental in the conception of *On Hearing the First Cuckoo in Spring*. On their very first meeting (see p. 212) the Australian had introduced himself to Delius with a performance of Grieg's op. 66 piano interpretations of *Norske folkeviser* (*Nineteen Norwegian Folk Songs*), of which 'I Ola-dalom, i Ola-tjønn' ('In Ola Valley, in Ola Lake') is number fourteen. Here is the start of the theme as Grieg used it:

Example 11.6 'I Ola-dalom, i Ola-tjønn', 3–6

In Delius's working for small orchestra, the Norwegian folk melody is the work's second theme. It is introduced in various snatches from bar 19 (fig. 3), and in full as Grieg wrote it after fig. 7 (bar 7). Commentators have suggested that the opening theme of Delius's miniature tone-poem (Example 11.7) also may derive from a different work by Grieg, 'The Students' Serenade' from op. 73, *Moods*:[21]

Example 11.7 *On Hearing the First Cuckoo in Spring*, fig. 1, 1–5

[20] Postcard from Delius to Percy Grainger, undated, probably January 1914 (GM).
[21] Although Grieg's and Delius's interpretation of the folk song are very different, Trevor Hold thought that with *On Hearing the First Cuckoo in Spring* Delius 'paid his greatest homage to his friend and mentor', and details harmonic subtleties that might support his theory. See 'Grieg, Delius, Grainger and a Norwegian Cuckoo' in *Tempo*, New Series, No. 203 (January 1998), 11–19.

Adhering to an instrumental tradition upheld by composers from Beethoven to Saint-Saëns, Rimsky-Korsakov and Mahler, Delius imitates the cuckoo itself on a solo clarinet, its first entry starting two bars before fig. 6. Imitation of birdcall in general was a musical way of tapping into the Romantic trope of distance used throughout the nineteenth century. But the cuckoo's call, emanating from the heart of the woods – *Le coucou au fond des bois*, to quote the Saint-Saëns title – has additional depth, and can convey a sense of spatial distance similar to Delius's mountain herding calls.

In one extraordinary score, begun around the same time as he was completing *On Hearing the First Cuckoo in Spring*, Delius combines both of these spatial indicators, the cuckoo and the mountain call, in a single musical sequence. His *Requiem* seems to have had a long gestation period. As early as 1902, the composer was developing ideas for a work that he called a *Requiem*. It seems likely that these plans were subsumed into *A Mass of Life*, which at one stage in the writing process was intended to open with a 'Marche Funèbre' or an orchestral introduction bearing the subtitle 'In Memoriam'. But who was being commemorated? Considering that the textual material of the *Mass* is from *Also sprach Zarathustra*, it does not seem far-fetched to presume that it was Friedrich Nietzsche, who had died in 1900. Indeed, Delius would later describe the *Mass* as 'a transcription of Nietzsche's spirit'.[22] If we now fast-forward to 1913, Delius was ready to write another non-Christian 'mass' in Nietzsche's spirit, and revived the *Requiem* title. He worked to a text that was penned in German by his friend Heinrich Simon, a farrago of everything Delius found most distasteful in religious faith and most profound in Nietzsche's poetry – served up in a quasi-biblical, quasi-Zarathustra and quasi-Hans Bethge mélange.[23] At times the text is sermonising and crass, at others poetical and visionary. The finishing touches were not put on the *Requiem* until 1916, including a dedication, not to Nietzsche, but 'To the memory of all young artists fallen in the war'.

The finale of the *Requiem* is the most uplifting part of the score, an exalted hymn to the eternal seasonal cycle – or, in another light, to Nietzsche's theory of Eternal Recurrence, as represented in the metaphor of the seasons: 'Everything on earth will return again, ever return again. Springtime, Summer, Autumn and Winter: And then comes Springtime – and then new Springtime'. As the vocal forces hail this final 'Springtime' and horns suffuse the texture with a waving haze of sound, the oboe introduces a lilting theme that seems to be almost an amalgam of Examples 11.6 and 11.7 from *On Hearing the First Cuckoo in Spring*, while the solo clarinet tries to make itself heard with plaintive

---

[22] Diary of Marie Clews, quoted in LC2, 206.

[23] Lionel Carley has drawn attention to the striking similarities in parts of Simon's text to lines chosen by Mahler for *Das Lied von der Erde*. These were selected from Hans Bethge's poetic interpretations of ancient Chinese verses. See 'Delius's *Song of the Earth*' in *Fanfare, Journal of the Royal Philharmonic Society* (Spring 1994), 3.

cuckoo calls (three bars after fig. 42). The music rises to a climax of alternating *ff* and *p* chords for the orchestra (fig. 45–fig. 46) before Delius – a master of lovingly crafted farewells ever since *Hiawatha* – adds a contemplative coda. High herding calls in the woodwind roll and roll against repeating horn and trumpet calls, this time literally distant, for the composer instructs them to be played from outside the concert stage. As in *The Song of the High Hills*, the call-metaphor here is a symbol of the immutability of nature over time. In the earlier work, the calls are associated with great mountain expanses, in the *Requiem* with the seasonal and biological cycle. At the close here, Delius also lets onstage horns imitate the pealing of heavy bells. Yes, it is another spatial indicator at work. But more specifically, this is the devoted pupil making his last farewell to the philosopher-poet who had changed his life with the sayings of Zarathustra. As it had done throughout *A Mass of Life*, the midnight bell tolls the death of the old wisdom and the dawn of the new.

The warmth and lyricism of the Two Pieces for Small Orchestra and the new ending to *Fennimore and Gerda* was not sustained in the *Requiem*, nor in the composer's suite *North Country Sketches* (1913–14), an orchestral depiction in four movements of shifting seasonal moods. Again, the emphasis here was on texture in fragmentary episodes rather than sustained motivic development. The chill of the north had returned to his orchestral music. Delius's English commentators have robustly argued that the north country in question can only be the countryside and moorland where the composer grew up.[24] For the first performance in May 1915, however, Delius asked Philip Heseltine – with whom he spent much time in this period – to prepare programme notes, and in these we can read that the four pieces 'reflect moods and emotions engendered by various aspects of nature in northern lands. No particular "north country" is specified, though the influences of Yorkshire, the composer's native country, and of Norway have probably contributed these musical impressions in no small degree.'

In the first two movements, 'Autumn (The wind soughs in the trees)' and 'Winter Landscape', the composer revisits the bleak moods and sinewy textures that informed the emotionally pinched episodes of *Fennimore and Gerda* and *An Arabesque* – Scandinavian works with the chill of the north on them. A more vibrant energy is released in the final movement, 'The March of Spring. Woodlands, Meadows and Silent Moors', and there are stylistic fingerprints that we have previously associated with Delius's Norwegian scores, such as the herding call of a shepherd's pipe (after fig. 43) and, as the work reaches its close, the distant *coucou au fond des bois*. Perhaps here, as with *On Hearing the*

---

[24] Guinery and Lee-Browne even go so far as to claim that 'there can really be no doubt that Delius was thinking of Yorkshire'. See *Delius and His Music*, 322.

First Cuckoo, we should keep in mind his statement: 'Spring always means for me a longing for Norway'.

1913–1914: 'This is the country for me – the Høifjeld'

> Next Saturday I leave for Norway – sail from Antwerp & go straight up to the mountains – My wife joins me a month later & we then go up to the Lofoten Islands. I am looking forward immensely to the trip.[25]

For a man who for so many years had steadfastly held to his favoured mountain regions of Southern Norway, Jotunheimen in particular, the Lofoten archipelago north of the Arctic Circle is a surprising choice of destination. It involved a four-day coastal trip from Bergen – a distance, as the crow flies, as far as from Grez to Kristiania. It may reflect a preference of Jelka's, the extraordinary summer light so far north having always attracted artists. Equally likely, the Deliuses' curiosity had been piqued by reports received from Bartók. Having been inspired in the first place by Delius to visit Norway, Bartók and his wife had toured the west coast for five weeks in 1912, declaring Lofoten the highlight of their visit.[26]

Delius would meet up with Jelka in Bergen on 1 August; before then, he would have three weeks alone on the Gol and Hardangervidda plateaus, a journey in large part frustrated by poor weather and hordes of tourists. Before leaving home, he had arranged to meet Edvard Munch in Kristiania on 9 July, his only full day in the city. In the event, the friends' reunion seems to have been postponed: the painter had been pinned down for weeks in his Kristiania Fjord studio at Grimsrød, Moss, by waves of wealthy German art collectors, a source of stress and annoyance for him. Delius did, however, get to enjoy Munch's work, enjoining Jelka that she must get to see 'the Munchs in the National Gallery – all the best ones of years ago. They are wonderful – Also the Viking Queen Ship. Perfectly marvellous with all sorts of ornaments & a carved sledge & a carved carriage drawn by 2 reindeer & gold and iron ornaments.'[27] In the evening Delius still had time to visit Milly Bergh in Slemdal on the city's outskirts.

At the tourist agency, he was informed that the mountain hotel he was heading for, Fossheimseter in Valdres, was fully booked. Instead, the agency made travel arrangements to get him part of the way to Jotunheimen, and let him

[25] Letter from Delius to Philip Heseltine, 28 June 1913 (BL).

[26] See Béla Bartók Jr, 'Béla Bartók i Norge', trans. Vince Sulyck, in *Norsk Musikktidsskrift*, No. 2 (June 1978), 97–8.

[27] Postcard from Delius to Jelka, 10 July 1913 (GM). The Viking ship is the Oseberg Ship, recovered from a burial mound on the west coast of the Kristiania Fjord in 1905. It is the pride of Oslo's Viking Ship Museum today, along with the Gokstad Ship, which the young Delius had seen on his visit to the city in 1887 (see p. 27).

improvise from there. On 10 July, he travelled west to Kongsberg, then next day was transported by car up Numedalen to Geilo – he and the driver stopping along the way to fish a couple of trout from a mountain tarn. 'This is the country for me – the Høifjeld', he wrote home to Jelka of the Geilo hills.[28] Having moved on next day to Gol, Delius spent the night at the Oset høyfjellseter, a lodge on the Gol Plateau, having to make do with a sofa for a bed. The attraction exerted by the country on the English and German middle classes was at its peak. 'Norway has become *very dear*', he exclaimed. 'The West Coast is crammed with tourists & every Sanatorium in Norway is full up.'[29] It was a dispiriting state of affairs that even discouraged him from continuing into Jotunheimen; the charm of hiking in the Norwegian mountains was in danger of being ruined by the swarms of visitors drawn to the region. It was at this moment the solution suddenly became obvious to him – and Jelka concurred: 'It would be lovely if we had a little hut of our own.'[30] Because of the approaching war, it would be another ten years before they had their own cottage, at Lesjaskog.

Having informed his host at Oset that the only way he would leave was if they picked him up and threw him out, a 'very primitive' room finally became available for Delius and he could enjoy several contented days fishing and walking in the complete stillness of the Gol Plateau, with the snow-flecked mountain peaks in the distance: 'The sun sets just behind Jotunheimen & the beautiful long meandering Lake – the colors are simply wonderful.'[31]

On 19 July, Delius moved down to Aurdal, spending a night in the same valley where, sixteen years earlier, he, Knut Hamsun and Halfdan Jebe had caroused their way around hotels and sanatoriums. Over the next week, he slowly made his way westwards towards the mountain hotel at Finse, stopping several nights at the Tyin and Maristova lodges, waiting in vain for better weather. 'It appears the sooner we go to Lofoten the better', he sighed in a postcard to Jelka.[32] Arriving at Finse on 27 July, Delius sat down and wrote to Nina Grieg, informing her that he and Jelka would be in Bergen a few days later. In the reply he received from Nina she promised to do everything she could to be able to receive them at Troldhaugen on 1 August.

The station at Finse opened in 1908; at 1,222 metres it is still the highest point in northern Europe served by a railway. This exotic location ensured that the Finse Hotel flourished, trains carrying the artistic and social elites of Kristiania and Bergen up to experience remote and frozen nature.[33] At a desolate

---

[28] Postcard from Delius to Jelka, 12 July 1913 (GM).
[29] Letter from Delius to Jelka, 13 July 1913 (GM).
[30] Letter from Jelka to Delius, 20 July 1913 (GM).
[31] Letter from Delius to Jelka, 13 July 1913 (GM). The lake is Tisleifjorden.
[32] Postcard from Delius to Jelka, 27 July 1913 (GM).
[33] The railway also enabled the most famous polar explorers of the day, including Shackleton, Amundsen, Nansen and Scott, to come to Finse to test themselves and their equipment in the plateau's polar conditions.

spot on the edge of Hardangervidda, Finse had snow much of the year and the eternal glacial ice of Hardangerjøkulen rose up nearby. The hotel's guestbook reveals that, around the same time as Delius was staying there, Norwegian author Sigrid Undset was a guest, as also was the German naval commander Reinhard Scheer, who three years later would lead the German fleet at the Battle of Jutland. It is likely that Delius stayed for three or four days before continuing to Bergen to meet Jelka on 1 August.

From this point and until they were back home in Grez five weeks later, we have no trace of the Deliuses' movements in Norway. The only certainty is that there was a reunion with Nina Grieg at Troldhaugen, for she would later mention their visit in a letter to a mutual friend. In fact, Delius was not the only foreign acquaintance of Nina to arrive in Bergen on 1 August. The day before, Kaiser Wilhelm II had unveiled a huge statue of the saga hero Frithjof the Bold on the shore of the Sognefjord. Wilhelm was a great friend of Norway, visiting the country most summers, and the statue was a gift he had commissioned. Late in the evening of 1 August, the imperial yacht *Hohenzollern*, accompanied by two German warships and saluted with fireworks from passenger ships, steamed into Bergen harbour. Invitations to a reception on board the yacht were immediately sent out to the city's eminences, including Edvard Grieg's widow. For Nina, who earlier in the summer had bemoaned the neglect in Norwegian media of what would have been Grieg's seventieth birthday, the Kaiser's courtesy would have been gratifying.

With our complete 'blackout' as to where Frederick and Jelka spent the next weeks, we do not know whether they continued up the west coast to enjoy a Lofoten adventure or returned to the mountains. Edvard Munch was in Norway until 6 September, so the postponed meeting would have been possible on the Deliuses' way home. However, right up to his departure, the painter and his German investors had been engaged in what he called 'the great Battle of Grimsrød'. 'I see my future eclipsed by these people', Munch complained, 'who endlessly come up here to annoy me and ruin my summer. My nerves can't stand this for days on end.'[34]

To Delius's delight, there arrived in 1913 news of his other close Norwegian friend, Halfdan Jebe, who several years previously had disappeared into the towns of the American Midwest. In April, he heard from Adey Brunel in London that Jebe had been in contact:

My dear Mrs Brunel –
I was very pleased & astonished to receive a letter from you – I almost thought you had gone to join Jebe in the South Sea Islands or the 'hereafter'! So you really received news from our dear old Jebe! I need not tell you how much this

[34] Quoted in Ludvig Ravensberg's diary (MM).

interests me; & would it be too much to ask you to send me the letter so that I may be able to form an idea of how he is & has been faring – Jebe is the only man I ever loved in all my life & I would fair believe that he has passed entirely out of my life – He seems to be making a reality of his life & living all the music that he has in him – With me it is just the contrary – I am putting everything into my music – all my poetry & all my adventures.[35]

Jebe's letter does not seem to have survived. Delius grasped the opportunity to write to Jebe himself and in early July, while he was in Norway, a reply arrived at Grez and was immediately forwarded to Delius, *poste restante* Kristiania. Thanks to Jelka also quoting some of its contents in her own letter to her husband, we gain once more a fleeting glimpse of the elusive Norwegian (in words we noted in an earlier chapter): 'How northern he is in spirit, how he loved what you wrote about mysterious influences or forces – he always comes back to it; and how he hates the Norwegians – and "Eisklumpen in seinem Herzen" – I love him.'[36]

Where had he been? In an interview many years later with a Norwegian paper, Jebe informed the journalist that he had 'trawled through pretty much every state in America, holding concerts in the larger towns and cities, and in pockets of Norwegian and Scandinavian culture. He had stayed in Chicago and New York for several years. He had also been concertmaster of several orchestras, making tours with them.'[37] Up to this point his wife, Sofie, seems to have stayed with him, and in New York she had made a reputation for herself as actor-manager at the Norwegian Theater. In mid-1915, however, she returned to Kristiania to pursue her career at home and without her husband.[38] Around the same time, the itinerant Jebe placed himself under the management of an impresario in Atlanta, and continued to tour widely.[39]

In the year and a half before the outbreak of war, the two months in Norway in 1913 stand out as a hiatus in the exacting, and often exciting, life Delius led in the musical world of Germany and England, travelling widely to prestigious performances of his works, and lionised in the finest social circles. These are some of the signal events he attended:

Jan. 1913	*A Mass of Life*	Munich
March 1913	*A Mass of Life*	London
June 1913	*In a Summer Garden*	Jena

---

[35] Letter from Delius to Adey Brunel, 27 April 1913 (CB).
[36] Letter from Jelka to Delius, 8 July 1913 (GM).
[37] *Dagbladet*, 19 January 1932.
[38] Sofie Bernhoft-Jebe would establish herself as one of the leading actresses of the early Norwegian cinema.
[39] See Don Gillespie, 'Halfdan Jebe in Atlanta', in *Journal of the Delius Society*, No. 149 (Spring 2011), 34–40.

June 1913	*Appalachia*	Paris
Oct. 1913	Two Pieces for Small Orchestra	Leipzig
Nov. 1913	*An Arabesque*	Vienna
Feb. 1914	*A Mass of Life*	Wiesbaden
Feb. 1914	*A Mass of Life*	Frankfurt
July 1914	All-Delius concert	London

At the outbreak of war, there were also wheels in motion for productions of *A Village Romeo and Juliet* in Frankfurt and *Fennimore and Gerda* in Cologne and London. Nijinsky was considering staging Dance Rhapsody with his newly-formed company. And in Delius's birthplace, Bradford, the prodigal son was due to be welcomed home in November 1914 with a large concert of his music. All of these were cancelled.

The Nijinsky connection gives a hint of the circles in which Delius was moving in Europe's capitals of musical culture. If we were to choose one moment from this period that typifies the exalted artistic company he was keeping, it might be the evening of 23 May 1913, on which Delius was to be found in Paris, eager to experience Diaghilev's staging of *Boris Godunov*. Not only did he meet Diaghilev and Nijinsky, but also 'a lot of old friends' with whom he retired to a restaurant after the opera. At the same table with Delius were gathered composers Igor Stravinsky, Maurice Ravel, Florent Schmitt and Oscar Klemperer. A few days later we find him writing to Stravinsky to suggest that he would pick him up at his hotel on the evening of 29 May so that they could go together to that evening's performance of the Ballets Russes at Théâtre des Champs-Élysées – the small matter of the première of *The Rite of Spring*.[40] The London social elite had also warmed to Delius, and visits to the city turned into rounds of luncheons and soirées with the leading artistic and political names of the day, including, on at least one occasion, with Prime Minister Asquith at Downing Street.

By late July 1914, the political situation in Europe was careering out of control, and Delius wrote to Heseltine: 'I do hope War will not break out & knock all Art and Music on the head for years'.[41] A period of fifteen years in Grez – a period of disciplined creative routine that had fully released his potential as an artist – was about to be dramatically interrupted.

1915–1918: 'It is dreadful that we are cut off from Norway'

To the French inhabitants of Grez-sur-Loing, Frederick and Jelka Delius were just two of the many artists that had enlivened the village since the early 1880s. With the outbreak of war, however, the couple's German ancestry turned

---

[40] For further details of Delius's meetings with the Russians in Paris, see LC2, 106–7.
[41] Letter from Delius to Philip Heseltine, 30 July 1914 (BL).

suspicious minds poisonous and life in Grez quickly became uncomfortable. Delius asked Scandinavian friends, such as Helge Rode, to write in Danish or English. With the enemy's startling advance into France in late August 1914 refugees started to flee south, as Delius related to Rode:

> [The] high road from Fontainebleau to Nemours was a terrifying sight – thousands of fugitives in every sort of vehicle & on foot – Automobiles, carts, wheelbarrows & perambulators with little blond heads sticking out from amongst provisions etc. We sat every afternoon for 2 hours watching this extraordinary cavalcade go by – they all had terrifying tales of german soldier brutalities.[42]

On 5 September, the first day of the First Battle of the Marne, the Deliuses could look on no longer and joined the flow of refugees, travelling by cattle truck to Orléans and taking with them a few possessions, including their most treasured paintings in a roll. A week later, the Allies had repelled the German sweep into France and Frederick and Jelka could make their way back to Grez again, shocked by having seen many wounded and dying soldiers being brought back from the lines. The unease they felt in their village was likely only to escalate, so in November they accepted a generous offer of accommodation from Thomas Beecham; for the next seven months their home would be an old house outside London, on the outskirts of Watford.

Four testing years had begun. Delius's standing as a composer would not be hugely affected by the war, for influential friends – not least Percy Grainger and Josef Stransky in America – ensured that his works continued to be performed, and after the conflict his reputation was quickly revived in England and Germany/Austria. The flow of royalties was, however, suspended for the duration and the Deliuses rapidly found themselves struggling to pay their way. Delius had arrived in England 'in a highly nervous and agitated state', related Beecham.[43] It was perhaps in this bleak time that Jelka carefully chose a book she could read to her husband: Asbjørnsen and Moe's Norwegian folk tales in the original language. She recalled reading them 'one whole winter during the war, a sort of relief from the dreadful tension'.[44] When, in early 1915, Delius felt capable of creative work again, it was indeed to ideas for an orchestral work inspired by trolls and goblins, eventually called *Eventyr*, that he applied himself.

Unsurprising in the circumstances, the state of Delius's health – so fragile at its core – began once more to deteriorate. A London specialist was consulted, who strongly recommended that the composer escape from the tensions of war to a remote place where his nervous condition might be calmed. On 6 July,

---

[42] Letter from Delius to Helge Rode, undated, November 1914 (KB).
[43] Beecham, *Frederick Delius*, 172.
[44] Letter from Jelka to Eric Fenby, 27 October 1933 (DT).

their trunks were therefore taken on board the Newcastle–Bergen ferry. Jelka explained to Heseltine: 'Norway is Fred's land'.[45]

Frederick and Jelka found themselves in a prelapsarian Norway. 'Crammed with tourists' in 1913, the country experienced in 1915 a summer without the swarms from Britain and Germany that had been the backbone of its tourism industry – although Norwegians did take up some of the slack. The Deliuses' three-month sojourn can be divided up thus:

July	travelling north up the coast then east into the mountains
August	Sandane, at a fingertip of the Nordfjord
September	Geilo, on the north-eastern periphery of Hardangervidda

From Bergen, they travelled first up to Sandane and spent some days at Hotel Gloppen. Around mid-July they continued up the west coast to Molde, from where Jelka wrote to Frederick's sister, Clare: 'Up here we are just opposite the Snow Mountains and the air is lovely and we get the most extraordinary appetite and the good people give one such a lot of food and everything so good and clean and fresh that it is quite a treat. If only one could really forget that the rest of humanity are all fighting!'[46] The view from Molde across the Romsdalsfjord to the Sunnmøre Alps was one that her husband had longed to share with her since 1908 (see p. 218). From here they seem (details being few and far between) to have travelled slowly south-eastwards towards the inland mountains, eventually arriving at the mountain post house of Hjerkinn. This was a route Delius had covered on his first great hike around the country in 1887 (see p. 26); it would also have taken them through Lesjaskog, where they would build a summer home a few years later.

Their first week in Sandane had given them a taste of the beauties of Vestlandet, the fjord country in the west, and in the first week of August they returned to Hotel Gloppen. The beautiful situation of Sandane, right by the calm waters of the inner fjord, would have been beneficial for the composer's nerves. Ever the keen angler, Delius likely availed himself of the hotel's licence to fish nearby mountain tarns, such as Traugdalsvannet:

> The lake lies beautifully between rows of mountains. It is rich in fish. On one dreamy summer night, the flickering of a large bonfire was reflected in its waters, there was the sound of cowbells from the hillsides and the herding calls of the girls with their red blouses and snowy white arms, and hundreds of cows rested on the green pasture.[47]

[45] Letter from Jelka to Philip Heseltine, 29 June 1915 (BL).
[46] Letter from Jelka to Clare Black, 13 July 1915 (DT).
[47] Ole Wilhelm Fasting, *Perler* (Bergen: Grieg forlag, 1904), 78.

For the hotel proprietor it was, indeed, unusual not to have the rooms full of Englishmen, as he explained to the local newspaper:

> In other years Englishmen make up the majority of our guests, and the fishing cabins in the valleys of Traudalen and Myklebustdalen are always full of English sports fishermen. There were none at all this year. Only a couple of English could be noted, the well-known composer Fredr. Delius and his wife, who settled here 3 weeks ago and who hopefully will be staying until October.[48]

It was not to be. In mid-August, the weather blowing in from the North Sea turned inclement and finally at the end of the month Frederick and Jelka packed up and left the rain behind them. They probably took the coastal steamer back to Bergen and from there the train east towards Kristiania, alighting at the halfway point. Geilo (794m), at the western end of Hallingdalen and on the incline down from Hardangervidda, was a village that had expanded with the arrival of the railway, trains bringing city dwellers up to the clean mountain air. Dr Holm, a canny Kristiania physician and entrepreneur, contrived for his hotel to open here in 1909 as the railway station was entering service.

In the month that Delius enjoyed these hills, he again felt his constitution strengthening. 'When you came to Norway, how splendidly well you got', Jelka would later recall, 'how you walked up at Geilo'.[49] To Percy Grainger, Delius poured out the elation he was feeling: 'It has been heavenly here all September – Not a cloud, no wind & hot sun all the time [...] the fjeld is simply a marvel of colors, russet gold & scarlet & down below where the forest begins the woods are in their brightest autumn tints'.[50] When Delius went out hiking, people would stop him 'to ask me if I were English & all about the war – Their sympathies are violently pro allies'.[51] The couple's plans were changing all the time. They had to take account of the shifting tide of the war and prolonged their stay at Geilo when they learnt that German submarines were stopping passenger ships and removing English passengers. A plan to return to Norway 'for the lovely winter', after visiting Denmark, never came to pass, nor the alternative of spending the winter in Copenhagen: their longing to return to Grez gradually trumped every other consideration.

At the end of September, Frederick and Jelka began the trip south from Geilo, spending a few days in the Norwegian capital. For his book on Delius and Munch, John Boulton Smith interviewed Inger Alver Gløersen, whose parents had been close to Edvard Munch. She had faint recollections of Delius coming to the artist's studio at Grimsrød to discuss the purchase of a picture. Presuming it happened, circumstantial evidence points to this visit taking place in 1915, when Gløersen was twenty-three years old. Grimsrød Farm lay

[48] *Nordfjord*, 10 September 1915.
[49] Letter from Jelka to Delius, 11 July 1917 (GM).
[50] Letter from Delius to Percy Grainger, 26 September 1915 (GM).
[51] Letter from Delius to Percy Grainger, 11 January 1916 (GM).

by the Kristiania Fjord outside the town of Moss, some sixty-five kilometres south of the capital. At the time, Munch was working in a small studio in Kristiania on his painting *Bohemens død* (*The Death of the Bohemian*). Having expressed an interest in purchasing a picture, Delius and Munch may have travelled together down to the farm. This was likely to have been the first time the two had met since the painter's full-blown crisis in 1908 when, after nearly drinking himself to death, he was a patient at a Copenhagen clinic for eight months. He emerged a quieter, older, less nervous man, who was perhaps never again inebriated:

> Yes, alcohol has had its day – with all the pain and pleasure it brought with it – a strange world is now closed off to me […] I must learn the habit of staying at home – that too has its charms – it's peaceful and then there's reading – As for women, I will leave them in their heaven – as did the old Italian masters – The thorns of the rose are too cruel – [52]

There is also every possibility that the friends saw a good deal of each other in Copenhagen a few weeks later – although, again, we have only circumstantial evidence. The Deliuses left for Denmark around 7 October, as did Munch. He was bound for Copenhagen and the Autumn Exhibition, they for three weeks in the peace and quiet of Palsgaard, the Schous' residence on the east coast of Jutland where they had first stayed in 1909. When, in early November, Frederick and Jelka continued to Copenhagen, Munch was still in the city. In fact, he had prolonged his stay there for a few days, finally departing on the same day as the Deliuses. The likelihood that they spent the time together is further supported by the fact that Delius had arranged to meet their mutual friend, Helge Rode, while in the Danish capital. Munch, Rode, Frederick and Jelka Delius – it would be the first time they had all met since the summer of 1898 in Åsgårdstrand, on Jelka's first trip to Norway.

'I cannot work in Hotels & private houses & want to get back home again', Delius wrote to Grainger,[53] and by a convoluted route to avoid the theatre of war they arrived back in their Grez home around 19 November 1915, exactly a year after abandoning it for Watford. They had risked mines and submarines to get to Norway and home again, and now they intended to see the war out in Grez. Delius's health had again been shored up and fortified:

> Since I left England my spirits have been gradually rising & in the highlands of Norway, away from all humans I really got my old self back again […] before leaving England – a certain depression had absolutely taken possession of me – I luckily could forget as long as I was working; But Watford is like an unpleasant dream to me now.[54]

[52] Letter from Munch to Jappe Nilssen, 28 December 1908 (NB).
[53] Letter from Delius to Percy Grainger, 26 September 1915 (GM).
[54] Letter from Delius to Philip Heseltine, 12 October 1915 (BL).

*

Strange though it seems, the war in Europe led to the next year and a half being one of the more contented periods of Delius's life. With food becoming scarce and local men to help with the garden away fighting, Jelka and Frederick rolled up their sleeves and turned their flowerbeds into vegetable patches. There was little correspondence to interrupt them, nor any trips to concert venues around Europe. Delius's daily routine of work at his piano, toil in the garden and walks in the countryside went undisturbed for long periods and his health seemed settled and robust. The absence of music-making in their lives became, of course, a sorely trying deprivation. In fact, before the escalating submarine threat closed off the Atlantic, Percy Grainger had succeeded in persuading the couple to come to America, where musical society, he assured them, was primed and ready to discover Delius in a big way. Delius's deeply-lying affections for the country and people that had so powerfully stimulated his creativity were also brought sharper into focus through the blooming of a new friendship.

Henry Clews Jr was an American millionaire who had turned his back on Wall Street to devote himself to his considerable talents as a painter and sculptor. He had married his second wife Marie in 1914 and the couple had moved to Paris. In periods of 1916 and 1917 when the cultivation of vegetables did not demand Frederick's and Jelka's immediate attention, they would travel up to Paris and enjoy for a week or two a life of leisure as guests of the Clewses, taking in restaurants and cinemas. Only with the deployment in 1917 of German long-range bombers in the night skies over Paris did the war seriously impinge on their visits.

Abruptly around midsummer 1917, Delius's condition took a turn for the worse. The strength in his legs failed and throughout July he underwent a course of spa treatments at institutions on the Normandy coast. On all other occasions when his health had troubled him, he had sought and benefited from the restorative powers of Norwegian highlands. 'It is dreadful that we are cut off from Norway', Jelka wrote to her disconsolate husband, 'I never felt so strongly that it is really a necessity to you'.[55] His condition responded well to the therapy and the couple could enjoy August together in a seaside resort in Brittany. The respite was short-lived, and in January 1918 he was admitted again to a sanatorium for several weeks, this time outside Paris. The spring in Grez aided his recovery, as did two summer months in Biarritz, where they enjoyed bathing in the sea. It was while they were there that Frederick and Jelka received news that their house in Grez had been requisitioned by French officers, and on their return in August they were appalled to discover their home vandalised, their belongings ransacked and their woodpile burnt. Feel-

---

[55] Letter from Jelka to Delius, 11 July 1917 (GM).

ing their lives defiled, and in any case not wishing to risk a winter without fuel, they again removed to London, conductor Henry Wood renting them a house while they looked for a suitable flat.

The arrival of Frederick and Jelka in London in September coincided with a performance under Wood of Dance Rhapsody, probably the first time in three years Delius had heard his music. His musical life was already returning to a semblance of normality by the time the armistice was declared on 11 November. He immediately rushed off a letter to his German publisher, Universal Edition: '*At last* the war has come to an end and it is now possible – thank God – to resume our relations.'[56] The curtain on 1919 was to be lifted with the first performance of an important new Delius score: *Eventyr*.

Eventyr: 'the very longing of his heart to go to Norway'

Eventyr is the last overtly Norwegian score to come from Delius's pen. It was started, we noted above, in 1915 when he and Jelka had decamped to Watford to escape the war in France and had no way of knowing how long their exile would be or whether routes to Norway would remain open. Work on the composition was resumed in 1916 and completed in the autumn of 1917, after two years away from Norway, when travel was too dangerous and any cessation in hostilities seemed remote. Shortly after the first performance in January 1919, Jelka recorded in a letter that the work was based on Norwegian folk tales – *eventyr* – collected by Peter Christen Asbjørnsen:

> [The] music is quite adorable – so Norwegian – the little trolls cantering along on the 'Vidders', the Huldre, the Peasants – The spirit of the whole thing was there out in that beloved nature. I think he has realized all that so well in the very longing of his heart to go to Norway – impossible on account of the War.[57]

The tone-poem *Eventyr*, which Delius initially referred to as 'a ballad for orchestra', was a *tour de force* of the composer's talents as a musical painter of moods in orchestral colour. Paul Guinery has pointed out that it is 'the nearest thing he wrote to a Straussian, or even more aptly, a Sibelian tone poem'.[58] *Eventyr* would also be Delius's one Norwegian work in which he, so to speak, steps to one side to let folklorists tell us something of the country, which he then interprets. In this respect it is the closest Delius came to the stance most often adopted by Grieg in approaching the Norwegian landscape and culture. While Delius had dwelled exclusively on personal emotional responses to the wilderness, Grieg had preferred to employ the connecting agency of rural people – the milkmaids and shepherds of the mountains. And Grieg was, of

---

[56] Letter from Delius to Universal Edition, undated, November or December 1918 (UE).
[57] Letter from Jelka to Rose Grainger, 14–16 January 1919 (GM). A *hulder* (plural: *huldre*) is a seductive female creature of Norwegian folklore.
[58] Guinery and Lee-Browne, *Delius and his Music*, 385.

course, fascinated by their superstitions about the fearful trolls. Almost half a century before Delius's *Eventyr*, Grieg had brilliantly set to music Peer Gynt's encounters with folklore figures such as the Woman in Green and the Bøyg, with Peer's journey into the mountain lair of the troll king and his deliverance through the power of church bells over troll magic. For all of these, Ibsen's primary source had also been Asbjørnsen's collections of folk tales.

Delius's title has given publishers and audiences a few headaches. During the prolonged process of composition, he had consistently referred to the work as *Once Upon a Time*,[59] opting finally for the Norwegian title only days before its first performance, with the English phrase as a subtitle. For publication, a further explanatory subtitle was added: *After Asbjørnsen's Folklore*. In information that Jelka supplied for a programme note for the work, she emphasised, with her husband's approval, that it was not inspired by any particular folk tale, but was rather 'a résumé-impression' of the old legends that were still alive with lonely peasants, hunters and mountaineers:

> These people have a naïve belief in the 'Underjordiske' (the Underearthly ones) Trolls, Heinzelmännchen, hobgoblins; who either help the humans or, if provoked, become very revengeful. A boy alone in a forest would imagine he heard them trotting after him, and get very frightened. At a wedding or a Xmas meal a little dish of cream porridge is put on the loft for these underearthly ones, or else they might be offended – they have been known to fetch girls (even the bride of a wedding) in such cases and dance with them furiously till they fall down unconscious.[60]

While Delius did not wish *Eventyr* to be regarded as a programmatic work, his and Jelka's efforts to lead his audience away from the details of Asbjørnsen's tales seem rather disingenuous. On hearing a composition so neatly structured into episodes, and those episodes full of such vivid characterisation, it would be a listener of scant imagination who did not wish to know more of the imagery and literary influences working on the composer. In fact, for parts or all of *Eventyr* Delius was faithfully depicting in music narrative events in Asbjørnsen's tales. Barrie Iliffe has identified three passages in the score that he thought could be directly connected to specific moments in Asbjørnsen – of which the present writer feels that two are indisputable.[61] This still leaves the

---

[59] Delius's growing friendship with Henry Clews may have nourished the period of composition. Both men were fascinated with legendary creatures. In 1918, Henry and Marie Clews started on the restoration of Château de la Napoule on the French coast near Cannes, turning it into a fairy-tale castle. Above one of the main doors he sculpted a lintel with the text: *ONCE UPON A TIME*.

[60] Letter from Jelka to Philip Heseltine, 28 September 1929 (BL).

[61] Barrie Iliffe, '*Eventyr* and the Fairy Tales in Delius', published in Lionel Carley (ed.), *Frederick Delius: Music, Art, and Literature* (London: Ashgate Publishing, 1998), 273–89. Iliffe also narrowed down the version of the tales Delius and Jelka were reading to one of three possible editions: *Norske Folke- og Huldre-Eventyr*, published by Gyldendalske Boghandel in either 1896, 1909–10 or 1911.

bulk of the music 'untainted' by relationship to a specific literary impulse, too indistinct to be regarded as overtly programmatic. Considering the popular appeal of a work like Rimsky-Korsakov's *Scheherazade*, Delius's reticence to disclose his 'programme' may have led to an opportunity slipping through his fingers to create a much wider audience for the music.

Eventyr opens 'slow and mysteriously', a brooding, modal folk music-like theme (Example 11.8) in the cellos and basses answered by apprehensive bars in the woodwind.

Example 11.8 *Eventyr*, opening

This is an ominous 'opening title sequence', as if our camera is slowly panning from a dark forest before finally, after twenty bars, moving towards the lights of a house. A warm theme is introduced by the string section, expressing – according to Eric Fenby – 'the idea of the warm-hearted superstitious peasantry':

Example 11.9 *Eventyr*, 21–4

In other words, Delius is employing a frame narrative to set up the main body of the work, following Asbjørnsen's example. Most of the tales narrated by the folklorist are sandwiched between framing tales: friends who meet in the thick of the woods, walkers who come across some wise old crone in the country, or an extended family gathered of a winter evening by the open fire, as in the following extract from 'An Evening in the Squire's Kitchen' – all these figures were primed to hear stories of the uncanny:

> A great fire blazed on the large open hearth and lighted up the room even in its farthest corners. By the side of the hearth presided the squire's wife with her spinning wheel. [...] Along the edge of the hearth sat the children, and cracked nuts. Round about them was a circle of girls and wives of the neighbouring tenants [...] In the passage outside the door, the threshers, who had done their

day's work, were stamping the snow off their feet before they came in, – their hair full of chaff.[62]

The composer's storytelling is light-hearted at the outset. An extended episode follows, introducing cackling woodwind phrases and ungainly shuffling and falling themes that seem to rush at us out of the texture. Various trolls and goblins are being described, the night is drawing in, the scene is being set for a tale of terror and danger. But first the composer breaks off again (thirteen after fig. 4), brings us back to the warmth of the fire and the comfort of the assembled company. Perhaps we are too frightened to hear any more? A pleading motif (actually marked *pleading* in the cor anglais, one bar before fig. 5) tells us that the children, though wide-eyed, are hungry for more. And so it begins.

The narrative that Delius's music follows at the heart of *Eventyr* comes from the folk tale 'Enkesønnen' ('The Widow's Son').[63] It tells of an unfortunate boy who is apprenticed to a cruel master, a wicked troll, and on a magic horse he finally makes his bid for freedom. Starting at fig. 6, driving triplets in woodwind and brass suggest we are galloping along at a brisk pace. In the deep instruments the ominous theme of the troll magic (Example 11.8) is growing stronger and stronger.

> No sooner had the boy mounted the horse than they galloped off so he hardly knew what was happening.
> He rode for a while, then the horse said: 'I think I hear a rumbling noise. Look behind, can you see anything?'
> 'We're being followed, and there's an awful lot of them, at least a score', said the boy.
> 'Yes, that's the troll alright', said the horse, 'he and his pack are giving chase'.

A few bars after fig. 8, the gallop turns into a furious chase and, at its climax, Delius scores a group of off-stage men to shout at the top of their voices: 'Hei!'[64] This is the troll pack that has been thwarted by the cunning of the horse:

> They rode for a while more, until their pursuers were getting close.
> 'Now take your briar twig and throw it over your shoulder', said the horse. 'And be sure to throw it as far from me as possible'.
> This the boy did, and at once a huge, dense briar thicket sprang up behind them. The boy continued his gallop for another great distance, while the troll had to turn back home to fetch an axe to hog a way through the briars.

In the music the same procedure begins again: the galloping rhythm, the even wilder chase and at its climax another wild shout from the thwarted trolls. In

---

[62] P. Chr. Asbjørnsen, 'An Evening in the Squire's Kitchen' from *Round the Yule Log: Norwegian folk and fairy tales*, trans. H. L. Brækstad (London: Sampson Low, 1881), 250–1.

[63] 'Enkesønnen' was one of the stories that had been collected, not by Asbjørnsen, but by his friend Jørgen Moe.

[64] Not a *Hi!* in salutation, but as an exclamatory *Hey!*

the story, we are told that the horse commands the lad to throw behind him a magic rock, from which a steep mountain immediately rises. The trolls have to retire once more, fetching tools to mine their way through the mountain between them and their prey. Around fig. 12 in *Eventyr* the pursuit is on again for the third and last time. This time the trolls are hindered when the contents of a magic water bottle are spilled in their path, becoming suddenly a huge lake, and we hear the flood in Delius's exciting music before fig. 13.

As every superstitious Norwegian would have known, the only way to turn wild trolls from their wicked ways is through the chiming of church bells. In a climactic passage of *Eventyr*, beginning at five bars after fig. 13, Delius lets the whole orchestra ring out the holy sounds of pealing bells. This superstition provides the key moment to several tales collected by Asbjørnsen from villages on the outskirts of Jotunheimen, an area with which Delius was intimately acquainted. The folklorist related the legends in his 1848 collection, *Norske Huldreeventyr og Folkesagn* (*Norwegian Fairy Stories and Folk Tales*),[65] each of them concerning young village girls who were stolen away from their homes, taken by trolls into their lair in the mountains. In one, young Rundborg is stolen away on her wedding day:

> So the priest was summoned. He said they should fetch the church bells from Vågå Church, carry them up into Jøndalen and ring them for three days. Well, they carried them from Vågå across Jettafjellet and up onto a large rock in Jøndalsbråtom which ever since has been called Bell Rock. They rang the bells for three days, but the bride had vanished and remained vanished.

The villagers of Øyer have more success when the eight-year-old Kari is abducted and the bells of Øyer Church are carried up to the mountains:

> So they let the bells chime, and deep in a remote corner of the mountain fortress an old man with a long, long beard raised himself up in his bed.
> 'Get her out again!', he shouted, so the echoes thundered through the mountain. 'When the bell cows of Øyer are grazing on the mountain, it makes my skull fit to burst.'

Even if Asbjørnsen's retelling of these tales was unknown to Delius, he would still have been familiar with the ritual of the bells from Ibsen's *Peer Gynt* and Grieg's music for the play. Indeed, the whole scene from Act II that culminates in Peer being chased by small trolls from the hall of the Mountain King and saved at the last moment by the distant chiming of church bells is a harbinger of the climactic passages of Delius's tone-poem. Into *On Hearing the First Cuckoo in Spring* he had also introduced a folk song from Valdres, 'I Ola-dalom, i Ola-tjønn', which relates the story of villagers carrying bells up into the mountains to try and recover a missing boy. It is unknown whether or not Delius was

---

[65] Not the *Norske Folke- og Huldre-Eventyr* collection from which 'Enkesønnen' was borrowed; the titles are confusingly similar.

acquainted with the legend behind the song, and no bells chime in the work. He would, however, have known Grieg's op. 66 version of the song – a wonderful little tone-poem created from bell effects throughout the piano texture.[66]

Delius's trolls are defeated by the power of Christian faith, and two bars after fig. 16 the effusive string theme (Example 11.9) returns. We are back with the peasant family sitting safely together around the fire. Christianity and home comforts: strange ways indeed for the composer – Nietzsche acolyte and great interpreter of the Norwegian mountain wilderness that he was – to let his musical interpretations of Norway's nature and culture chime away into silence.

Wistful and lyrical

During the war, a further transformation took place in the musical language of Frederick Delius. We have seen that, following a period of serious illness in 1910, a northern chill had entered his music. In the war years, and for the rest of his career, the chromaticism of that bleak philosophy was further developed; now, however, it was always counterbalanced by extended passages of quiet, wistful lyricism, couched in a simple harmonic language warmed with added sixths and ninths. So quickly did this style flourish in his instrumental works that by the time *Eventyr* came to performance in 1919, its exuberance and extrovert posturing was an exception to a rule, almost an anachronism in the timeline of his musical development. There are examples of this lyrical, autumnal melancholy in most scores Delius wrote after 1914. Ostensibly uncomplicated passages, they are beautifully crafted to achieve an emotional effect on the listener, not least in the way they function as clearings in thickets of chromatic writing. We might cite the pentatonic passage at the heart of the Double Concerto for violin and cello (1915), the middle section of the 'Late Swallows' movement of the String Quartet (1916), the lyrical centre of the Cello Sonata (1916), the Scotch-snap passage at the core of the Violin Concerto (1916) and the *Lento* melody that opens the third movement of Sonata No. 3 for violin and piano (1930). It was a language that would be perfected in the Cello Concerto of 1921. In almost all instances Delius introduces pentatonic melodic phrases with the guilelessness of folk music, strongly reminiscent of the quasi-American songs that typified his earliest scores. Musical associations, in other words, with a time of innocence and youth.

---

[66] Grieg would return frequently to troll legends for his inspiration: *The Mountain Thrall*, op. 32; 'March of the Dwarfs', op. 54 no. 3; 'Puck', op. 71 no. 3; 'The Goblins' Bridal Procession at Vossevangen', op. 72 no. 14 and the piano variations on 'Sjugur and the Troll Bride' that became op. 51. Edvard and Nina Grieg also chose to call their house Troldhaugen (Troll Hill) – not on account of a particular affection for the elves, but because the small gully that ran round the plot was known to locals as Trolldalen, or Troll Valley.

Most striking in this regard is the recurrence in the 'Late Swallows' movement of the String Quartet of a theme he had written for his Florida opera *The
Magic Fountain*. The composer instructs the players to perform this movement
'wistfully'. Wistful – for what? It would be too easy to say that it was a reaction
to the loss of a youthful generation in the war. Even less appropriate to imagine
that Delius mourned the passing into history, with the war, of an old world in
which the bourgeoisie had run society as they saw fit; despite his dependence
on the patronage of the moneyed classes, his political leanings remained left
wing.[67] Far more likely, this was a secondary stage of his reaction to the place
he had arrived at in life, an existential repositioning. To recall the words of
Schopenhauer cited in connection with *The Song of the High Hills*, there occurs
in us a distinct shift 'when we have crossed the summit [and] actually catch
sight of death that was hitherto known only from hearsay'. It is always fascinating to study in these late works how successful the alloy is – of the young man's
heart and the older man's art. One of the finest examples was also the last in
the sequence of works for solo string instrument before illness silenced for a
time the composer's creative voice: Sonata No. 2 for violin and piano (1923).
Here, two of the principal themes seem to be the offspring of passages in much
earlier works, but these are embedded in one of the most perfectly evolving
textures he wrote, a gem of his late style. Example 11.10 is as Griegian a motif
as Delius ever penned, its first three notes and general shape bound to rouse
associations with the opening of the Norwegian's Piano Concerto.[68] In the way
these dotted rhythms drive the music, there are also shades of the unpublished
violin sonata of 1892, a work saturated with Delius's 'Mountain Music' of the
period (see p. 94):

Example 11.10 Sonata No. 2, 23–6

Introduced by the piano, Example 11.11 might also have been one of the composer's rising, pentatonic horn themes typical of his music of the 1890s.

[67] 'In between these concerts we have been attending labor meetings & hearing Shaw & Ramsay
Mcdonald & Henderson & Mrs Snowdon speak – We are coming to it old boy, & it is coming
to us! as I told you once in Paris – Bolschevism.' From a letter from Delius to Henry Clews, 4
February 1919 (DT).
[68] This Grieg 'fingerprint' is not uncommon in Delius works with a Nordic coloration – see, for
example, Example 11.1, the opening bars of *The Song of the High Hills*.

Example 11.11 Sonata No. 2, 75–6

The fact that this development in Delius's language occurred during war-time seems, then, to be a coincidence, the conflict serving only to intensify his sense of exposure. Indeed, the backward-looking gaze is perhaps first strongly identifiable in a *pre-war* composition, Sonata No. 1 for violin and piano (1914),[69] his first solo work for the instrument of his youth in almost twenty years.

A further powerful catalyst seems to have been his chance discovery of two young female musicians with the talent to fire his imagination and the youthful beauty to pique his sense of loss. Delius became immediately enamoured of May and Beatrice Harrison when he heard them performing the Brahms Double Concerto with the Hallé in Manchester in December 1914. Violinist May was then twenty-four, cellist Beatrice was twenty-one and Delius fifty-two years old. After the concert, the composer introduced himself and declared his intention of writing a double concerto for them. Both this concerto and the other works for solo string instrument mentioned above were composed for the Harrisons, with the exception of Sonata No. 1 for violin and piano, which was written shortly before he met them. With the decline of Delius's health, the Harrison sisters came to have an unforeseen effect on the composer's attitude to the country of his birth. In them he saw represented the noble virtues of an England he had previously spurned. Finally, after Delius's death, the Harrisons would be instrumental in bringing his remains back to England.

During the war years, however, the advance of his disease had been stalled. Delius still hoped to fully restore his health and to build a permanent summer home – not in England, but in the land for which he constantly longed. Norway.

---

[69] The early violin sonata from 1892 was posthumously published in 1977.

12

1919–1934
Myth and reality in Lesjaskog

'At last we are here in Norway – the land of Fred's constant longing'
Letter from Jelka Delius to Marie Clews, 18 August 1919

Prior to 1919, Delius had been to Norway sixteen times, but only once in consecutive summers (1898 and 1899). From 1919 to 1923, however, he and Jelka spent four of the five summers in the country, the last three of them in Lesjaskog, first planning for, then enjoying a secluded life in their own cottage. The story of these visits becomes gradually less and less about 'light summer nights & all the poetry & melancholy of the Northern summer', and more about the rapid deterioration in Delius's health. With the advance of his disease and paralysis, many admirable and attractive traits of Delius's personality were curtailed, 'collateral damage' in his battle to preserve the innermost core of himself. The commentators who got to know the composer in this period have left us some of the best known and, unfortunately, prevailing descriptions of him as an abrasive and difficult individualist. Before embarking on these years, then, it would be timely to quote from some of the many people who, prior to his illness, were irresistibly drawn towards his light.

Percy Grainger, composer
Delius, as I knew him, was remarkable for his gracious and graceful companionship, for the gaiety and lightness of his moods, for his good-humoured delight in fair and open-minded argument, for his unfailingly humane outlook on world affairs.[1]

Thomas Beecham, conductor
[There] was nothing in Delius of that vague indetermination associated traditionally with musical genius; in practical affairs he was as hardhearted as any to be found in his native county, and his knowledge of the world, both men and women, was searching and profound. He was sceptical and cynical where the

---

[1] Percy Grainger, 'About Delius', a text written 'At sea, June 23–25, 1950' for the 1952 edition of Philip Heseltine, *Frederick Delius*, 180.

majority of people were concerned, and he never wasted a word of sympathy or encouragement on those who in his opinion were not deadly in earnest over their job. But he was frank and cordial with the few he really cared for, and in general company he loved passionately to engage in highly controversial discussions on every subject imaginable.[2]

Clare Delius, sister
His sense of humour was highly developed and his laugh was infectious. He was entirely devoid of mannerisms, and when he took the call at the St. James's Hall his modesty and simplicity – his naïve air of being delighted at having been able to introduce his audience to the heights of beauty which he had scaled – attracted everybody's attention.[3]

Margaret Harrison, violinist, youngest of the Harrison sisters
In those days Delius was full of fun; nobody could realise what a happy soul he was then. He was always so very thin, but he had such charm and he was a good smiler too. He had a great sense of humour, of a very quiet kind but always straight to the point.[4]

1919–1921: The good life in Valdres and Lesjaskog

In the first two years after the war, things returned surprisingly quickly to normal in the musical life of both England and Germany, at least as far as Delius was concerned. There was a huge appetite for music, and the composer, with a backlog of scores awaiting performance, again found himself courted by opera houses and concert producers. The Deliuses were also awaiting the unfreezing of their royalty assets from Germany/Austria and America, until which point their financial situation remained precarious. So, in the spring of 1919, they determined to travel to Norway and, while there, try to sell their Gauguin painting, *Nevermore*, through the auspices of art critic Jappe Nilssen, one of Edvard Munch's closest friends. Early travel enquiries curbed their enthusiasm. 'Norway seemed exorbitantly dear, also the actual journey', Jelka wrote to Philip Heseltine in mid-June, 'so we had to give it up for the moment. Besides it is said to be packed full.'[5] Instead, they left London for the coast of Cornwall, staying for six weeks in a cottage at Land's End. Four years had now passed since the war had closed Norway off to Delius, and by the end of a chilly July the desire to be among the Jotunheim mountains had become too strong. Before they could travel north, however, Jelka had to attend to important and difficult business. She had returned to France to demand from the authorities compensation for the damage caused to their home at Grez by billeted

---

[2] Beecham, *A Mingled Chime*, 117–18.
[3] Clare Delius, *Frederick Delius*, 133.
[4] Margaret Harrison, 'Margaret Harrison Remembers' in *Journal of The Delius Society*, No. 87 (Autumn 1985), 13.
[5] Letter from Jelka to Philip Heseltine, 19 June 1919 (BL).

soldiers. While she was away, Delius made the final travel arrangements, once more with the help of Milly Bergh in Kristiania, and on 5 August the couple were at last crossing a North Sea that had been swept clear of mines.

They found accommodation at Fossheimseter in Valdres, south of Jotunheimen and not far from Bagn, where Delius had spent a happy summer in 1896. The mountain hotel was perched high above the Strondefjord lake. Jelka wrote to Marie Clews: '[It] is so beautiful, so fresh and invigorating and we need only climb up for an hour or so and then we see the whole chain of Snowmountains. The food is gorgeous here [...] After a winter of Margarine in London this is most enjoyable.'[6] Delius's days of nine-hour hikes were over. Until they moved on to Kristiania a month later, the couple relaxed in the relatively gentle countryside, taking short walks in the surrounding hills. From the summit of nearby Ålfjell (1,100m) there was a panoramic view of the mountains of central Norway, with the white Jotunheim peaks on the northern horizon.

In early September, they travelled south to the Norwegian capital, but were not yet ready to come down from the heights, taking rooms at Anna Kures Hotell high above Kristiania in the woods of Voksenkollen, with a spectacular view down to the fjord. No matter how lovely the surroundings, they would have been unable to ease the pain it must have caused Delius to deliver one of his most prized possessions into the hands of Jappe Nilssen. For *Nevermore*, the composer was asking 28,000 crowns – a huge sum, but Nilssen was confident he could find a buyer among the shipping magnates who had profited handsomely from Norwegian neutrality during the war.[7] While in Kristiania, the Deliuses got together with Edvard Munch, probably at their hotel. Years later the artist would recall: 'I think the last time [I met Delius] in Norway was at Holmenkollen – where he stayed with his Jelka – I drew then the lithograph that was later shown at my exhibition in London. His disease had by then begun to take its toll on him.'[8] With his superb lithograph of the composer (see Illustration 23), Munch captured the duality of his appearance – the clean, but drawn features of the nose, cheekbones and chin offsetting the soft eyes that are fixed in reverie on some internal horizon.

Directly from Norway, Frederick and Jelka proceeded to Frankfurt for a prolonged stay during the preparations for the first production of *Fennimore and Gerda*, the première brought off on 21 October with marked success. Four

---

[6] Letter from Jelka to Marie Clews, 18 August 1919 (DT).

[7] A year later the painting was still unsold. It was finally sold to the Manchester shipping merchant Herbert Coleman in 1922. In 1927, it was purchased by art collector Samuel Courtauld as the jewel in his Gauguin collection. See Martin Bailey, 'Gaugin's *Nevermore* Was Offered to Swiss Collector', published online in *The Art Newspaper*, 22 June 2013.

[8] Memoir note by Munch (MM N 218) (MM). Munch, making notes from his life, was writing at least ten years after this meeting. Earlier biographers of Delius have written that the two friends also met in Kristiania in 1922 (see p. 292) – a meeting that must be discounted if Munch's memory serves him well. Voksenkollen and Holmenkollen are parts of the same hill. The London exhibition took place at the Royal Society in 1928.

23. Edvard Munch, *Frederick Delius* (1920). The artist had sittings with Delius during his stay in Kristiania in 1919, and made this lithograph the following year.

days later, Delius was back in his music room at Grez for the first time for a year. With concerts and opera productions ramping up, however, there seems to have been little opportunity for him to resume the peaceful routine from which he had profited during the war. In February and March 1920, he made prolonged visits to London, finally hearing a magnificent first performance of *The Song of the High Hills*, eight years after its composition, and a production by Beecham of *A Village Romeo and Juliet* at Covent Garden. Momentous though such occasions were in Delius's career, they inevitably placed severe strain on his fragile nervous system, and signs of a developing paralysis in his arms and legs became evident. One planned holiday in Brittany was cancelled, another in the Basque country was cut short by bad weather. The fine autumn in Grez brought Delius some comfort, but when he sent a letter to Edvard Munch, urging him to come down from Paris for a few days, it was written in Jelka's hand.

The same taxing level of activity continued into the winter of 1920–21, spent in Frankfurt, and the spring of 1921, when they took a flat in London. Here the composer worked on his Cello Concerto and a commission to supply incidental music to *Hassan*, a verse drama by James Elroy Flecker. Using all their influence with British authorities, the Deliuses were delighted when some of the funds that had been held back since early in the war began to be released. It meant that on 17 June 1921 they could again leave England for Kristiania and a Norwegian summer.

Throughout the war years, the Deliuses exchanged New Year greetings with Nina Grieg. The final item in their correspondence is from New Year 1920, with Nina hoping that they soon would meet again, perhaps in Grez, but no evidence of any further meetings has come to light. She would outlive both Frederick and Jelka, dying in December 1935 at the age of ninety.

In the early 1920s, the wanderings of Delius's Norwegian kindred spirit, Halfdan Jebe, were finally coming to an end, at least for a period. For ten years or more he had lived a life playing in theatre orchestras and giving recitals and then, once he had some money to live on, leaving on new travels around the Americas. One such adventure brought him in 1920 to countries of Central America and, while there, he got in touch with Delius to request assistance in buying a violin. More details followed later in the year, as Jelka related to Adey Brunel:

> He wrote to Fred from Panama in November and told about his assault and subsequent illness and that he wanted to work his way to N. York as a stoker. He really did, and then wrote again from N. Y. that he was now perfectly well and that the heat of the engine quite cured his lungs and rheumatic pains and he had bought a violin and was now going to work southward again playing in Hotels etc.[9]

In 1922, Jebe renewed his fascination with the cultures of Central America, drawn to Mexico – he would later recall – both by the desire to visit the ruins of ancient civilisations and to witness the sweeping social reforms that were being implemented in the wake of the recent revolution.[10] Around January 1923, he extended his travels out to the region where the Mayan population was most strongly represented, the Yucután Peninsula. Here in the capital city, Mérida, he settled down, living for the first two years in an abandoned chapel. He became acquainted with the state governor, the champion of the indigenous Mayan people Felipe Carrillo Puerto. It was probably Carrillo Puerto himself who persuaded Jebe to devote himself to the same cause, offering him a position as professor of composition, violin and piano in a new regional conservatory. Far from the pretensions of European cultural life that he so despised, Halfdan Jebe had finally found a meaningful purpose. When the

---

[9] Letter from Jelka to Adey Brunel, 19 January 1921 (CB).
[10] The fascinating story of Jebe in Yucután was the part-subject of Ricardo Pérez Montfort's article 'Three Norwegian Experiences in Post-Revolutionary Mexico: Per Imerslund, Halfdan Jebe and Ola Apenes' in Steinar A. Sæther (ed.), *Expectations Unfulfilled: Norwegian migrants in Latin America, 1820–1940* (Leiden: Brill, 2015), 198–217.

military uprising of 1923 targeted the socialist oasis that Carrillo Puerto was creating, Jebe too was twice imprisoned. In 1924, on the execution of Carrillo Puerto, Jebe composed his Symphony in A minor, subtitled *The Path of Destiny Towards the Ideal*, dedicating it to his friend's memory. And in the ensuing years he devoted himself to developing the musical life of Mérida: he was a founding member of the regional symphony orchestra, he led chamber ensembles, he was more prolific as a composer than ever before and, in due course, Jebe would also become a naturalised Mexican.

'Yet he could not cut himself off from his heritage', writes John Bergsagel, 'works such as *Lad vaaren komme* (*Let Spring Come*) and *Norvegia* reveal continuing ties with Norway'.[11] These ties would indeed draw him back one last time to Europe and – as we shall see – to the door of his old friend in Grez-sur-Loing.

Frederick and Jelka checked in to Mølmen Hotel in Lesjaskog around 21 July 1921 and, in a postcard to Henry and Marie Clews, described their lodgings as 'the nicest little place we've ever been in – quite patriarchal – the family running the Place'.

> We are up here in the high mountains in the most heavenly sunshine and fresh snow-mountain air. After London's strenuous season this is perfectly delicious. [...] Fred is doing a little trout fishing and we wander about in the lovely birch and pinewoods gathering lilies of the valley. It is only spring here, and the snow melting making the little brooks all rush down the hillsides. It is so light we read in bed at 11 p.m.[12]

The choice of Mølmen Hotel as a base for the summer of 1921 reflects the fact that Delius was making allowances for his state of health. He was now having to walk with the aid of a cane, so it was prudent that, instead of travelling between mountain lodges or staying at a remote sanatorium, the couple selected a hotel that doubled as a post house, and therefore was on a main road. Lesjaskog lies roughly halfway along the important artery joining the western coast, at the town of Åndalsnes, to the main inland trunk road running north–south, at Dombås – the crossroads at the mountain heart of central Norway. Lesjaskog also straddles the watershed between west and east. Today a bypass has ensured that the village lies sleepily off the highway; Mølmen Hotel received its last guests in 1985 and was demolished in 2013. In Delius's day, the hotel was a favourite haunt of English anglers, due to its proximity to the Rauma river and Lesjaskogvatnet. Nevertheless, the hotel's guestbooks make it clear that

---

[11] John Bergsagel, 'Halfdan Jebe', Grove Music Online, accessed 26 January 2016 at www.oxford-musiconline.com.

[12] Postcard from the Deliuses to the Clewses, 4 July 1921 (DT). In a subsequent letter, Jelka wrote: 'He dreams and does nothing and I shall send you a photo I made of him fishing – a poet fishing, not an excited sports-fisherman. Also he catches no fish.'

the problem of overcrowding common along the most popular tourist routes was never an issue here.

'I have been so lazy enjoying the wonderful scenery & air up here', Delius wrote to Philip Heseltine, revealing, however, that his creative imagination was not dormant: 'We intend building a little house up on the mountain for next summer as we expect our money shortly.'[13] The Deliuses' pre-war dream of owning a cottage in the Norwegian mountains was revived during their stay in Lesjaskog in 1921. If Delius's struggle to regain health could be bolstered by visits to the country, then this place offered them the climate, geography and ease of transport that were optimal for their needs.

Climate: Although the summer is short, it is typified by a dry inland climate with invigorating chill breezes blowing off the surrounding snow-topped mountains.

Geography: At Lesjaskog, the North Gudbrandsdal is wide, making for light, open vistas east towards the waters of Lesjaskogvatnet. The village is surrounded by gently rising hills, not steep mountain cliffs. The whole valley environment was one of tranquillity.

Transport: When Frederick and Jelka arrived in Lesjaskog in 1921, construction was far advanced for a branch line of the railway network from Dombås to Åndalsnes. Indeed, in November that same year the first train would stop at the new Lesjaskog station. The ease and comfort of communication from Kristiania to Lesjaskog, some 400 kilometres, was one thing, but for a composer needing to freight a hired piano back and forward it would be a godsend.

On the north side of the valley, beyond the white frame of the small Lesjaskog Church, the incline of Liahovdane rises to 1,296 metres above sea level.[14] Øverli Farm lies a third of the way up the hillside. In 1921 the estate was run by Mathias Øverli, and he was approached by Delius with a proposition to purchase a small plot of land. According to a brief memoir by Ola O. Mølmen, Delius's health problems were not immediately evident, 'except that his walk seemed rather unsteady. He used a cane and wore glasses with very thick lenses, and often took walks. He must have gone on foot up to Øverli many times before he decided on a lot for the cottage.'[15] By the time Frederick and Jelka left Lesjaskog for Kristiania on 20 August, a sum of 500 crowns had been agreed upon for one *mål* of land on the hillside – 1,000 square metres, about a

---

[13] Letter from Delius to Philip Heseltine, 6 August 1921 (DT).

[14] Liahovdane (literally, The Tops of the Slope) is today the official name of the hill. Alternative versions that are widely used locally are Liahovda and Liahovdan.

[15] Ola O. Mølmen, *Recollections of Composer Frederick Delius and Narrative of His Stay in Norway in the Years 1921–24*, trans. Kristin Feyling, copy now in Delius Trust archive. Mølmen, the eldest child of the hotel owner, was ten years old in 1921. He wrote down these memories of the Delius visits to Lesjaskog in 1968.

quarter of an acre.[16] Frederick and Jelka had spent their evenings making plan drawings of the cottage, such as they envisaged it, and left these with Øverli for the local builders who would be engaged.

It had been mooted since before the outbreak of war, and finally at the end of October 1921 it was realised: the attendance of the composer at a performance of his music in his Yorkshire birthplace, Bradford. 'I saw a lot of old friends & it was quite fun', he reported back to Jelka.[17] This letter, however, was the last one his enfeebled hands were ever to write to his wife. From now on, his condition was too precarious for him to travel on his own.

1922: The search for health

In January 1922, Delius, now sixty years old, experienced a new health setback. The general weakness in his limbs worsened in the course of a few weeks, so Frederick and Jelka left home in search of a cure, travelling first to the spa town of Wiesbaden in central Germany. Physicians there prescribed a period of complete rest for him, and even forbade him to walk. While recuperating, he had a chance meeting with one of his closest friends, Edvard Munch, who later noted:

> I was strolling along the main thoroughfare when I heard a voice that seemed to come from below
> Good day, Munch – with that light, always cheerful voice –
> It was Delius – He sat in a wheelchair that was being pushed by an orderly
> His legs were lame
> He would sit every day in the Wiesbaden park and listen to the music [18]

Edvard Munch was passing through on his way to Frankfurt, but stayed long enough to make two sketches of the composer as he sat in his wheelchair in the park, listening intently to a concert on the bandstand. From these he would create the lithograph *Delius i Wiesbaden*. The meeting with Munch took place in early April, at a time when Delius was beginning to feel the benefit of his treatment. Further improvements were marked when the Deliuses moved on in mid-May to take the spa waters of Wildbad in the Black Forest. However, all of these worrying journeys, involving treatments and ever-increasing expenses, placed a heavy burden of care on the shoulders of Jelka: 'With Fred an invalid it is impossible for me to do anything but take care of him and life is so expensive. [...] He is better upon the whole and can now walk 10 minutes on my arm, sitting down 3 or 4 times in between, he can not dress himself nor

---

[16] Øverli Farm consisted of some 20 acres of cultivated land, 25 acres of forest and 70 acres of brush land. The farm had been in the family's possession since 1750.
[17] Letter from Delius to Jelka, 28 October 1921 (DT).
[18] Memoir note by Munch (MM N 218) (MM).

do anything really without help – '[19] A little relief was on its way. On 24 June, they arrived in Hamburg to take the ferry to Kristiania, meeting up at the ferry terminal with the young Tyrolean cook and maidservant they had employed before the war. Senta Mössmer would prove an invaluable helper for the next two years.

In the last days of June 1922, Frederick, Jelka and Senta arrived at Lesjaskog, staying again at Mølmen Hotel for the first week while final preparations were made for them to move into their cottage. 'We are quite delighted with our little hut up here – it was a tremendous moment, when we saw it standing quite finished on the hillside.' However, a secluded life brought with it many challenges:

> Tomorrow the pianino we hired in Kristiania has to be pulled up the steep hill-side by 2 horses – it will be an awful affair and they are first going to take up a big trunk and the Kitchen stove as a sort of rehearsal. There is a lovely big Verandah in front of our hut and the view all around is perfectly exquisite and ever changing – and the absolute stillness up there. But there are English Fisher-men coming to the hôtel and they will come up and see us and bring trout, I hope!! Senta is sewing all the towel dusters and sheets, making herself a sack of straw to sleep on; carrying up things etc, and planning all the good things she will cook for Fred. The piano is spending the Sunday standing in its case outside the railway station in the landscape in the pouring rain with a canvass over it and an admiring crowd around!![20]

Their degree of seclusion was, of course, relative. The cottage was surrounded by the grounds of Øverli Farm, separated from the farmhouse by a narrow neck of field, and, in the manner of friendly neighbours, the Øverli family included Frederick and Jelka in the daily life of the farm. Mathias was himself a competent performer of folk melodies on the violin, and would come to the cottage and entertain the Deliuses.[21] His wife Petra would bring plates of her homebaked breads and cakes to the cottage and the three young Øverli sons – Sigurd, Peder and Olav – would run errands for the Deliuses down to the village shop. The children would also have been fascinated to hear Delius at the piano and see Jelka painting at her easel in the fields and farmyards.[22]

From the first legal documents regarding the sale of the plot and cottage, it is clear that the Deliuses had chosen for their property the name Høifager-li.[23] It stood at 755 metres above sea level. From the hills above Høifagerli the

---

[19] Letter from Jelka to Norman and Adine O'Neill, 15 June 1922 (DT).

[20] Letter from Jelka to Adine O'Neill, 2 July 1922 (DT).

[21] Several of the tunes for which he was known have been preserved in folk music collections.

[22] See Gudrun Haraldsen Faukstad, 'Frederick Delius: Et verdensnavn på Lesjaskog' ('Frederick Delius: A world-famous name in Lesjaskog') in Årbok 2011 (Yearbook 2011) (Otta: Lesja histo-rielag, 2011), 110.

[23] The name has three components: høi means high, fager means beautiful and a li is a hillside. In local dialect the first adjective høi has a concluding g: høg. Øverli means simply Upper

Mølmså stream rushed down to the valley, passing just a few yards to the east of the cottage. The large front and side windows of the small house afforded spectacular views south across the valley to the slopes of what today is Reinheimen National Park, east to the waters of Lesjaskogvatnet, south-west to the Tafjord mountains and west to the snow-topped peaks crowding in on the rugged Romsdal. Immediately to the north, directly up behind Høifagerli, were the foothills to mountains that today are part of the Dovrefjell National Park. The Delius cottage was about a third of the way up the slope of Liahovdane and the path to the summit, frequently trodden by the tourists who stayed at Mølmen Hotel, went through the Øverli estate. In his memoir, Ola O. Mølmen recalls that Jelka was fond of gathering wild plants, berries and mushrooms, her enthusiasm carrying her unheedingly into cultivated fields, much to the annoyance of Mathias Øverli.

Frederick and Jelka were greatly encouraged by the effect on his health: 'I am walking about with 2 Sticks now out of doors and with one stick in the rooms, which is a great improvement and I hope my legs and arms will continue to get stronger gradually.'[24] When the weather turned cold and damp, however, the couple were housebound and the burden of care on Jelka was doubled. She wrote to Philip Heseltine that

> all these months I have been busy *only* for Fred, to read to him, to help correcting, correspondence, in fact to keep him from depression etc. in this lonely place! I am grieved that I had quite given up my piano playing. I have now to stumble to it again with the greatest difficulty and out of sheer devotion so as to help him, as he has such difficulty about using his hands.[25]

In an effort to prolong the creative life of her husband, Jelka was taking down small compositions by dictation. The arrival in early September of composer Balfour Gardiner, one of Delius's closest friends from England, would have helped to lift their spirits somewhat.

None of the legal process concerning the conveyance of the land and cottage to Delius had been carried out before his arrival there in 1922. In fact, Mathias Øverli had taken out a land loan in March, no doubt to cover the expenses of surveying and preparing the plot and building the house.[26] On 19 August, Delius and Øverli registered their survey of the plot with the Land Register, and on 30 August the Deed of Conveyance was itself registered. Delius had become a man of property in Norway.

Hillside.

[24] Letter from Delius to Norman O'Neill, 20 August 1922 (DT).

[25] Letter from Jelka Delius to Philip Heseltine, 2 September 1922 (BL).

[26] Delius paid 500 crowns for the land, but it is unknown what he paid for the finished house. When he sold it on in 1924, the sum agreed was 7,500 crowns.

Both on their way up to Lesjaskog and down again, the Deliuses had sent word
to Edvard Munch of when they would be in Kristiania, but it seems unlikely
that any meeting was possible. The painter arrived back in Norway a little
too late to meet them at the end of June; in early September he was at home,
but struggling with a serious bout of bronchitis. Another intimate friend had
just arrived in the city, however, and his reunion with the Deliuses would be
marked by deep emotion. In April, the mother of Percy Grainger, with whom
he had always had a very tight bond, had killed herself by jumping from the
window of a New York office building. Grainger was now about to embark on
a piano concert tour, his billed performance in Kristiania on 8 September the
first recital since the tragedy. Frederick and Jelka were no doubt in attendance that night, before embarking on the ferry to Hamburg the next day. Just
how crucial the Deliuses' solicitude would be for Grainger became clear in
the course of 1923, when his attachment to them was reflected in a selfless and
touching devotion.

1923: 'Percy in front, Senta and I at the back, all strapped in like horses'

With Delius's health so frail, the couple elected to spend the winter in the comfort of Frankfurt, where there were to be two Delius concerts during their stay.
For much of their four months in the city, Percy Grainger was also nearby.
No doubt concerned about the welfare of their friend, Jelka had suggested
that Grainger come to Frankfurt and prepare the choir for a Delius choral
and orchestral concert in March. Delius had once written to Grainger: 'As I
have so often told my wife & others, I feel that you are the only real individual,
with an original & daring line of thought & conduct, who I have ever met – &
the only musician of genius – bar Grieg – who I ever came in contact with'.[27]
Their friendship with Edvard Grieg and common admiration for his music
was crucial for the two men. As Delius grew older he seems to have become
ever more willing to put on record the admiration he felt for his old Norwegian
mentor.[28] In Frankfurt, he encouraged Grainger to come and play to him as
often as he could, Grieg's music in particular. Delius had also at this time the
deepest concerns regarding his own music, not least the need to tidy up loose
ends if blindness and paralysis were to bring his career, perhaps also his life,
to a premature close. 'I often think of your birthday in 1923', recalled Grainger
some years later, 'when we went out on the "Promenade" in Frankfurt with
your chair and when you talked to me about your sketches and unfinished

---

[27] Letter from Delius to Percy Grainger, 23 June 1917 (GM).
[28] In a talk about her visits to Delius in Grez, the violinist May Harrison recalled: 'Norway was
undoubtedly Delius's spiritual home, and he told me that Grieg was the greatest and most
loved friend he ever had'. Printed as 'The Music of Delius' in *Journal of the Delius Society*,
No. 87 (Autumn 1985), 35.

works'.[29] It is likely that Delius, even at this stage, was probing the possibilities of finding a musician of suitable gifts who might take on the task of amanuensis. That would eventually be the destiny of a different man, with a personality dissimilar to that of the restless Australian.

From early April to late June, the Deliuses decamped to the spa town of Bad Oeynhausen, where they were greatly encouraged by the beneficial effect the waters had on his condition. From there they travelled directly to Norway and by the end of June were back in their own Høifagerli cottage, high above Lesjaskog village.

Two weeks of splendid summer weather greeted them, the good relationship with the Øverli family continued and in mid-July Delius could declare himself to be 'extremely happy'.[30] Ominous clouds were, however, gathering on the horizon. Now far less mobile than he had been when they chose the plot in 1921, Delius needed flat ground to persevere with walking sticks and was frustrated by the steep slope and rocky paths around the cottage. The fine weather broke, turning 'chilly, cloudy, rainy and changeable and most trying', reported Jelka.[31] Most challenging of all, the Flecker play *Hassan*, for which Delius had written incidental music, was billed to open in London in September, and the theatre director now found that he needed more music. For a composer having to dictate every note to his wife, this was slow and exhausting work. Happily, the ideal assistant arrived at Høifagerli on the evening of 21 July. In the pocket diary he kept during his stay, Percy Grainger recorded just one phrase for the days Tuesday 24 July to Friday 27 July: 'Scoring "Hassan" Dance'.[32] This was a new movement he not only scored, but in fact composed for the incidental music.

The activities of the next day, Saturday 28 July, were recorded in greater detail by Grainger. The diary entry is a matter-of-fact listing of times and participants – the barest skeleton of what would come to be regarded as a momentous event in the relationship of Frederick Delius to his spiritual homeland. Here Grainger simply recorded that he, together with Jelka and Senta, had carried Delius to the top of the mountain behind Høifagerli 'on chair bound to poles'. They had left Høifagerli at 1.30 and arrived at the summit at 6.20. After only twenty-five minutes they had started back down again, and arrived back at the cottage at 9.15. A mythology has accumulated around this extraordinary day. In biographies of Delius it is stated that the ascent alone took over seven hours. We can see from Grainger's timings that this is incorrect, the whole journey taking seven hours and forty-five minutes. It has also been widely accepted by his biographers that the purpose of the adventure was

---

[29] Letter from Percy Grainger to Delius, 29 January 1932 (GM).
[30] Letter from Delius to Universal Edition, 16 July 1923 (UE).
[31] Letter from Jelka to Marie Clews, 4 August 1923 (DT).
[32] The diary is today kept in the archive of the Grainger Museum.

24. Looking west from the summit of Liahovdane, Delius would have seen the peaks of the Tafjord mountains.

to let Delius see for the final time a sunset over the mountains he loved. This too is incorrect. Seen from Liahovdane, the sun on this day dips behind the western mountains of Reinheimen around 10.30. By this time the party was back in the cottage.

By any definition this is a remarkable and singular feat, and has no need of the embroidery of added mythologies. Not least among the many astonishing facts surrounding it is what it reveals of the love which Frederick Delius inspired in those who were closest to him. Throughout his career he had been a singer of songs of these high hills, and now he felt the need to see them one last time. Jelka and Percy Grainger were so devoted to him that they do not seem to have questioned either the practicality or wisdom of the endeavour and, with the aid of Senta, found a way to transport Delius to the summit of Liahovdane. The ascent was a modest climb for any unencumbered hiker. For a group carrying a man in a low-slung chair the accomplishment seems barely credible, particularly in the first half of the ascent, where the mountain path rises steeply through brush and woodland. At least two stretches of the climb are so steep it is difficult to imagine the party being able to proceed, unless Delius was physically carried by Grainger. It is from a letter Jelka wrote a few days later that we have more details of this endeavour:

> Fred was *longing* to go up the mountain side and up a high mountain back of our hut, because there is a heavenly view on the High Snow-mountains and a great solitude with no human trace up there. So Percy arranged a chair and two poles thro it and straps and ropes for us all three, Percy in front, Senta and I at the

back, all strapped in like horses and so we carried Fred up to the top and down again. With wraps and overcoat, our lunch etc. to carry it was an awfully heavy job. But we could not get any Norwegians to do it.[33] It took us 7 ½ hours, as we had to rest so often and we had to go over stones and rocks, up the steep mountain, thro' snowfields, rainclouds, bogs, becks – a tremendous job. I cannot boast for myself as Percy and Senta had the heaviest carrying; but being quite out of training I found it all I could do. But we came home in triumph at 9 p.m. having been watched from below with telescopes and marvelled at by the inhabitants, Fred very cold and tired, but all the better for the beloved mountain-air and sight and we all rather stiff but alright next day.[34]

Although Jelka refers only to the 'sight', this might be taken to support later accounts of the rainclouds parting to reward the party with a brief view of the panorama. From the summit of Liahovdane all the distant peaks of Reinheimen and Romsdalen are visible to the south and west, and in the north the barren *vidde* – the mountain plateau – leads off to the escarpments of the Dovrefjell peaks.

The chair on which Delius was carried – a simple wooden stool with a curving backrest – has been preserved as a family treasure by succeeding generations of the Øverli family (see Illustration 25).

Would Frederick Delius have been aware that this would be his final ascent in the Norwegian highlands? And this visit to Norway his last? All evidence points in that direction. The depression into which he soon would fall, even on the ferry on his way home from Norway, and the rapid sale of Høifagerli the following year, coupled with all the details of his deteriorating health in Jelka's letters, suggest that the twenty-five minutes Delius spent at the summit of Liahovdane would have been marked with the poignancy of a farewell. For over forty years of his life he had returned to Norway to restore his self-confidence in his creative powers. Before the turn of the century he had sought the double effect of fjord and fell, but as he grew older nothing would do other than the wide expanses of the mountain *vidde*: the great solitude. The summer of 1923 in Lesjaskog was his twentieth and last visit to Norway.

---

[33] Although the accounts of Jelka and Grainger are in unison regarding who carried Delius, a slightly different version has persisted in the local community to this day. According to this, a young, well-educated teacher from Lesjaverk, Ola Nordsletten, was in attendance during the Liahovdane climb. The first printed account of the ascent came in Eric Fenby's *Delius as I Knew Him* (1936), and in this narrative – which does contain factual errors – Grainger and Jelka took the front and there were 'two servants at the back'. In the Mølmen memoir from 1968, Nordsletten is specifically mentioned as helping to carry Delius up Liahovdane. Questioned in 1976 by Lionel Carley, Mølmen said that it was a detail of which he was unsure, that his memory may have been at fault. In summary: it seems unlikely that Nordsletten was part of the group, but if he was, it might have been in the capacity of porter for clothing and refreshments.

[34] Letter from Jelka to Marie Clews, 4 August 1923 (DT).

25. Percy Grainger adapted this simple rustic chair to be carried on two poles. He took the front, Jelka Delius and Senta Mössmer the rear.

Percy Grainger left Lesjaskog soon after his Liahovdane exploits and a week later, around 14 August, Frederick and Jelka also left Høifagerli. The weather had compelled them to abandon their cottage a month earlier than planned. From their ferry to Antwerp, Jelka wrote to Grainger: 'Øverli and Senta carried Fred down, Øverli could hardly manage to do it, and Senta had to take the front and he the lighter back!!! So without your glorious energy and devotion Fred would never have been taken to the top.'[35]

The Deliuses did not, however, leave Kristiania without visiting Marie Beyer, the widow of Frants Beyer, who had died in 1918. For a few hours, happy memories were revived of Delius's visits to Troldhaugen in 1889 and 1891 as the guest and intimate friend of Edvard Grieg. They sailed from Kristiania for the last time. An era was passing not only for Delius, but also for the city. In 1897, the composer had been embroiled in the country's fierce fight for

[35] Letter from Jelka to Percy Grainger, 17 August 1923 (GM).

independence from the political and cultural domination of its neighbours. In a final gesture, the city of Kristiania was casting off the last remnants of its Danish heritage, and from 1 January 1925 would be known by its ancient name: Oslo.

Høifagerli had all too briefly afforded the Deliuses the mountain retreat for which they had longed. The sale of the property would also bring with it unpleasant surprises and complications. In the spring of 1924, it seems that Delius engaged as his intermediary a lawyer who is only referred to in sources as Mr Dybwad. In all likelihood he had made use of ties of friendship with Vilhelm Dybwad, head of a leading law practice in Kristiania and a highly popular author of cabaret songs.[36] Dybwad found a buyer for the property, a salesman called O. Chr. Onsrud, and at the end of July he and Delius exchanged signed contracts for the sale. In August, the Deed of Conveyance was registered with the Lesja Municipality and Onsrud agreed to pay 7,500 crowns. This was money that was sorely needed by the Deliuses as they embarked on new rounds of sanatorium treatments, with the value of German royalties plummeting during a period of hyper-inflation in the Weimar Republic. Unfortunately, the money did not arrive. A despairing Jelka wrote to Mathias Øverli in November 1924:

> I hear from Dybwad that considerable difficulties have arisen with regards to the deeds and that Onsrud is therefore in his right not to pay us for the house. Would you be so kind, dear Øverli, to explain this to me, what is the problem? We completed all our deed formalities and you have never mentioned that there was a mortgage and that you were not legally permitted to sell it. For us it is just painful, for we have not received payment and Onsrud has lived there all summer without paying.[37]

It seems that Vilhelm Dybwad made several trips to Lesjaskog on Delius's behalf during 1925, to meet with Øverli and to go through the records.[38] He would have discovered that Mathias Øverli had indeed acquired the farm from his father in 1898 – not by inheritance, but by a symbolic document of sale. Unfortunately, the contract was never registered officially, most likely because Mathias had two older brothers with prior claims to the farm, who had emigrated to America. Without their acquiescence to the right of Mathias to assume ownership of the farm, his purchase was not binding. It was probably Dybwad who suggested a solution: that Øverli default on taxes accruing on

---

[36] When Delius met Norwegian cabaret singer Bokken Lasson in London in 1908, Dybwad was courting her (see p. 216). The couple married in 1916.

[37] Letter from Jelka to Mathias Øverli, 11 November 1924 (ØV).

[38] Dybwad's trips are mentioned in Mølmen's memoir, but he remembers them as having been made in connection with the building of Høifagerli in 1922. This seems improbable, the construction of a small house by a farmer on his own property unlikely to require the oversight of a high-flying Kristiania lawyer.

the farm, instigating thereby a compulsory sale of the property. At the official auction in March 1926, Mathias was the only bidder for Øverli Farm and was entered into the Land Register in June as its rightful owner. Whether or not the result of this was that Onsrud was compelled to pay Delius what was due on Høifagerli is unknown.

In 1932, Onsrud had the name of the house officially changed from Høif-agerli to Utsikten (The View), and the property remained in his possession until he died in 1939. It was then sold to railway engineer H. F. Haraldsen and his wife Ragnhild for 2,500 crowns, and has remained in their family ever since. His daughter, Gudrun, has written of the cottage's fate:

> [My parents] used the cottage both during the summer and Easter holidays, but gradually realised that it was difficult to keep warm in winter months. In 1959, therefore, it was demolished and replaced with a smaller, insulated cottage a few metres higher up. The new house could not accommodate all the furniture, so some of it was given away. Our neighbours on Øverli Farm received Delius's large rocking chair and the chair in which he was carried up Liahovda.[39]

Music has remained part of the fabric of the cottage. Gudrun Haraldsen Fauk-stad holds a university degree in musicology and is a skilled pianist. She mar-ried Jon Faukstad, who held a professorship of classical accordion and folk music at the Norwegian Academy of Music.

1924: Health failure

Never doubting that the right balance of sunshine, rest and a healthy diet could halt the deterioration of Delius's condition, the couple travelled to the warmth of the Mediterranean for the winter of 1923–24. They stayed for a couple of months at the Ligurian coastal town of Rapallo, then travelled west to stay for over a month at La Napoule, near Cannes, where their friends Henry and Marie Clews were renovating a fortified château. They travelled in some com-fort, having invested in a chauffeur-driven car from the royalties of *Hassan*, which had been a huge success in London. While at Rapallo, Delius was examined thoroughly by a German specialist who insisted that the composer should be brought to his sanatorium for further treatment. In mid-May 1924, therefore, Frederick and Jelka arrived full of optimism in Cassel. Their faith in the treatment, which involved the use of electricity to reinvigorate inactive glands, seemed to be well placed, for it was a much improved Delius who was sent home to Grez in August with the doctor's assurance that 'Fred will con-tinue to improve there, and, in fact, forget that he has been ill'.[40] Instead, his eyesight continued to deteriorate throughout the autumn and in November

---

[39] See Haraldsen Faukstad, *Frederick Delius*, 110.
[40] Letter from Jelka to Sydney Schiff, 2 August 1924 (BL).

Frederick and Jelka were compelled to seek further succour in 'the general atmosphere of hope and good cheer'[41] at the Cassel sanatorium. None of this good cheer carried over into the first months of 1925, spent in a depressing round of consultations with eye specialists. While the sanatorium team had been able to effect some passing improvement on the patient's limbs, there was nothing it could do with his failing eyesight. Jelka, tireless and selfless in her efforts to lift her husband's spirits, took him out of the sanatorium for a few days in March to experience a thrilling performance of *A Mass of Life* in Wiesbaden, the performers and audience pouring their adulation onto the wheelchair-bound composer. Disillusioned with their doctors, the Deliuses cut their losses in Cassel and returned home.

In the summer of 1925 the last phase of the composer's life began, he and his devoted wife confined to their house and garden in Grez. Jelka summed up their situation in a letter to Marie Clews:

> *He can not see at all.* [...] He therefore cannot walk at all. We have a man[42] who carries him up and down, and he lies most of the day in the garden on his chaiselongue. That lovely garden all full of flowers and he cannot see it! His mind is as lucid and as active as ever and of course to keep him from depression I read to him a tremendous lot.[43]

Delius had been diagnosed in December 1910 as suffering from the prolonged effects of syphilis. Conclusive though those findings were, he had been reluctant even at the time to accept them. Having since enjoyed long periods of good health, including vigorous mountain holidays in Norway in 1913, 1915 and 1919, he had in his own mind distanced himself wholly from the syphilis diagnosis and was unwilling to countenance it. As his health collapsed during the 1920s, he and Jelka offered – or were offered by physicians working in branches of alternative medicine – an astonishing gamut of explanations. During the war, Delius was congratulated by one 'expert' on having an excellent constitution and informed that the tiredness in his legs was caused by varicose veins.[44] Later, Delius would express his opinion that 'the whole trouble has been nervous, caused by the tremendous strain & anxiety of the War'.[45] Jelka expressed disgust with 'the stupidity of almost all doctors. They mostly put Fred's illness down to a disease of the spine and I do not believe it is that at all.'[46] Their specialist at Cassel diagnosed the condition as multiple sclerosis,

---

[41] Letter from Jelka to Sydney Schiff, 25 November 1924 (BL).
[42] 'We have the good religious "Bruder" as nurse and he fits exceedingly well into the place', Jelka wrote in a letter to their friends Sydney and Violet Schiff. From 1925 and until the end of Delius's life, a series of male nurses – lay brothers hired out by a German charitable organisation – were employed.
[43] Letter from Jelka to Marie Clews, 31 August 1925 (DT).
[44] Letter from Delius to Jelka, undated, probably 25 July 1917 (GM).
[45] Letter from Delius to Philip Heseltine, 18 September 1924 (BL).
[46] Letter from Jelka to Adine O'Neill, undated, spring 1923 (DT).

resulting from a malignant influenza. As the patient's eyesight began to cloud, however, Jelka looked in desperation for a further explanation: 'Can he have eaten poisoned meat?'[47]

It could, of course, be regarded merely as a reflex of our wisdom after the event, that we wonder at the Deliuses' refusal to accept that syphilis was at the root of his condition, and to apply the new effective treatments medical science had developed. There were, however, also those close to the composer at the time who despaired of his blind faith in homeopathy and his intransigence with regard to conventional medicine. Thomas Beecham went so far as to have a specialist brought over from London who prescribed for Delius a course of treatment: 'But once again the blind belief in homeopathy prevailed and nothing came of it.'[48]

1924–1933: 'our calm and almost posthumous existence'

After the terrible years of stressful journeys between sanatoriums and the exhausting search for some glimmer of hope, Delius's acceptance of his fate brought with it unexpected peace and quiet to the garden and house at Grez. If it was characteristic of this advocate of the Nietzschean spirit that he should refuse to bemoan his plight, it was equally untypical that, as long as his mind was active and sharp, he should resign himself to the fact that creative activity was impossible. In his music room were advanced sketches for unborn works, their growth suddenly arrested, but their image in his imagination still animate and vivid. In his better periods, attempts were made at dictation to Jelka. Now and then there would be a welcome break in the daily routine – 'our calm and almost posthumous existence', as Jelka called it[49] – when one of the many friends of Delius came to Grez, often specifically to play music for him, including Percy Grainger, Balfour Gardiner, Norman O'Neill and the Harrison sisters. After the visit of the young Nadia Boulanger and friends, Jelka noted that 'the great calm of the garden with its touching central figure made a great impression on them.'[50]

The house was wired for electricity in 1926, making possible the introduction of other 'visitors' into the couple's seclusion – the concerts that were a staple of radio broadcasts, many with Delius compositions on the programme. It was one such BBC broadcast of *On Hearing the First Cuckoo in Spring* that would play a part in bringing the most significant guest to Grez. Early in 1928, Eric Fenby, a 22-year-old Yorkshire musician, had been spending an evening playing chess with a friend, and giving him little competition. 'My friend as

---

[47] Letter from Jelka to Percy Grainger, 28 March 1925 (GM).
[48] Beecham, *A Mingled Chime*, 314–15.
[49] Letter from Jelka to Marie Clews, 22 January 1928 (DT).
[50] Letter from Jelka to Marie Clews, 10 August 1927 (DT).

a final gesture got up and turned on the radio. From the loudspeaker came music of exquisite invention, such as I'd never heard before.'[51] After studying the score of *A Mass of Life*, Fenby wrote to Delius to thank him for the pleasure his music gave him, and was gratified to receive immediately a warm and appreciative reply. To Fenby's enthusiastic mind, the plight of the composer was intolerable: '[The] real tragedy of it all, or so it seemed to me, was to hear that the composer was worried and unhappy because it was physically impossible for him to continue and finish his life's work.'[52] Finally, in August 1928, Fenby wrote to Delius and proposed that he come to Grez and devote himself to this task for three or four years. 'I am greatly touched by your kind and sympathetic letter', came the reply, 'and should love to accept your offer.'[53] So familiar now is the narrative of the young amanuensis and the irascible, disabled composer – thanks in most part to Fenby's own account of it in his 1936 memoir *Delius as I Knew Him* – that it has become all too easy to lose sight of just how extraordinary the two men's achievement was. Delius, defying obstacles that would have extinguished the last flicker of resistance in the spirit of lesser mortals, regenerated dormant compositions, applying himself with almost inhuman focus to the challenge. Fenby, for his part, owned in equal abundance the musical talent and personal humility to be able to attune himself perfectly to the creative wavelengths of the composer. Off and on for exactly four years this unparalleled partnership worked together, with the following scores among the more important they produced:

Unfinished works completed
Cynara
A Late Lark

Works that were substantially new
Songs of Farewell
Sonata No. 3 for violin and piano
Caprice and Elegy
Fantastic Dance

Revised works
A Song of Summer (revision of *Poem of Life and Love*)
Idyll (music extracted by Fenby from *Margot la Rouge*, words by Walt
  Whitman)

---

[51] Eric Fenby, 'Delius as I Knew Him', BBC radio talk, 5 June 1974, published in Stephen Lloyd (ed.), *Fenby on Delius: Collected writings on Delius to mark Eric Fenby's 90th birthday* (London: Thames Publishing, 1996), 91.
[52] Fenby, *Delius as I Knew Him*, 8–9.
[53] Letter from Delius to Eric Fenby, 29 August 1928 (DT).

Although the quality of these works varies greatly, the variation is not significantly greater than in the rest of the composer's output. When at their best, they are undoubtedly – to borrow Fenby's own words about *Songs of Farewell* – 'a monument of what can be done when, the body broken, there still remains in a man the will to create'.[54]

Finally unable to travel to Norway, we can assume that Delius's sense of loss was profound. Eric Fenby became quickly aware that Norway had been a second home to Delius and that 'when illness prevented him travelling there he kept in touch through Norwegian newspapers read aloud to him by his wife up to a month before his death'.[55] He also reflected on 'the flavour of Scandinavian thought which permeated the Delius household. There was so much talk of Norway, of Edvard Munch, Grieg, Sinding, Jacobsen and others'.[56]

One of the more positive moments of the early years of enforced confinement at Grez was the renewed contact in 1926 between the Deliuses and Edvard Munch. The painter, visiting Paris in October, sent a greeting to Grez, to which Jelka immediately responded, imploring Munch to come and visit them: 'Delius was so indescribably pleased to hear from you from Paris!'[57] On his return to Norway, Munch composed a letter to his friend, of which we have a draft: 'I am so delighted that I managed to get to see you and your wife again – And it especially delighted me to see that you have retained your lovely, cheerful voice – That you have your good optimistic humour which I so often envied you – '[58] In mid-November 1928 they were in correspondence again, Munch writing first a letter that has not survived, perhaps reminding Delius of his visits to Norway, for he replied: 'Sadly my Jotunheim days are past, which I miss very much'.[59] He also assured the painter that 'your room is always ready'.[60] To this letter, Jelka added her own lines. The painter in Jelka could not ignore the visual impact of the invalid artist any more than she could after the visit of Nadia Boulanger:

> I cannot look at him without thinking of *you* for I am always convinced that *nobody* could make a picture of him as *you* could. He is now so beautiful, so expressive, and especially when he listens to music he becomes so wonderfully engrossed, peaceful, quite extraordinary. You could paint or draw this so

---

[54] Fenby, *Delius as I Knew Him*, 101.

[55] Eric Fenby, sleeve note to HMV ASD 2804 (1972), reprinted in Lloyd, *Fenby on Delius*, 148.

[56] Eric Fenby, 'Some Changes of Mind', talk published in *Journal of The Delius Society*, No. 71 (April 1981), 7.

[57] Letter from Jelka to Munch, 19 November 1928 (MM).

[58] Letter draft from Munch to Delius (MM).

[59] Letter from Delius to Munch, 19 November 1928 (MM).

[60] Presumably the room to which Eric Fenby had been assigned. In *Delius as I Knew Him* he describes the room as being full of 'fantastic creations by Munch, dark with suicide' (p. 14). The composer possessed at the end of his life twelve prints by Munch, seven in this small bedroom and five of them lining the staircase.

wonderfully. [...] Here you have peace and quiet, a studio, and good red wine
and us two, your faithful friends. [...] But you have to paint the image of the sick
Delius. You would render it a masterpiece.[61]

Jelka's proposal did not fall on deaf ears. As Munch planned for the summer
of 1929, he wrote to one friend: 'I am thinking of visiting my blind and lame
friend, composer Frederick Delius, in Paris – I would also like to paint him'.[62]
In a drafted letter around the same time to Delius, it is clear that the painting
had begun to take shape in Munch's imagination: 'I am considering making a
short trip to Paris – but not until the summer [...] I would have painted you. It
would have been a very beautiful image.'[63] What might have turned into a late
masterpiece by the painter was not to materialise. The two friends were never
to meet again.

Delius had not seen Halfdan Jebe since the Norwegian had turned his back on
Europe in 1906. Any letter from him or even news of him was always a cause
for celebration, for he held a unique place in Delius's heart. News may well
have reached Delius of Jebe's devotion to the cause of the indigenous Maya
population of Mexico. If so, he would no doubt have resigned himself to never
meeting again the friend with whom he had shared so much after their first
meeting at the Leipzig Conservatory. He and Jelka were, then, unprepared for
the Norwegian's startling reappearance in Grez around New Year 1931. At the
time, Delius's young niece was staying with them, and she would later recall
the scene:

[The] maid came into the room in a state of great agitation to say that a filthy old
man was at the door, giving the name of Halfdan Jebe.
    'Bring him in!' cried Delius, pleased at the thought of meeting an old friend
who had led the orchestra at his first London concert.
    'But sir,' replied the worried girl, 'he smells, he is incontinent, and I believe
that he is on drugs.'
    Nevertheless, Delius insisted on inviting Jebe into the house, and would
not let him go until he had been provided with a good meal and a change of
clothing.[64]

---

[61] Letter from Jelka to Munch, 19 November 1928 (MM).
[62] Letter draft from Munch to Elsa Glaser, 1929 (MM).
[63] Letter draft from Munch to Delius (MM). The letter has not survived, but Munch made three
     drafts of it, so it is highly likely that a letter was finally sent.
[64] Memories of Margaret de Visci, as related to Christopher Redwood and published in 'Delius's
     Last Known Relative' in *Journal of the Delius Society*, No. 60 (July 1978), 19–20. Musicians
     who played with Jebe in the orchestra pit of the Mérida opera house also had occasion to
     remember his poor personal hygiene and eccentric habits. When he took his violin from its
     case, pungent odours of cod and onion were often released into the confined space. 'He had
     stored them in the violin case for the intermission, along with a bottle of wine and a French
     loaf. As soon as the curtain closed for the interval, Jebe took out his salty fish and onion and

In Jelka's letters to Fenby, who was in England at the time, it is abundantly clear that this unfortunate visit came at a moment when she was close to collapse under the strain of caring for her patient. Having to cope with Jebe was almost too much for her:

> The Norwegian friend from Mexico turned up in a terrible state like the most abject dirty beggar. It affected us very much. His state was so impossible that after 2 days I had to take him to hospital in Fontainebleau and from there we got him to Paris after the most fatiguing difficulties and we are now sending him back to Norway where he has his brother.[65]

In March 1931, she could report that their 'Norwegian-Mexican friend has arrived safely in Oslo – a great relief for us. It nearly killed me when they handed him back to me at the hospital, and I knew I daren't bring him back here.'[66]

Jebe had not been in Norway for twenty-five years. Now he had taken a two-year sabbatical from his position as violin and composition tutor at the Mérida conservatory, presumably with the goal of testing the level of interest he could generate in his homeland with the substantial compositions he had written in recent years, all inspired by Mayan and Mexican culture. He persuaded the Oslo Philharmonic Orchestra to devote an evening to his works in late January 1932, which he was to conduct. Considering his earlier disparagement of Norwegian culture, it is astonishing to read in an Oslo newspaper his statement: 'I have only come back home to visit, and to give – in gratitude to the country where I had my best years – this concert.'[67] It seems improbable that the 'abject dirty beggar' who had turned up at Grez one year earlier would lead a philharmonic concert and, in the end, Jebe's addictions and nervous state seem to have prevented his appearance. 'Halfdan Jebe's Composition Evening, which he was to conduct, met with misfortune', wrote one newspaper. 'He was indisposed and Olaf Kielland had to step in as conductor with only half an hour's warning.'[68] Jebe returned to Yucatán and Mérida and renewed his efforts to reinforce the musical institutions, not least with the establishment of a regional opera house. At the end of 1937, his alcoholism brought his extraordinary life to an end.

If the young Fenby was helping Delius round off his creative work, the man who had been his staunchest champion in England was again doing his utmost to ensure that the composer's name remained bright in the perception of the

---

bit greedily into them.' José Enrique, *Hafdan* [sic] *Jebe tenía especial predilección por Yucatán*, accessed 10 February 2016 at www.poresto.net.

[65] Letter from Jelka to Eric Fenby, 19 February 1931 (DT).
[66] Letter from Jelka to Eric Fenby, 7 March 1931 (DT).
[67] *Morgenposten*, 20 January 1932.
[68] *Dagbladet*, 22 January 1932.

musical public. Throughout 1929, Thomas Beecham, with the aid of Philip Heseltine, worked towards a highly ambitious Delius Festival in London, with six concerts in October devoted entirely to his works. So, for the last time, the involuntary recluse left his French village to hear his music. Delius's plight made for gripping copy for London newspapers and touched a nerve with many people. The concerts quickly sold out and at the composer's every appearance he attracted the celebration and adulation of crowds of well-wishers. He was doubtless aware that this was the last time he would attend an orchestral performance.

By the end of 1932, Eric Fenby's work at Grez was done, and he left the household in the summer of 1933.

1934: Finally at rest in a 'Norwegian' churchyard

For several years, Delius's condition had remained relatively stable, only severe disruptions to the daily routine – such as the deep shock of Philip Heseltine's suicide in December 1930 – threatening to upset once and for all the fragile equilibrium of the composer's mind and body. At New Year 1934, Frederick and Jelka sent Edvard Munch a greeting in Norwegian, asking: 'Won't you come in the spring and visit us?'[69] However, the health of both Delius and his long-suffering wife took a serious turn for the worse in the early part of the year. When they lost, in the spring, the friendships of Norman O'Neill, killed in a traffic accident, and then Edward Elgar, with whom Delius had belatedly developed a warm understanding, the blows were felt especially hard. In April, the composer's health deteriorated further, and for most nights he was in pain.

On 16 May, Jelka had to go into hospital in Fontainebleau for a colostomy operation, and she wrote to Fenby imploring him to come and watch over Delius: 'I have gone on till I could not any more.'[70] Fenby arrived three days later and stayed at Delius's bedside, reading to him day and night as his condition worsened. Jelka was brought back from her sick-bed in Fontainebleau in the hope that it might help Delius to rally, but to no avail. He died early on Sunday 10 June.

Much of the responsibility for the funeral arrangements had to be placed on the shoulders of Eric Fenby. There were many considerations to take into account, as he related:

> It had long been Delius's wish to be buried in the garden of his house, but, as this was not possible, he had said that he would like to rest in a country churchyard

---

[69] Postcard from the Deliuses to Munch, 5 January 1934 (MM).
[70] Letter from Jelka to Eric Fenby, 16 May 1934 (DT).

somewhere in the South of England, for there the churchyards had always reminded him of those he had loved up in Norway.[71]

As early as 1918, the Harrison sisters had persuaded Delius that his final resting place should be in the country churchyard of their local parish in Limpsfield in Surrey. Delius's body was buried temporarily in the churchyard at Grez, only to be disinterred for reburial at Limpsfield on 26 May a year later. Jelka, deteriorating rapidly, travelled to England to be at the ceremony, but was too ill to attend. She died two days later, on 28 May. Later in life, Fenby looked back on his involvement in bringing Delius to Surrey as a mistake; if the composer felt he belonged anywhere, it had been in Norway and France: 'Delius, free from national prejudices, had played no part in English life beyond visits to London to hear his music. […] The countryside round Grez had nurtured his genius and given him peace to pursue his ideals and realize on paper his meditations in Norway.'[72] Whatever the merits of the case, Frederick Delius was surrounded in Limpsfield by the graves of artists who loved his music, including the Harrison sisters and Thomas Beecham.

The news of Delius's death barely registered in the country which biographers have called 'his spiritual home'. In the leading Oslo daily *Dagbladet* a short notice appeared on 15 June 1934 with the headline:

The composer Delius is dead
Old theatre memory from Christiania will live on

Nearly forty years after the *Folkeraadet* scandal – years during which he had scaled the heights of European musical life – Norwegians were still upset about his playful rendition of the national anthem. It would not have surprised him. Not once since the scandal of 1897, when he was declared 'the most unpopular man in Norway', did Delius seek to promote his music there. Nor, however, did he ever lose sight of the fact that the music that made his name in Germany and England was dependent on his visits to the Norwegian wilderness. For his searching, creative spirit there was little of value in provincial Kristiania; he needed to get back to the high hills where he could make sense of himself and his place in the world. Looking out on *the wide far distance – the great solitude.*

As this singer of Norwegian mountain songs prepared for death, perhaps his mind wandered, as it had done one day in 1923, when he woke from a short sleep and turned to Jelka:

I have had such a beautiful dream – glorious scenery. I walked over a big 'Vidde'. There was a full moon and it was quite warm – It was lovely.[73]

---

[71] Fenby, *Delius as I Knew Him*, 227.
[72] Fenby, *Delius*, 91.
[73] Sayings of Delius noted by Jelka (GM).

Appendix I

List of visits to Norway
With principal places visited

1881	Commercial journey to Sweden and Norway
1882	Commercial journey to Norway; Hardangervidda (?)
1887	Western fjords; Hardangervidda; Malmøya
1889	Hamar; Fredriksværn; Bergen; Jotunheimen
1891	Aulestad; Bergen; Lofthus; Haukeli; Fredriksværn; Kristiania
1893	Drøbak; Kongsvinger; Åsgårdstrand; also short visit to Sweden
1896	Bagn; Røros; Valdres; Jotunheimen; Rondane
1897	Kristiania
1898	Åsgårdstrand (?); Kristiania;
1899	Åsgårdstrand; Jotunheimen
1902	Nevlunghavn; Åsgårdstrand; Dovre; Jotunheimen
1906	Fredriksværn; Åsgårdstrand; Østerdalen
1908	Vågå; Geiranger; Sunnmøre; Jostedal Glacier; Jotunheimen; Fredriksværn; south coast villages
1911	Lauvåsen; Gålå; Jotunheimen
1913	Geilo; Gol Plateau; Tyin; Hardangervidda; Bergen; Lofoten (?)
1915	Nordfjord; Hjerkinn; Geilo; Kristiania
1919	Valdres; Kristiania
1921	Lesjaskog; Kristiania
1922	Lesjaskog; Kristiania
1923	Lesjaskog; Kristiania

Appendix II

Works with Norwegian and Danish texts and associations

Works are listed with English title, if well established; in these cases the alternative or original title is also given (where applicable)

Works without Norwegian text, but with Norwegian associations

1887	*Sleigh Ride/Norwegischer Schlittenfahrt*
1889	*Idylle de Printemps*
1890	*Summer Evening/Sommer Abend*
1890–01	*On the Mountains/Paa Vidderne*
1892	Violin Sonata in B Major
1896–97	*Over the Hills and Far Away*
1897	*Folkeraadet*, incidental music (later: *Norwegian Suite*, extracted from *Folkeraadet*)
1900–02	*A Village Romeo and Juliet/Romeo und Julia auf dem Dorfe* (orchestral intermezzi)
1904–05	*A Mass of Life*: Part I, 1st movement; Part II, Prelude ('Auf den Bergen') and 1st movement
1911–12	*The Song of the High Hills*
1912	*On Hearing the First Cuckoo in Spring*
1913–16	*Requiem* (closing sequence)
1917	*Eventyr – Once upon a time (after Asbjørnsen's Folklore)*

Works with texts by Norwegian authors

1885	Over the Mountains High	Bjørnson
1887 (?)	Song of Sunshine/Sonnenscheinlied	Bjørnson
1888	*Paa Vidderne*	Ibsen
1888	Hochgebirgsleben	Ibsen
1888–90	*Five Songs from the Norwegian/Fünf Lieder aus dem Norwegischen*	
	Slumber Song/Der Schlaf	Bjørnson

	The Nightingale/Sing, Sing	Kjerulf
	Summer Eve/Am schönsten Sommerabend war's	Paulsen
	Longing/Sehnsucht	Kjerulf
	Sunset/Beim Sonnenuntergang	Munch
1888–90	*Seven Songs from the Norwegian/Sieben Lieder aus dem Norwegischen*	
	Cradle Song/Wiegenlied	Ibsen
	The Homeward Way/Heimkehr	Vinje
	Twilight Fancies/Abendstimmung	Bjørnson
	Young Venevil/Klein Venevil	Bjørnson
	The Minstrel/Spielmann	Ibsen
	Hidden Love/Verborg'ne Liebe	Bjørnson
	The Birds' Story/Eine Vogelweise	Ibsen
1891(?)	Here we shall feast/Her ute skal gildet staa	Ibsen
1890–01	Softly the Forest/Skogen gir susende langsom besked	Bjørnson
1892–03	I once had a newly cut willow pipe/Jeg havde en nyskaaren seljefløjte	Krag

Also:

1890–02	*Irmelin* (purportedly based on Norwegian fairy tales)

Works without text with Danish associations

1899	*La Ronde se déroule* (overture to *Dansen gaar* by Dano-Norwegian Helge Rode), revised as *Lebenstanz*

Works with texts by (or based on texts by) Danish authors

1885	Two Brown Eyes/Zwei Bräune Augen	Andersen
1889	Sakuntala	Drachmann
1891	Dreamy Nights/Lyse Nætter	Drachmann
c. 1895	The Page sat in the Lofty Tower/Pagen højt paa taarnet sad	Jacobsen
1897	*Seven Danish Songs*	
	Silken Shoes/Seidenschuhe	Jacobsen
	Irmelin/Irmelin Rose	Jacobsen
	Summer Nights (1893–95)	Drachmann
	In the Seraglio Garden/Im Garten des Serails	Jacobsen
	Wine Roses	Jacobsen
	Red Roses (Through long, long years)	Jacobsen
	Let Springtime come, then/Den Lenz lass kommen	Jacobsen
1898	In bliss we walked with laughter/Im Glück wir lachend gingen	Drachmann

1900	*Two Songs from the Danish*	
	The Violet/Das Veilchen	Holstein
	Autumn/Herbst	Holstein
1901	I hear in the night/Jeg hører i natten	Drachmann
1902	Summer Landscape/Sommer i Gurre	Drachmann
1908–10	*Fennimore and Gerda*	Jacobsen
1911	*An Arabesque*	Jacobsen

Selected bibliography
and archival sources

Agawu, V. Kofi. *Playing with Signs: A semiotic interpretation of classic music* (Princeton: Princeton University Press, 1991)

Aksdal, Bjørn, and Sven Nyhus (eds). *Fanitullen: Innføring i norsk og samisk folkemusikk* (Oslo: Universitetsforlaget, 1993)

Alnæs, Karsten. *Historien om Norge, III: Mot moderne tider* (Oslo: Gyldendal, 1998)

Andersson Greger (ed.). *Musik i Norden* (Stockholm: Kungl. Musikaliska Akademien, 1997)

Arbo, Jens. 'Arve Arvesen 60 år' in *Tonekunst*, No. 18 (1929), 246–7

Bartók Jr, Bela. 'Béla Bartók i Norge', trans. Vince Sulyck, in *Norsk Musikktidsskrift*, 15 (No. 2, June 1978), 97–8

Beecham, Thomas. *A Mingled Chime* (New York: G. P. Putnam's Sons, 1943)

Beecham, Thomas. *Frederick Delius* (London: Hutchinson, 1959)

Beecham, Thomas, Robert Threlfall, Eric Fenby and Norman Del Mar (eds). *Collected Edition of the Works of Frederick Delius* (London: Delius Trust, 33 volumes and 5 supplementary volumes edited and published between and 1951 and 1993)

Benestad, Finn (ed.). *Edvard Grieg: Brev i utvalg 1862–1907, I: Til norske mottagere* (Oslo: Aschehoug, 1998)

Benestad, Finn (ed.). *Edvard Grieg: Brev i utvalg 1862–1907, II: Til utenlandske mottagere* (Oslo: Aschehoug, 1998)

Benestad, Finn. *Johan Svendsen: Mennesket og kunstneren* (Oslo: Aschehoug, 1990)

Benestad, Finn, and Bjarne Kortsen (eds). *Edvard Grieg: Brev til Frants Beyer 1872–1907* (Oslo: Universitetsforlaget, 1993)

Benestad, Finn, and Dag Schjelderup-Ebbe. *Edvard Grieg: Mennesket og kunstneren* (Oslo: Aschehoug, 1980; revised 1990)

Benestad, Finn, and Hanna de Vries Stavland (eds). *Edvard Grieg und Julius Röntgen, Briefwechsel 1883–1907* (Utrecht: Koninklijke Vereniging voor Nederlandse Muziekgeschiedenis, 1997)

Bergsagel, John. 'J. P. Jacobsen and Music' in F. J. Billedskov Jansen (ed.), *J. P. Jacobsens spor i ord, billeder og toner* (Copenhagen: C. A. Reitzels forlag, 1985), 283–313

Bird, John. *Percy Grainger* (Oxford: Oxford University Press, 1999)

Bjørgo, Narve, Øystein Rian and Alf Kaartvedt. *Selvstendighet og union: Fra middelalderen til 1905* (Oslo: Universitetsforlaget, 1995)

Bjørndal, Arne. 'Edvard Grieg og folkemusikken' in *Frå Fjon til Fusa: Årbok for Nord-og Midt-Hordaland Songlag* (Flesland: Nord- og Midt-Hordaland Songlag, 1951), reprinted in Mydske, *Grieg og folkemusikken*, 9–29

Blanc, T. *Christiania Theaters historie 1827–1877* (Christiania: Cappelen, 1899)

Boulton Smith, John. *Frederick Delius and Edvard Munch: Their friendship and their correspondence* (Rickmansworth: Triad Press, 1983)

Boyle, Andrew J. 'A Quest for Innocence: The music of Frederick Delius 1885–1900', Ph.D. dissertation, University of Sheffield, 1984

Bryne, Arvid. *Christian Krohg: Journalisten* (Oslo: Unipub, 2009)

Bødtker, Sigurd. *Kristiania-premierer gjennem 30 aar* (Kristiania: Aschehoug, 1923)

Carley, Lionel. *Delius: A life in letters, I: 1862–1908* (London: Scolar Press, 1983)

Carley, Lionel. *Delius: A life in letters, II: 1909–1934* (London: Scolar Press, 1988)

Carley, Lionel. *Delius: The Paris years* (London: Triad Press, 1975)

Carley, Lionel. *Edvard Grieg in England* (Woodbridge: Boydell Press, 2006)

Carley, Lionel. 'Folkeraadet: performance and history' in Carley, *Delius: A Life in Letters, II*, 211–59

Carley, Lionel (ed.). *Frederick Delius: Music, Art, and Literature* (London: Ashgate Publishing, 1998)

Carley, Lionel. *Grieg and Delius. A Chronicle of their Friendship in Letters* (London: Marion Boyars, 1993)

Dahlhaus, Carl. *Nineteenth-Century Music*, trans. J. Bradford Robinson (Berkeley and Los Angeles: University of California Press, 1989)

Delius, Clare. *Frederick Delius: Memories of my brother* (London: Ivor Nicholson & Watson, 1935)

Dreyfus, Kay (ed). *The Farthest North of Humanness: Selected letters of Percy Grainger 1901–1914* (Melbourne: Macmillan, 1985)

Dybsand, Øyvin. 'Johan Halvorsen (1864–1935): En undersøkelse av hans kunstneriske virke og en stilistisk gjennomgang av hans komposisjoner. Med en tematisk verkoversikt og en kronologisk fortegnelse over Halvorsens konsertvirksomhet', Ph.D. dissertation, University of Oslo, 2016

Eggum, Arne. *Edvard Munch: Livsfrisen fra maleri til grafikk* (Oslo: J. M. Stenersens forlag A. S., 1990)

Eggum, Arne, and Sissel Bjørnstad (eds). *Frederick Delius og Edvard Munch*, exhibition catalogue (Oslo: Munch Museum, 1979)

Engberg, Hanne. *En digters historie: Helge Rode 1870–1937* (Copenhagen: Gyldendal, 1996)

Engen, Arnfinn. *Skysstell og skysstasjonar i Gudbrandsdalen* (Lillehammer: Bruket forlag, 2009)

Eriksen, Asbjørn. 'Griegian Fingerprints in the Music of Frederick Delius', paper presented at the 2007 conference of The International Grieg Society

Eriksen, Asbjørn. 'Halfdan Kjerulf (1815–1868), den mangfoldige liedkomponist – Et jubileumsessay' in *Studia Musicologica Norvegica*, Vol. 41, No. 1 (2015), 9–39

Fenby, Eric. *Delius* (London: Faber & Faber, 1971)

Fenby, Eric. *Delius as I Knew Him* (London: G. Bell & Sons, 1936)

Fjågesund, Peter, and Ruth A. Symes. *The Northern Utopia: British perceptions of Norway in the nineteenth century* (Amsterdam & New York: Rodopi, 2003)

Flaatten, Hans-Martin Frydenberg. *Måneskinn i Åsgårdstrand: Edvard Munch. Edvard Munchs sjelelandskap, scener, stemmer og stemninger i en småby ved sjøen* (Oslo: Sem & Stenersen, 2013)

Flatmoen, Arne. *Turist i Gudbrandsdalen på 1800-tallet* (Oslo: Cappelen Damm, 2007)

Foreman, Lewis (ed.). *The Percy Grainger Companion* (London: Thames Publishing, 1981)

Gillespie, Don C. *The Search for Thomas F. Ward, Teacher of Frederick Delius* (Gainesville: University Press of Florida, 1996)

Gillies, Malcolm, and David Pear (ed.). *Portrait of Percy Grainger* (Rochester: University of Rochester Press, 2002)

Gillies, Malcolm, and David Pear (ed.). *The All-Round Man: Selected letters of Percy Grainger* (Oxford: Clarendon Press, 1994)

Gjermundsen, Jon Ola. *Gard og bygd i Sør-Aurdal. Bind B* (Sør-Aurdal: Valdres Bygdeboks forlag, 1988)

Gjersvik, Martin. 'Hjalmar Johnsen' in *Spor dei sette, II: Form og farge* (Åkrehamn: Eige forlag, 1991), 15–70

Gløersen, Inger Alver. *Lykkehuset: Edvard Munch og Åsgårdstrand* (Oslo: Gyldendal, 1970)

Grimley, Daniel M. *Grieg: Music, landscape and Norwegian identity* (Woodbridge: Boydell Press, 2006)

Grinde, Niels. *Norsk musikkhistorie: Hovedlinjer i norsk musikkliv gjennom 1000 år* (Oslo: Universitetsforlaget, 1981)

Guinery, Paul, and Martin Lee-Browne. *Delius and His Music* (Woodbridge: Boydell & Brewer, 2014)

Haavet, Inger Elisabeth: *Nina Grieg: Kunstner og kunstnerhustru* (Oslo: Aschehoug, 1998)

Hagemann, Gro. *Aschehougs norgeshistorie, IX: Det moderne gjennombrudd 1870–1905* (Oslo: Aschehoug, 1997)

Herresthal, Harald. *Med spark i gulvet og quinter i bassen: Musikalske og politiske bilder fra nasjonalromantikkens gjennombrudd i Norge* (Oslo: Universitetsforlaget, 1993)

Herresthal, Harald, and Ladislav Reznicek. *Rhapsodie norvégienne: Norsk musikk i Frankrike på Edvard Griegs tid* (Oslo: Norsk musikforlag, 1994)

Heseltine, Philip (pseudonym Peter Warlock). *Frederick Delius* (London: John Lane, The Bodley Head, 1923; reprinted with additions, annotations and comments by Hubert Foss, London: The Bodley Head, 1952)

Hoeckner, Berthold. *Programming the Absolute: Nineteenth-century German music and the hermeneutics of the moment* (Princeton: Princeton University Press, 2002)

Hoem, Edvard. *Bjørnstjerne Bjørnson* (Oslo: Oktober, four volumes from 2009 to 2013)

Hope Nicolson, Marjorie. *Mountain Gloom and Mountain Glory: The development of the aesthetics of the infinite* (Seattle: University of Washington Press, 1997; first published Ithaca: Cornell University Press, 1959)

Huismann, Mary Christison. *Frederick Delius: A research and information guide* (New York & London: Routledge, 2005; revised 2009)

Hurum, Hans Jørgen. *Vennskap: Edvard Grieg og Frants Beyer i lys av glemte brev* (Oslo: Grøndahl, 1989)

Hutchings, Arthur. *Delius* (London: Macmillan, 1948)

Illbruck, Helmut. 'The Ranz-des-Vaches' in *Nostalgia: Origins and ends of an unenlightened disease* (Evanston: Northwestern University Press, 2012), 79–100

Jefferson, Alan. *Delius* (London: Dent, 1972)

Jenkins, Lyndon. *While Spring and Summer Sang: Thomas Beecham and the music of Frederick Delius* (London: Ashgate, 2005)

Jensson, Liv. *Biografisk skuespillerleksikon* (Oslo: Universitetsforlaget, 1981)

Johannesen, Ole Rønning. *Lillehammermalerne* (Espa: Lokalhistorisk forlag, 1990)

Johansen, David Monrad. *Edvard Grieg* (Oslo: Gyldendal, 1934)

Journal of the Delius Society (earlier, *Newsletter*) (London: 1962–present)

Jørstad, Finn R. *Historien om Finse: Om fangstfolk, jernbanebyggere, hotellgjester, friluftsfolk, filmfolk, forfattere, flora, fauna og hotellet, 1222 m.o.h.* (Bergen: Nord 4, 1998)

Kirk, Elise K. *American Opera* (Champaign: University of Illinois Press, 2001)

Kjelland, Arnfinn. *Bygdebok for Lesja, II: Gards og slektshistorie for nørdre del av Lesja hovudsokn* (Lesja: Lesja kommune, 1992)

Koht, Halvdan (ed.). *J. E. Sars: Brev 1850–1915* (Oslo: Gyldendal, 1957)

Kristensen, Rolf. 'Nygaards Grund 4: Eiendommen som ble verdensberømt museum' in *Broen: Aasgaardstrandiana* (Åsgårdstrand: Aasgaardstrand og omegn historielag, 2002), 14–19

Kronen, Torleiv. *De store årene: Fransk innflytelse på norsk åndsliv 1880–1900* (Oslo: Dreyer forlag, 1982)

Lande, Marit. *Edvard Munch: Liv og kunst* (Oslo: Aventura, 1995)

Lande, Marit. *På sporet av Edvard Munch: Mannen bak mytene* (Oslo: Messel, 1996)

Lind, Sverre. *Johan Selmer: En annerledes komponist i norsk musikkliv* (Oslo: Solum forlag, 2000)

Lindanger, Rita. 'Christiania Tivoli: En musikk- og teaterhistorie om et forlystelsesetablissement i Kristiania', Masters dissertation, University of Oslo, 1997

Lloyd, Stephen (ed.). *Fenby on Delius: Collected writings on Delius to mark Eric Fenby's 90th birthday* (London: Thames Publishing, 1996)

Lloyd, Stephen. *H. Balfour Gardiner* (Cambridge: Cambridge University Press, 1984)

Lowe, Rachel. *A Descriptive Catalogue with Checklists of the Letters and Related Documents in the Delius Collection of the Grainger Museum* (London: Delius Trust, 1981)

Lowe, Rachel. 'Delius's First Performance' in *The Musical Times*, Vol. 106, No. 1464 (March 1965), 190–2

Lowe, Rachel. *Frederick Delius 1862–1934: A catalogue of the Music Archive of the Delius Trust* (London: Delius Trust, 1974)

Lowe, Rachel. 'Frederick Delius and Norway', reprinted in Redwood, *A Delius Companion*, 167–86.

Lübbren, Nina. *Rural Artists' Colonies in Europe, 1870–1910* (Manchester: Manchester University Press, 2001)

Lucas, John. *Thomas Beecham: An obsession with music* (Woodbridge: Boydell Press, 2008)

Marum, Reidar A. *Teaterslag og pipekonserter* (Oslo: Cammermeyer, 1944)

Marx, Leo. *The Machine in the Garden: Technology and the pastoral ideal in America* (Oxford: Oxford University Press, 1964)

Meyer, Michael. *Henrik Ibsen* (London: Hart-Davis, three volumes from 1967 to 1971)

Millroth, Thomas. *Molards salong* (Stockholm: Forum, 1993)

Moksnes, Aslaug. 'Randi Blehr' in *Norsk biografisk leksikon*, accessed autumn 2015 at https://nbl.snl.no/Randi_Blehr

Monelle, Raymond. *The Musical Topic: Hunt, military and pastoral* (Bloomington: Indiana University Press, 2006)

Montfort, Ricardo Pérez. 'Three Norwegian Experiences in Post-Revolutionary Mexico: Per Imerslund, Halfdan Jebe and Ola Apenes' in Steinar A. Sæther (ed.), *Expectations Unfulfilled: Norwegian migrants in Latin America, 1820–1940* (Leiden: Brill, 2015), 198–217

Mydske, Maj-Liss G. (ed.). *Grieg og folkemusikken: En artikkelsamling* (Oslo: Landslaget Musikk i Skolen, 1992)

Myhre, Jan Eivind. *Norsk historie 1814–1905: Å byggje ein stat og skape ein nasjon* (Oslo: Det Norske Samlaget, 2012)

Møller, Arvid. *Gjendine* (Oslo: Cappelen, 1976)

Møller, Arvid. *Memurubu* (Lillehammer: Thorsrud lokalhistorisk forlag, 2010)

Nielsen, Yngvar. *Reisehaandbog over Norge* (Christiania: Alb. Cammermeyers forlag, 1888)

Nielsen, Yngvar. *Reisehaandbog over Norge* (Christiania: Alb. Cammermeyers forlag, 1907)

Nilsen, Knut A. *Gjendebu 100 år: Et streif gjennom hyttas historie* (Oslo: Den Norske Turistforening, 1971)

Norseng, Mary Kay. *Dagny Juel Przybyszewska: The woman and the myth* (Seattle: University of Washington Press, 1991)

Nygaard, Knut. *Gunnar Heiberg: Teatermannen* (Bergen: Universitetsforlaget, 1975)

Næss, Atle. *Munch: En biografi* (Oslo: Gyldendal, 2004)

Næss, Trine. *Christiania Theater forteller sin historie: 1877–1899* (Oslo: Novus, 2005)

Opstad, Gunvald. *Fandango!: En biografi om Vilhelm Krag* (Bergen: Vigmostad & Bjørke, 2006)

Palmer, Christopher. *Delius: Portrait of a Cosmopolitan* (London: Duckworth, 1976)

Pareyón, Gabriel. 'Halfdan Jebe' in Alfonso Nuño Rodríguez (ed.), *Diccionario Enciclopédico de la Música de Mexico* (Guadalajara: Universidad Panamericana, 2007), 537

Peattie, Thomas. *Gustav Mahler's Symphonic Landscapes* (Cambridge: Cambridge University Press, 2015)

Prideaux, Sue. *Edvard Munch: Behind the Scream* (New Haven: Yale University Press, 2007)

Randal, William. 'Frederick Delius in America' in *The Virginia Magazine of History and Biography*, Vol. 79, No. 3 (July 1971), 349–66

Ratner, Leonard. *Classic Music: Expression, form, and style* (New York: Schirmer Books, 1980)

Redwood, Christopher (ed.). *A Delius Companion* (London: John Calder, 1976, revised 1980)

Redwood, Dawn. *Flecker and Delius: The making of Hassan* (London: Thames Publishing, 1978)

Rogan, Bjarne. *Det gamle skysstellet: Reiseliv i Noreg frå mellomalderen til førre hundreåret* (Oslo: Det Norske Samlaget, 1986)

Röntgen, Julius. *Julius Röntgen og Edvard Grieg: Et musikalsk vennskap*, translated, expanded and edited by Hanna de Vries Stavland (Bergen: Alma Mater, 1994)

Rosen, Charles. *The Romantic Generation* (Cambridge, Mass.: Harvard University Press, 1995)

Rossi, Jérôme. *Frederick Delius ou Une célébration de la vie* (Geneva: Edition Papillon, 2010)

Rugstad, Gunnar. *Christian Sinding (1856–1941): En biografisk og stilistisk studie* (Oslo: Cappelen, 1979)

Sars, J. E. *Udsigt over den norske historie* (Christiania: Cammermeyer, four volumes from 1873 to 1891)

Schjelderup-Ebbe, Dag. *A Study of Grieg's Harmony: With special reference to his contributions to musical impressionism* (Oslo: Tanum, 1953)

Schulerud, Mentz. *Norsk kunstnerliv* (Oslo: Cappelen, 1960)

Skavlan, Einar. *Gunnar Heiberg* (Oslo: Aschehoug, 1950)

Smith, Barry (ed). *Frederick Delius and Peter Warlock: A friendship revealed* (Oxford: Oxford University Press, 2000)

Stabell, Waldemar. 'Edvard Munch og Eva Mudocci' in *Kunst og Kultur*, Årg. 56 (1973), 209–36

Stang, Ragna. *Edvard Munch: Mennesket og kunstneren* (Oslo: Aschehoug, 1977)

Stenersen, Rolf. *Edvard Munch: Nærbilde av et geni* (Oslo: Gyldendal, 1946)

Thiis, Jens. *Edvard Munch og hans samtid: Slekten, livet og kunsten, geniet* (Oslo: Gyldendal, 1933)

Threlfall, Robert. *A Catalogue of the Compositions of Frederick Delius. Sources and References* (London: Delius Trust, 1977)

Threlfall, Robert. 'Delius's Piano Concerto – A Postscript' in *Musical Opinion*, Vol. 95, No. 1129 (October 1971), 14–15

Threlfall, Robert. *Frederick Delius: A supplementary catalogue* (London: Delius Trust, 1986)

Threlfall, Robert. 'The Early Versions of Delius's Piano Concerto' in *Musical Opinion*, Vol. 93, No. 1115 (August 1970), 579–81

Thue, Oscar. *Christian Krohg* (Oslo: Aschehoug, 1997)

Torp, Arne, and Lars S. Vikør. *Hovuddrag i norsk språkhistorie* (Oslo: Ad Notam Gyldendal, 1994)

Vollestad, Per. *Christian Sinding* (Oslo: Solum forlag, 2005)

Vollestad, Per. 'Jeg bærer min hatt som jeg vil. Christian Sinding: En komponist og hans sanger', Ph.D. dissertation, Norges musikkhøgskole, 2002

Wallem, Fredrik B. *Det norske studentersamfundet gjennem hundrede aar* (Kristiania: Aschehoug, 1916)

Warlock, Peter: see Philip Heseltine

Woll, Gerd. *Edvard Munch: Complete graphic works* (Oslo: Munch Museum, 2001)

Woll, Gerd. *Edvard Munch: Complete paintings* (Oslo: Cappelen Damm, 2009)

Worm-Müller, Jacob S. *Ideer og mennesker* (Oslo: Aschehoug, 1954)

Østvedt, Einar. *Henrik Ibsen: Miljø og mennesker* (Oslo: Gyldendal, 1968)

Archival sources

Arne Bjørndal Collection (Bergen): Gjendine Slålien's correspondence

Bergen offentlige bibliotek/Bergen Public Library: Edvard Grieg's correspondence and account books, also Nina Grieg's correspondence

British Library (London): Delius manuscripts and correspondence

Delius Trust (London): Frederick and Jelka Delius's correspondence and photographs

Grainger Museum (Melbourne): Frederick and Jelka Delius's correspondence with each other and Grainger

Jacksonville University Library: Jutta Bell Ranske's correspondence

Kvinnemuseet/The Norwegian Women's Museum (Kongsvinger): letters and photographs of Ragnhild Juel

Munchmuseet/Munch Museum (Oslo): Munch's correspondence, notebooks and sketch books; also accessed at emunch.no

Nasjonalbiblioteket/National Library (Oslo): correspondence of leading Norwegian figures, newspaper records, music manuscripts; also accessed at nb.no

National Archives (UK): passenger lists, accessed at nationalarchives.gov.uk

Riksarkivet/The National Archives of Norway (Oslo): correspondence of Randi Blehr; archive also accessed at arkivverket/Digitalarkivet.no for church records, population censuses, property records

Index